# Employment and Health Benefits

## A Connection at Risk

Marilyn J. Field and Harold T. Shapiro, *Editors*

Committee on Employer-Based Health Benefits
Division of Health Care Services

INSTITUTE OF MEDICINE

NATIONAL ACADEMY PRESS
Washington, D.C. 1993

338.433621
I592e

**NATIONAL ACADEMY PRESS • 2101 Constitution Avenue, N.W. • Washington, D.C. 20418**

NOTICE: The project that is the subject of this report was approved' by the Governing Board of the National Research Council, whose members are drawn from the councils of the National Academy of Sciences, the National Academy of Engineering, and the Institute of Medicine. The members of the committee responsible for the report were chosen for their special competences and with regard for appropriate balance.

This report has been reviewed by a group other than the authors according to procedures approved by a Report Review Committee consisting of members of the National Academy of Sciences, the National Academy of Engineering, and the Institute of Medicine.

The Institute of Medicine was chartered in 1970 by the National Academy of Sciences to enlist distinguished members of the appropriate professions in the examination of policy matters pertaining to the health of the public. In this, the Institute acts under both the Academy's 1863 congressional charter responsibility to be an adviser to the federal government and its own initiative in identifying issues of medical care, research, and education.

Support for this project was provided by the Agency for Health Care Policy and Research, U.S. Department of Health and Human Services, under Contract No. 282-91-0020. The views presented are those of the Institute of Medicine Committee on Employer-Based Health Benefits and are not necessarily those of the funding organization.

**Library of Congress Cataloging-in-Publication Data**

Institute of Medicine (U.S.). Committee on Employer-Based Health
Benefits.
    Employment and health benefits : a connection at risk / Committee
on Employer-Based Health Benefits, Division of Health Care Services,
Institute of Medicine ; Marilyn J. Field and Harold T. Shapiro,
editors.
        p.  cm.
    Includes bibliographical references and index.
    ISBN 0-309-04827-3
    1. Insurance, Health—United States.  2. Voluntary employees'
beneficiary associations—United States.  I. Field, Marilyn J.
(Marilyn Jane)  II. Shapiro, Harold T., 1935-    .  III. Title.
HG9396.I57   1993
331.25'5—dc20                                           92-42468
                                                            CIP

介

The serpent has been a symbol of long life, healing, and knowledge among almost all cultures and religions since the beginning of recorded history. The image adopted as a logotype by the Institute of Medicine is based on a relief carving from ancient Greece, now held by the Staatlichemuseen in Berlin.

Printed in the United States of America

# COMMITTEE ON EMPLOYER-BASED HEALTH BENEFITS

*iii*

*Study Staff*

Marilyn J. Field, Study Director
Jo Harris-Wehling, Program Officer
Donna D. Thompson, Administrative Assistant
Karl D. Yordy, Director, Division of Health Care Services

# Preface

The many stunning and continuing achievements of American medicine and biomedical science and technology are widely understood and gratefully appreciated by many people in the United States and abroad. More recently, however, the focus of our attention has shifted—quite appropriately—to a set of equally startling problems that have come to characterize health care finance and delivery in this country. The most important of these complex and interrelated matters surround issues of access (too many Americans no longer have access to basic medical care), issues of value and cost (increasing concern that the value of the care received is not commensurate with its quickly escalating cost), and issues of social policy (how do we wish to share costs between the sick and the well and between the rich and the poor). Also quite sobering is the growing evidence of excess capacity in our inventory of hospital beds and of certain advanced diagnostic and treatment equipment.

Moreover, the widely different patterns of medical practice and their widely different resource requirements seem to suggest less than full understanding of the most effective way to deliver health care. Each of these issues is itself a complex mixture of many sub-issues, but there is little question in my mind that it is critical for America to develop private and public policies that not only insure the continued vitality of American medicine and biomedical science and technology, but do so in a manner that addresses—in a fundamental way—our concerns in the area of access, value, cost, and social policy.

One important piece of the policy puzzle is this country's system of voluntary employment-based health benefits. This was recognized by the Institute of Medicine's Board on Health Care Services, which began discussing the concept of this study over three years ago. The board was particularly concerned that the current and potential impact on our overall health care system of employer responses to their escalating problems in financing health benefits was not sufficiently appreciated or understood. As a result, the difficulties, for example, of preserving our voluntary employment-based health benefits system as a mechanism for sharing risk across the well and the ill and the rich and the poor often were being underestimated. Moreover, a careful understanding of the benefits and limitations of this voluntary, employment-based system could make a contribution to the current public policy debate on health reform.

In late 1990 the Committee on Appropriations of the United States Senate requested that the Agency for Health Care Policy and Research (AHCPR) contract with the Institute of Medicine for a study of voluntary employment-based health insurance. The request noted the severe strains facing this system. It cited double-digit inflation, employer doubts about the value of their increased spending, and deterioration of the employer group as a vehicle for sharing risk. One of the specific requests made by AHCPR was for a research agenda.

To oversee the study, the Institute of Medicine formed a committee that included individuals with a broad range of experience in health care delivery, business, union activities, health insurance, law, economics, and health services research and policy. The committee met four times between June 1991 and July 1992. Study activities included a public hearing; a round table discussion with leading consulting and insurer actuaries; a symposium for business and other leaders; two public opinion surveys planned with and sponsored by the Employee Benefit Research Institute; commissioned or committee papers on the legal context of employment-based benefits, the links between financing for patient care and medical education and biomedical research, and the relationship between health care costs and the productivity and competitiveness of American business; an extensive literature review; and consultation with a wide range of policy leaders, researchers, employers, and concerned parties.

As this study proceeded, health care reform once again began to emerge as a major public policy issue. Proposals for reform have proliferated and mutated so rapidly that the systematic identification, categorization, and analysis of their basic features has become a mini-industry (see, for example, Blendon and Edwards, 1991; Blue Cross and Blue Shield Association, 1991b; CBO, 1991a; EBRI, 1992b; Association of American Medical Colleges, 1992). The committee, because of its particular mandate, neither joined this new "industry" nor pursued its own special vision for health care reform. The committee chose rather to focus its limited time and resources on certain important characteristics of the current system that had received relatively little in-depth analysis.

The committee focused, in particular, on one of the defining characteristics of the U.S. health care finance system—its voluntary employment-based nature—and the particular implications this had for those with health care needs and for the role of public policy, medical care providers, the insurance industry, and other major participants in the health care system. The committee believed that the results of such an examination would be informative and thought-provoking for both those who favor the continuation of a voluntary employment-based health benefit system and those who favor its replacement by other arrangements.

Nearly all of the committee agreed on the findings and recommendations presented in Chapter 7. Unlike most National Research Council committees, however, this committee did not reach consensus on some central issues. For example, committee members could not agree on whether employment-based health benefits should be continued or abandoned or whether regulatory or market-based strategies for cost containment were preferable. On such matters the committee and, consequently, its report reflect the fundamental lack of consensus that has characterized the public debate over health care reform. Bringing agreement and commitment out of conflict and ambivalence will be a major challenge for this nation's leaders.

Although the committee members hold a wide variety of views on health care reform, it seems quite clear to me that major changes in current arrangements are necessary in order to achieve a more equitable and cost-effective system of health care. It is my own judgment that without major changes our system of voluntary employment-based health benefits will deteriorate further and may collapse. Indeed, as Chair of this effort over the nearly two years of the committee's work, I have—somewhat reluctantly—come to believe that a purely voluntary system cannot sufficiently expand access to health care benefits to retain its social viability as one of the cornerstones of our national health care system. I have also come to believe that all acceptable outcomes in the arena of health care will require that the healthy and the well-off share in the cost of covering the ill and the poor (i.e., reform cannot be fully financed from "waste"). Finally, I believe that additional public policy initiatives (e.g., subsidies, taxes, and regulations) are necessary to ensure that private markets function more effectively for the consumer of health care. These and other associated issues must be thoroughly debated and a national consensus achieved.

I hope the content of this report will help all its readers decide many of these issues for themselves.

Harold T. Shapiro
Chair, Committee on Employer-Based
Health Benefits

# Acknowledgments

In preparing this report, the Committee on Employment-Based Health Benefits and the study staff were assisted by many individuals and groups, most of whom we hope we have acknowledged here. Three meetings—a public hearing, a workshop on actuarial issues, and a symposium—sponsored by the committee were particularly useful sources of ideas and insights. Those who participated in these sessions are listed in Appendix C. Many of these individuals also assisted the study in other ways. Stephen Merrill, Lois Perolle, and Daniel Gross of the Academy Industry Program helped in organizing and jointly sponsoring the May 1992 symposium.

Initial direction for this study came from a planning group that met in June 1989. The meeting was chaired by Paul O'Neill, CEO of Aluminum Company of America. The other participants (and their affiliations at that time) were Howard Bolnick, Celtic Life Insurance Co.; Helen Darling, Mercer Meidinger and Hanson; Jerome H. Grossman, New England Medical Center Hospitals; Karen Ignagni, AFL-CIO; Stanley Jones, Consolidated Health Care, Inc.; Walter J. McNerney, Northwestern University; Thomas O. Pyle, Harvard Community Health Plan; William R. Roy, Women's Clinic; and Gail Warden, Henry Ford Health Care Corporation. Lynn Etheredge prepared the background paper for that meeting and contributed many more provocative ideas thereafter.

Throughout the project we also benefited from the experience and advice of Walter J. McNerney, chair of the Institute of Medicine (IOM) Board on Health Care Services, and other members of the board. Two members of the IOM Council, Joseph Newhouse and Harold Luft, reviewed major sections of the report and provided invaluable critiques.

The committee commissioned two papers that provided useful background for this report. Edward Shay prepared an overview of state and federal regulation of employee health benefits (Appendix B), and Ruth Hanft provided an overview of third-party payment issues related to biomedical research and medical education. David Brailar of the Wharton School of the University of Pennsylvania presented research results from that institution's work on health care and American competitiveness.

In addition, the Employee Benefit Research Institute (EBRI) graciously offered the committee the opportunity to help draft questions for two of the surveys it periodically conducts using the Gallup Organization. A summary of results is presented in Appendix A. Our collaborators at EBRI were Dallas Salisbury, William Custer, Laura Bos, and Jill Foley. In addition, Janette Hall and other staff at EBRI were excellent sources of information.

Beth Fuchs and Janet Kline of the Congressional Research Service also shared information and ideas based on their extensive work on health insurance and related issues. As project officer, Fred Hellinger of the Agency for Health Care Policy and Research (AHCPR) was helpful on many occasions, as was Michael Hagan, also of AHCPR. At the Department of Labor, Richard Hinz and Richard Lindrew helped clarify the intricacies of the Employee Retirement Security Act. Also at the Department of Labor, Jay Meisenheimer and William Wiatrowski helped us with many inquiries about Bureau of Labor Statistics data. Martin Lefkowitz at the U.S. Chamber of Commerce provided similar assistance.

Several panel discussions organized by Judith Miller Jones, Karl Polzer, and others at the National Health Policy Forum contributed a variety of important perspectives on problems of insuring employees of small organizations. Others who provided useful insights from their experience or research included Ellen Goldstein of the Association of Private Pension and Welfare Funds; Judith Feder of the Georgetown University Center for Health Policy Studies; Greg Scandlen of the Council for Affordable Health Insurance; Deborah Chollet of Georgia State University; Arlene Ash of Boston University; Sonia Muchnick-Baku of the Washington Business Group on Health; Uwe Reinhardt of Princeton University; Mark Rothstein of the University of Houston; and Robert J. Moses of Michaels and Wishner.

Within the Institute of Medicine, Kathleen Lohr reviewed the discussion of health status measures, effectiveness research, and quality of care. Gary Ellis provided helpful advice on the discussion of employer health promotion programs that originally formed a chapter in a early draft of this report. Elsewhere in the National Academy of Sciences and the National Research Council, Charles Starliper offered much advice on the case studies in Chapter 4. During the first few months of the study, Karen Onstad, an intern from the University of California at Berkeley, helped in assembling and analyzing a large volume of background materials.

On many occasions we received information, explanations, and other assistance from a number of individuals at the following organizations:

AFL-CIO, American Academy of Actuaries, Blue Cross and Blue Shield Association, Children's Defense Fund, Group Health Association of America, Health Insurance Association of America, Heritage Foundation, Midwest Business Group on Health, Milliman and Robertson, and National Association of Insurance Commissioners.

Finally, to publish this report, we relied on a great many people beyond the study committee and staff and those already acknowledged above. In particular, we want to acknowledge Holly Dawkins, who helped review the report proofs as they came back from the National Academy Press; Mike Edington, who helped smooth the publication process in innumerable ways; Roseanne Price, who copyedited the report; and Sally Stanfield, who managed publication of the report at the Press.

# Contents

SUMMARY                                                                    1

1  BACKGROUND AND INTRODUCTION                                            25
   Employment-Based Health Benefits in Context, 27
   Overview of Report, 34
   Why This Study?, 35
   Key Concepts and Terms as Used in This Report, 40
   Conclusion, 47

2  ORIGINS AND EVOLUTION OF EMPLOYMENT-
   BASED HEALTH BENEFITS                                                  49
   The Birth of Insurance for Medical Care Expenses, 51
   The Divergent Path of the United States, 57
   Early Cost Management Efforts by Insurers and Others, 73
   The Limits of Voluntary Health Benefits and Medicare
       and Medicaid, 77
   ' Federal Regulation and the Employer's Growing Role, 82
   Conclusion, 85

3  EMPLOYMENT-BASED HEALTH BENEFITS TODAY                                 87
   Data Sources, 88
   Who Is and Is Not Covered by Employment-Based
       Health Benefits?, 89
   What Types of Coverage Are Offered?, 98
   What Do Employment-Based Health Benefits Cost?, 106
   Who Bears the Risk?, 111
   What Other Health-Related Benefits Do Employers Offer?, 114
   Conclusion, 119

4  WHAT DOES EMPLOYER MANAGEMENT
   OF HEALTH BENEFITS INVOLVE?  OVERVIEW
   AND CASE STUDY                                          121
      Overview, 121
      Core Case Study, 128
      Contrasting Cases, 142
      Consequences for Employees, 145
      Consequences for Practitioners and Providers, 149
      A Note on Employers' Legal Liability for
         Managed Care, 152
      Conclusion, 153
      Addendum, 155

5  RISK SELECTION, RISK SHARING, AND POLICY               167
      Basic Concepts, 168
      Factors Contributing to Risk Selection, 170
      Evidence of Risk Selection, 177
      Policy Questions, 179
      Strategies for Responding to Risk Selection and
         Risk Segmentation, 187
      Conclusion, 200

6  HEALTH CARE COSTS:  MORE QUESTIONS
   THAN ANSWERS                                            202
      Health Care Spending:  Trends and Explanations, 204
      Public and Private Responses to Escalating
         Health Care Costs, 206
      Functioning of the Health Care Market, 220
      The Question of Value, 223
      Conclusion, 227

7  FINDINGS AND RECOMMENDATIONS                            229
      Recapitulation, 231
      Features, Strengths, and Limitations of the Current
         System, 234
      Future Directions, 242
      A Few Comments on Practical and Technical
         Challenges, 254
      Agenda for Research and Evaluation, 256
      Final Thoughts, 260
      Supplementary Statement of a Committee
         Member, 261

REFERENCES                                                 262

APPENDIXES
A  Opinion Surveys on Employment-Based Health Benefits
   and Related Issues   287
B  Regulation of Employment-Based Health Benefits:
   The Intersection of State and Federal Law   293
C  Participants in Meetings Held in Conjunction with Project   323
D  Biographies of Committee Members   328

GLOSSARY AND ACRONYMS   334

INDEX   347

## TABLES AND FIGURES

*Tables*

1  Broad Functions or Activities That May Be Undertaken by Employers Providing Health Benefits, Arrayed by Approximate Level of Administrative Difficulty or Complexity, 6
2  Summary of Committee Findings and Recommendations on Steps to Respond to Certain Current Limitations of Voluntary Employment-Based Health Benefits, 15
1.1  Nonelderly and Elderly Americans with Selected Sources of Health Insurance, Employee Benefit Research Institute Analysis of the March 1991 Current Population Survey, 28
1.2  Trends in Government, Individual, and Business Spending in Selected Years, 1965 to 1990, 29
1.3  Selected International Comparisons of Health Spending, for Selected Years, 1970 to 1989, 32
2.1  Key Dates in the Development of Employment-Based Health Benefits and Its Environment, 52
2.2  Standards Adapted by American Association for Labor Legislation in 1914 for Drafting Model State Medical Care Insurance Bill, 59
2.3  Summary of Positions on Health Care Coverage in the Majority and Minority Reports of the Committee on the Costs of Medical Care, 1932, 62
2.4  Standards for Blue Cross Plans Adopted in the 1930s, 68
2.5  Major Categories of "National Health Insurance" Proposals in the Early 1970s, 81
3.1  Percentage of Individuals with Selected Sources of Health Insurance by Own Work Status, 1990, 91
3.2  Variations by Size of Employer in Percentage of Wage and Salary Workers Aged 18 to 64 with Employer Health Coverage or No Coverage from Any Source, 1990, 96

3.3   Variations by Industry in Percentage of Wage and Salary Workers
      Aged 18 to 64 with Employer Health Coverage or No Coverage from
      Any Source, 1990, 97
3.4   Percentage Distribution of Employees Across Types of Health
      Benefit Plans, 1987 to 1990, 101
3.5   Selected Examples of State-Mandated Health Coverage, 102
3.6   Selected Types of Limits on Mental Health Services Among Several
      Health Benefit Plans, 105
3.7   Employer-Reported Percentage Premium Increases, by Plan Type,
      1989 to 1991, 109
4.1   Selected Types of Decisions, Tasks, and Options Faced by
      Organizations That Choose to Offer Employment-Based Health
      Benefits, 123
4.2   Sources of Variation in Employment-Based Health Benefits, 124
4.3   How Size May Affect How Employers Manage Health Benefits, 125
4.4   Selected Comparisons of Existing Health Plans in Case Study
      Organization, 132
4.5   Summary Evaluation of Responses to RFP, 139
4.6   Possible Tasks, Responsibilities, and Decisions for Employees, 147
5.1   Estimated Impact of Biased Risk Selection on Premiums in a
      Multiple-Choice Program, Individual (self-only) Coverage, Federal
      Employees Health Benefits Plan, 1989, 176
5.2   Some Possible Strategies for Responding to Biased Risk
      Selection, 188
5.3   Major Provisions on Which Proposals for Reform in Underwriting
      Practices May Differ, 189
5.4   Some Steps Proposed to Manage or Limit Health Plan Competition
      Based on Risk Selection, 192
6.1   Percentage of Surveyed Employers Reporting Selected Utilization
      Management Features, 1987 to 1991, 214
6.2   Percentage of Full-time Participants in Employment-Based Fee-for-
      Service Health Plans Subject to Selected Cost Containment
      Features, 215
7.1   Broad Functions or Activities That May Be Undertaken by
      Employers Providing Health Benefits, Arrayed by Approximate
      Level of Administrative Difficulty or Complexity, 233
7.2   Summary of Committee Findings and Recommendations on Steps to
      Respond to Certain Current Limitations of Voluntary Employment-
      Based Health Benefits, 244
7.3   Examples of Practical and Technical Issues in Drafting State or
      Federal Legislation and Regulations to Implement Major Changes in
      Employment-Based Health Benefits, 255

*Figures*

1.1 Percentage of expenditures for health services and supplies, by payer, 1965 to 1990, 30

3.1 Work status of the family head for the 35.7 million Americans under age 65 who were without health insurance, 1990, 93

3.2 Percentage of firms offering various types of health plans for firms offering a plan, by firm size, 1991, 99

3.3 Flow of funds from sponsors of health care into the health care system in the United States, 1990, 107

3.4 Growth in health plan costs, expressed in total dollars per employee for 1985 to 1991 and percentage increase from previous year, 109

3.5 Percentage of firms self-insured by total number of employees, 1991, 112

5.1 Variation in average annual plan premiums for the typical health plan, by age and gender, 1986, 173

6.1 Reasons for growth in personal health care expenditures, 1981 to 1990, 205

# Employment
# and Health Benefits

## A Connection at Risk

# Summary

To make the many accomplishments of modern medicine available to its people, the United States depends heavily on a voluntary system of employment-based health benefits. Although neither federal nor state law generally requires employers to finance health coverage for employees and their families, approximately 140 million people—nearly two-thirds of all Americans under age 65—receive health benefits through the workplace.

The United States is unique in relying on employers to do voluntarily what governments in most other countries either do themselves or require private parties to do on an extensively regulated basis. Not only are employers in this country free to offer or not offer coverage, they have extensive discretion in determining what specific benefits are to be offered, how they are to be administered, what share of benefit costs will be paid by employees, and what will be attempted to control the employer's costs.

Most of those with employment-based health benefits view them favorably and value them highly. Overall dissatisfaction with the U.S. health care delivery system is, however, quite strong. Among ordinary citizens, policymakers, providers, and business people, it is widely seen as too inequitable and too complex and not effective enough given the level of resources committed. Over 35 million Americans are uninsured, and for millions more coverage is precarious or inadequate. There is widespread feeling that medical care costs are out of control and that the patience of health care purchasers—public and private—is wearing thin. These feelings feed back as further reason to worry about the structure of health care delivery and financing, including its link to the workplace.

Many proposals for health care reform would replace existing arrangements with fundamentally different relationships among patients, medical

*1*

care providers, and those financers of care. Some would put a single national purchaser—the federal government—in charge. Others would put the cost-conscious individual consumer at the helm. Yet others would mix strong government regulations with market competition among certified health plans. Most of these proposals would leave employers with a more limited role than they have now.

The debate over health care reform raises many controversial questions involving the obligations of richer or healthier individuals to help poorer or sicker individuals, the role of the private versus the public sector in ensuring access to needed health care, the virtues of voluntary versus compulsory insurance, and the effectiveness of market versus regulatory strategies to contain costs and ensure value. Regardless of the stance taken in such debates, the central position of employment-based health benefits is a major factor to be reckoned with in considering the feasibility and specifics of proposals for change.

This report explores the following questions: How did the current system of voluntary employment-based health benefits develop? How does it relate to the overall structure of health care delivery and financing in the United States? What are its basic characteristics, strengths, and limitations? What might be done about the limitations? The committee believes that the results of this exploration will be informative and thought-provoking for both those who favor the continuation of a voluntary employment-based health benefit system and those who favor its replacement by other arrangements.

The findings and recommendations presented here do not constitute a blueprint for health care reform, even for reform that seeks to build on voluntary employment-based health benefits. In particular, the findings do not address the most effective means to limit the rapid escalation in health care costs and to define the appropriate role of advanced medical technologies, two issues that trouble all economically developed countries regardless of their system of financing medical expenses. Furthermore, the discussion here does not touch directly on the problems facing Medicare, Medicaid, and other public programs, although the committee recognizes that efforts to resolve those problems cannot go forward in isolation from the system examined here.

Rather, this report sets forth some steps that government, business, individuals, and health care practitioners and providers could take to alleviate certain problems related to the current link between the workplace and health benefits. These steps are grouped into two divisions: one that assumes the preservation of a voluntary system of employment-based health benefits and a second that assumes that a voluntary system cannot significantly extend access, control biased risk selection, or manage costs. This discussion does not constitute a general committee endorsement or rejection of either a voluntary or a compulsory system of employment-based health benefits.

Overall, the current system of voluntary employment-based health benefits earns both positive and negative marks. It is a dynamic system that continues to change in both constructive and destructive ways. The negatives are, however, becoming more significant. They need to be confronted through action, both public and private, if the nation wants to preserve a productive role for employment-based health benefits.

## EMPLOYMENT-BASED HEALTH BENEFITS IN CONTEXT

### Historical Development

In the United States, the strong link between health benefits and the workplace developed through a combination of historical coincidences and deliberate decisions. Its emergence depended on the voluntary initiative of many private individuals and groups, the largely unintended impetus of federal tax and labor laws, the collective bargaining strategies of trade unions, and the repeated failure of proposals for some kind of government-mandated health insurance. Beginning in the early 1930s, this system of voluntary employment-based health benefits experienced three decades of rapid growth. Only in the 1960s and 1970s were major government programs established to cover the elderly, the disabled, and some of the poor—all groups ill-suited to private insurance. Today, however, neither government nor employment-based coverage reaches many low-income or high-risk workers and their families, especially those who work for small firms or on a part-time or seasonal basis and those who are chronically ill.

Moreover, in recent periods, the continual exercise of employer and individual choice among private insurance or health plan options has diminished the degree to which the burden of health care expenses is shared among the well and the ill. Health care costs are highly skewed in their distribution. In any year, perhaps 5 percent of a population will account for 50 percent of expenditures, and 20 percent will account for 80 percent. Thus, any health plan (or employer) that is relatively successful at avoiding this group will have a significant competitive advantage, though not a socially constructive one.

### Key Statistics

The relative importance of private and public sources of health benefits and health care spending is suggested by the following statistics:

• Seventy-three percent of all Americans below the age of 65 have private health coverage, the great majority through programs sponsored by private and government employers and unions.

• Almost 36 million Americans below the age of 65—17 percent—have no health benefits. Of this group, 85 percent live in families headed by a worker, usually one who works for a firm with fewer than 100 employees and over half the time one who works full-time.

• Ninety-six percent of all Americans age 65 and over are covered by public programs, many have supplementary private coverage (some of it employer sponsored), and only 1 percent have no health coverage.

• Public program spending accounts for approximately 40 percent of all spending on health care services and supplies, and employers and households account for roughly equivalent shares of the rest.

• Households now directly finance a much smaller proportion of health care than they did 30 years ago, and government and business finance a greater share (although individuals still contribute indirectly to this financing, for example, through income taxes and forgone wages).

Although the proportion of the nonelderly population covered by employment-based health benefits leveled off during the 1970s and even decreased from 66 to 64 percent between 1988 and 1990, business spending on health benefits continues to grow as a fraction of total labor compensation. Business health spending stood at 7 percent of total labor compensation in 1990, up from 2 percent in 1965 and 5 percent in 1980. For the nation as a whole, about 12 percent ($666.2 billion) of the gross national product was accounted for by spending on health care (including noncommercial health research and construction) in 1990, up from 6 percent in 1965 and 9 percent in 1980 (Levit et al., 1991).

This high and increasing commitment of resources to health care reflects a generally rising standard of living, an aging population, more comprehensive health care coverage, an incentive structure that encourages high medical spending (e.g., third-party payments on an open-ended fee-for-service reimbursement basis), tax policy, and other factors. However, given the common pattern of rising costs across nations with greatly different health systems, the unique structure of the U.S. system cannot be held solely or perhaps even primarily responsible for increasing costs. The influence of new medical technologies and practices together with rising expectations, although extremely difficult to document, may be hard for any system to resist.

## International Comparisons

The United States stands out among economically advanced nations for its high overall level of health care spending, its large numbers of uninsured individuals, and its extensive segmentation of high- and low-risk individuals into separate risk pools. It is also noteworthy for the relatively low proportion of total health care spending that is accounted for by public sources, approximately 40 percent in the United States versus 95 percent in Norway (the highest), 87 percent in the United Kingdom, and over 70 percent in France, Germany, and Japan (Schieber and Poullier, 1991). Distinctiveness is often a matter of pride, as are high expenditures for a socially valued service. No pride can, however, be derived from the fact that this country spends so much more on health care than other countries while leaving a significantly larger fraction of its population uninsured and not appearing to achieve clearly superior health outcomes.

Nonetheless, virtually all economically advanced countries—regardless of how they finance and deliver care—worry that their health care costs are too high or at least increasing too quickly. Furthermore, given the nation's wealth, commitment to medical research and technological development, and other factors, it is quite likely that the United States would lead the world in the proportion of national resources devoted to health care even if 20, 40, or 60 years ago it had adopted some other system of health care coverage. If it had followed the pattern of other developed nations, however, it might not also lead in the proportion of the population uninsured.

## Scope and Functions

Within the United States, the offering of health benefits to employees and their families is virtually universal in large and medium-sized organizations (those with 100 or more employees). Only about half of all workers are, however, employed by these organizations, and this fraction is declining. Among the smallest organizations (those with fewer than 25 employees), only about one-third of workers receive coverage directly from their employer, former employer, or union. The reasons are diverse: many small employers feel that even limited coverage is too expensive, others believe their employees do not need or want it, and some do not see its provision as an employer's responsibility. In general, those who manage and work for small organizations operate in environments with problems and options regarding health coverage that differ in significant ways from the environments faced by larger firms.

Large organizations generally cover a large portion of the cost or premium for employee coverage, but their contributions for family coverage vary considerably. In addition, they often help employees understand their health coverage and resolve problems with specific health plans. Moreover, large employers have become increasingly active in health benefit management by offering employees choices among competing health benefit plans, limiting employee choice of health care practitioners, adding managed care features to indemnity health plans, and developing workplace health promo-

**TABLE 1**   Broad Functions or Activities That May Be Undertaken by
Employers Providing Health Benefits, Arrayed by Approximate Level of
Administrative Difficulty or Complexity

| LEAST DIFFICULT OR COMPLEX | | MOST DIFFICULT OR COMPLEX |
|---|---|---|
| | | Direct Contracting with Health Care Providers or Direct Provision of Health Care Services |
| | Direct Administration of Claims, Utilization Review, and Other Management Functions | |
| | Extensive Tailoring and Detailed Oversight of Health Benefit Program | |
| Contributing to Plan Premium, Monitoring Basic Aspects of Health Plan Performance, Assisting Employees with Problems | | |
| Facilitating Participation in Health Plan: Enrollment, Information Distribution, Payroll Deduction | | |

tion programs.  At the same time, large employers are focusing—more
than ever before—on how they can have employees pay a larger share of
costs directly, how they can get the best possible rates from health care
providers regardless of the impact on others in the community, and how
they can avoid sharing the risk for medical care and benefit costs for
anyone other than their employees and, perhaps, their dependents.  For
small employers that offer coverage, options and involvement tend to be
quite limited.

Table 1 depicts some of the important functions assumed by employers
and the relative difficulty or complexity of these functions.  It does not
attempt to list the positive and negative effects on employees or the community that may follow from specific steps taken by employers in carrying out
these functions.  In general, the participation by employers in these functions falls off sharply between the first and second functions—particularly
among small employers—and also between the second and third functions
(reading across the table from left to right).

## Access to Health Services

Coverage is not the same as access, which has been defined in another Institute of Medicine report as the timely use of personal health services to achieve the best possible health outcomes. Some who have coverage still face access problems by virtue of their location, race, education, or other personal characteristics or as a result of specific characteristics of their coverage, such as low rates of payment for physician services. Likewise, even those who lack health insurance have some access to care on an emergency basis for serious illness or injury, and some needy individuals receive primary and preventive services through public and private programs and charity care offered by individual practitioners. Access overall is, however, often not timely and is rarely coordinated, and the financial burden of uncompensated and public care for the uninsured is very unevenly borne across communities.

## Costs in Context

For more than two decades, concerns about high and escalating medical care expenditures and strategies to control those costs have been a major focus of health policy. The continuation of the former and the ineffectiveness of the latter not only have made it more difficult to extend health coverage to those now uninsured and underinsured but also have been partly responsible for the growth of this pool.

High health care costs are frequently portrayed as the nation's number one health policy problem, but the problem is more complex. That is, the country is spending a greater share of national resources on medical care and making such care less affordable for many without having much evidence or confidence that it is achieving better health outcomes or other equivalent value for its increased investment. Efforts to accumulate such evidence, to evaluate and compare the costs and benefits of alternative medical practices, and to generally assess the quality of medical care are increasing in numbers and sophistication. Nonetheless, the public and private resources devoted to these efforts are minuscule compared with those devoted to developing more advanced treatments and technologies.

The health care market is in a variety of respects not currently structured to achieve the efficiency expected of properly functioning markets. The debate over health care reform centers on several questions: Can major changes in public policy create an effectively functioning market? Should the employer have a major role in a market-oriented approach? Would, on balance, the projected effects of one or another kind of reformed market be better or worse than the effects of major alternatives, which occupy a spectrum of possibilities from the current system on the one hand to a single payer, single national health plan on the other hand?

## DISTINGUISHING FEATURES OF THE CURRENT SYSTEM

Any concise statement of key features of employment-based health benefits in the United States must simplify and generalize from a world that is neither simple nor uniform nor static. Nonetheless, on the basis of descriptions and analyses presented in the first six chapters of this report, several characteristics stand out. Most of these characteristics distinguish the system in the United States from systems in other advanced industrial nations and from what is envisioned by proposals for a fully public system of health insurance or for a private health insurance market based on individual choice and responsibility or some combination of these principal alternatives. They are not, however, purely a function of voluntary employment-based health coverage. If the link between employment and health benefits were abandoned or retained only as a conduit for financing health benefits, some of the features discussed below would likely disappear, but others might persist—or even become more prominent—depending on the specific changes made. Reforms that retained a significant role for employers might bring significant or only marginal changes, again depending on their specifics.

### Voluntary Group Purchase

The very subject of this report is a defining, indeed unique, feature of the U.S. health care system: reliance on health benefits voluntarily sponsored by employers—or collectively bargained between employers and unions—to cover the majority of nonelderly individuals. Voluntary group action has offered an alternative to government mandates but still created purchasers with more leverage than single individuals can normally bring to bear in buying health insurance, identifying and resolving problems, and securing some efficiencies in program administration. Once an employer opts to offer health benefits, some governmental limits on its discretion may apply, but they are relatively modest.

### Lack of Universal Coverage

More than 30 million uninsured Americans, the great majority of those without health benefits, are workers or their family members. In contrast, virtually every other advanced industrial nation covers all, or all but a very small fraction of, its population. Most require employers—and employees and taxpayers generally—to finance coverage, and most subsidize low-income workers and make special arrangements for seasonal or other workers with limited connections to the workplace. Absent such compulsion and support, many U.S. employers choose not to offer health benefits to all or some of their employees. Such employees are especially likely to work part-time, seasonally, or in low-wage jobs for small employers. Some workers, if offered a choice of health benefits versus higher wages or the opportunity to work full-time, might decline the former—as do a small percentage of workers today when they have a choice, even if they have no other coverage.

## Risk Selection and Discrimination

Biased risk selection is always possible when individuals, employers, or other groups can choose whether or not to buy health coverage or whether to select one health plan rather than another. Unfortunately, this continual exercise of choice—a valued feature of individual liberty and of markets generally—can create both philosophical and practical problems in the health care arena. In particular, it can seriously diminish the degree to which the burden of health care expenses is shared among the well and the ill.

Employment-based health insurance was initially a powerful vehicle for spreading risk among the well and the ill. It is becoming less so, however, most notably for employees of small organizations but increasingly for those who work or seek to work for larger organizations. For some employers as well as insurers, the selection of low-risk workers or enrollees or the use of rules regarding preexisting conditions to exclude high-risk workers from health plans can be more attractive than trying to manage health care utilization or prices. Although federal law limits the use by employers of medical examinations and questionnaires, employers can generally obtain from their health plans extensive medical information about individual employees and their families. They have the potential to use that information to make overt or covert decisions about individual's continued employment, a particularly troublesome form of risk selection. Rapid advances in genetic technologies for identifying individual risk for various diseases is making information available that could be used by insurers to reject or limit coverage for an ever-larger proportion of the population.

## Dispersed Power and Accountability

It is in the nature of both voluntarism (as a mechanism for decisionmaking) and federalism (as a form of government) to disperse power, although the degree and nature of this dispersion can be quite variable. The current structure of voluntarism in the health sector concentrates a great deal of discretion at the employer level. With power dispersed to organizations of vastly different sizes and resources, large purchasers have had much more leverage than small employers to negotiate with health care providers for discounts and other favorable payment arrangements. Because the national government has precluded state regulation of employee benefits (except as they are indirectly affected by state insurance regulation) and simultaneously chosen to leave many important aspects of these benefits unregulated, the power to provide, negotiate, and restrict such benefits devolves to thousands of self-insured employers of widely differing competence, outlook, and accountability. At their best, employers are available—and have a direct financial incentive—to act as ombudsmen for their employees and to support them in making informed decisions and resolving problems. Such assistance is less readily available to those with Medicare, Medicaid, or individually purchased private insurance. At their worst, employers may arrange coverage through corrupt or incompetent sources, discriminate against employees on the basis of health status, and terminate benefits unilaterally.

## Diversity

Although patterns have developed that are associated with variations in employer size, region, industry, and other factors, virtually every employer's program of health benefits differs from every other employer's program in some aspect (e.g., who is eligible for coverage, through what kinds of health plans, for which kinds of services, with what level of employee cost sharing and other cost containment features, and at what overall cost). For health care providers, employment-based health benefits have promoted diversity in the prices paid by different purchasers and, as described below, in the administrative practices with which providers have to comply.

## Innovation

Compared with other nations, the United States has witnessed great innovation and entrepreneurship in the creation and marketing of health plans and coverage options and in the design or modification of cost containment and quality assurance strategies. For a variety of reasons that have little if anything to do with employment-based health benefits, the United States is also a leader in many areas of clinical and health services research. Although their specific influence cannot be easily identified, the country's largest employers and unions probably have helped encourage selected fields of research, for example, methods to measure health status and quality of care, to assess the benefits and costs associated with specific medical services, and to compare the performance of health care providers.

## Discontinuity

Although many of the above characteristics produce positive social products, they can also promote discontinuity of health coverage and health care. They are thus a mixed blessing. From one year to the next, an employer may add or drop health plans, increase or decrease the types of services covered, increase (but rarely cut) the level of employee cost sharing, change provider networks, or make other major and minor changes in the health benefits offered to employees. Some individuals lose some or all coverage when they voluntarily or involuntarily change jobs or move from welfare to working status. Others suffer "job lock" or "welfare lock" rather than voluntarily give up medical coverage. Sometimes financial protection is continuous following a job change, but the continuity of medical care is still disrupted because the new job's health plan requires a change of health care practitioner. Such discontinuity of care for those with serious health problems is likely to become an increasingly important issue as more employers and health plans attempt to restrict individuals to defined networks of health care practitioners and providers. Through their national health plans or regulatory standards for sickness funds and similar organizations and their general commitment to universal coverage for basic health services, other countries limit the likelihood that changes in job status or employers' policies will interrupt care or coverage.

## Barriers to Cost Management

Whether the measure is health spending as a percentage of the gross national product or spending per capita, the United States is noted for spending considerably more on health care than other nations. Employers' capacities and incentives to manage health benefit programs effectively are quite uneven and will remain so. Managing health benefits is a secondary issue in most employers' visions of their future and in their priorities, and some seem to feel that pressing hard on health care costs may, at some point, actually undermine employee morale and other values. At their best, employers' skills in health benefit management can be quite sophisticated, but this sophistication is generally limited to the largest employers. At their worst, employers rely for cost containment on risk segmentation, discrimination, and excessive intervention in patient-clinician decisionmaking. Direct evidence that employers' cost containment efforts make a difference, especially for overall health care costs, is very limited . On the other hand, the track record for public cost containment strategies is not dramatically more positive.

## Complexity

Several of the features singled out above—diversity, discontinuity, risk segmentation—contribute to another distinctive feature of the U.S. health care system: the immense complexity of its public and private methods for providing and managing health benefits. A great array of differing coverage features and administrative procedures have been devised by insurers, claims administrators, and others in response to different employer priorities, employee values, and government policies. Individually purchased insurance, while certainly not simple for consumers to evaluate, is less administratively complex in some respects—if only because individuals lack the leverage and the desire to obtain the customized cost management, data collection and reporting, and other health plan features that many employers successfully demand from insurers and providers. On the other hand, government control is no guarantor of simplicity. Medicare, for example, has created a complex maze of accountabilities and administrative procedures that dismays both beneficiaries and health care providers and that equals or exceeds the complexity of individual employer programs. Nonetheless, if an equivalent of today's Medicare program covered the entire population, the result would undoubtedly be the elimination of some existing regulations (e.g., primary and secondary payer rules), a reduction in the total volume of rules, forms, and other burdens on various parties, and a decline in the confusion created by inconsistent rules.

## Strengths and Limitations of These Features

The above discussion portrays a system with both positive and negative features that are related at least in part to this nation's distinctive reliance on employment-based health benefits. Many of the negatives are experienced most acutely by small employers and their employees, and certain of the positives may accrue mainly to larger employers and their employees.

Some or most of the negative features of the U.S. system are nonexistent or less serious in other economically advanced countries and might be completely or partly resolved by certain kinds of health care reforms, including some that would retain a significant role for employers. Depending on their specifics, however, reforms in the U.S. health care system might leave other negative features untouched, make some problems worse, or weaken certain positive features of the current system.

Certainly, individuals who have employment-based health benefits are by and large satisfied with them, although satisfaction with the health care system overall is relatively low. Moreover, even though employers generally report that they are very worried about the cost of health benefits and pessimistic about their ability to control these costs, most employers appear reluctant to give up their sponsorship of these benefits, particularly if the alternative is a government-based system.

The committee found it impossible to characterize several of the features described in the preceding sections as simply strengths or simply limitations. It did, however, place lack of universality, discontinuity of coverage and care, risk segmentation, barriers of cost consciousness, and complexity on the negative side. Each of these may be viewed, to some degree, as a generally unwanted but necessary consequence of efforts to achieve some more positively viewed objective. The committee acknowledges that others might not even agree that these are real or at least serious limitations, but it believes that few would argue that public or private decisionmakers have deliberately sought these ends or view them positively.

The exception may be risk segmentation, which is viewed by many insurers and some economists as fair and efficient. Many employers reject that view as it applies within their employee group but support it as it applies to outside individuals and groups. This committee rejects the argument for risk segmentation on both philosophical grounds (believing that the least vulnerable should share risk with the most vulnerable) and practical grounds (believing that competition based on risk selection should be discouraged in favor of competition based on effectiveness and efficiency in managing health care and health benefits).

Most of the other characteristics discussed above have both positive and negative aspects. Americans tend to value voluntary initiative and distributed power as barriers to overweening government control of individual and business life. Diversity is one face of this country's generally treasured pluralism, and innovation is regarded as a source of wider choice and improved medical care. However, there are negative sides to each of these features, for example, when innovation focuses on ways to avoid insuring the high-cost or high-risk individual or when expensive new techniques are disseminated with little evidence of their practical impact. These kinds of innovations are unproductive and distract from more socially productive creativity to improve the efficiency and effectiveness of health services.

In sum, today's system of voluntary employment-based health benefits earns both high and low marks. It is a dynamic one that continues to change in both positive and negative ways. This committee believes that the negatives are becoming more significant and need to be confronted through both public and private action if the nation wants to preserve a constructive role for voluntary employment-based health benefits.

## FUTURE DIRECTIONS

In response to the limitations identified above, what changes might be undertaken in employment-based health benefits that would not do appreciable damage to the system's strengths? The committee's findings and recommendations are presented in two parts. The first part assumes the continuation of a voluntary system. The second part sets aside this assumption and briefly examines the options for some form of mandatory coverage. Both make only limited reference to Medicare and Medicaid, quality improvement, data systems, and other areas in which policy changes have been recommended by the IOM and others. Neither significantly addresses the fundamental technological and social trends that are troubling the health care delivery and financing systems of most economically advanced countries, regardless of their system of medical expense protection.

Nearly all members of this committee[1] believe that without the first set of changes described below, the system of voluntary employment-based health benefits will significantly deteriorate and even collapse in some sectors. They also believe that even with these changes, a voluntary system will be unable to either significantly expand and subsidize access to health benefits for those in need or manage the problems of risk selection that so undermine the current system. Indeed, piecemeal change could further destabilize rather than strengthen the small-group market. Thus, although committee members are not united on a single specific strategy that either involves or excludes employers, nearly all believe some form of universal, compulsory coverage accompanied by major financing reforms is essential.

The committee agreed that what follows should not be interpreted as either an endorsement or a rejection of employment-based health benefits. On the one hand, a substantial minority of the committee believes employment-based health coverage is, on balance, not socially desirable, except perhaps as a financing vehicle and a supplement to a national health plan. In contrast, other committee members believe that an employment-based system can—if significantly restructured—serve the country as well or better than the likely alternatives and that such restructuring is the most workable strategy for securing reforms that move the nation toward universal coverage.

## To Improve a Voluntary System

Table 2 summarizes the committee findings and recommendations that are discussed in this section and the next and links them to the limitations in the current system identified earlier. The emphasis in the first subsection below is on the problems created by risk selection and risk segmentation in both large and small employee groups. The final four subsections emphasize the committee's concerns about the affordability of coverage, its continuity, and its stability.

### *Reducing or Compensating for Risk Selection*

As a first priority, if a system of voluntary employment-based health benefits is to be maintained and improved, risk selection and risk segmentation must be significantly reduced as they affect both large and small em-

---

[1] One member prepared a supplementary statement. See page 261.

**TABLE 2**   Summary of Committee Findings and Recommendations
on Steps to Respond to Certain Current Limitations of Voluntary
Employment-Based Health Benefits

| Current Limitation | Responses that Continue a Voluntary System |
|---|---|
| • Risk Segmentation<br>• Lack of Coverage | Risk selection should be controlled as it affects individuals in large and small employee groups through steps that<br>• prohibit insurance companies from denying coverage to groups and individuals within groups based on their past or expected health status or claims experience;<br>• price coverage to individuals without regard to medical risk or claims experience;<br>• amend the Employee Retirement Income Security Act (ERISA) to prohibit medical underwriting practices in employee health benefits;<br>• amend ERISA (through provisions analogous to those contained in the Americans with Disabilities Act) to regulate employer access to individual medical information collected in connection with employment-based health benefits;<br>• devise methods and mechanisms (such as purchasing cooperatives) for risk adjusting employer and government contributions to health plans to reflect the risk level of enrollees; and<br>• extend public subsidies to help employers, employees, or both purchase health coverage for workers and their families. |
| • Discontinuity<br>• Complexity | National (ERISA) regulations or national standards for state regulation should be adopted to fill selected gaps and achieve more uniformity in the oversight of employee health benefits (e.g., solvency regulations, medical expense payments as percentage of total health plan expense, definition of basic benefits, coverage for workers changing jobs, and data collection protocols). |
| Current Limitation | Responses that Go Beyond a Voluntary System |
| • Lack of Coverage<br>• Risk Segmentation | The above responses will not significantly extend access or control risk segmentation and thus should be augmented by policies that<br>• require that all individuals have coverage through a mandated employer program, mandatory individual purchase, public provision, or some combination of these approaches; and<br>• minimize the financial burden of such coverage on low-income individuals and low-wage organizations. |

ployee groups. Movement in this direction will require a set of interrelated actions affecting (1) underwriting practices, (2) employers' access to personal medical information, and (3) methods and mechanisms for risk adjusting employer or government contributions to health plans and for monitoring health plan behavior. Because these changes will do little to make health benefits more affordable and will likely increase costs for some, new subsidies to help lower-income groups (or their employers) purchase health benefits will be necessary. Even then, some will choose not to purchase coverage.

*Medical underwriting in the small-group market.* To reduce risk segmentation in the insurance market for small groups, one step that policymakers can take is to prohibit insurance companies from denying coverage to groups and individuals within groups on the basis of their past or expected health status or claims experience. In addition, what an individual pays for health coverage should not, in principle, be based on her or his health status, past medical expenses, or similar factors, although the initial stages of policy change and implementation may concentrate on the narrowing of price differentials. The committee recognizes that, by itself, eliminating or further regulating these medical underwriting practices could encourage some insurers or health plans to be even more energetic in their efforts to attract the well and avoid the ill and could encourage some low-risk individuals to drop coverage if their premiums increased. Some of the steps discussed below address these problems.

The committee sees some merit in the argument that individual prudence may be encouraged by relating health status or health behavior to individual payments for health benefits. Nonetheless, most members believe that such risk rating of health coverage is, on balance, neither fair nor productive given the myriad genetic, cultural, economic, and other factors that shape individual behavior and limit self-determination. Moreover, identifying a risk factor is not the same as identifying a reliable and successful strategy for reducing the risk and its health consequences.

*Medical underwriting among larger employers.* Steps to modify the small-group insurance market would not affect risk selection as it is practiced among larger, self-insured employers, where the committee sees disturbing signs that the concepts of medical underwriting and risk segmentation are becoming more attractive to financially pressed employers. To prohibit medical underwriting within self-insured groups would require federal action to amend the Employee Retirement Income Security Act (ERISA). If action on the small-group insurance market were undertaken at the federal level, then provisions related to medical underwriting affecting both small and large groups could be explicitly coordinated.

*Protection of personal medical information.* Even if explicit medical underwriting disappears, the health benefit costs of experience-rated and self-insured employers will be affected by the health status, age structure, and other characteristics of the work force. Thus, some employers may still be tempted to reduce their exposure to high health care costs by using information obtained through their health benefit plans to discriminate against high-cost and high-risk workers.

To discourage this form of risk selection, employer access to certain kinds of information collected in connection with employment-based health benefits should be limited through provisions analogous to those contained in the Americans with Disabilities Act of 1990 (ADA). Although ADA prohibits certain employer-required physical examinations and questions about employee or family health status and restricts access to permitted sources of information, it does *not* restrict access to information available from claims data, medical underwriting questionnaires, or other sources of data associated with employment-based health benefits. This information, which involves covered family members as well as workers, can be as revealing and potentially damaging as that covered by ADA. Information restrictions that are analogous to those in the ADA might define what kind of individual-specific information insurers, claims administrators, or similar entities may share with employers; what employer uses of the information are permissible (e.g., detecting fraud or developing programs to target specific health problems such as premature births); which staff may have access to the information; and how shared information is to be stored. They might also have to define more specifically the rules for employers who choose to self-administer claims and who thus have the greatest access to personal information about employees.

As long as employers' payments for employee health benefits vary depending on the health status of their workers, employers will still have an incentive to avoid high-risk or high-cost workers or dependents above and beyond that related to their concerns about workers' compensation, absenteeism, and similar costs. Bringing self-insured and experience-rated employers back into a broader community risk pool would lessen the motivation for discrimination. Absent movement in that direction, regulatory, educational, and other efforts to discourage discrimination by both employers and health plans have an important role, although covert discrimination is always difficult to detect and eliminate.

*Risk-adjusted employer or government contributions to health plans.* An end to medical underwriting may diminish one source of risk segmentation in a competitive market, but it would leave other sources unaffected. As long as health plans can reap sizable financial advantages from favorable risk selection, they will have an incentive to devise creative and difficult-to-regulate tactics to do so. To discourage these tactics and encourage stability, some protection is needed for health plans that have existing high-risk enrollments, services, or features that attract sicker individuals, or other characteristics that do not warrant marketplace penalties. One protection is risk-adjusted contributions to health plans by employers and governments (for enrollees from public programs), although additional protections involving very high cost individuals will still be needed.

Unfortunately, the methods to assess relative risk or determine appropriate payment adjustments are still in their infancy. They are relatively weak, often require data not readily available when needed, and may incorporate unwanted incentives for inefficient behavior. Several employers are using different methods to make risk-adjusted payments to health plans, and a number of public and private research projects are under way to build better methods. Slow progress in risk-adjustment methodologies is probably the single greatest barrier to making competition a more positive force in the health care arena.

*Purchasing cooperatives.* The mechanisms as well as the methods needed to make risk-adjusted payments are inadequate in significant respects. For example, small employers lack the resources to manage risk-adjusted contributions for the plans they offer to employees. Some kind of external mechanism is needed to handle the process, for example, as the government does in its administration of capitated payment for HMOs enrolling Medicare beneficiaries. Purchasing cooperatives have been suggested as one such mechanism. Such cooperatives might also reduce marketing and other costs and allow employees of small employers a choice among health plans. However, if multiple, competitive purchasing cooperatives were created rather than the single entity envisioned by most managed competition proposals, then problems of risk selection across cooperatives would likely arise and savings in marketing and other costs would diminish.

Taken together, the above steps should provide individuals with new protection from restrictions on their access to health coverage related to their past, present, or expected future health status. However, they are unlikely to eliminate completely the advantages health plans receive from favorable risk selection and the incentives for plans to engage in the selection strategies described in Chapter 5. To further discourage discrimination against higher risk individuals or "skimming" of lower risk individuals, it will probably be necessary to monitor health plan enrollment and disenrollment patterns and their marketing, management, and other strategies. The design of practical and reasonably effective policies will be a challenge.

### Subsidizing Coverage

As noted above, eliminating or significantly reducing medical underwriting and risk segmentation will in the short term do little to make health benefits more affordable for many employers and employees, especially those in low-wage industries. Costs might even increase for some groups and individuals now in low-risk pools, and some low-risk individuals might avoid buying insurance until they thought they needed costly health care services. Overall, in the absence of some financial assistance to some employees or employers or both, access to health benefits is not likely to improve. The committee therefore concludes that some public subsidies are necessary to extend coverage to more workers and their families. The policy dilemma this creates in the current fiscal environment is discussed further below.

*Other Regulatory Issues*

If the above actions were taken, they would go some distance toward making health benefits "portable," alleviating the phenomenon of "job lock," and discouraging efforts by some employers to gain a competitive advantage by restricting or not offering health benefits. However, further action would be necessary—probably through amendments to ERISA—to limit the use of waiting periods and other health plan provisions that may interrupt coverage and thereby discourage labor mobility and permit some continued degree of risk selection by employers and health plans.

*ERISA.* The above findings taken together point to the need for amendments to ERISA or other legislation that would limit medical underwriting, restrict employer access to sensitive health plan information, reduce barriers to labor mobility, and monitor certain health plan practices. In addition, most members of this committee believe that the system of voluntary employment-based health benefits could be further strengthened by more coherent, uniform, and protective regulatory oversight of employee health benefits, whether they are conventionally insured or self-insured and whether they involve a single employer or a multiple employer benefit plan. The current regulatory vacuum, whereby states cannot regulate employee health benefits and the federal government largely refrains from doing so, needs at a minimum to be filled in selected areas such as plan solvency and data collection protocols. Oversight could be extended either as part of a policy of uniform national regulation or as part of a policy that permits some state discretion within national guidelines or standards.

*Defining basic benefits.* The committee would not favor a proliferation of federal or state mandates for coverage of individual treatments, providers, or sites of care. Such movement could be curtailed by a government commitment to define a basic benefit package developed through processes that weigh the advantages expected from coverage against its costs and risks. Ideally, this package should apply to public and private programs. If the value of the basic benefit package is to be constrained by some kind of cap on its expected actuarial cost, the problems in defining the package become particularly acute, as Oregon's recent experience in trying to set coverage priorities demonstrates. Because the committee does not agree that current methods and definitions are sufficient for this formidable and sensitive task, particularly given the variability in individual patients and the extra decisionmaking burdens imposed by a budget constraint, the research agenda discussed below returns to this issue.

*The Financing Dilemma*

Although the combination of the steps described in this and the next section would address important weaknesses in the current system, they would do nothing to control the rate of increase in health care spending. Moreover, some would impose new financial obligations for federal or state governments, employers, or employees. Any broad new policy of subsidized voluntary (or compulsory) coverage will be costly, probably cannot be financed primarily at the state level, and will therefore have to compete with other demands in a federal budget process that is already severely stressed. New subsidies to employers or individuals or both could be financed by cutting health care spending, by shifting resources from other areas, by increasing taxes in some fashion, or all three.

In principle, as described in Chapter 6, costs may be reduced in many ways, for example, by controlling prices, eliminating inappropriate use of services, controlling the introduction and use of new technologies of untested cost-effectiveness, and reducing administrative costs. In practice, most members of the committee believe it is unrealistic to expect such good performance in these areas that all the costs of extending coverage could be offset.

Committee members have quite different views on what cost containment strategies show the most potential to be effective, equitable, and compatible with good quality care and on whether these strategies should include an important role for employers. Thus, this report includes no recommendations on the major obstacle to any form of universal health insurance. In addition, this report makes no recommendations on the use of payroll, income, or other taxes to finance coverage or on the amount individuals ought to contribute directly for health coverage. It saw the issues in this area as so intertwined with the broader health care reform agenda that detailed recommendations would go beyond the committee's charge. The committee, however, acknowledges that the changes discussed in this section—and the next—are unlikely as long as policymakers lack a realistic financing strategy that they feel is feasible politically.

Furthermore, it may be important to consider employer reactions to health care reforms that limited employers' involvement in managing employee health benefits and assigned them only a voluntary or nonvoluntary financing role (e.g., a direct premium contribution or payroll tax). Employers might more vigorously oppose increases in their financial obligations for a health benefits program over which they had no control, and some might withdraw altogether from a voluntary role.

*Beyond Voluntary Coverage*

The steps described in the first part of Table 2 could encourage some employers that do not offer coverage to begin to do so and could help some workers afford coverage that is now beyond their reach. Nonetheless, some employers and workers would still choose not to offer, purchase, or accept health coverage, even if substantial (but not total) subsidies were provided to assist vulnerable small employers and lower-income workers. For most of the committee, therefore, an important finding is that these steps alone—difficult as they may be to achieve in today's environment—cannot significantly extend access or control risk selection. To do so, in the view of the majority of the committee, will almost certainly require that some form of compulsory and subsidized coverage be imposed on the employer, the employee, or both. In fact, without universal participation, the problems facing the small group market could get even worse. Although the committee did not examine the problems of the self-employed and those with no connection to the workforce, it believes that the arguments for universal coverage apply to these groups as well.

One rationale for requiring health coverage lies in a major limitation of a voluntary system that precludes medical underwriting. That is, some individuals or groups would choose not to purchase coverage until faced with a health problem. Such action is like buying fire insurance while one's house is burning down or life insurance once terminal illness has been diagnosed. Although this kind of behavior can be controlled by leaving some medical underwriting in place, the majority of this committee believes, on balance, that leaving individuals and families without coverage is not a desirable strategy, especially since low-income groups—even if subsidized—are likely to be overrepresented in the excluded class.

Another rationale is that although those without coverage can generally obtain health care once medical problems have become emergencies, such care tends to come late in the course of the problems, many of which could have been prevented or treated more effectively with more timely care. Emergency care also tends not to be coordinated to meet other important but less immediately pressing health care needs. Moreover, because much care for the uninsured is written off as charity service or bad debt, health care providers seek to finance it by shifting the cost to other parties, particularly those who lack market leverage. Although some states have created special schemes (e.g., earmarked taxes on hospital services, regulated hospital rates) to help cover uncompensated care in hospitals and have established limited programs to provide primary and preventive care to the uninsured, these are second-best strategies in the view of this committee—especially given the current vulnerability of these schemes to ERISA challenges. Again, most members of this committee believe that extending health benefits is preferable on grounds of improving health status and achieving equity.

Greatly different approaches are possible to implement compulsory and subsidized coverage, and provisions for some form of mandated coverage are embedded in reform proposals that span the political spectrum. Not all would continue a significant role for the employers. For example, some strong advocates of market-oriented strategies urge a move toward mandatory individual purchase of insurance, some government subsidy for lower-income individuals, and an optional and limited role for employers. In contrast, some advocates of a strong government favor a unified social insurance program that would make health coverage near-universal and compulsory and would largely restrict employers to a financing role.

Both these approaches would resolve many of the complexities associated with mandated employer coverage, for example, treatment of different categories of workers (e.g., part-time, seasonal, and free-lance) and discontinuity of specific benefits or sources of health care related to changes in job status. Depending on its specific features, an individual mandate could make universal the problems of risk selection now found in the individual purchase of insurance or it could attempt to control them through the kinds of features described in the preceding section. A unified national system following the Canadian model would eliminate risk selection by eliminating choice among health plans (but not choice among individual practitioner or provider). A national nonemployment-based program that allowed for choice among health plans would, however, require some mechanisms for controlling or compensating for selection.

The primary appeal of proposals that provide a significant role for employment-based health benefits is that they would continue a familiar structure that is, in general, viewed favorably by most Americans. This structure provides many employees with an accessible source of information and assistance in making health plan choices and resolving problems. It also encourages employer interest in the link between health care and worker productivity and well-being and the link between health spending and health outcomes.

Again, this committee does not take a specific position about broad options for health care reform. It does, however, agree that the strengths of the current system should be appreciated and the potential for preserving these strengths while reducing the system's weaknesses should be thoughtfully considered.

Facing problems and trade-offs squarely will be an immense challenge for the policy process. Data analysis is helpful but limited and, in any case, not conclusive given that powerful interests and values are at stake. The nation's inability to decide whether access to basic health care and medical expense protection is a collective obligation or a private responsibility encourages impasse rather than action and rhetoric rather than reasoned problem solving. Surveys indicate considerable public misunderstanding of health care cost and access problems, and this misunderstanding could be a significant obstacle to change if not successfully addressed by a careful public education strategy. These constraints are reinforced by the oppressive persistence of large federal budget deficits, slow economic growth, and the view that effective cost controls must precede expanded access. The committee grants these difficulties, but it is, in general, a group of optimists who believe that this nation's policymakers and its citizens have met equal challenges in the past and can do so again.

## Research Agenda

Implied or stated in the committee's findings are several important research questions. Some are already the subject of much attention, whereas others have, as yet, been little emphasized. In summary, they involve the following five areas:

- methodologies for risk adjusting payments to health plans,
- consequences of underwriting reforms,
- challenges and options in defining basic benefits,
- employer assistance with employee decisionmaking and problem resolution, and
- continuity of patient care in the context of multiple choice among network health plans.

## FINAL THOUGHTS

The United States is unique in its reliance on employers to provide voluntarily health benefits for workers and their family members. This constantly evolving arrangement has its pluses and minuses, although the limitations of the system are becoming considerably more visible and worrisome. In particular, the dynamics of risk segmentation, the potential for increased discrimination, the persistence of millions of uncovered individuals through economic upturns and downturns alike, and the increasing complexity generated by employer—and government—cost containment efforts have led to many proposals for health care reform. Some retain a central role for employment-based health benefits—voluntary or mandatory—whereas others eliminate them (relegate them to a minor position) in favor of a government health plan or a market for individually purchased insurance. As the details of specific proposals are emerging and being subjected to increasing critique and analysis, the arguments about their particular characteristics, expected consequences, and apparent tradeoffs are growing more specific.

Do employment-based health benefits offer sufficient "value added" to make their continuation, indeed their mandating, worthwhile even if some important limitations of the system cannot be fully corrected? Each member of the committee has a somewhat different answer to this question, one affected to varying degrees by the practical reality that this system is what is in place and is familiar and perceived as valuable to most Americans. Nonetheless, most committee members foresee a continued deterioration in the quality and scope of health coverage unless major steps are undertaken to reduce or correct the serious weaknesses in the system. Most believe it unlikely that a larger proportion of small employers will voluntarily and independently provide the coverage and assistance offered by large employers.

Overall, policymakers and reform proponents of all stripes may both overstate and understate the advantages and disadvantages of current arrangements, a circumstance made easy by the diversity of these arrangements. As noted above, those who would limit employer involvement in health benefits largely or entirely to a financing role may overestimate the degree to which employers will acquiesce in funding increased spending under such circumstances.

Despite the diversity of its views on specific directions for health care reform and the role of the employer, the committee would not like to see lost the help that employers can provide to employees facing problems with their health coverage. Because imperfect performance can be expected from a single national system or a competitive market based on individual (not employer) choice, employers might very well see advantages in a new kind of "employee assistance program." This program could provide employees with aid in understanding their health plan coverage or help in resolving problems with denied claims, bureaucratic inertia, or whatever similar difficulties a reformed system might present.

Furthermore, the committee would not like employers to become unconcerned about the link between health coverage, health status, and worker well-being and uninterested in efforts to improve assessments of the cost-effectiveness of specific medical services and health care providers. Because workplace and community health promotion programs, local health care initiatives and institutions, and other health-related activities have attracted employees' and employers' support for reasons beyond any specific tie to their health benefit programs, some continued support can be expected and fostered.

Given the creativity shown by both public and private sectors in the past and the considerable accomplishments of employment-based health benefits, there is reason to be optimistic that decisionmakers—if they can agree on a basic framework for reform—can find a positive role for employers. That role may be larger or smaller than it is today, but in either case it should be designed to support the country's broad objective of securing wider and more equitable access to more appropriate health care at a more reasonable cost.

# 1

# Background and Introduction

*Lloyd and Anne Ridge's daughter, Beth, is doing well 12 months after being diagnosed with acute lymphoblastic leukemia. Although she experiences some side effects from maintenance chemotherapy, Beth's prospects are good—over half the children with the disease achieve long-term remission and probable cure. Lloyd is profoundly grateful for the advances in chemotherapy that have made this possible. He remembers his childhood friend who died 40 years ago when this leukemia was invariably and quickly fatal. Lloyd is also grateful for the health insurance offered by his employer. It paid for care from top-notch physicians and hospitals and kept the family from financial hardship. The personnel office also helped sort out a couple of problems with insurance claims for Beth's care.*

* * * *

*One year later, Beth Ridge continues in good health. However, Lloyd Ridge has new worries. Lloyd knows his employer is concerned about its increasing costs and is considering a new health plan. It could force the Ridges to use a limited network of physicians and hospitals or pay a much higher proportion of the ongoing costs for Beth's checkups and maintenance chemotherapy. Even more threatening is the small but real chance that the company will reduce its work force. If Lloyd lost his job, the family could not switch to coverage through Anne's job because she works as a free-lance editor with no fringe benefits. They could, under federal law, continue group coverage, at their own expense, for at least 18 months, but Lloyd worries that he would face covert discrimination by another employer or insurer because of Beth's history. Lloyd and Anne do not even think about their old dream of going into business for themselves. Individually purchased health insurance to cover Beth would be expensive or perhaps not even available at any price.*

To make the many accomplishments of modern medicine available to Americans such as Beth Ridge, the United States depends heavily on a voluntary system of employment-based health benefits. Although neither federal nor state law generally requires employers to finance health coverage for employees and their families, almost two-thirds of all Americans under age 65 receive health benefits through the workplace.

Sixty years ago, when the full capacity of modern medicine was just beginning to be mobilized, such benefits barely existed. Indeed, few had access at that time to health insurance from any private or public source. Since World War II, most American workers and their families have come to rely on health insurance provided through the workplace. Recent trends in the general economy and in the health sector have, however, generated considerable uncertainty about the continued availability of such coverage. An individual's probability of losing health benefits, being trapped in a job or on welfare because a new job comes without health coverage, or facing disruptions in established relationships with physicians is growing. Many employees and employers are increasingly concerned—even fearful—about their inability and the inability of governments, insurers, and medical professionals to deal effectively with problems related to the availability, cost, and quality of health benefits and health care.

The United States is unique among advanced industrialized nations in the way it relies on employers to voluntarily sponsor and finance health benefits for workers and their families. In this system, not only are employers free to offer or not offer coverage, most have extensive discretion in determining what specific benefits are to be offered, how they are to be administered, whether employees must participate, what share of the cost employees must pay, and what will be done to control costs. As a consequence, American workers have particular reason to factor the availability and quality of workplace health benefits into employment decisions, collective bargaining, and other interactions with employers.

An understanding of the link between employment and health benefits and the relationship between private and public spheres of decisionmaking about health care delivery and financing is essential to an informed debate about restructuring the nation's health care financing and delivery system. Such an understanding, in turn, requires an appreciation of the social, economic, and political dynamics that created employment-based health insurance and the advantages and disadvantages that accrue to its sponsors and participants and the society as a whole. This report is intended to help build this necessary understanding by

  • describing employment-based health benefits and their relationship to the overall structure of health care financing and delivery in this country;
  • identifying the important features, strengths, and limitations of this system;

• assessing strategies or actions that might improve the performance of this system; and

• defining an agenda for future research.

## EMPLOYMENT-BASED HEALTH BENEFITS IN CONTEXT

In the United States the strong link between health benefits and the workplace developed through a combination of historical coincidences and deliberate decisions. Its emergence depended on the voluntary initiative of many private individuals and groups, the largely unintended impetus of federal tax and labor laws, the collective bargaining strategies of trade unions, and the political failure of proposals for universal, public health insurance. Beginning in the early 1930s, this system of voluntary employment-based health benefits experienced three decades of rapid growth. In the 1960s and 1970s, major government programs were established to cover the elderly, the disabled, and some of the poor—groups ill-suited to private insurance. Today, neither government nor employment-based coverage reaches many low-income or high-risk workers and their families, especially those who work for small firms, those who are employed on a part-time or seasonal basis, and those who are chronically ill but not disabled.

The relative importance of private and public sources of health benefits and health care spending is summarized in Tables 1.1 and 1.2 and Figure 1.1. These tables reveal a number of facts:

• Seventy-three percent of all Americans below the age of 65 have private health coverage, the great majority through programs sponsored by private and government employers and unions.

• Almost 36 million Americans below the age of 65—17 percent—have no health benefits.

• Of the uninsured, 30.5 million—85 percent—live in families headed by a worker, most of whom work for firms with fewer than 100 employees.

• Ninety-six percent of all Americans 65 and over are covered by public programs, many have supplementary private coverage (some of it employer sponsored), and only 1 percent have no coverage.

• Public program spending accounts for nearly 40 percent of all spending on health care services and supplies, and employers and households account for roughly equivalent shares of the remainder.

• In the past three decades, health care expenditures have become a considerably larger fraction of government and business spending, but out-of-pocket consumer expenditures have increased more modestly as a share of personal income. As a result, households now directly finance a much smaller proportion of health care than they did 30 years ago, and government and business finance a greater share.

**TABLE 1.1**   Nonelderly and Elderly Americans with Selected Sources of Health Insurance, Employee Benefit Research Institute Analysis of the March 1991 Current Population Survey

|  | Nonelderly (below age 65) | | Elderly (age 65 and over) | |
| --- | --- | --- | --- | --- |
|  | No. (millions) | % | No. (millions) | % |
| Total population | 215.9 | 100 | 30.1 | 100 |
| Total with private health insurance | 158.3 | 73 | 20.6 | 68 |
| Employer coverage | 138.7 | 64 | 10.0 | 33 |
| Other private coverage | 19.7 | 9 | 10.6 | 35 |
| Total with public health insurance | 29.2 | 14 | 28.9 | 96 |
| Medicare | 3.5 | 2 | 28.8 | 96 |
| Medicaid | 21.6 | 10 | 2.6 | 9 |
| CHAMPUS/CHAMPVA[a] | 5.9 | 3 | 1.1 | 4 |
| No health insurance | 35.7 | 17 | 0.3 | 1 |
| In family headed by worker | 30.5 | 15 | NA[b] | NA |
| In family headed by nonworker | 5.2 | 2 | NA | NA |

NOTE:  Details may not add to totals because individuals may receive coverage from more than one source.

[a]Includes only the retired military and members of their families provided health coverage through the Civilian Health and Medical Program for the Uniformed Services and the Civilian Health and Medical Program for the Department of Veterans Affairs.  Excludes active duty military personnel and members of their families.

[b]NA = not available.

SOURCE:  Adapted from EBRI, 1992d, Tables 1 and 8.


Although the proportion of the nonelderly population covered by employment-based health benefits leveled off during the 1970s and even decreased from 66 to 64 percent between 1988 and 1990, business spending on health benefits continues to grow as a fraction of their total labor compensation and after-tax profits (Levit et al., 1991).  Business health spending stood at 7 percent of total labor compensation in 1990, up from 2 percent in 1965 and 5 percent in 1980.  For the nation as a whole, about 12 percent ($666.2 billion) of the nation's gross national product was accounted for by spending on health care (including noncommercial health research and construction) in 1990, up from 6 percent in 1965 and 9 percent in 1980.

This rising commitment of resources to health care services reflects a complex set of interacting influences.  These include a generally rising standard of living, an aging population, more comprehensive health care coverage, the influence of new technologies and medical practices, an incentive structure that encourages high medical spending (e.g., third-party

**TABLE 1.2** Trends in Government, Individual, and Business Spending in Selected Years, 1965 to 1990

| | Government Health Spending as Percentage of Total Government Spending[a] | | Individual Health Spending as Percentage of Adjusted Personal Income[b] | Business Health Spending as Percentage of Total[c] | |
| | | | | Gross Private Domestic Product | Total Labor Compensation |
| --- | --- | --- | --- | --- | --- |
| | Federal | State | | | |
| 1965 | 9 | 12 | 4.2 | 1.0 | 2.0 |
| 1970 | 15 | 12 | 4.1 | 1.7 | 3.1 |
| 1975 | 17 | 14 | 4.3 | 2.1 | 3.9 |
| 1980 | 18 | 14 | 4.1 | 2.7 | 4.9 |
| 1985 | 17 | 15 | 4.7 | 3.3 | 6.1 |
| 1986 | 16 | 15 | 4.7 | 3.4 | 6.3 |
| 1987 | 16 | 15 | 4.9 | 3.4 | 6.2 |
| 1988 | 16 | 15 | 4.9 | 3.6 | 6.5 |
| 1989 | 17 | 15 | 4.9 | 3.7 | 6.9 |
| 1990 | 18 | 15 | 5.0 | 3.9 | 7.1 |

[a]For detailed definitions and data sources, see Levit et al. (1991), especially Table 2 and accompanying discussion.

[b]For detailed definitions and data sources, see Levit and Cowan (1991), especially Table 4 and accompanying discussion of tables and revisions in methods.

[c]For detailed definitions and data sources, see Levit and Cowan (1991), especially Table 3 and accompanying discussion of tables and revisions in methods.

SOURCE: U.S. Health Care Financing Administration, Office of the Actuary, and other sources, as presented in Levit et al. (1991).

payments on an open-ended fee-for-service reimbursement basis), tax policy, and growing administrative costs (including malpractice costs).

Although international comparisons can provide a useful context for discussion, they can also be misleading, given the different ways in which nations provide health care and report health care spending and the complexities in calculating appropriate exchange rates. Table 1.3 presents trend data for six advanced industrial countries using three different measures of health spending: total health expenditures as a percentage of gross domestic product;[1] an index (1970 = 1.0) of the cumulative change in per capita health spending (in national currencies); and per capita spending denomi-

---

[1]Different analyses use different measures of national economic output. The analysis reported here uses the gross domestic product (GDP), which is the value of all goods and services produced in a country. Analyses reported earlier in this chapter used the gross national product, which is the value of all goods and services produced in a country plus income earned in foreign countries less payments to foreign sources.

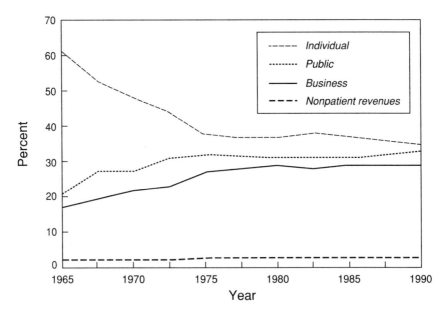

**FIGURE 1.1**   Percentage of expenditures for health services and supplies, by payer, 1965 to 1990.   See Table 1.2 for description of differences in categorizing of public and private spending.   SOURCE:   Based on analysis by the Health Care Financing Administration, Office of the Actuary; data from the Office of National Health Statistics as presented in Levit and Cowan, 1991.   (The legend for this table in the source document inadvertently switched the labels for the business and public spending curves [HCFA, personal communication, June 4, 1992].)

nated in U.S. dollars.   The United States stands out for its high overall level of health care spending, although other countries have generally shared the experience of rapid growth in per capita spending in recent decades.   This country is also noteworthy for the relatively low proportion of total health care spending that is accounted for by public sources.   That figure is just over 40 percent in the United States (with workers' compensation counted as public spending) versus 95 percent in Norway (the highest), 87 percent in the United Kingdom, and over 70 percent in France, Germany, and Japan (Schieber and Poullier, 1991).

The trends in U.S. health care spending have focused national attention on the question:   what contribution do such high and growing expenditures make to the health status and quality of life of the U.S. population and the productivity of its work force?   To date, health services research has not documented this contribution very precisely, but it has raised serious questions about the appropriateness and effectiveness of many health care services.   These questions have prompted government, employers, and others to seek better methods for judging the value of specific medical services, assessing the performance of health care providers, and evaluating whether medical resources—from surgery to pharmaceuticals—are appropriately priced by existing markets and practices.

Although employers both here and abroad often have an important role in financing health benefits, U.S. employers are unique in the discretion they have in determining whether and how to offer health coverage to current and former employees and their family members. This voluntary system of employment-based health insurance has helped bring many Americans advantages that may not be so widely experienced elsewhere. It has encouraged creativity in the design of health benefit plans to suit different preferences and circumstances. Some major employers have played a visible role in the movement for more research on the outcomes of medical care and for more accountability from providers for the cost and quality of the care they offer. In addition, some have used their purchasing power and skills to reinforce consumers' and patients' efforts to articulate and follow through on demands that health plans be sensitive to enrollees' concerns, questions, and problems. The growth and structure of employment-based health benefits (including the methods used to pay for medical care) have undoubtedly been important—albeit hard to document—stimuli for the advances in biomedical science, medical education, and medical services and technologies. These advances have made the U.S. health care system overall the most technically and clinically sophisticated and dynamic in the world.

Moreover, despite widespread public concern about health care costs and the problems of the uninsured, most of those with employment-based health benefits find them satisfactory or highly satisfactory and rate them most important among workplace benefits. When a recent public opinion survey developed by the Employee Benefit Research Institute and the Institute of Medicine asked who should bear the most responsibility for providing health benefits for full-time employees and their dependents, 48 percent of those surveyed identified employers, 31 percent the federal government, 14 percent individuals, and 3 percent said "all the same" (Appendix A). Employers too appear to favor a continued employer role—though generally not a mandatory one—rather than a fully public system of health coverage (Cantor et al., 1991). Although the public is ambivalent about the desirability of many government actions, they clearly favor government requirements that employers provide health benefits for full-time workers and dependents (Appendix A).

On the other hand, countries that leave employers with little but a statutory financing role in health benefits are afflicted less or not at all by issues that greatly worry decisionmakers here—for example, millions of working people without health benefits, high administrative costs and com-

**TABLE 1.3** Selected International Comparisons of Health Spending, for Selected Years, 1970 to 1989

| | Canada | | | France | | | Germany | | |
|---|---|---|---|---|---|---|---|---|---|
| | %GDP[a] | NPCS[b] | US$[c] | %GDP | NPCS | US$ | %GDP | NPCS | US$ |
| 1970 | 7.1 | 1.0 | 274 | 5.8 | 1.0 | 192 | 5.9 | 1.0 | 199 |
| 1975 | 7.2 | 1.96 | 478 | 7.0 | 2.21 | 365 | 8.2 | 2.12 | 422 |
| 1980 | 7.4 | 3.63 | 806 | 7.6 | 4.60 | 656 | 8.5 | 3.16 | 749 |
| 1985 | 8.5 | 6.46 | 1,315 | 8.5 | 8.61 | 991 | 8.6 | 3.98 | 1,046 |
| 1986 | 8.8 | 7.08 | 1,427 | 8.5 | 9.31 | 1,036 | 8.5 | 4.16 | 1,082 |
| 1987 | 8.8 | 7.67 | 1,507 | 8.5 | 9.82 | 1,088 | 8.6 | 4.34 | 1,139 |
| 1988 | 8.6 | 8.27 | 1,581 | 8.6 | 10.63 | 1,173 | 8.9 | 4.72 | 1,250 |
| 1989 | 8.7 | 8.97 | 1,683 | 8.7 | 11.57 | 1,274 | 8.2 | 4.63 | 1,232 |
| 1970–80[d] | | 13.8 | | | 16.5 | | | 12.2 | |
| 1980–89[d] | | 10.6 | | | 10.8 | | | 4.3 | |
| 1970–89[d] | | 12.2 | | | 13.8 | | | 8.4 | |

[a]Percentage of gross domestic product.
[b]Growth in nominal per capita health spending. Index year is 1970. The value for later years is 1.0 plus the percentage increase in spending over 1970. Thus, the 3.63 figure for Canada in 1980 means that per capita spending in Canada in 1980 was 263 percent higher than in 1970.

plexity, and insurer refused to cover high-risk individuals. Because health coverage is not portable (i.e., does not continue automatically from job to job), many U.S. workers feel locked into jobs they would rather leave. Increasing numbers worry that unilateral actions by their employer will put them and their families into the ranks of the uninsured. Small employers face many difficulties in providing any coverage at all. Many larger employers are now dubious about their capacity to manage costs, anxious about legal liability that could arise from some of their cost containment measures, and worried that their health benefit costs make them less competitive. In addition, state officials are frustrated because federal laws limit their ability to regulate (directly or indirectly) the health benefits offered by self-insured employee benefit plans and complicate programs to finance care for the uninsured, underinsured, and uninsurable. Rounding out the litany of disaffected parties, health care practitioners and institutions object to what they see as misguided and ineffective bureaucratic micromanagement of medical practice generated by employer, insurer, and government efforts to control costs and increase accountability.

For many, the most troubling element in national comparisons is not that the United States is different or even more expensive. Distinctiveness is often a matter of pride, as are high expenditures for a socially valued

| | Japan | | | United Kingdom | | | United States | | |
|---|---|---|---|---|---|---|---|---|---|
| | %GDP[a] | NPCS[b] | US$[c] | %GDP | NPCS | US$ | %GDP | NPCS | US$ |
| 1970 | 4.4 | 1.0 | 126 | 4.5 | 1.0 | 146 | 7.4 | 1.0 | 346 |
| 1975 | 5.5 | 2.51 | 252 | 5.5 | 2.49 | 272 | 8.4 | 1.79 | 592 |
| 1980 | 6.4 | 4.72 | 515 | 5.8 | 5.74 | 454 | 9.3 | 3.35 | 1,059 |
| 1985 | 6.5 | 6.30 | 785 | 6.0 | 9.10 | 658 | 10.6 | 5.65 | 1,700 |
| 1986 | 6.7 | 6.66 | 828 | 6.0 | 9.79 | 697 | 10.8 | 6.08 | 1,813 |
| 1987 | 6.8 | 7.10 | 907 | 5.9 | 10.75 | 747 | 11.1 | 6.62 | 1,955 |
| 1988 | 6.7 | 7.47 | 978 | 5.9 | 11.81 | 793 | 11.3 | 7.32 | 2,140 |
| 1989 | 6.7 | 7.79 | 1,035 | 5.8 | 12.85 | 836 | 11.8 | 8.12 | 2,354 |
| 1970–80[d] | | 16.8 | | | 19.1 | | | 12.9 | |
| 1980–89[d] | | 5.7 | | | 9.4 | | | 10.3 | |
| 1970–89[d] | | 11.4 | | | 14.4 | | | 11.7 | |

[c]Per capita health spending in denominated U.S. dollars.
[d]Compound annual rate of growth over the time period.

SOURCE: Schieber and Poullier, 1991. For further definitions and descriptions, this reference should be consulted.

service. No pride, however, can be derived from the fact that although this country spends so much more on health care than other countries (nearly 40 percent more per capita in 1989 than the second ranking nation, Canada), it leaves a larger fraction of its population uninsured and has not achieved clearly superior health outcomes.[2]

People in other economically advanced nations are not without concerns about their systems for financing and delivering health care. They, too, worry about increased health care spending and about access problems

---

[2]For a variety of reasons, this discussion should not be read as implying that changes in the health care financing and delivery in the United States will necessarily lead to improved health status. For example, explanations for differences in international mortality and morbidity statistics are a subject of contention. In the United States, demographic and cultural characteristics may in part account for the country's lower rankings on such outcome measures as life expectancy and infant mortality (Davis, 1989; Schieber et al., 1991; Liu et al., 1992). In general, increases in spending for medical care do not appear to have a great impact on easily measured health outcomes in economically advanced countries. Such spending may, nonetheless, benefit specific categories of individuals or improve population health status and well-being in ways that are not readily measured. Other problems with international comparisons involve differences in the way health care expenditures are counted and adjusted across nations (e.g., treatment of capital costs, price changes, research spending, spending for long-term care and other specific services) (Poullier, 1989, 1992).

experienced by special population groups. These common concerns—shared by countries with quite different ways of organizing and financing health care delivery—suggest that some of the challenges are not primarily a function of particular national institutions. Instead, they may be related to other influences, such as the developments in biomedical science and medical technology that affect a nation's definition of what constitutes appropriate health care.

Policymakers elsewhere are weighing the merits of market-based approaches versus communitywide regulatory responses to costs, access, and quality, and some are considering the adoption of hospital payment methodologies, quality assessment tools, and other innovations developed here. Nonetheless, few if any of these nations seem likely to assign employers a major role beyond financing coverage. All appear certain to retain an explicit or implicit social contract that links individuals to each other and their government in a collective agreement that basic health services should be available to all and that those who are better off—economically, physically, and mentally—should assist those who are less well off. No such social contract links Americans.

## OVERVIEW OF REPORT

The rest of this chapter discusses the rationale for this study, explains how it relates to the debate over health care reform, and defines the key concepts and terms used in this report. This last discussion is lengthy and involves sometimes tedious or intricate distinctions among terms that are used in widely differing and often confusing ways by insurers, health services researchers, and policymakers. An understanding of the report's terminology is necessary for a clear understanding of the analyses and recommendations presented in later chapters.

In Chapter 2, the committee recognizes the importance of understanding the historical roots of current conditions and debates. It examines how voluntary employment-based health benefits have evolved in this country over the past century and how various efforts to establish state or national health insurance programs have fared. Both this chapter and Appendix B discuss the Employee Retirement Income Security Act of 1974, which has significantly increased the discretion employers have in structuring and administering their health benefit programs.

Chapter 3 provides an overview of employment-based health benefits today: who is covered for what services at how much cost and under what conditions? In Chapter 4, which includes a case study, the focus turns to the decisions and tasks faced by employers as they manage a program of health benefits and some of the implications of these decisions for employees and health care providers. Chapter 5 examines the problems of risk selection and risk segmentation created when individuals, employers, or others can choose whether or not to offer or accept health coverage or whether to choose one health plan over another.

Chapter 6 considers the issue of health care costs—how to understand them, what employers and others are doing to control them, and why it is important to focus on the value obtained for health care spending rather than simply on total expenditures. The final chapter presents the committee's findings on the key features, strengths and weaknesses of the current system, possible directions for change, and research issues.

## WHY THIS STUDY?

Given the virtual blizzard of recent reports and proposals on health care reform, what purpose is served by an Institute of Medicine study of employment-based health benefits? The principal justification for this study, which was requested by the Senate Appropriations Committee, is that surprisingly little exists in the way of a broad analysis of the strengths and weaknesses of organizing health coverage around the workplace on a voluntary basis. The problems facing the uninsured and the small employer and its employees have been fairly thoroughly described, although not resolved. However, the core of the employment-based system—large employer groups—has been less systematically examined. The situations of both large and small groups and the interrelations between them need to be considered.

A broader examination of employment-based health benefits is certainly relevant for public officials, private groups, and policy analysts who wish—for whatever reasons—to build on the present system. Even for those who believe in fully public insurance, this study may suggest some advantages in employment-based insurance that they are overlooking or some defects that are unwittingly being built into their proposals for change. The same holds true for those devoted to the kinds of market solutions that would abandon employment-based health benefits in favor of a focus on the individual consumer. Should particular advocates not find any reasons to modify their own proposals, they might nonetheless profit from a clearer understanding of what they propose to replace, the transition questions posed by such replacement, and the potential for seriously overstating the comparative advantages of their favored strategies.

### Relation to the Debate over Health Care Reform

It was in the highly charged context of an intensifying national debate about health care reform that this study was conducted and the committee's report developed. This committee, however, was not charged with developing a proposal for general reform in health care financing and delivery, nor was its mission to prepare a comprehensive description and analysis of such proposals. (The preface discusses the origins and activities of this study in more detail.) There is no shortage of such descriptions and analyses by other parties (see, for example, Blendon and Edwards, 1991; Blue Cross and Blue Shield Association, 1991b; CBO, 1991a; EBRI, 1992b; Association of American Medical Colleges, 1992). Because there is, however, little in-depth analysis of voluntary employment-based health benefits, the committee chose this as its focus, believing that such analysis would be useful to analysts and policymakers regardless of their views about health care reform.

Members of the committee disagreed among themselves about the merits of continuing to rely on voluntary, workplace-based health coverage, as is discussed further in Chapter 7. Such differences of opinion notwithstanding, the committee has attempted to devise analyses and findings related to employment-based health benefits that are cognizant of and relevant to the debate over health care reform.

In this report, the U.S. system of voluntary employment-based health benefits is from time to time compared with other nations' systems and with proposals for health care reform in this country. When this report describes another country's system or a particular reform proposal as employment-based, it means that employers have or would have some significant discretion in designing or managing health benefits for their employees. A governmentally mandated health insurance program in which the employer's involvement is limited to administering a payroll tax and handling routine paperwork is employment-based in only the narrowest technical sense. As a system or proposal moves away from this limited role and adds discretion for the employer, there is a grey area where analysts can and do disagree in their categorizations.[3,4]

Health care reform proposals and health care systems in other countries vary greatly in important details. Some of the major dimensions of varia-

---

[3]Such disagreement has arisen about the German system, in which most of the population is covered by nonprofit sickness funds that are financed primarily through payroll taxes that vary in level from fund to fund but that are shared equally by employer and employee. According to Glaser (1991), 44 percent of fund subscribers are assigned to one of 269 "area sickness funds," 34 percent subscribe to one of 15 funds for white-collar and management workers, 11 percent are covered by one of 722 "workplace sickness funds," and most of the rest are distributed among 155 craft-based funds and 19 agricultural funds. Membership in one of these funds is legally required for all but high-income workers, and fund discretion in defining benefits and other important matters is significantly limited. Germany is generally described as having a social insurance system, not an employment-based or even a private system. However, opinion is not uniform on whether the system is basically public or private. Thus, one source categorizes 72 percent of all personal health spending in Germany as public spend-

tion include whether the approach (1) is compulsory or voluntary; (2) if compulsory, mandates employer provision or individual purchase of coverage; (3) provides for competitive private health plans or a single public plan; (4) involves extensive or limited regulation; (5) perpetuates, expands, or eliminates separate means-tested, age-related, or other special public programs; (6) continues a significant role for some or all employers; (7) places the major direct financing burden on the individual, the employer, or the government; (8) relates an individual's cost for coverage to his or her income; and (9) relates the individual's cost for coverage to his or her health status or expected level of medical expenses.

Although specific proposals for U.S. health care reform may involve various combinations of positions on these dimensions, some combinations are more common than others in the most frequently mentioned proposals (see detailed comparisons of a variety of specific proposals in the references cited earlier in this section). Broad alternatives include

• compulsory public or statutory plans, which (1) cover all or most of those in an area under a single program and (2) rely on employers for some financing but little else (example: Canadian system);

• systems based on competitive markets for the mandatory individual purchase of insurance with little or no incentive for employer involvement and limited regulation (examples: Heritage Foundation proposal; Responsible National Health Insurance plan);

• systems based on competitive markets for the mandatory or voluntary purchase of insurance by individuals with extensive regulation of competitors and variable roles for employers and public programs (examples: several "managed competition" proposals; proposal from California Insurance Commissioner John Garamendi);

• systems that either mandate employer-provided coverage *or* give employers the option of either providing coverage or contributing to a public program for their employees (examples: Hawaii for the first; Pepper Commission for the second); and

• voluntary systems that expand subsidized or public coverage and extend regulation of insurance practices (examples: Steelman Commission; U.S. Chamber of Commerce).

---

ing (Schieber et al., 1991), whereas another source gives a figure of 12 percent (Schneider et al., 1987, cited in Reinhardt, 1990).

[4]In the United States, workers' compensation programs are hard to classify. If one focuses on their mandated employer financing and benefits, the "public" label seems fitting. If one focuses on employer options in insuring and managing their programs and, to some degree, their costs, then the programs look more private and employer-based and less public.

With the exception of access, many of the central questions about alternative systems are not expressly touched on by the above distinctions. For example, most comprehensive proposals include—indeed emphasize—specific cost containment strategies, processes for monitoring the quality of care, and principles for determining what care will be covered.

Proposals that are otherwise quite different may be similar in some respects. For example, formal procedures to define covered benefits based on evidence of effectiveness appear in proposals for single national health insurance programs and so-called managed competition proposals (third option above). Similarly, some form of global budgeting has accompanied proposals for mandatory employment-based coverage and proposals for a single health program.

Another IOM report (forthcoming) discusses quality, cost, financing, and other issues that should be addressed explicitly in specific proposals for health care reform. This report takes a different approach in Chapter 7, one more inductive than deductive. It identifies steps policymakers could take to ameliorate some of the problems with the current system of voluntary employment-based health benefits.

## Issues and Concerns

To guide its examination of voluntary employment-based health benefits, the committee identified several key issues and concerns. Briefly stated, these issues and concerns involve

- access to appropriate health care services and improved health status;
- risk sharing for medical care expenses among the well and the ill, the high-cost and the low-cost individual, and those at higher and lower risk of future expenses;
- portability of medical expense protection and continuity of medical care for individuals;
- desirable innovation in health care, biomedical science and technology, and health care administration;
- privacy of information about individual health status and health benefit costs and potential misuse of that information;
- total health care costs, costs for health services of no or limited value, and overall productivity of resource allocation; and
- complexity for individuals, employers, practitioners, and others.

Although the emphasis in this report is on voluntary employment-based health benefits rather than the entire system of health care financing and delivery in the United States, it was often difficult to separate the role of such benefits from other factors. This was particularly true in the examination of health care costs and cost containment strategies.

The committee did not assume that equity in health coverage ensured equity in access to health care nor that either coverage or access ensured equity in health outcomes.[5]   Moreover, equity in coverage for those with some attachment to the work force does not imply equity for those without such an attachment.

In addition, the committee recognizes that trade-offs among objectives must be considered in any evaluation of the present system and alternatives to it.  Improving access to health coverage and health care for workers now uninsured or underinsured will tend to mean increased costs, even if actions are taken to reduce unnecessary care, limit payments to providers, and otherwise try to contain some kinds of costs.

The committee endeavored to consider the perspectives of the individual, the employer, the health care provider, and the public policymaker and also tried to understand the particular values that inform these views.  Each perspective reflects broadly different experiences, needs, philosophies, and objectives.  Nonetheless, much variation exists within each category, and substantial overlap is present across categories.

For example, in some respects, large employers may have less in common with very small employers than with their own employees.  Individuals who are insured undoubtedly differ from the uninsured in the nature and intensity of their concerns about employment-based benefits, and any given individual may reflect one set of concerns when considering the purchase of insurance and another when faced with an acute need for health care.  Likewise, leaders of health care institutions not only differ among themselves but also may experience role conflicts as they act as provider, employer, health insurer, or consumer.  The same holds true for a large number of other firms and service organizations involved to some degree in the provision of health-related services and products.  With over 12 percent of the gross domestic product generated in the health sector, many organizations, communities, and governmental bodies become very "anxious" about prospective adjustments in resources committed to health care.  After all, if health care costs are high, so are health care incomes, and those who receive them can be expected to protect their positions.  To the extent that public policymakers strive to represent the interests of different groups, they naturally find conflicting as well as common ground.

Policymakers here and elsewhere face difficult and fundamental questions about alternative uses of limited resources and about directions for health care policy.  One of the most explosive is:  how is health care to be rationed (whether explicitly or not) in a society that is unable or unwilling to pay for all medical services that contemporary medical science can pro-

---

[5]Another Institute of Medicine report (1993) has defined access as the timely use of personal health services to achieve the best possible health outcomes.

vide?  How will the paradox be dealt with that consumers, providers, and policymakers desire high-quality medical care but disagree about the proportion of national resources that must be transferred to the health sector to achieve this result?  How will public policy deal with the tendency for new developments in medical science to increase the demand for care and its costs?  Can technological innovation be maintained but directed in greater part to areas in which significant gains in health outcome or other values can be achieved at lower cost?  These questions are critical to decisions about the specific future role of employment-based health benefits.

At this time, broad goals for improved access, equity, effectiveness, and efficiency in health care garner general endorsements but no clear agreement on how the tensions among these goals should be resolved.  The country is not yet near consensus on the specific policies and actions needed to move from general goals to actual improvements in the performance of the health care system.

## KEY CONCEPTS AND TERMS AS USED IN THIS REPORT

The language of insurance can be quite arcane, and insurers, researchers, and others do not always use terms in the same way when they discuss the roles and functioning of insurance.  Even a single source can switch between more and less technical usage, treat technically distinguishable terms as synonyms, or fail to make definitions explicit.  A number of concepts and terms that are particularly central to this report and its analyses are discussed below.  Others are discussed in later chapters, in particular, Chapters 3 and 5.  In addition, a glossary at the end of this report provides definitions for other terms the committee thought might not be widely understood or might be understood somewhat differently among readers of this document.

Early on, the Institute of Medicine decided to describe this project as a study of employment-based *health benefits*, not as a study of employment-based *health insurance*.  One rationale was to reinforce the project's emphasis on the role of the employer—not the insurer or other agent—as the major private sponsor and purchaser of health benefits.  This rationale notwithstanding, much of this report is about insurance in one form or another.

### Employment-Based Health Benefits

Although this report often refers to "an" employer as sponsor and decisionmaker, the reality is more complex than implied by this linguistically convenient phrasing.  For example, several million individuals are covered by multiple employer plans of various sorts, some of which are administered jointly by representatives of the employers and employees (see Chapter 2 for further discussion). In addition, some unions sponsor health benefit programs, and many employers negotiate their health plans with unions. Other employers make unilateral benefit decisions, with direct employee input ranging from nil to modest.

Health benefits for most of those under age 65 are defined as employment based because employers in the United States, particularly large and nonunionized employers, have substantial discretion in making decisions about the existence and features of health benefits for workers and their families. Even small employers have considerable discretion in a few areas such as deciding whether or not to offer health benefits or how much to pay of the cost of any coverage offered. As noted earlier, a governmentally mandated or statutory health insurance program in which the employer's involvement is limited to administering a payroll tax and handling routine paperwork is employment-based in only the narrowest technical sense.

## Social Insurance and Private Insurance

Definitions of social insurance vary.[6] For purposes of this report social insurance for health care expenses is broadly and perhaps ideally defined as a national policy, backed by statutes, with the following features (see, for example, Glaser, 1991; Saltman, 1992):

• Most or all individuals are protected against the costs of health care, most often under arrangements that are either compulsory or automatic.

• The amounts that individuals pay for this protection are not explicitly linked to their use of or need for care.

• A standard, fairly comprehensive level of benefits or services is available to covered individuals without regard to income.

• Most covered individuals make earmarked contributions for coverage through payroll taxes or similar devices.

• Government tax and other policies directly or indirectly generate the revenues and subsidies to make all this possible, in particular, for the poor.

To use several other important concepts, social insurance—in ideal form—is *universal* (or very nearly so), *compulsory* or *automatic* (or very nearly

---

[6]One insurance textbook cites this definition of social insurance from the American Risk and Insurance Association: it is "a device for pooling risks by transfer to a governmental service organization" (Mehr, 1983, p. 365). In this country the Social Security Administration (SSA) would qualify as such an organization, and Medicare would generally qualify as a social insurance program for a population subgroup. However, this definition and its accompanying list of further defining characteristics would appear to exclude Germany—the birthplace of social insurance—from the list of nations with social insurance programs because risk is transferred not to the required governmental service organization but to hundreds of regulated sickness funds.

so), largely *uniform* in basic benefits, and *community rated* (that is, priced without regard for individual characteristics such as age or health status). Purely means-tested programs, such as Medicaid, are not covered by the definition. Also, direct government provision of health care, such as is undertaken in Britain, is generally not considered to fit the definition of social insurance. In addition, Switzerland, where all but 2 percent of the people are covered under subsidized voluntary insurance or canton-based compulsory insurance (Glaser, 1991), has no explicit national policy of automatic or compulsory insurance and therefore does not conform.[7]

Under a social insurance scheme, private organizations can be involved in program administration and health care delivery. In addition, private health insurance may coexist with social insurance. For example, in Germany, higher-income individuals, who are not required to join the statutory sickness funds, may purchase coverage privately, and members of sickness funds may also supplement their statutory health benefits with additional private coverage.

The United States lacks a social insurance policy for health care expenses except for certain limited groups (primarily the elderly). For most of those under age 65, health insurance is not compulsory or automatic. Many are unwillingly without coverage, and some choose not to protect themselves when they could. Individuals or groups with high past use or high expected future use may be charged more for coverage with the implicit or explicit backing of public policy. Public policy also allows substantial competition and variation among private insurers with respect to enrollment, benefits, premiums, and other matters.

### Small and Large Groups

Much of the debate over health care reform involves the problems faced by small employers and their employees in obtaining and affording health insurance. In actuarial terms, smallness is a problem because the predictability of expenses for health care increases as a function of group size, and insurance depends on such predictability. In policy terms, small groups are often seen as more economically vulnerable and less administratively capable of dealing with regulatory requirements than larger employers and therefore as warranting special policy treatment. Many laws do not require compliance by employers below a certain size, which often but not always is defined as 24 or fewer employees. On the other hand, for data collection

---

[7]Compulsory national insurance has been voted down several times by the Swiss, but the national government has since 1911 subsidized health insurance provided by a sickness fund (but not a mutual or stock insurance company) that "accepts any citizen, offers certain minimum benefits, pays providers according to certain [government] rules, is a nonprofit legal entity, and reports its accounts to the national government" (Glaser, 1991, p. 516).

purposes, the Department of Labor uses 99 or fewer employees as the break point for small groups, and some insurers may not experience-rate or even sell to groups with fewer than 100 or 200 members. For insurance and public policy purposes, coverage for an entity with only one or two employees is usually categorized as individual rather than small-group coverage.

In sum, definitions of small and large groups are somewhat arbitrary and contingent on the concerns of those doing the defining. In this report the definitions used in major sources of data are indicated as appropriate.

## Risk, Insurance, and Benefits

*Risk* is the chance of loss; its essence is uncertainty (see, generally, MacIntyre, 1962; Donabedian, 1976; Mehr, 1983; HIAA, 1992). In the case of health insurance, risk relates to the chance of health care expenses arising from illness or injury.[8] People attempt to deal with such risk in many ways: by avoiding it (no hang gliding), reducing it (no french fries), carrying it themselves (no claims for small expenses), or transferring it. *Insurance* is widely used by individuals and organizations as a mechanism for transferring risk.

In order to function as a method for transferring and spreading risk, insurance requires the *pooling* of individuals at risk. What is highly uncertain for a single individual can often be predicted reasonably well for a reasonably large group. When individuals buy insurance, they accept a predictable "small loss (the premium) in order to lessen or eliminate uncertain heavy losses; average loss is substituted for actual loss" (MacIntyre, 1962, p. 20).

In conventional terms, insurance may be defined as the protection against significant, unpredictable financial loss from defined adverse events that is provided under written contract in return for payments (premiums) made in advance. The contract may be with an individual or a group.

*Benefits* are conventionally defined as the amounts payable for a loss under a specific insurance contract (indemnity benefits) or as the guarantee that certain services will be paid for (service benefits). Here, health benefits may broadly refer either to covered services or to the amount of financial protection available. The latter is typically expressed with reference to various financial limits such as deductibles, coinsurance, copayments, and maximum amounts payable.

---

[8]This report uses the term *health insurance* in connection with expenses arising from medical care and reserves the term *disability insurance* for protection against the loss of income due to illness or injury. Some traditionally oriented insurance texts use *health insurance* to cover both forms of protection (Mehr, 1983), as may state insurance laws; older texts may use the term to describe insurance that provides only for income protection (see, for example, Faulkner, 1960).

As used in this report, employment-based health benefits include conventionally insured programs and programs that are fully or partly self-insured by employers (who retain risk and cover net losses through internal resources). Self-insured programs may be fully or partly administered by the employer, by an insurer offering administrative services only (ASO), or by an independent or third-party claims administrator (TPA). In addition, employment-based benefits may come in the form of health services provided directly through employer-owned clinics or other arrangements.

The term *prepayment* has sometimes been used interchangeably with the term insurance. Other times, it is reserved for arrangements whereby a health plan agrees to provide defined health services (as a health maintenance organization has traditionally done) or to pay for defined health care services (as most Blue Cross plans have traditionally done). In these latter senses, prepayment is contrasted with indemnity insurance, in which the agreement is to make defined cash payments for expenses incurred.

The term *health plan* has no unique technical meaning. It is sometimes used interchangeably with health benefits, but it also incorporates the notion of management or sponsorship, particularly as reflected in the growth of geographically delimited networks of health care practitioners and institutions, utilization management programs, and similar elaborations on older insurance programs. This report adopts a broad use to cover traditional insurance and network arrangements. When referring generally to the health plan or plans offered by employers, this report sometimes uses the term *health benefit program*.

## Insurable Events

A central insurance concept is that of the *insurable event* (Faulkner, 1940; MacIntyre, 1962; Donabedian, 1976). Conventional insurance principles describe an insurable event as one that is (1) individually unpredictable and unwanted, (2) relatively uncommon and significant, (3) precisely definable and measurable, (4) predictable for large groups, and (5) unlikely to occur to a large portion of insured simultaneously.

The relatively slow development of private health insurance (in comparison with private fire and life insurance) and its current complexity can in part be explained by the deviation of medical care and associated expenses from all but the last of these principles. Medical care use is not necessarily beyond control by the insured, unwanted, uncommon, or precisely definable. Several examples can illustrate the insurability problems presented by quite ordinary aspects of medical care:

• Some services such as physician office visits are not individually unpredictable and may be very much at the discretion of a patient; patient preferences certainly influence courses of treatment for many medical problems.

- Some services such as a yearly physical or an extra day in the hospital following surgery or childbirth may be welcome to some patients.
- Although some insured services (e.g., major surgery) are relatively uncommon, others (e.g., physician visits and prescriptions) are not.
- Determining the specific content, value, or necessity of a particular medical service is a continuing challenge, as demonstrated by the growth of utilization management and technology assessment programs, the ongoing refinement of nomenclature systems and payment schedules for physician services, and similar developments.
- The promotion or mandating of coverage for routine, relatively low cost preventive services and for events that may be planned, such as pregnancy, has led to further departures from the principle of insurance for significant unpredictable losses toward a policy of entitlement to coverage for a wide array of services.

### Moral Hazard, Biased Selection, Risk Segmentation, and Underwriting

The features just described make insurance for health care particularly vulnerable to what is sometimes called *moral hazard*, a value-laden term for the tendency of insured individuals to behave differently from uninsured individuals (Donabedian, 1976; Mehr, 1983; Arnott and Stiglitz, 1988, 1990). In its most traditional usage, moral hazard is identified with an increased probability of loss due to various kinds of unethical or imprudent behaviors on the part of an insured individual. These behaviors include extravagance, malingering, indifference to accident avoidance, claims fraud, dishonest failure to disclose a known hazard as part of an application for insurance, and imprudent failure to purchase insurance until the hazard is at hand (e.g., one's house is burning down).

In the health insurance arena, moral hazard has been most widely used to label a rather different behavioral effect of insurance: the propensity of insured individuals to seek and accept more medical care than they would if they lacked insurance. Such higher use of health care by the insured need not be the result of profligacy, carelessness, or other morally dubious behavior on the part of patient or practitioner, although it may be in some instances. It is no easy task for even the most well-intentioned of patients, clinicians, and health insurers to distinguish between necessary and unnecessary care, and unequivocal evidence about the effectiveness of specific services for special problems is in short supply. Furthermore, discussions of the problems of the uninsured and underinsured make clear that increased access to and use of needed care are central objectives of providing health coverage to these individuals. In this report, the term *moral hazard* is avoided in favor of more neutral references to the expected (but difficult to control or regulate) effect of health insurance on the demand for and supply of medical services.

Nor does this report apply the term *moral hazard*, as is sometimes done, to the tendency of individuals to make choices among different health insurance plans based on which plan best meets their needs. In this usage, the hazard for insurers is that individuals make health insurance choices using knowledge of their risk status that is more complete than that available to (or even sought by) insurers. Those who expect to need dental care or complicated surgery may choose health plans with coverage to fit these needs and may typically do so without behaving dishonestly or deceptively. Those who do not expect to need care may take a chance on a high-deductible health plan without being irresponsible or imprudent. In this analysis, individuals making these kinds of decisions are regarded as rational consumers, although the combined effect of these decisions may have consequences such as risk segmentation that many would regard as undesirable.

Whether characterized as moral hazard or rational decisionmaking, the behavior just described is one aspect of an especially difficult problem in health insurance, *biased risk selection*. Biased risk selection is a nonrandom process that occurs (1) when the individuals or groups that purchase insurance differ in their risk of incurring health care expenses from those who do not or (2) when those who enroll in competing health plans differ in the level of risk they present to each plan. When a health plan, an insurer, or—in some cases—an employer attracts a less risky or costly group than the average (or the competition), it has experienced *favorable selection*. A group with a more risky or costly membership has experienced *unfavorable* or *adverse selection*.

The committee does not view the term biased risk selection as pejorative, and it views the factors or behaviors contributing to biased risk selection (described further in Chapter 5) as sometimes desirable or at least acceptable and sometimes undesirable. Again, reasonable individual and organizational behavior can sometimes have undesirable social consequences. In any case, for the sake of simplicity, the remainder of this report refers just to risk selection.

For purposes of this report, risk selection is viewed as a *process* related to individual or group choices that is influenced by a variety of individual, employer, and insurer characteristics. Its most serious potential *consequence*—the clustering of higher- and lower-risk individuals in different health plans or the exclusion of higher-risk individuals from coverage altogether—is described here as *risk segmentation*.[9] In other discussions, the terms are

---

[9]Risk segmentation also can occur in systems in which insurance is largely compulsory and the opportunity to choose among health plans is quite limited, as it is in Germany. Risk segmentation among the German sickness funds occurs because plans draw or are assigned their membership from occupational and other groups that differ in age, income, and other risk factors (Wysong and Abel, 1990).

often used interchangeably, but some use the term selection to describe individual behavior and the term segmentation to describe insurer practices.

Risk segmentation, in the sense used here, can also result from the strategic or competitive business practice of experience rating, wherein insurers offer better rates (premiums) to groups with lower claims experience (expense) than to groups with higher past or anticipated experience. Experience rating has largely replaced *community rating*, which—at its purest—rates all risks equally across a particular community.

Another kind of risk segmentation happens when larger, relatively low risk employers choose to self-insure and leave conventional insurers with populations more heavily weighted toward riskier (in the sense of less predictable) individual and small-group purchasers. In turn, risk segmentation can result within a self-insured group when employees are offered a choice of health plans.

To control, discourage, or preclude selective enrollment by high-risk, high-expense individuals, insurers have developed an array of *underwriting* practices to classify, price, and otherwise set the terms under which they select those they will insure. These practices include medical examinations and questionnaires that provide information about an applicant's health status or past use of care, required waivers of medical record confidentiality, limits or exclusions on coverage for preexisting health problems, exclusions or limits on coverage for certain types of businesses or industries, waiting periods before coverage applies, and higher rates for higher-risk categories of individuals or groups. It is these practices that have been targeted for modification or elimination by many proposals for small-group reform.

In this report the term *risk rating* is used to broadly describe the linking of an individual's health risk to some individual financial penalty or reward, whether it be a higher or lower premium or a rebate for low users of care or other approach. Chapter 5 considers risk rating as a business practice, a fairness issue, and a tool for behavior modification.

To control costs stemming from the effects of insurance on the behavior of consumers and providers, insurers and others have devised a variety of practices, in particular, requirements that individuals share part of the cost of using services covered by insurance. Chapter 6 describes these and other strategies to limit the use of health care, to control health care costs in general, and to relate both use and cost of care to its expected value in improving health status and function.

## CONCLUSION

As the twenty-first century approaches, there is a widespread sense that the entire U.S. health care system, including the system of employment-based health benefits, needs significant restructuring. This perception has reinvigorated debates in the United States about the obligations of richer or healthier individuals to help poorer or sicker individuals, the virtues of voluntary versus compulsory insurance, the role of the private versus the public sector in ensuring access to needed health care, and the effectiveness of market versus regulatory strategies to contain costs and ensure value. For some, the conclusion is that market forces are not being allowed to work and need to be strengthened by various regulatory changes (hence the term *regulated* or *managed competition*). Others conclude that market forces have not worked and cannot work given the nature of health care and health insurance and that existing market structures should therefore be replaced in part or whole by public programs of various sorts. For all, the current, central position of employment-based health benefits is a major factor to be reckoned with in considering the feasibility and specifics of proposals for health care reform.

# 2

# Origins and Evolution of Employment-Based Health Benefits

*History is a record of "effects" the vast majority of which nobody intended to produce.*

Joseph Schumpeter, 1938

The current U.S. system of voluntary employment-based health benefits is not the consequence of an overarching and deliberate plan or policy. Rather, it reflects a gradual accumulation of factors: innovations in health care finance and organization, conflicting political and social principles, coincidences of timing, market dynamics, programs stimulated by the findings of health services research, and spillover effects of tax and other policies aimed at different targets.

The major innovation, as described below, was the creation of alliances and mechanisms that made the employee group a workable vehicle for insuring a large proportion of workers and their families. That the employee group existed for purposes other than the provision of insurance (that is, to produce a product or service) was an important although not sufficient condition for dealing with biased risk selection and some of the other problems described in Chapter 1 and discussed further in Chapter 5.

This chapter provides a rather detailed overview of some important bases for present public and private arrangements for insuring health care. From this overview, five broad points emerge:

1. Insuring medical care expenses is difficult for several reasons, and making private insurance workable for large numbers of workers and their families has taken considerable creativity, leadership, and some luck.

2. A constituency for broad access to health coverage has existed for nearly a century, pressuring both public and private sectors to find new and better ways of extending that access.

3. The path taken by the United States has diverged from that of other developed nations, particularly since the end of World War II.

4. The debate about private versus public strategies for medical expense protection is longstanding and has, with the exception of programs for special populations, repeatedly been resolved in the United States in favor of private approaches.

5. The central role of employment-based health benefits and the very substantial discretion accorded employers rest, in considerable measure, on federal laws and regulations (in particular, the Employee Retirement Income Security Act of 1974) that did not explicitly plan or envision that structure.

Many of the values, pressures, and conflicts that have shaped the evolution of employment-based health benefits persist and should be factored into evaluations of this system and proposals for restructuring it. Moreover, it is important to recognize the forces that have led people in this country and elsewhere to expect both more medical care and more protection against its rising cost. These forces, which affect both public and private provision of health coverage, include

• an ever-accelerating pace of scientific and technological discovery that has offered new relief from pain and suffering and heightened expectations about the value of new medical technologies, products, and practices;

• a century's worth of professional and institutional development in health care that has made possible the delivery of biomedicine's new achievements;

• an increase in medical care costs that has been fueled both by economic growth and by advances in clinical capabilities and organizational resources; and

• a system of private and public health coverage that has for most of the last 50 years increased financial access to these advances but placed few controls on medical price inflation or overuse of medical services.

On almost every front, the thrust in the United States is still expansionist—the uninsured want basic protection, the insured want restrictions on coverage eased, and researchers, providers, and entrepreneurs devise new technologies and services that further stimulate demand for care. Hence, health care consumes a greater share of national resources each year.

The expansionary thrust has, however, stalled in some areas. In particular, the proportion of the U.S. population covered by private health benefits has leveled off and even shown signs of decline in the employment-based sector. Furthermore, many now question whether current medical practices and technological advances produce improvements in health and well-being commensurate with their cost. These questions reinforce policymakers' wariness about new initiatives to improve equity and access given two decades of unsuccessful efforts to moderate the flow of resources to the health sector.

Although this chapter is lengthy, it is not intended to be comprehensive.[1] Rather, the object is to provide sufficient detail to make clear that current arrangements, problems, and controversies have deep roots. By way of brief overview, Table 2.1 highlights key dates in the evolution of employment-based health benefits in the United States and in the environment that shaped its development.

## THE BIRTH OF INSURANCE FOR MEDICAL CARE EXPENSES

In Europe and the United States, modern insurance for medical care expenses has its origins in diverse actions undertaken by unions, fraternal organizations, employee associations, employers, commercial insurers, governments, and other less easily categorized entities. The primary objective of most of these initiatives was not reimbursement for medical expenses but protection against the loss of income due to illness or injury.

### Early Voluntary Initiatives

By the beginning of the nineteenth century in Europe, guilds, unions, mutual aid societies that crossed occupational lines, fraternal associations, and other private groups had already developed various forms of collective action to protect group members and members' families against such economic catastrophes as death of the breadwinner (Anderson, 1972; Glaser, 1991). Such efforts became more widespread as the Industrial Revolution took hold and the hazards of workplace injury and related wage loss became a major concern.

Although these efforts were often described as sickness insurance, sick benefits, or health insurance, they usually did not cover medical care expenses (Faulkner, 1940; Glaser, 1991). In the latter part of the nineteenth century, however, some European mutual aid societies and other groups did offer limited medical expense coverage, and several employed or contracted with physicians and created clinics or hospitals to serve their members. In general, the voluntary nature of the programs and the often meager financial resources of their participants limited their scope. In England, where mutual aid societies were particularly strong, voluntary sickness insurance covered less than one-seventh of the population in the period just before the country adopted its first social insurance measures in 1911 (Starr, 1982).

The early lack of emphasis on medical expense insurance is not surprising. Truly effective medical services were limited—and sometimes even

---

[1]The sources cited here are not always consistent and unambiguous, especially about the period before 1960, but the committee has attempted to determine what is accurate insofar as possible within its resources.

**TABLE 2.1**   Key Dates in the Development of Employment-Based
Health Benefits and Its Environment

| | |
|---|---|
| 1798 | U.S. Marine Hospital Service established; deductions from seamen's pay cover costs |
| 1847 | First (short-lived) company to issue health insurance organized in Boston |
| 1849 | New York passes first general state insurance law |
| 1853 | French mutual aid society establishes prepaid hospital care plan in San Francisco |
| 1863 | Travelers Insurance Company offers accident insurance in the United States |
| 1870s | Railroad, mining, and other industries begin to provide company doctors funded by deductions from workers' wages |
| 1877 | Granite Cutters Union establishes first national sick benefit program |
| 1906 | American Association for Labor Legislation founded to promote workers compensation and other social insurance programs |
| 1910 | Flexner report on need for improvements in medical education |
| 1910 | Montgomery Ward enters into one of the earliest group insurance contracts |
| 1910s | Physician service and industrial health plans established in Northwest and remote areas |
| 1912 | First model state law developed for regulating health insurance |
| 1913 | International Ladies Garment Workers Union (ILGWU) begins first union medical services program |
| 1915–1920 | Efforts to establish compulsory health insurance programs fail in 16 states |
| 1927 | Committee on the Costs of Medical Care established |
| 1929 | Stock market crash followed by Depression |
| 1929 | Baylor group hospitalization plan founded (first Blue Cross plan) |
| 1935 | Social Security Act passes without health insurance provisions |
| 1937 | Blue Cross Commission established |
| 1940 | Predecessor of Group Health Association of America established |
| 1943 | War Labor Board rules wage freeze does not apply to fringe benefits |
| 1945 | Kaiser Foundation Health Plan opens to non-Kaiser groups |
| 1947 | Taft-Hartley Act requires collective bargaining on wages and conditions of employment |
| 1948 | McCarran-Ferguson Act gives states broad power to regulate insurance |
| 1949 | Supreme Court upholds National Labor Relations Board ruling that employee benefits are subject to collective bargaining |
| 1954 | Revenue Act confirms employer-paid health benefits are not taxable as employee income |
| 1965 | Medicare and Medicaid legislation adopted (effective 1966) |
| 1968 | Firestone Tire and Rubber Co. begins to self-fund health benefits |
| 1971–1974 | Economic Stabilization Program (wage-price controls) in effect for health sector |
| 1973 | HMO Act requires most employers to offer federally qualified HMOs |
| 1974 | Employee Retirement Income Security Act passed |
| 1974 | Washington Business Group on Health organized (predecessor) |
| 1978 | General Motors cost-containment reports initiated |
| 1985 | Budget Act requires employers with 20 or more employees to offer continued health coverage to terminated employees and dependents for 18 or 36 months |
| 1990 | Financial Standards Accounting Board requires companies to record unfunded retiree health benefit liabilities on balance sheets (effective late 1992) |

SOURCES: Somers and Somers, 1961; Munts, 1967; Anderson, 1968; Wilson and Neuhauser, 1974; Brandes, 1976; U.S. Department of Health, Education, and Welfare, 1976; Starr, 1982; Stevens, 1989; Health Insurance Association of America, 1991b; Employee Benefit Research Institute, 1992c.

suspect—well into the nineteenth century (Somers and Somers, 1961; Anderson, 1968; Poynter, 1971; Ebert, 1973; Knowles, 1973; Starr, 1982; Stevens, 1989). Hospitals were, to a considerable extent, sick houses for the poor and those infected with contagious diseases. Medical practices had little capacity to prevent or alter the course of disease. At best, the goal or reality of medical care was "to cure seldom, to help sometimes, and to comfort always."

By the turn of the century, advances in public health and, to a lesser extent, biomedical science had brought significant changes in what medical care could accomplish. For example, developments in bacteriology and anesthesiology were making safer and less painful surgery a reality. As modern medicine helped transform hospitals into places where the sick could be effectively treated, numbers of hospitals and capital investments in them multiplied. Their growing stature and value were suggested by the fact that some hospitals began to advertise, establish prices, and actually charge fees to those patients who could afford it.

Still, in 1900, physicians remained limited in what they could actually do for many patients. In a telling statement made that year, one physician argued to his colleagues that the practice of medicine is "'not only diagnosis and autopsy but the treatment and care of patients'" (Jacobi, 1900, quoted in Hill and Anderson, 1991, p. 52). Although hospital costs were on the verge of becoming an important concern for workers and their families, protection against income lost due to illness and injury remained a more significant objective than medical expense protection.[2]

As European ideas and institutional forms diffused to the United States, often through immigrants, various kinds of mutual aid or benevolent associations, fraternal organizations, workers clubs, unions, and other similar concepts and structures were adapted to this country's circumstances and culture (Munts, 1967; Anderson, 1968, 1972; Brandes, 1976; Weir et al., 1988). Quite early in this process, in 1853, La Société Française de Bienfaisance Mutuelle established the first prepaid hospital care arrangement, which was linked to the hospital it founded. A German association started a year later and began to offer hospital services in 1855. Patients with lifetime care contracts purchased during the 1930s from the latter plan were still being cared for in the 1960s by the restructured, surviving hospital (Trauner, 1977).

Notwithstanding some exceptions, most American benevolent societies and similar organizations, like their European counterparts, focused on income, not medical expense, protection. For example, the 179 national fra-

---

[2]Although data are scarce, one figure for the pre-World War I period suggests that wage losses due to worker illness and injury were 2 to 4 times greater than worker expenses for medical care. For families as a whole, lost income and medical costs were about equal because dependent wives and children might incur medical expenses but generally had little or no income to lose (Starr, 1982).

ternal organizations in the United States paid out $97 million for benefits in 1917, but only 1 percent of this amount went for medical expenses (Starr, 1982).

Among unions, the Granite Cutters Union is cited as establishing in 1877 the first national sick benefit program. It was probably, like most early efforts, more an income protection than a medical expense plan. The International Ladies Garment Workers Union followed a different approach, creating the first union medical services program in 1913 and incorporating the first union health center four years later. (Later, in 1940, the garment workers began the first multiemployer welfare funds to avoid lost benefits due to job changes or company failures.) Important as such union initiatives were, the main focus of union activities and concerns tended to be on organizing members and on surviving employer resistance to a restructuring of the fundamental relationship between workers and management.

Early employer programs include frequently cited examples from the mining and lumbering industries and the railroads (Somers and Somers, 1961; Munts, 1967; Anderson, 1968; Brandes, 1976; Starr, 1982). These employers had a practical interest in the provision of medical services to injured or ill employees who often worked in isolated geographic areas. The scope of some of these efforts is suggested by the fact that, by the turn of the century, there were an estimated 6,000 railway surgeons (Starr, 1982). In some—perhaps most—situations, employers arranged for the services, but workers paid for them through an innovative wage "checkoff" system. Another innovation was the development of contracts between employers and closed physician panels or prepaid plans allowing free choice of physician.[3]

Although these early programs represented advances in some respects, they were also criticized for using unqualified, overworked "contract" physicians and providing dismal physical facilities in some areas (Somers and Somers, 1961; Munts, 1967). After the passage of workers' compensation legislation, "industrial medicine" became more prominent and focused because companies had stronger financial incentives to identify and reduce workplace hazards.

Employment-related medical programs occasionally covered not only work-related injuries but also general medical care for workers, their families, and even the larger community (Somers and Somers, 1961; Munts, 1967; Brandes, 1976). In the early part of this century, company medical services could be one component of "welfare capitalism," a range of hous-

---

[3]For example, the Pierce County (Washington) Industrial Medical and Surgical Service Bureau was created in 1917 as a for-profit stock company that could "make contracts with employees of labor and their employers" (Pierce County Medical, 1992, p. 3). In its first quarter, it signed contracts with 21 businesses. In 1946, it reorganized as a nonprofit organization, and in 1964, it became a Blue Shield plan. It describes itself as the first successful prepaid health plan.

ing, education, social assistance, and other programs intended to socialize workers, bind them to their employer, and discourage unions. Instead of or in addition to providing company hospitals and doctors, some employers assisted employee mutual benefit associations with financial and clerical aid. Most general accounts of these associations do not make clear whether they protected against medical care expenses, and to what extent, or simply against loss of income due to injury or illness. In any case, although a few companies, such as Eastman Kodak, made large contributions to these employee programs, a 1916 Public Health Service survey found only one company of 425 that fully funded such a program, and most assistance was quite limited (Munts, 1967; Brandes, 1976).

For the most part, physician organizations opposed company-provided medical care as a threat to their autonomy and income. During the early part of this century, this opposition discouraged many companies from expanding their involvement in medical care. For example, after the company doctor at Sears, Roebuck resigned because the county medical society refused him membership, his successor persuaded the company to stop providing services to workers' families at reduced prices and to provide only periodic examinations and other limited care to employees (Starr, 1982).

Workers had different concerns (Brandes, 1976). Company doctors were often seen as serving the company before the patient, for example, in reporting illnesses discovered during physical examinations and in making judgments about whether injuries were work-related and thus required some compensation to the employee. Also, many workers preferred to choose their own physician. As a consequence of these and other concerns, unions often pressed for cash benefits instead of company medical services (Starr, 1982).

Finally, in addition to the programs devised by voluntary associations, employers, unions, and other employee groups, disability and sickness insurance products created by commercial insurers constituted another institutional base for modern health insurance (Faulkner, 1940, 1960; Somers and Somers, 1961; MacIntyre, 1962; Anderson, 1972). Such products began to appear in England around 1850 to provide insurance against accidental injury, in particular, injury arising from railway and steamship travel.[4] This insurance initially provided cash payments (indemnities) in the event of

---

[4]In an interesting example of the diffusion of an innovation, Faulkner (1940) describes how architect James Batterson, the founder of the Traveler's Insurance Company, purchased an accident insurance ticket while in England in 1859 to cover him on a train trip from Leamington to Liverpool. Interested in this concept, Batterson visited both the insurance company (the Railway Passenger's Assurance Company of London) and a leading English actuary. Four years of further investigation, capitalization efforts, and legal work passed before Traveler's was chartered in 1864 in Hartford, Connecticut. Among the coverage exclusions in the earliest policies were injuries arising from disease, surgical operations, dueling, war, or intoxication.

death or total disability and gradually expanded to cover various kinds of accidents and illnesses. These early products employed the standard actuarial principles and techniques that had been developing in the fields of life, fire, and marine insurance.

Efforts to extend commercial accident-and-sickness insurance, as it was often called, to expenses for medical care were intermittent and limited during the latter part of the nineteenth century and first third of the twentieth century (Faulkner, 1940, 1960; Somers and Somers, 1961; Starr, 1982). Life insurers made some efforts to add medical expense benefits to their newly developing group life insurance programs aimed at employers, but these attempts were sporadic. In general, insurers considered medical expense benefits to be actuarially dubious and a "frill" (Faulkner, 1940; Somers and Somers, 1961).[5] Overall, as a vehicle for and influence on health insurance, commercial insurers played a relatively limited role in most European countries. They became major actors in the United States largely after World War II, once community-based organizations, hospitals, physician groups, and government policies provided evidence that private medical expense coverage was feasible.

## Early Public Action

It was on the foundation of the early but limited initiatives of union, mutual aid, and other groups that most European governments created their policies of compulsory, subsidized medical expense protection beginning in the late nineteenth century (Anderson, 1972; Starr, 1982; Glaser, 1991). This foundation remains visible in some countries, for example, in the sickness funds of Germany. In yet other countries, it has largely been replaced by alternative structures, for example, the National Health Service in Britain.

Generally, the building of publicly supported arrangements for medical expense protection was embedded in the broader development of social insurance and other policies to protect workers, their families, and others against various harms, in particular, the loss of earning ability due to old age, disability, or workplace injuries (Flora and Heidenheimer, 1981; Weir et al., 1988).[6] As described in Chapter 1, social insurance for medical expenses shares common features with other social insurance programs. It is universal or nearly universal; coverage is virtually automatic or compulsory for most of the population; common basic benefits are available with-

---

[5]Funeral expense protection, on the other hand, was so valued that millions of people paid weekly premiums for individual "industrial life" policies, which were a backbone of companies such as Metropolitan Life and Prudential (Somers and Somers, 1961).

[6]A more thorough history would also cite as foundations for the policies of different nations the development of public health initiatives (e.g., sanitation and quarantines) and sick houses or hospitals.

out regard to income; payments for basic coverage are not explicitly priced to reflect the individual's level of risk; and tax or other revenue-generating policies subsidize coverage, particularly for the poor.

The creation of a comprehensive array of social insurance programs was, however, uneven in its pace across nations and piecemeal in its formulation within nations (Anderson, 1968, 1972; Glaser, 1991). Bismarck is cited as the originator of statutory health insurance, which was one of the social insurance programs he initiated in Germany in the 1880s. A major objective was to defuse worker unrest. Like many later programs, this system was a product of compromises that, in this case, left the national government with far less administrative power than Bismarck had proposed. The existing sickness funds retained administrative responsibilities that persist to this day. As with many other social insurance programs, Germany's became universal in fits and starts. White-collar workers were not covered initially, and farmers were not included until after World War II. In 1907, only 21 percent of the German population was covered by sickness insurance (Starr, 1982). By the end of World War II, however, most European countries had social health insurance or other government health programs in place for major segments of their population.

## THE DIVERGENT PATH OF THE UNITED STATES

As noted in the preceding chapter, the United States is almost alone among developed countries in lacking some governmentally mandated form of comprehensive health coverage for all or nearly all its population. Its divergent path became apparent primarily after World War II, when most other countries moved to adopt, restructure, or complete their schemes for protecting most of their population against expenses for medical care.

The seeds for a more typical evolution were not totally absent in the United States. For example, the government established the U.S. Marine Hospital Service in 1798 and deducted 20 cents a month from each seaman's wages to pay for it. Unlike somewhat similar initiatives in Sweden and elsewhere, it did not become the cornerstone for a government medical care delivery or insurance program for the citizenry at large (Anderson, 1972; Mullan, 1989). The marine system eventually did evolve into an important research and public health organization, the U.S. Public Health Service.

Early in this century, the instability and inadequacy of voluntary health benefit programs and the need for broad government action became a subject of public debate and agitation in this country, as it had elsewhere (Anderson, 1968, 1972; Harris, 1969; Starr, 1982). As noted above, many early employer-sponsored programs were not well regarded, and the financial instability of union and mutual aid programs and the conservatism of commercial insurers also contributed to negative opinions of voluntary private insurance.

Many were aware of the public schemes evolving in Europe and the arguments behind these developments.

The Progressive Party under President Theodore Roosevelt included national health insurance in its platform for the 1912 election (Harris, 1969), and some key officials of the U.S. Public Health Service supported compulsory insurance in the belief that it would encourage more backing for public health measures (Starr, 1982; Mullan, 1989). Legislation to study and plan for national unemployment, old age, and sickness insurance was introduced in Congress in 1916 and 1917 by its only Socialist member. Hearings were held, but the legislation never passed, in part because of the pressures and distractions presented by World War I and in part because of interest group opposition (Anderson, 1968; Starr, 1982).

Reflecting the federalism of the times, most initial efforts to secure government action focused on state rather than national initiatives. The following discussion first traces early attempts to secure state health insurance legislation and then examines subsequent efforts to achieve national health insurance. It turns last to initiatives in the private sector and the stimulus provided to employment-based health coverage by federal decisions affecting employee benefits and employer-employee relationships generally.

### Unsuccessful Early State Initiatives

After workers' compensation or disability insurance for work-related injury, medical care insurance was one of the earliest targets for groups in the United States advocating social insurance against the hazards of modern industrial society (Anderson, 1968, 1972; Starr, 1982). Particularly prominent in behalf of both was the Committee on Social Insurance of the American Association for Labor Legislation (AALL), the organizing of which began in 1905 at the annual meeting of the American Economic Association.[7] The AALL, whose prestigious administrative council included Jane Addams, Louis Brandeis, and Woodrow Wilson, drafted a model state medical care insurance bill in 1915, and some 16 such bills were introduced at the state level by 1920.

The standards for these proposals, which were set forth by AALL in 1914 (Anderson, 1968), are summarized in Table 2.2. The actual benefits provided by the model bill included sick pay (at two-thirds of wages for up to 26 weeks); medical coverage for physician, hospital, and nursing care; maternity benefits for working women and workers' wives; and a $50 ben-

---

[7]The social activism of social scientists in this period is suggested by the program of the 1916 annual meeting of the AALL, which included joint sessions with the American Economic Association, the American Political Science Association, the American Sociological Association, and the American Statistical Association (Anderson, 1968).

**TABLE 2.2** Standards Adapted by American Association for Labor Legislation in 1914 for Drafting Model State Medical Care Insurance Bill

*Coverage*
- Compulsory participation for workers.
- Voluntary participation for the self-employed.
- Emphasis on illness prevention when possible.

*Organization and Operation*
- Financing through contributions from employer, employee, and the public.
- Administration by employers and employees under public supervision.
- Separate program of disability insurance to replace lost income.

SOURCE: Anderson, 1968.

efit for burial expenses (Starr, 1982). Two-fifths of the cost would come from workers, two-fifths from employers, and one-fifth from state government; the total cost was estimated at 4 percent of wages. The objectives were to reduce the social costs of illness through effective medical care and incentives for disease and injury prevention.

In 1916 the American Medical Association (AMA) established its own Committee on Social Insurance to cooperate with the AALL in studying the issue and drafting legislation (Anderson, 1968; Harris, 1969; Starr, 1982). The group was chaired by Theodore Roosevelt's personal doctor (Alexander Lambert) and staffed by a Socialist physician (I. M. Rubinow). In the same year the AMA elected as its president Dr. Rupert Blue, then surgeon general of the United States. Dr. Blue called for adequate health insurance in his presidential address (Mullan, 1989). Moreover, an AMA trustees' report argued that it was better that they "'initiate the necessary changes than have them forced on us'" (Harris, 1969, p. 5). The AMA Committee on Social Insurance concluded that voluntary health insurance under private control was unworkable and urged support for state legislation.

By 1920, however, the stance of organized medicine switched from cautious cooperation to forceful opposition that lasted decades.[8] One explanation is that the academically oriented leadership of the AMA was countered by "grass roots" practitioners who were reacting to the immediate reality of

---

[8]The American Medical Association now supports legislation that would (1) strengthen Medicaid to ensure "that no poor person is left without access to needed health care," (2) require "employer provision of health insurance for all full-time employees and their families, with tax help to employers," and (3) create state risk pools to cover the medically uninsurable and those who cannot afford or otherwise obtain coverage (Todd et al., 1991, p. 2504). A number of other physician groups have developed their own reform proposals, most of which include some type of required coverage and some public funding.

legislative proposals and initiatives in states such as New York, California, Illinois, and Michigan (Anderson, 1968). Foreshadowing the tone of later vehement opponents of national health insurance, one physician wrote in 1917 of a New York proposal: "'Nowhere has the swinish greed of the debasing propaganda of state socialism been more brazenly exposed than in this merciless attempt to steal the livelihood of the most unselfish profession in the world'" (quoted in Anderson, 1968, p. 75).

In addition to medical opposition, explanations for the uniform failure of the early state-directed initiatives in the United States usually cite several other factors (Anderson, 1968; Starr, 1982; Weir et al., 1988). World War I diverted attention from social welfare programs and gave opposing groups time to organize. The impact of medical care costs on individuals and families had not been systematically documented, and the public was relatively uninterested and uneducated about the concept of health insurance. Hospital, nursing, and public health interests expressed some support for health insurance but were largely passive. Organized labor was not united. Some business groups argued that if any public action were taken it should be in behalf of public health measures, which would do more to increase productivity than would sickness benefits. Economic elites were not spurred by the specter of socialism to establish state welfare programs, and the U.S. civil service was too underdeveloped to provide the intellectual and organizational activism seen in many European countries. Altogether, opposition from commercial insurance companies (who were primarily protecting related lines of business, because medical expense insurance was almost nonexistent), the medical profession, big business, and drug companies overwhelmed the labor interests at the state level and the economists, lawyers, political scientists, and other "do-gooders" who made up the AALL (Anderson, 1968, p. 75).

### Proposals for National Health Insurance in the Depression and Postwar Years

Much of the motivation for the next major push for public—and private—medical expense insurance in the United States came from another private committee, the Committee on the Costs of Medical Care (CCMC).[9] This committee was established in 1927 with private funding from six major foundations: the Carnegie Corporation, the Josiah Macy, Jr., Foundation, the Milbank Memorial Fund, the Russell Sage Foundation, the Twentieth Century Fund, and the Julius Rosenwald Fund. It was chaired by Ray Lyman Wilbur, a former president of the AMA and then president of Stanford

---

[9]This section draws on Anderson, 1968; Rorem, 1982; Starr, 1982; and Weeks and Berman, 1985.

University. With the cooperation of many major organizations such as the AMA and Metropolitan Life and a $1,000,000 research budget, the 42-member committee (which included 17 physicians in private practice) and 75-person technical staff issued a series of 27 field studies and a final report between 1928 and 1932.

The field studies and household surveys conducted for the CCMC provided a clearer understanding of the incidence of illness and disability, the appropriate forms of medical treatment (as judged by a panel of physician experts), the distribution and organization of health care services, the nature of health care expenditures, and the efforts of various groups to help individuals gain access to health care and protect themselves against the financial costs of illness. A vast array of information was compiled, presented, and relied on for years after. The following points are particularly relevant here:

• Insufficient medical care (as judged by medical panels) was widespread even among higher-income groups.

• Per capita spending on health care in the United States averaged $25 to $30 per year (about 4 percent of national income), but 3.5 percent of families bore about one-third of the total spending burden.

• Almost 30 percent of medical care spending went to physicians, about 24 percent to hospitals, 18 percent for medicines, 12 percent to dentists, and 3 to 5 percent each to nurses, cult practitioners, and public health services.

• One-third of those receiving hospital care had that care paid for by a government or philanthropy.

• Unions, lodges, and commercial insurance companies focused on disability insurance and provided little in the way of insurance for medical expenses.

• Some innovative employment-based arrangements for medical expense protection were developing that offered health benefits for as little as $6 to $12 per year, depending on the scope of benefits.

• About 150 multispecialty medical groups existed, many of which were developing innovative health care delivery and financing methods that could coordinate patient care across different settings and clinical problems.

As summarized in Table 2.3, the CCMC's analyses and majority report provided a vision of health care delivery and financing that has echoes in today's policy discussions. Although the majority endorsed the concept of private or public voluntary insurance, they argued—with dissents from several liberal members—against compulsory insurance as too costly for either taxpayers or employers.

The committee minority report vehemently attacked the majority statement, in particular, its call for sweeping reorganization of medical practice. The minority vigorously supported fee-for-service and solo practice medicine and attacked care organized around medical centers as "'big business,

**TABLE 2.3** Summary of Positions on Health Care Coverage in the Majority and Minority Reports of the Committee on the Costs of Medical Care, 1932

---

*Majority Report*
- Costs of medical care should be placed on a voluntary group payment basis through the use of insurance, through the use of taxation, or through the use of both these methods.
- The continuation of medical service provided on an individual fee basis should be available for those who prefer the present method.
- Medical service, both preventive and therapeutic, should be furnished largely by organized groups of physicians, dentists, nurses, pharmacists, and other associated personnel.
- Groups should be organized, preferably around a hospital, to provide complete office and hospital care.
- Organizations should encourage high standards and a personal relation between patient and physician and should not compete with each other.

*Minority Report*
- State or county medical societies should establish and control voluntary nonprofit medical care plans, which should be separate from disability insurance payments and physician certifications and which should not compete with each other.
- Plan enrollees should have free choice of physicians and should pay directly for the care they can afford.
- Plans should maintain the confidentiality of the patient–doctor relationship.
- Participation in plans should be open to all medical society members willing to meet plan conditions, and plans should include all or most medical society members.
- Public care for the indigent should be strengthened and should be assisted (but not paid for) by the medical plan.

---

SOURCE: Anderson, 1968, pp. 94, 98; Starr, 1982.

that is, mass production'" and "'pernicious'" (quoted in Anderson, 1968, p. 98). They conceded, however, that private insurance might have merit if based on plans created by state or county medical societies. These plans would have to operate in accord with several "safeguards," as listed in Table 2.3. The first of the listed provisions related to problems identified in the CCMC study of insurance in Europe.

Both the majority and the minority agreed that competition among physicians and organized plans was destructive (Starr, 1982). Interestingly, both the majority and the minority report argued against administration of medical plans by private insurance companies (rather than prepaid group practices or similar entities). The majority report stated that such administration would "'forfeit . . . effective professional participation in the formulation of policies'" and also increase costs (quoted in Anderson, 1968, p. 95). On this point, both camps on the committee were influenced by a study of European health insurance that stated that "'a comparative study of many insurance systems seems to justify the conclusion that the evils of insurance decrease in proportion to the degree that responsibilities with

accompanying powers and duties are entrusted to the medical profession'"
(Simons and Sinai, quoted in Anderson, 1968, p. 98).

The response of organized medicine to the CCMC majority report is
colorfully represented in a 1932 editorial by Morris Fishbein, editor of the
*Journal of the American Medical Association*:

> "The alignment is clear—on the one side the forces representing the great
> foundations, public health officialdom, social theory—even socialism and
> communism—inciting to revolution; on the other side, the organized medi-
> cal profession of this country urging an orderly evolution guided by con-
> trolled experimentation." (quoted in Anderson, 1968, p. 101)

Some responses from the medical community were, however, less hostile. For example, in 1934 the American College of Surgeons endorsed
voluntary, nonprofit prepayment plans for hospital and medical care (Davis,
1988). The AMA condemned "'this apparent attempt . . . to dominate and
control the nature of medical practice'" (quoted in Davis, 1988, p. 497). In
1935 the California Medical Association came out in favor of a compulsory
state program, a position it revoked after pressure from the AMA. Even the
AMA reluctantly supported government payments for the indigent as a "'temporary expedient'" (quoted in Starr, 1982, p. 271), and it came to accept
certain forms of voluntary insurance, as is described in the next section of
this chapter. These positions reflected the hard times for many physicians
during the Depression. One study indicated that physician incomes dropped
47 percent between 1929 and 1933 (Starr, 1982).

By the time the CCMC final report was published, the American Hospital Association had already picked up on the voluntary hospitalization insurance concept. It was seen as a way to counter "'more radical and potentially dangerous forms of national or state medicine'" (quoted in Anderson,
1968, p. 102).

Given the powerful opposition of the medical profession and the hospital industry to national or state government financing and delivery of medical care and the many crises facing government in the 1930s, it is understandable that national health insurance did not figure in the social policies
pressed by the New Deal (Anderson, 1968; Starr, 1982). Nonetheless, the
President's Committee on Economic Security (CES), established in 1934,
did include medical care in its charge to make recommendations for a program "'against misfortunes which cannot be wholly eliminated from this
man-made world of ours'" (quoted in Anderson, 1968, p. 106). The CES
insurance section and medical advisory committee had at least four former
CCMC members or staffers.[10] However, the CES was mainly concerned

---

[10]According to Starr (1982), Warren Hamilton, chair of the CES medical care subcommittee, and Edgar Sydenstricker, its technical study director, were both members and liberal
dissenters from the CCMC. According to Anderson (1968), I.S. Falk, associate study director

with unemployment compensation, old age insurance, maternal and child health, certain disabled children, and the blind. Its 1935 report and recommendations scarcely mentioned health insurance except to say that a report was expected in a few months. At President Roosevelt's behest, that report (which recommended an optional state program) was never made public (Starr, 1982).

The Social Security Act passed in August 1935 with no provisions for health insurance, but it provided some support for state public health programs including maternal and infant care. A provision in the original Social Security bill calling merely for further study of the health insurance problem provoked so much controversy that it was deleted (Anderson, 1968). However, the financial implications of a comprehensive program of public health insurance provided another rationale for inaction in 1935. If health insurance had been included, one estimate is that it would have doubled the amount of the payroll deduction required to fund the new programs (Anderson, 1968, p. 196). The late 1930s saw further studies and committees and some vague endorsements of more adequate medical care from President Roosevelt. Public programs for special groups were created on an emergency basis for short periods. One was the federal Emergency Maternity and Infant Care Program. This program developed the first nationwide uniform program for paying for hospital care on the basis of the "actual per diem cost of operating the hospital" rather than on the basis of hospital charges (Law, 1974, p. 60). The policy prompted the preparation of a cost accounting manual by the American Hospital Association (AHA) (Anderson, 1975).

The 1940s saw new legislative proposals but no action (Anderson, 1968; Harris, 1969; Starr, 1982). Senators Robert Wagner, Sr., and James Murray and Representative John Dingell, Sr., introduced the first of a series of national health insurance bills in 1943. (A 1939 proposal had emphasized state programs.) None got very far. President Truman actively supported national health insurance, for example, in his state of the union address in 1948. "What the New Deal had ignored, the Fair Deal now embraced" (Fein, 1986, p. 45). Congress, however, never brought a compulsory national health insurance bill out of committee, and various less extensive proposals[11] also got nowhere in the face of a strong public relations cam-

---

of CCMC, was also involved in CES work on health insurance. Falk later helped interest Senator Robert Wagner and others in sponsoring a series of national health insurance proposals in the 1940s (Harris, 1969).

[11]These included a proposal from Senator Jacob Javits, Representative Richard Nixon, and other Republicans for a "locally controlled, government-subsidized, private nonprofit insurance system, with premiums scaled to subscribers' incomes" (Starr, 1982, p. 285). It had no means test.

paign by the AMA against "socialized medicine." In contrast, without much notice, the 1950 Social Security Amendments, in addition to expanding the old age and survivors insurance program, provided states with matching funds to pay physicians and hospitals for caring for welfare recipients.

In the early 1950s the Eisenhower administration, opposed to the "socialization of medicine" but concerned because voluntary insurance still left many unprotected, repeatedly proposed a government reinsurance program. It was labeled by the Secretary of the Department of Health, Education and Welfare as the "keystone" of the administration's health program (Anderson, 1968, p. 145), and its goal was to support the provision of private insurance to the poor and to high-risk groups. As described in 1954, reinsurance would have worked as follows:

> "The premium charge for reinsurance of any health service contract of any approved association would be 2 per cent per year of the gross payments received by the association on all health contracts. A Health Service Reinsurance Corporation would be set up, with a hospital service reinsurance fund of $25 million. The federal government would pay two-thirds of any hospital bill in excess of $1,000 a year for any individual. The premiums would be scaled according to income." (*The New York Times*, quoted in Anderson, 1968, p. 223)

This relatively comprehensive concept failed, "'caught in cross fire by the conservative wings of both parties from one direction and by New Deal and Fair Deal Democrats from the other'" (Morris, quoted in Anderson, 1968, p. 144). Attention and debate then shifted to other proposals aimed more narrowly at the elderly, the poor, and other groups that had been left aside by the growth of private health insurance as described below. The eventual result was the establishment of the Medicare and Medicaid programs in 1965, which are discussed later in this chapter.

### Innovation in the Private Sector

The Committee on the Costs of Medical Care had documented a number of interesting private sector initiatives to provide medical expense protection or prepaid medical services but revealed that their scope was limited. One study cited approximately 400 businesses that had established "more or less complete medical services for their employees" under widely differing financing, service, and other arrangements (Rorem, 1982, p. 64, reprinted from Rorem, 1932). Some employers or employee groups had entered into agreements with clinics, group practices, and hospitals to make monthly payments for medical care provided to employees or to assist employees in making such payments. One agreement, which began in 1929 and involved Baylor University Hospital and Dallas public school employees, is conventionally cited as the first Blue Cross plan, although that term did not come into use until 1934. Another plan involved the employees of the Los Angeles water and power departments and what became the Ross-Loos Clinic, often cited as the first prepaid group practice. Nationwide, by 1930, plans sponsored by employers, employees, or both covered only an estimated 1.2 million employees and 1 to 2 million dependents (Somers and Somers, 1961).

At the same time that some former members and staff of the Committee on the Costs of Medical Care were trying to secure for health insurance a place in the New Deal, others followed up on the CCMC's recommendations with respect to group practice and voluntary health insurance and sought to build on the models identified in the CCMC's reports.[12] One CCMC staff member and employee of the Rosenwald Fund, C. Rufus Rorem, exercised particular leadership by formulating principles and operating practices for group hospitalization plans and working with leaders in many communities to make these principles a reality.[13]

The concept of the community-based, voluntary, nonprofit group hospitalization or prepayment plan—what became Blue Cross—began to spread with start-up funding from foundations, community chests, loans, and hospital contributions. The development of Blue Cross in the 1930s was strongly influenced by the early coordinating and technical assistance role played by the AHA to which C. Rufus Rorem served as a part-time consultant. Rorem had sought—to no avail—to interest the Rosenwald Fund, the Twentieth Century Fund, and the Community Chest in playing this role before he turned to the fledgling AHA in 1936. It is interesting to speculate whether support from one of the former organizations would have added more force to the community service concept, diminished the influence of hospital interests, and, in any fundamental sense, altered the path of Blue Cross and health insurance generally in subsequent decades.

By 1935, 15 Blue Cross plans existed in 11 states, with 6 more estab lished in the following year (Anderson, 1975). The founder of the plan in St. Paul had developed a blue cross logo (replacing the image of a nurse in

---

[12]This section is drawn largely from Somers and Somers, 1961; Law, 1974; Anderson, 1975; Rorem, 1982 (which includes many essays published in the 1930s and 1940s); Starr, 1982; Weeks and Berman, 1985; Stevens, 1989; also see *Journal of Health Policy, Politics and Law*, Winter 1991 issue, for several historical assessments of Empire Blue Cross and Blue Shield (New York) that refer to broader developments.

[13]When the Rosenwald Fund ended its medical economics work, it gave Rorem (a certified public accountant and Ph.D. economist) a "nest egg"—$100,000 for four years. A larger amount was given Michael Davis, a more senior Rosenwald employee, who then established the Committee for Research in Medical Economics, which promoted national health insurance. Davis also founded the first journal of medical economics research, *Medical Care* (Anderson, 1975).

a blue and white uniform), and this logo gave rise to the name, which was adopted first by the St. Paul plan and then others. The growth of these plans prompted the search for a coordinating scheme that resulted in 1938 in an AHA-associated Council of Plans and in 1941 in the Hospital Service Plan Commission, a separate financial entity within the AHA corporate structure. (AHA and Blue Cross ended this formal affiliation in 1972.)

Influenced by a variety of personal convictions, practical considerations, and political sensitivities, the standards developed in the 1930s for Blue Cross plan operation and membership reflected a mix of influences.[14] These principles, which had some points in common with those set forth in the CCMC minority report, are summarized in Table 2.4. The most significant departure from CCMC majority principles involved the exclusion of Blue Cross payment for physician services and the lack of emphasis on group practice. This was a practical accommodation to organized medicine, which in particular opposed payment to hospitals for physician services for pathology, radiology, and anesthesiology (Stevens, 1989).

Although they disregarded or were in partial ignorance of many insurance principles, the founders of voluntary health insurance plans in the 1930s understood that the composition of the risk pool is critical to the cost and survival of a plan. If the people who buy health insurance are disproportionately those who expect high expenses for health care, then insurance will be, at best, a form of group budgeting for the ill without the critical feature of risk sharing with healthy individuals.

The choice of the employee group as the foundation for private health insurance was a key element in managing the risk pool and avoiding disproportionate participation by higher risk individuals. The employee group was attractive because it existed for reasons other than the purchase of insurance. One provision that emerged in most group plans was a requirement that a substantial majority of employees participate in the program, another guard against adverse risk selection. Many of the early nonprofit health insurance plans were also committed to what has come to be called "community rating." That is, they charged the same amount per individual based on the projected expenditures for all those covered in the community.

Initially, employees often paid the full premium, with employers supplying organizational support and the payroll deduction mechanism, which greatly cut expenses for collecting premiums from individuals. Although hospitals played a major role in helping early Blue Cross plans get started, the other necessary condition was employer interest. For example, J.L. Hudson, the large Detroit-based department store, and Ford Motor Com-

---

[14]Even into the 1980s, the Blue Cross and Blue Shield Association preferred to describe its organizations not as insurers but rather as prepayment or service benefit organizations, despite the substantial blurring of the distinctions between the two concepts.

**TABLE 2.4**   Standards for Blue Cross Plans Adopted in the 1930s

*Conditions of Coverage*
   • Widest possible coverage as to types of subscribers, minimum of exclusions, and low annual subscription rates (even if benefits must be limited to use of lower-priced hospital accommodation).
   • Free member choice of hospital.
   • Hospital admission only upon recommendation of a physician and for treatment only while under physician care.
   • Hospital benefits in the form of services (guaranteed by hospitals) rather than cash payments.
   • Uniform adequate payments to hospital on a basis that would not jeopardize quality.

*Organization and Operation*
   • Nonprofit sponsorship and commitment to public service.
   • Economic soundness of the plan.
   • Avoidance of competition among plans.
   • Representation on plan governing boards of members of the general public and the medical profession.

SOURCES:  Anderson, 1975; Rorem, 1982.

pany were two employers important to the early development of the Blue Cross plan in Michigan (Weeks and Berman, 1985).

The growth of Blue Cross plans was impressive. By 1940, 6 million members were enrolled in 56 plans; this number grew to 19 million in 80 plans by 1945 and to 52 million in 79 plans by 1958 (Somers and Somers, 1961; Anderson, 1975).

Although early Blue Cross plans stayed away from coverage for physician services in order to decrease physician opposition to group hospitalization insurance, the demand for such coverage and the growing interest of commercial insurers helped prompt a somewhat parallel source of nonprofit benefits for physician services. What is considered the first Blue Shield plan, the California Physicians Service, was organized in 1939—with leadership from Ray Lyman Wilbur, who had chaired the CCMC (Starr, 1982).[15] This plan helped pioneer a number of innovations, including the relative value system for pricing physician services (still surviving—albeit much altered—in the Resource-Based Relative Value System adopted by Medicare in 1989) and assessments of new technologies based on both scientific and community input.

---

[15]Earlier medical society plans were organized by county medical societies in Oregon and Washington before 1920, partly in reaction to the opening to the public of the contract medical services organized by the lumber and railroad industries. Some of these plans, such as those in Washington's King and Pierce counties, later became Blue Shield plans (Somers and Somers, 1961).

Blue Shield enrollment stood at 2.5 million in 22 plans in 1945 and at 41 million in 65 plans in 1958 (Somers and Somers, 1961). Enrollment in Blue Cross and Blue Shield plans, collectively, peaked at 86.7 million in 1980 and now stands at about 70 million (HIAA, 1991b).

One other noteworthy stream of innovation in the 1930s and 1940s involved prepaid group practice and similar arrangements, which the CCMC had strongly endorsed (Somers and Somers, 1961; Anderson, 1968; Rorem, 1982; Starr, 1982). Some believed group practice was the only foundation on which voluntary insurance could successfully be based, and they worked vigorously to promote its growth.

The Ross-Loos plan, started in 1929, was cited above. In 1933, Dr. Sidney Garfield organized a similar prepaid arrangement for injuries suffered by workers constructing an aqueduct in the Southern California desert. Garfield then undertook in 1938 a like effort for Henry J. Kaiser's workers at the Grand Coulee Dam. In 1945 and 1946 as Kaiser's work force was declining with the war's end, Kaiser opened its plans to enrollment by workers in other organizations rather than close the plans. To promote acceptance, Kaiser adopted an innovative "dual-choice" policy that required employers offering the Kaiser plan to also offer a fee-for-service plan. Practical as this policy was and attractive in the choice it offered employees, it helped provide the basis for biased risk selection to operate within the employee group.

Sponsorship of early prepaid group practice plans was quite varied. Some early plans were initiated by employers (e.g., Kaiser); some by employee groups, unions, or consumers (e.g., Group Health Association of Washington, D.C., which was organized by employees of the Federal Home Loan Bank, and the Health Alliance Plan of Detroit, which was organized by the United Auto Workers); some by individual physicians (e.g., Ross-Loos); and some by government (e.g., the Health Insurance Plan of New York City, which was promoted by Mayor Fiorello LaGuardia with start-up help from the Rockefeller, New York, and Lasker foundations). Even the federal government was involved, through the short-lived rural prepayment plans started by the Farm Security Administration. As early as 1940, the movement for prepaid group practices had developed enough to warrant establishment of the trade association that eventually became the Group Health Association of America (not to be confused with the individual Group Health Association plan in the nation's capital).

Overall, however, these plans grew slowly because of fierce opposition from the medical profession. This opposition was codified in many state laws and in medical society rules that excluded prepaid group practice physicians from membership. Twenty-six states eventually prohibited consumer-controlled medical plans, and 17 states required that plans allow free choice of physician (Starr, 1982). In addition to this legislative front, medical societies in many places organized boycotts, got hospitals to deny admitting privileges to prepaid plan physicians, and otherwise sought to eliminate such plans.  In 1938 the Justice Department indicted the AMA and the District of Columbia medical society for antitrust violations stemming from their efforts against the Group Health Association.  The Supreme Court upheld the convictions in 1943, and similar activities continued to be identified and challenged by the Justice Department in succeeding decades.

### Employment-Based Benefits, Federal Regulations, and Union Policies

During and after World War II, the growth of voluntary health insurance and the interest of commercial health insurance were powerfully accelerated by two forces:  federal policy and union activism.  Both helped tie health coverage even more closely to the workplace.

One of the most important spurs to growth of employment-based health benefits was—like many other innovations—an unintended outgrowth of actions taken for other reasons during World War II (Somers and Somers, 1961; Munts, 1967; Starr, 1982; Weir et al., 1988).  In 1943 the War Labor Board, which had one year earlier introduced wage and price controls, ruled that contributions to insurance and pension funds did not count as wages. In a war economy with labor shortages, employer contributions for employee health benefits became a means of maneuvering around wage controls.  By the end of the war, health coverage had tripled (Weir et al., 1988).

For a variety of reasons, unions began a push for employer provision and funding of health and other benefits that employers strongly resisted. In an action that was a blow to union control of health plans and a stimulus to employer-controlled programs, the Taft-Hartley Act of 1947 banned union control of welfare funds based on employer contributions.  On the positive side, an attempt to explicitly exclude employee benefits from the require ment for collective bargaining failed, and the law retained the vague language of the 1935 National Labor Relations Act that required management to bargain on "wages and conditions of employment."  The law also established regulations for joint employer-union control of plans involving multiple employers.

Health and welfare benefits were major factors in a wave of postwar strikes and other conflicts with employers over what bargaining on "conditions of employment" involved.[16]  Key National Labor Relations Board

---

[16]The most extensive union program of direct services and coverage, that operated by the United Mine Workers Welfare and Retirement Fund, emerged from a bitter labor-management confrontation that prompted repeated federal intervention (including seizure of the mines in 1946) to establish and secure the fund (Somers and Somers, 1961; Munts, 1967).

(NLRB) rulings in 1948 clarified the matter. The NLRB held, in a case involving Inland Steel Company and the United Steel Workers, that federal law required employers to bargain over pensions. Shortly after that, the board ruled likewise for health insurance benefits. The Supreme Court upheld the NLRB in 1949. Still, over half the strikes in 1949 and the first part of 1950 were related to health and welfare issues (Weir et al., 1988). During the 1949 steelworkers strike, a fact-finding board appointed by the President firmly supported the union position on bargaining, and the steel companies began to settle.

Health insurance and other fringe benefits were on their way to becoming a standard feature of employment. A number of unions continued to sponsor health centers and other programs, but most focused on the employer-sponsored programs. A further important boost to these programs came in 1954 when the Internal Revenue Code made it clear that employers' contributions for health benefit plans were generally tax deductible as a business expense and were to be excluded from employees' taxable income. Between 1950 and 1965, employer outlays for health care rose from 0.5 to 1.5 percent of total employee compensation.[17]

## Growth and Change in Health Insurance Products

The importance of these developments—that is, the defeat of national health insurance, government decisions favorable to employer-based insurance, the success of the Blue Cross concept, and the switch of unions from opposition to support for employer-based insurance—led to further rapid growth of employment-based health benefits in the 1950s. (Unions did not, however, abandon their preference for national health insurance.) By 1958 an estimated three-quarters of the 123 million Americans with private health coverage were participants in employment-based programs, and about 36 million of this group participated in plans that were collectively bargained (Somers and Somers, 1961). In 1960, 79 Blue Cross and 65 Blue Shield plans had been established, 250 to 300 prepaid group practice and other independent plans existed, and over 700 commercial insurance companies were selling individual or group coverage or both (Somers and Somers, 1961).

The growth in commercial insurance was particularly notable after World War II. At the end of the 1940s, Blue Cross plans had larger enrollment

---

[17]These data were compiled by the Department of Commerce, which changed its methods for analyzing data in 1959. According to the department's current methodology, 6.3 percent of employee compensation was accounted for by employer health care spending in 1990 (EBRI, 1992a). As calculated by analysts in the Health Care Financing Administration of the Department of Health and Human Services (and cited in Chapter 3), the 1965 figure is 2.0 percent and the 1990 figure is 7.1 percent.

than individual and group insurers combined; by the end of the next decade, commercial group enrollments exceeded Blue Cross group enrollments.[18] The serious entry of commercial insurers brought important changes: new products, different rating practices, and significant competition.

Firm and fast generalizations about differences between Blue Cross and other nonprofit plans and commercial insurance are risky given the variability that has characterized both. However, reflecting its roots in property, casualty, and life insurance practices and principles, commercial insurance brought to the provision of health insurance a perspective that is quite different from that of the Blue Cross and Blue Shield plans, with their ties to health care providers and their nonprofit, community orientation (Faulkner, 1960; Somers and Somers, 1961; MacIntyre, 1962; Anderson, 1975; HIAA, 1991b). This perspective was reflected in

- a business and even ideological commitment to insurance premiums that reflected a specific individual's or group's level of risk (based on past or expected claims experience) in isolation from the broader community;
- a greater emphasis on consumer cost sharing through deductibles and other traditional devices to eliminate small, expensive-to-process claims and to control consumers' tendencies to use more of a good for which they do not bear the full cost;
- a reliance on indemnity products that paid cash to the individual and were not linked to contracts for payment and other arrangements that involved health care practitioners and institutions directly;
- a proliferation of products that included, most notably, major medical benefits (combined coverage for hospital and physician services with high overall limits on coverage) and, less constructively, low-benefit, high-profit products such as so-called "dread disease" policies;
- greater marketing expertise and resources; and
- for the larger national companies, a greater ability to provide uniform and efficient service for employers with workers at multiple sites in multiple states.

Many of these features were attractive to employers and workers, and they also influenced the practices of the nonprofit organizations. Arguably, the first of the above features, rating premiums according to risk or experience, had the most significant influence on the course of voluntary insurance over the next several decades.

---

[18]Commenting on the growing involvement of commercial insurers in this field, one observer stated in a 1956 text on casualty insurance, "'In large part, . . . this new business has been manna from heaven or Washington or Mars; it has yet to stand the test of adversity'" (Kulp, quoted in Somers and Somers, 1961, p. 261).

## Federal Government as Sponsor of Employee Health Benefits Program

Because it has been both cited and criticized as a model for national health policy for the last two decades and because it is the country's largest employment-based program, a note on the history of the Federal Employees Health Benefits Program (FEHBP) is in order (Somers and Somers, 1977b; Fleming, 1973, cited in Enthoven, 1989; Enthoven, 1978, 1988a, 1989; Moffit, 1992). FEHBP was established in 1959 so that the federal government could compete more effectively with private employers to recruit and retain a productive work force (CRS, 1989, especially Appendix B). Until that time, only a fraction of federal agencies sponsored health plans, although between 1947 and 1959 some 30 bills had proposed creation of a program.

The FEHBP program was unusual in that its congressional sponsors wanted to encourage competition and employee choice among health plans. It provided for three types of plans: (1) governmentwide plans, including both a service benefit plan (Blue Cross and Blue Shield) and an indemnity plan; (2) employee organization plans (several of which were already in place by 1959); and (3) comprehensive medical plans such as prepaid group practices. By 1961, there were already 55 approved options, and there are over 300 today. Initially, the government paid 40 percent of a plan premium (rather than the 33 percent proposed by the Bureau of the Budget and the Civil Service Commission), subject to certain minimums and maximums. The contribution formula was revised in 1971 so that the government contribution would equal 60 percent of the average of the premiums of the six big FEHBP high-option plans, not to exceed 75 percent of any specific plan premium.

FEHBP remains unusual in two particular respects. One is the large number of choices provided. All employees have at least 20 plans to choose among, and those in urban areas may have more than 30 options. The program is also unusual in that the fee-for-service plans are all privately insured rather than self-insured by the government. Thus they compete with HMOs on the same "at risk" basis. As discussed in Chapter 5, FEHBP has had significant problems with biased risk selection that are in considerable measure a function of its wide-open multiple-choice structure.

## EARLY COST MANAGEMENT EFFORTS BY INSURERS AND OTHERS

Between 1920 and 1965, many of the basic elements of today's strategies for managing health benefit costs were identified, even if they were not persuasively articulated or successfully applied.[19] These elements include

---

[19]Much of this section appeared in IOM (1989).

- management of the risk pool,
- design of the benefit plan,
- controls on payments to health care providers,
- constraints on the supply of health care resources, and
- review of the appropriateness of utilization.

## Management of the Risk Pool

As noted above, the founders of health insurance plans in the 1920s and 1930s used the employment group, community rating, and other steps to make insurance affordable and sustainable by spreading risk broadly. Subsequently, competition in insurance markets brought experience rating and medical underwriting as means to reduce premiums for healthier groups and thereby attract their business. Neither strategy for premium cost containment directly targets the price, use, or intensity of health care services, although it is claimed that making individuals with poorer health status or health behavior pay more for coverage encourages more prudent and thereby less costly behavior.

## Design of the Benefit Plan

Like management of the risk pool, the centrality of benefit design was also quickly appreciated as a vehicle to control health plan costs. One way to limit expenses is to require patients to bear some of the cost of care themselves through such mechanisms as deductibles, coinsurance, and dollar maximums on benefits for all services or specific categories of service. Cost sharing has two objectives—first, to transfer some liability for costs to the patient and, second, to discourage patient demand for care. Plan administrators also concluded that premiums could be held in check by excluding coverage for experimental and ineffective treatments, for treatments whose use was highly discretionary or difficult to monitor, for extended or custodial care for chronic conditions, and for relatively low cost services that could be scheduled and budgeted. For the most part, these provisions built from principles developed in more traditional forms of insurance, as discussed in Chapter 1.[20] Relatively slower to develop was the hope that payment for and timely use of certain low-cost services (e.g., preventive

---

[20]The most notable exceptions to these traditions were what came to be called the "first dollar" service benefits for hospital care offered by Blue Cross plans and their participating hospitals. Nonetheless, statistics from a 1944 monograph on these plans indicate that they covered, on average, about 75 percent of the hospital bill (cited in Stevens, 1989). The other 25 percent presumably involved such things as specific uncovered services and very long hospital stays, which exceeded the limit of 60 or 120 days covered by many contracts.

and outpatient care) could avoid higher total payments for inpatient and acute care.

## Controls on Payments to Providers

During the financially difficult years of the 1930s, contracting and risk sharing with providers were important economic elements of prepaid group practice arrangements and some health insurance plans. For example, most Blue Cross plans through their guarantee of service benefits rather than indemnity payments had provisions for some sharing of risk by their contracting hospitals (Donabedian, 1976). Strong contractual relationships that included some risk sharing or limits on payments to providers, however, were hard to establish and maintain (Werlin, 1973; Anderson, 1975; Hellinger, 1978; Weeks and Berman, 1985).

The expansionary postwar decades stimulated hospital restiveness with the contractual relationship that guaranteed service to Blue Cross enrollees at a negotiated price. Physicians, moreover, continued to fight prepaid group practice plans and other forms of contracting and risk sharing. Some physician associations took a less negative approach. To compete with prepaid group practices, they established foundations for medical care (FMCs), beginning with the San Joaquin County Foundation (in California) in 1954. By 1973, there were 61 FMCs in 27 states (Egdahl, 1973). Those FMCs that involved physician acceptance of limited financial risk are predecessors of today's independent practice associations (IPAs). The push for prepaid group practices, IPAs, and similar health plans—collectively christened HMOs in 1970—as a cost containment strategy began in earnest in the 1970s (Ellwood et al., 1971; Brown, 1983; see also Chapter 6 of this report).

## Constraints on Supply

Another approach to cost containment was developed under the rubric of health planning. Health planning had received much of its initial nationwide impetus as a tool for guiding the expansion in community hospital resources under the Hill-Burton program established after World War II. Beginning in the late 1950s, however, the growing supply of hospital resources came to be viewed as a source of rising health care costs (Roemer and Shain, 1959), and health planning was supported by many—including some insurers and some employers—as a way to limit excessive capital investment (Somers and Somers, 1961). As of 1961, 14 health planning agencies had been established (Stevens, 1989). In 1964, New York adopted the first state certificate-of-need law, which required state approval for hospital construction projects. Using a tactic pioneered by Blue Cross of Northeast Ohio as early as 1950 (U.S. Department of Health, Education and Welfare,

1976), some insurers warned that unless hospitals cooperated with public or voluntary health planning "we will not pay full reimbursement or continue our contract with a hospital" (Walter McNerney, quoted in Somers, 1969, p. 138).

## Utilization Review

Historically, third-party payers tended to concentrate their cost containment energies on the unit price of medical services and to pay less attention to the volume of those services provided by institutions and practitioners and sought by patients. However, some early physician organized health plans established a form of peer review.[21] Although some hospitals used committees to monitor utilization in an effort to cope with the short supply of hospital beds during World War II, the first explicit use of retrospective utilization review to control fee-for-service payments for unnecessary and inappropriate hospital services seems to have been in the 1950s (Payne, 1987). In 1954, Fred Carter, a physician, wrote in *The Modern Hospital*, "'Why not appoint a standing hospital staff committee designated as the "hospital utilization committee" to do in the field of hospital and medical economics what the tissue committee does . . . in the field of surgery. Abuses in the use of hospital services and facilities coming to the attention of this hospital utilization committee could be disciplined to the point of near deletion'" (quoted in London, 1965, p. 77). Apparently, high optimism about the impact of utilization review was born with the idea itself.

The 1950s also appear to have seen the first attempt by health plans to encourage or require second opinions about the need for proposed surgery. The United Mine Workers Union tried to institute such a program but failed because of resistance from organized medicine (Rutgow and Sieverts, 1989). It was not until the 1970s that such provisions were successfully introduced by the Store Workers Health and Welfare Fund and other union programs (McCarthy and Widmer, 1974).

The San Joaquin County Foundation for Medical Care, founded in 1954, not only served as a model for many IPAs but also helped inspire several medical societies to organize peer review of health care utilization and quality. FMCs pioneered many utilization review tools, including model treatment profiles to assess physician performance, protocols for reviewing ambulatory care, and computerized screening of claims (Egdahl, 1973).

---

[21]For example, soon after its creation in 1917, what is now the Pierce County (Washington) Blue Shield plan established a Consultation Committee and required that physicians check with a committee member to determine whether an operation was appropriate before they would be paid. The plan also warned physicians about their overuse of prescription drugs and private duty nurses.

By the early 1960s, more than 60 Blue Cross plans reported programs to review claims for the appropriateness of hospital admissions, and more than 50 looked at the length of stay. Some required physicians to certify at admission that hospital care was necessary for cases such as diagnostic and dental admissions, and more than two dozen required physicians to certify the need for continued hospital care after a specified length of stay (Fitzpatrick, 1965; Young, 1965). In a prescient comment, Odin Anderson noted in 1968 that as payers showed increasing interest in medical practice patterns, "the central concern of the medical profession today and in the years ahead might well be 'bureaucracy'" (Anderson, 1968, p. 161).

## Impact of Early Cost Management Efforts

The various tools used to control costs from the 1930s into the 1960s may have had some impact, but they often were neither rigorously applied nor rigorously evaluated. In general, concerns about controlling costs were still overshadowed by society's desire to expand access and improve health outcomes through the development and implementation of advances in medical care. Government was not a major actor, but neither had marketplace competition emerged as a rallying point for private sector cost containment strategies. Community-oriented programs and cooperative work with health care providers were more prominent themes in this period. Further discussion of private and public efforts to control health care costs, which greatly expanded in the 1970s and 1980s, is deferred until Chapter 6.

## THE LIMITS OF VOLUNTARY HEALTH BENEFITS AND MEDICARE AND MEDICAID

As the growth of employment-based health benefits was making such coverage an expected feature of personal life for many Americans, some limitations of voluntary private insurance were simultaneously being identified. The elderly were singled out as a special problem, having greater medical needs but less financial protection than younger individuals still in the work force (Somers and Somers, 1961; Feingold, 1966; Harris, 1969; Marmor, 1973). In 1960, about half of those aged 65 to 74 were thought to have some form of private health insurance—frequently more limited than that available to younger individuals—but only one-third of those over 75 had any protection. Somers and Somers (1961) estimated on the basis of data acknowledged as fragmentary that health insurance met perhaps "one sixth of total medical costs of the insured [but] one fourteenth of the total for all the aged" (p. 445).

The consequences of being uninsured had become more significant as the medical advances associated with World War II and the postwar commitment of significant resources to biomedical science and hospital construction expanded both the problems medicine could treat and the costs of treatment. Moreover, growth in personal income, private insurance, and open-ended third-party reimbursement practices and constrained growth in the supply of physicians combined to place inflationary pressure on medical care prices.

Between 1950 and 1960, employment in the health care sector rose by over 50 percent, compared with only 10 percent for employment in total (Fuchs, 1968). The amount of per diem hospital costs accounted for by salaries went from $5.11 in 1946 to $20.56 in 1960, an increase of 300 percent, compared with an increase of about 160 percent for other expenses (Colman, 1968). The number of outpatient prescriptions tripled from 1945 to 1966, but prescription expenditures went up tenfold (McEvilla, 1968). In addition, between 1950 and 1965, medical care prices rose twice as fast as consumer prices overall, and consumer expenditures for health care went from $8.5 billion to $28.1 billion (Gorham, 1968).

The late 1950s and early 1960s saw persistent efforts to expand state and federal government programs to cover medical expenses for the elderly, poor, and other groups. The first legislation to provide health insurance for Social Security beneficiaries was introduced in 1952, and a national program for certain aged and other poor individuals was passed in 1960. The adoption of a more comprehensive national program for the elderly and a state-federal plan for certain low-income groups took another five years.

## Medicare

The events leading up to the passage of Medicare, Title 18 of the Social Security Act, are well documented (Feingold, 1966; Harris, 1969; Somers and Somers, 1967, 1977a, 1977b; Anderson, 1968; Marmor, 1973; Starr, 1982). The legislation, which was passed in 1965 (to take effect in July 1966), reflected the bitter political battles and varied compromises that preceded final agreement. In 1972, Medicare was extended to disabled individuals and certain others (who now constitute about 10 percent of all beneficiaries). In 1982, employers who offered a health plan were required to cover workers aged 65 to 69.

For both practical and political reasons, the program reflected and built on structures and practices developed in the private insurance sector. In its design and implementation, Medicare continued the division between hospital and physician services coverage that had accompanied the growth of Blue Cross and Blue Shield. It maintained free choice by beneficiaries of physician and hospital. It essentially took the hospital insurance and cost reimbursement approach from Blue Cross (except that it included a deductible for hospital care) and adapted the medical insurance approach from commercial insurers. However, Medicare adapted from Blue Shield the participating physician concept and the method for paying physicians based on reasonable charges.[22] Participating physicians had to agree to accept these payments as payments in full, but physicians could choose not to participate and bill patients for the balance. In addition, the original Medicare legislation had special provisions allowing Medicare beneficiaries to enroll in prepaid group practices (but not on a capitated basis). Congress did not follow the suggestion of a Kaiser official that the program be structured along the lines of the Federal Employees Health Benefits Program (Somers and Somers, 1972, reprinted in Somers and Somers, 1977b).

For program administration, Medicare used private organizations, known as intermediaries for Part A and carriers for Part B. On the hospital, or Part A, side, most of the intermediaries were Blue Cross plans. On the Part B side, carriers were initially split about 50-50 between commercial insurers and Blue Shield plans, although the Blue Shield share has since grown. Payment for Part A services relies on payroll taxes paid by employers and employees and deductibles and other expenses borne by beneficiaries using services. Part B, which is a voluntary but still near-universal program, is financed through beneficiary premiums (to cover 25 percent of program costs) and general revenues (to cover the other 75 percent).

Enrollments in Medicare Part A grew from 19.5 million in 1967 to 33.1 million in 1989; Part B enrollments grew from 17.9 to 32.1 million in the same period (HIAA, 1991b). Total spending for Part A and Part B has gone from $3.1 billion in 1967 to $94.3 billion in 1989. Real spending per beneficiary (in 1987 dollars) rose from $939 in 1970 to $2,671 in 1988 (CBO, 1991b). As is described in the next chapter, many elderly individuals receive additional coverage from former employers.

## Medicaid

The Medicaid program, created at the same time as Medicare, did not build on the social insurance principles that guided the latter program. Rather, it continued the charity care approach of its predecessor, the 1960 Kerr-Mills Act (Marmor, 1973; Starr, 1982; Stevens, 1989).

---

[22]This general approach was first experimented with by the Blue Shield plan in Wisconsin in 1954 and spread rather slowly to other plans until labor unions began pushing the method in the 1960s and Medicare gave the method a further boost (Showstack et al., 1979). Simply described, Medicare would pay the physician whichever charge was lowest: the actual charge for a service to a Medicare beneficiary, that physician's usual charge for the service, or the prevailing fee for all physicians providing the service in the same geographic area. The major alternatives at the time (for fee-for-service practitioners) were payment according to a fixed schedule of fees or payment of a percentage of actual charges.

Title 19 of the Social Security Act created a complex program that was to be (1) financed by federal and state funds, (2) aimed primarily at poor individuals who were eligible for certain other welfare benefits, in particular, Aid to Families with Dependent Children, and (3) administered by the states under federal rules. These rules provided considerable latitude for states to determine who would be eligible, what services would be covered, and how much providers would be paid. The result has been substantial state-to-state variation (PPRC, 1990). For example, states have varied in the extent to which their Medicaid programs cover low-income workers and their families. For a welfare recipient, employment often means an end to Medicaid without the beginning of employment-based coverage, although federal requirements provide some exceptions. Overall, Medicaid generally has covered less than half of the poor (that is, those with incomes below the federally defined poverty level).

The 1965 law provided that federal financing for Medicaid, which comes from general revenues, would be dispensed to states on a matching basis related to state per capita income and claims submitted by states.[23] Today, the federal contribution to program expenditures constitutes about 56 percent of the total, but the share varies from 50 to nearly 80 percent of the total for individual states (GAO, 1991c).

In 1972, Medicaid covered about 17.6 million people, versus 25 million individuals in 1989, but total program costs grew from $6.3 to $64.9 billion during the same period (HIAA, 1991b; EBRI, 1992a). Real payments per user (1990 dollars) rose from $1,200 in 1975 to $2,600 in 1990 and ranged from $6,700 per user for the 3.2 million aged participants to $800 per user for the 11.2 million children from low-income families (CBO, 1992c).

In 1990, Medicaid was the second-largest component of state spending and was increasing faster and less predictably than other costs. At 12 percent of total state spending, it was exceeded only by spending on elementary and secondary education at 23 percent (GAO, 1991c, 1992a). In 1989, 49 governors asked Congress for a two-year moratorium on federally mandated expansions of Medicaid eligibility and services.

## National Health Insurance Revisited

In the 1970s, some kind of national health insurance program was widely believed to be imminent (Starr, 1982). A 1977 summary by Herman and Anne Somers listed four basic categories of proposals (Table 2.5).

The greatest opportunity for action came in 1974, when the Nixon ad-

---

[23]States may require local governments to cover up to 60 percent of program costs, but only 14 states did so in 1990, and the local burden was significant in only 3 states (PPRC, 1990).

**TABLE 2.5** Major Categories of "National Health Insurance" Proposals in the Early 1970s

*Tax Credits*
• Purchase of private insurance subsidized through tax credits for premiums paid for insurance meeting established standards.

*Employer Mandate*
• Employers required to provide an approved level of private insurance for full-time employees and their dependents.
• Premiums for the poor and unemployed subsidized by the government.

*Expanded Medicare-Type Program*
• Private insurers act as administrative agents for universal national health plan financed by payroll and other taxes.

*Fully Public Program*
• National government directly administers universal health plan financed by payroll and other taxes.

SOURCE: Adapted from Somers and Somers, 1977a.

ministration and congressional leaders (in particular, Senator Kennedy and Representative Mills) appeared willing to compromise on a broad national health insurance program. They proposed private insurance for workers and their families and public coverage for others. Labor and some other liberal groups still favored a fully public program, but organized medicine and traditional opponents of government action appeared to have accepted that the time for a comprehensive national health program had come.

Nevertheless, none of the major proposals introduced in the 1970s were successful. At the time of writing this report, just before the 1992 presidential election, health insurance had appeared as a noteworthy campaign issue for the first time since 1976. Although they vary in specifics, many current proposals still fit the basic categories identified in Table 2.5. Even one missing category, what now goes under the rubric *managed competition*, had been quite clearly described (and endorsed) by Somers and Somers as early as 1971. After calling for "pluralistic and regulated competition" and "consumer options . . . [among carriers approved by a national board] . . . on an informed and meaningful basis," they warned that the policy debate threatened to degenerate into "doctrinaire position-taking" among those attached to "old ideologies" that pitted "public" against "private" strategies (pp. 193, 198, 200). In fact, the 1970s and 1980s did see a debate that was framed in terms of market versus regulatory strategies (as described further in Chapter 6), and the same rhetoric continues to be heard in the 1990s.

## FEDERAL REGULATION AND THE EMPLOYER'S GROWING ROLE

### Federal and State Roles Before 1974

The federal structure of the U.S. political system has produced a particularly complex and uneven mix of state and national regulation of health insurance and related matters. Before 1974, states generally regulated private health insurance, whether it was individual or employment-based, insured or self-insured. State insurance regulation began in the mid-1800s and was upheld by a Supreme Court decision in 1868, which ruled that insurance contracts were not part of interstate commerce and therefore were subject to state not federal regulation. In 1944 the Court reversed its decision, holding that insurance transactions did involve interstate commerce and were subject to federal antitrust and other laws. This decision, in turn, was overruled in 1945, when Congress passed the McCarran-Ferguson Act. The act returned to the states many regulatory powers but left the option of national regulation of insurance if states did not act. In order to promote systematic state action and avoid federal regulation, the National Association of Insurance Commissioners was formed to assist in the development and passage of model state legislation.

Until the 1970s the national government largely confined its attention to employment-based health benefits to two policy issues: collective bargaining and taxation. Faced with rising Medicare and Medicaid costs in the 1970s, the federal government instituted an array of cost management initiatives, including federal wage-price controls, health resource planning, HMO promotion, and quality and utilization review of health care services (see Chapter 6 for a discussion of these programs). With the exception of the HMO Act of 1973, which mandated that most employers offer their employees a federally qualified HMO if one was available, these initiatives did not touch employment-based health benefits very directly. (Legislation adopted in 1988 calls for the HMO mandate provision to expire in 1995.)

### The Employee Retirement Income Security Act of 1974

In 1974 the division of federal and state regulatory authority with respect to employee benefits changed fundamentally with the passage of the Employee Retirement Income Security Act (ERISA). Since then, the relevance of state regulation to employment-based health plans has declined dramatically—without any significant expansion in substantive federal regulation of plan operations and characteristics.

ERISA was aimed primarily at private employer pension plans, and most of its provisions and implementing regulations are directed at such pension plans with little explicit attention to health plans. As interpreted by the courts over the years since its passage, however, ERISA has preempted an increasing number of state regulations affecting employment-based health plans (Appendix B; Moses, 1992). Despite some pressure to do so, Congress has refused to enact legislation that would overrule these interpretations.

States can indirectly reach some employers through their regulation of insured health plans, including insured HMO plans, but the group of insured employers has grown smaller every year as more employers—including quite small employers—have seen the advantages of self-insuring to avoid such regulation. Multistate employers are free to establish uniform health benefit programs across state lines and no longer have to modify their programs to conform to the myriad different details of state laws.

For self-insured employers the major regulatory consequences of ERISA are that such plans are exempt from several requirements: state taxes on insurance premiums; state mandates that certain types of benefits be provided; state limits on certain kinds of utilization management and provider contracting arrangements; solvency and prefunding requirements; defined claims settlement procedures; state law claims for various kinds of damages; and mandatory participation in state risk pools or uncompensated care plans. The last protection is now one of the most controversial, as many states try to maintain or establish these kinds of programs. A recent federal court decision in a case brought by 14 union health and welfare plans held that ERISA precluded the state from requiring such plans to pay hospital bills that included subsidies for uncompensated and undercompensated care (*United Wire Health and Welfare Fund* v. *Morristown Memorial Hospital*, 15 EBC 1625 [1992])(Firshein, 1992b).

In addition, ERISA has been interpreted as exempting those administering claims for employee benefit plans from punitive damages for bad faith denials of claims. Further, in a case decided in June 1992, a federal appeals court held that ERISA precluded a malpractice action against a company that provided utilization review services to an ERISA-covered plan (*Corcoran* v. *United Health Care, Inc. and Blue Cross and Blue Shield of Alabama*, 1992 U.S. App. LEXIS 14621 [5th Cir., June 26, 1992]). (See Chapter 4 for further discussion of the legal liability of employers.)

Although ERISA precludes state regulation of self-insured employer-sponsored health benefits, it does not replace diverse state policies with an equivalent set of consistent national standards. The requirements it imposes on employers are quite limited. They primarily involve information reporting and disclosure, prudent exercise of fiduciary responsibilities, limits on disproportionate benefits for highly compensated employees, and (since 1985) continued coverage for certain former workers and others. There is no provision for waivers from ERISA requirements, and only one state, Hawaii, has obtained a statutory waiver.

The point that ERISA preempts state regulation without substituting explicit federal regulation of some basic dimensions of health benefit plans can be illustrated with several specific examples, which are discussed further in Appendix B. Unlike many or all state laws, ERISA

•  sets no solvency, reserve, funding, financial management, or backup insurance requirements for health plans to protect employees in the event of employer bankruptcy;
•  specifies no standards for health coverage or minimum benefits;
•  establishes no requirements that certain categories of employees or family members be generally eligible for coverage (except for the continued coverage requirements described below); and
•  contains no prohibitions against unilateral reduction or termination of benefits by an employer during the plan year nor any limits on medical underwriting practices such as exclusions of coverage for preexisting conditions.

With respect to this last point, although ERISA did not set funding and vesting requirements for health benefit plans as it did for pension plans, other statutes and the general law of contracts may limit employers' freedom to reduce or terminate benefits in some cases. For example, employers may need to prove that their right to terminate retiree benefits was specifically stated and widely known to employees (EBRI, 1991d). This constraint is particularly significant for employers considering their options given recent nongovernmental rules established by the Financial Accounting Standards Board (FASB). These rules require that benefits promised to retirees be recognized as liabilities on a firm's financial statements. (See Chapter 3 for further discussion.)

ERISA did establish somewhat more extensive regulatory provisions for one type of employment-based health benefits involving multiple employers, but the results have not been satisfactory to many (CRS, 1988h; McLeod and Geisel, 1992; National Health Policy Forum, 1992; U.S. Senate Committee on Governmental Affairs, 1992a). *Multiple employer plans* were originally defined as plans to which more than one employer contributes but which are not collectively bargained. Then in 1982, Congress redefined this category as multiple employer welfare arrangements (MEWAs), and made such plans subject to special regulations intended to control abuses fostered by the lack of applicable federal or state regulation. Fully insured MEWAs are subject to direct state insurance regulation related to the adequacy of contribution and reserve levels. MEWAs that are not fully insured are subject to all state insurance regulations, to the extent that they are not inconsistent with ERISA. Abuses and outright fraud by some third parties marketing MEWAs have led to calls for further legislation to strengthen regulation of such plans at the state or federal level or both.

Further complicating the regulatory picture are *multiemployer plans*, which, as defined by statute, are plans to which more than one employer contributes pursuant to collective bargaining agreements. They generally have joint labor-management boards, are regulated under the 1947 Taft-Hartley Act, and are explicitly excluded from coverage under the ERISA amendments related to multiple employer welfare arrangements.

Federal laws enacted since ERISA have imposed a limited number of mandates on employers. The most important emerged from the Consolidated Omnibus Budget Reconciliation Act (COBRA) of 1985. That act requires employers with 20 or more employees who offer health benefits to offer continued coverage to most former employees, their dependents, and certain others for 18 or 36 months or until coverage under another plan begins.[24] Employers can charge no more than 102 percent of the average cost to the employer of providing coverage to all its employees.[25] An earlier federal law, the Tax Equity and Fiscal Responsibility Act of 1982, requires employers with 20 or more workers to cover certain employees (those aged 65 to 69, the disabled, and those with end-stage renal disease) who would otherwise be eligible for Medicare coverage.

Overall, ERISA gave a powerful boost to employer discretion and involvement in the management of health benefits. It diminished the position and influence of states and insurers and eliminated some protections for insured individuals but provided little in the way of explicit national standards for employee health benefits. As states' concern about the uninsured and the financial problems of health care institutions providing uncompensated care has grown, ERISA has also limited states' efforts to develop state risk pools, set minimum standards for certain kinds of health benefit programs, and act generally in areas in which the federal government has not taken the initiative.

## CONCLUSION

Although the link between occupation or workplace and assistance with the costs of illness dates back to the last century and before, it has generally been tenuous and limited by its voluntary character and by the limited financial resources of those involved. In most countries the result has been the gradual mandating by governments of compulsory, near-universal, publicly subsidized coverage. These mandates have sometimes built on work-related insurance organizations and employer and employee deductions to

---

[24]COBRA does not require a former employee or other eligible individual to accept coverage under another plan, for example, a plan available from a new employer.

[25]One recent study indicated that claims costs for those who elect COBRA coverage are 120 percent of the cost for the non-COBRA group (A. Foster Higgins, 1992).

cover "premiums," but employers have been left with relatively little discretion regarding the details of health benefit programs and with limited involvement in health care cost management.

The exception to this pattern is the United States, where voluntary private action has managed—with some assistance from facilitating national legislation—to extend coverage to the majority of the nonelderly population. Although the concept of workers' compensation had become widely accepted and broadly accommodated in state laws by the second decade of the century and other social insurance concepts were adopted at the national level during the 1930s, insurance for medical care expenses did not follow these precedents. Opposition by important interests outside and inside government to an expanded government role has limited public health insurance programs to the elderly and a segment of the poor. Millions of individuals are not covered by either public or private programs.

The next four chapters of this report describe the current status of employment-based health benefits and discuss developments over the last two decades. Among the key features cited are the

• extensive involvement by business (primarily large employers) in the design of health plans and efforts to influence the delivery, price, and overall cost of health care;

• significant responsibilities and administrative complexity for employers, employees, health care providers, and public officials resulting from the expansion and diversity of employers' efforts to manage their health benefit programs;

• troublesome segmentation of high- and low-cost or high- and low-risk individuals into different insurance pools and growing debate about what constitutes an equitable spreading of risk for medical care expenses;

• continued escalation in medical care expenditures and uncertainty about the value of this spending despite many efforts to contain medical care prices, limit unnecessary or marginally beneficial use of health care services, and otherwise control costs; and

• persistent controversy about the merits of public, private, or mixed strategies for achieving a more satisfactory allocation of resources for health care.

# 3

# Employment-Based Health Benefits Today

*[Employment-based benefits are] . . . the shotgun marriage of medical care and industrial relations.*

Herman Somers and Anne Somers, 1961

As described in the first two chapters of this report, the special union between the workplace and medical expense protection is a major and distinctive feature of the U.S. health care system. Despite the leveling off in the proportion of the population covered by employment-based health benefits in the 1970s and 1980s and, indeed, the decrease in coverage from 66 percent in 1988 to 64 percent in 1990, employer spending on health benefits continues to increase as a fraction of business receipts and labor compensation. The persistent escalation of health benefit costs has prompted employers to become ever more involved in the design and management of their health benefit plans and to experiment with an ever-wider variety of techniques in an effort to contain their costs.

Although the employers' role in financing health benefits is important, their role in determining whether and how to offer coverage is equally significant. This chapter provides a detailed picture of employment-based health benefits in the late 1980s and early 1990s. It examines the following six questions:

• Who is covered by employment-based health benefits and who is not?

• What kinds of health plans are offered and what services and providers do these plans cover?

• What limits are placed on this coverage?

• What do employment-based health benefit programs cost employers and employees?

• Who bears the financial risk for employment-based programs?

• What other kinds of health-related benefits do employers offer?

Although this kind of summary discussion can cover general patterns and major sources of variability in employee health benefits, it cannot portray the full diversity that currently characterizes employment-based health benefits in the United States.[1] Chapter 4 elaborates on the theme of diversity and on the complexities employers face in making and implementing decisions about health benefits in different organizational environments.

## DATA SOURCES

This chapter relies on data from four basic sources: the Bureau of the Census in the Department of Commerce, the Bureau of Labor Statistics in the Department of Labor (DOL), the Health Insurance Association of America (HIAA), and the Health Care Financing Administration (HCFA) in the Department of Health and Human Services. Although information from these sources is generally consistent, differences in definitions of terms, sampling procedures, and units of analysis require that some care be taken in interpreting data and analyses from different sources. Even data drawn from the same source may be subjected to somewhat different analytic procedures by different analysts, who are then likely to develop somewhat different inferences. Readers who want a more detailed understanding of the data sources used here should consult the methodology sections and table notes in the relevant source documents.

The Current Population Survey (CPS) of the Bureau of the Census is directed at households and does not include individuals in nursing homes, prisons, and other institutions. Because of changes in questions and population groups surveyed starting with the March 1988 survey, data covering health insurance status in 1987 and later are not comparable with data for earlier years. For analysis of the CPS data on health coverage collected during March of each year, this report relies on the analysis of the March 1991 data published by the Employee Benefit Research Institute (EBRI, 1992d).[2]

DOL statistics refer only to workers (not family members) who participate in an employer-sponsored health plan; the numbers include those em-

---

[1] Chapter 1 notes that employment-based health benefits typically involve a single employer sponsor but that some involve multiple employers and unions. The data and discussion in this chapter do not distinguish sponsor characteristics.

[2] For the March CPS, the basic question on private health insurance status asks respondents whether—other than government-sponsored policies—health insurance can be obtained privately or through a current or former employer or union and whether anyone in the household was covered by health insurance of this type at any time during the preceding calendar year. Follow-up questions ask who in the household was covered, what the specific source of coverage was, and whether it was financed in part or whole by an employer or union. In addition, the May CPS asks whether the respondent's employer offers a health plan, whether the respondent and dependents are covered by it, and if not, why. The analysis by Long and Marquis (1992) cited later in this chapter combines information from the March and May surveys.

ployees who have not yet completed any required waiting periods. DOL's Bureau of Labor Statistics now surveys small private establishments (under 100 employees) and state and local governments during one year and medium and large private establishments in alternate years.

The data generated by HIAA also come from surveys of employers, but the unit of analysis is, for the most part, the firm rather than the individual (HIAA, 1990, 1991a,c). The estimates of aggregate health care expenditures come from the HCFA. HCFA bases these estimates on its own data, information from the Census Bureau and the Bureau of Economic Analysis in the Commerce Department, and results from surveys conducted by the U.S. Chamber of Commerce.

This chapter also uses certain additional sources, including surveys conducted by the Department of Health and Human Services, the General Accounting Office (GAO), the Treasury Department, the U.S. Chamber of Commerce, and private consulting firms. Surveys conducted by consulting firms may provide the only relatively recent information on issues such as use of self-insurance arrangements, decisions about retiree health benefits, or use of financial incentives to reward or penalize off-the-job behavior. Unfortunately, these surveys, which generally question firm benefit managers and use the firm as the level of analysis, often have low response rates overall and even lower response rates for certain specific questions (DiCarlo and Gabel, 1989).[3]

## WHO IS AND IS NOT COVERED BY EMPLOYMENT-BASED HEALTH BENEFITS?

The first parts of this section report generally on who has employment-based coverage and who does not.[4] A discussion of factors affecting the availability of coverage follows.

### Covered Workers and Family Members

Employment-based health coverage may be provided directly through one's own employer or union or indirectly through a family member's workplace.[5]

---

[3]For example, one study of mental health insurance costs (Frank and McGuire, 1990) noted that only 18 percent of the benefits managers who responded to a frequently cited employer survey actually answered the questions on mental health costs. Half of this group said they did not know what their cost experience was. From the remaining small number of respondents came the news that mental health costs rose between 18 and 27 percent from 1988 to 1989. The survey in question was undertaken by A. Foster Higgins & Co., Inc., whose latest survey (A. Foster Higgins, 1992) is cited at several points in this chapter.

[4]Unless otherwise indicated, the data in this section come from EBRI (1992d).

[5]The term *family member* is used broadly here to describe those eligible for health coverage by virtue of their relationship to a worker who is directly eligible for coverage. Some eligible individuals are technically "dependents," as the Internal Revenue Service (IRS) code defines

In 1990, almost two-thirds of all Americans under age 65, an estimated 138.7 million people, were covered by employment-based health benefits (see Table 1.1, Chapter 1). This group was about evenly split between those who received coverage directly from their employer and those who received it indirectly through a family member. Analyses from the Rand Corporation using March 1988 CPS data indicate that 11 percent of those eligible for direct employer coverage turn it down because they have other coverage and only 2 percent decline coverage without having other coverage (Long and Marquis, 1992). Many employers require employee participation unless the employee has other coverage.

In 1990, only 9 percent of the nonelderly had private insurance that was not employment based; another 14 percent were covered by Medicaid or some other public program. Virtually all of the elderly are covered by Medicare, although—as discussed below—some have supplemental benefits from a former employer. For the relatively small percentage of those aged 65 through 69 who are employed, federal law requires that any employment-based health benefits serve as primary coverage.,

Employment-based coverage is most common for full-time, full-year workers (Table 3.1). Among individuals aged 18 to 64 who were working on a full-time, full-year basis in 1990, some 70 percent had employment-based coverage directly from their own employer, former employer, or union, and another 10 percent of this group received such coverage indirectly through a family member. In contrast, among those who worked on a part-time, full-year basis, only 22 percent reported direct employment-based coverage, whereas 38 percent reported indirect coverage. Among nonworkers aged 18 to 64, just over 40 percent had employment-based coverage, and, not surprisingly, most of this coverage was indirect, although some nonworkers have coverage through former employers. Almost one-third of this group, moreover, had coverage through Medicaid or some other public program.

Virtually all organizations that offer coverage to employees also offer coverage to family members, although such coverage is less likely than individual coverage to be fully financed by the employer. In 1990, in addition to nonemployed adults with indirect coverage, about 60 percent of children received employment-based coverage indirectly through a family

---

the term for purposes of allowing deductions and exemptions on personal income tax returns. However, individuals eligible for health benefit coverage are not always dependents (as defined by the IRS), and dependents are not necessarily eligible for coverage. Two examples illustrate these points. On the one hand, a small number of employers have expanded access to health benefits by extending coverage to domestic partners, some covering only same-sex partners and others covering both same-sex and opposite-sex partners (Schachner, 1992). On the other hand, some states have mandated coverage for individuals who clearly qualify as dependents (e.g., newborns) but who have sometimes been excluded from conventional insurance plans. Table 3.5 shows categories of eligibles mandated by some states.

**TABLE 3.1**  Percentage of Individuals with Selected Sources of Health Insurance by Own Work Status, 1990

| | Number (millions) | Private Health Insurance | | | | | Publicly Sponsored | | No Health Insurance Coverage |
|---|---|---|---|---|---|---|---|---|---|
| | | Total | Total employer | Direct employer | Indirect employer | Other private | Total | Medicaid | |
| Own Work Status, Ages 18–64 | | | | | | | | | |
| Full Year, Never Unemployed | 96.2 | 85.6 | 77.4 | 63.3 | 14.1 | 8.2 | 4.0 | 1.4 | 12.7 |
| Full time | 83.6 | 86.9 | 80.0 | 69.6 | 10.5 | 6.9 | 3.6 | 1.1 | 11.7 |
| Part time | 12.6 | 76.8 | 59.9 | 21.8 | 38.1 | 16.9 | 7.0 | 3.6 | 18.8 |
| Full Year, Some Unemployment | 13.9 | 58.5 | 50.3 | 35.0 | 15.3 | 8.2 | 10.1 | 7.0 | 34.2 |
| Part Year | 13.7 | 68.4 | 51.6 | 16.1 | 35.6 | 16.8 | 14.2 | 9.9 | 21.5 |
| Nonworker | 27.8 | 53.2 | 40.8 | 8.0 | 32.7 | 12.5 | 31.6 | 21.1 | 21.6 |
| Own Work Status, All Nonelderly | | | | | | | | | |
| Child | 64.2 | 67.9 | 60.4 | 0.1 | 60.3 | 7.6 | 20.6 | 18.7 | 15.3 |
| Family-head worker | 75.6 | 79.9 | 71.3 | 66.7 | 4.6 | 8.6 | 6.4 | 3.5 | 16.3 |
| Nonfamily-head worker | 48.3 | 81.9 | 71.7 | 36.3 | 35.4 | 10.2 | 4.9 | 2.1 | 15.7 |
| Nonworker | 27.8 | 53.2 | 40.8 | 8.0 | 32.7 | 12.5 | 31.6 | 21.1 | 21.6 |

SOURCE:  Adapted from EBRI, 1992d, Tables 2 and 22.  Based on EBRI analysis of March 1991 Current Population Survey.

member's plan. Of the 72 percent of workers who had employment-based coverage in 1990 but who were not classified as head of household, about half were directly covered by their own employer and another half were covered indirectly by another's employment-based plan. Data from the 1977 and 1987 National Medical (Care) Expenditures Surveys (NMES) indicate that 63 percent of spouses in two-worker families who were eligible for coverage from both employers chose dual coverage in 1987, down from 80 percent a decade earlier (Schur and Taylor, 1991). The decline is attributed in part to the decrease in coverage that is fully paid by the employer and the increase in overall premium costs.

News reports suggest that some employers are deliberately encouraging their employees to switch their coverage to a spouse's plan or are trying to protect themselves from such practices or both (Block, 1992). A few organizations no longer offer family coverage if the family member has coverage available from his or her own employer. Others now require extra payments for coverage of family members who decline coverage elsewhere (sometimes modifying or eliminating charges if the other worker's wages are low or the premium contribution is very high). Others use flexible benefit plans (discussed later in this chapter) to discourage this option. Overall, the employed individuals most affected by such restrictions are thought to be "secondary" wage earners who work for organizations that offer less comprehensive benefits than those available to "primary" wage earners.

Although the increased participation of women in the work force and the growth of two-worker families might have been expected to increase the availability of health benefits to individuals and families, this does not appear to have happened. Data from the NMES surveys show that (1) "the percentage of households in which both spouses were offered employment-related coverage has remained constant over the decade [1977 to 1987]" and (2) "the proportion of households in which neither spouse has job-related health benefits available has actually increased" (Schur and Taylor, 1991, p. 161).

### Uninsured Workers and Family Members

For 1990, some 35.7 million nonelderly Americans, nearly 17 percent of those under age 65, reported that they had no private or public health benefits during the year. About 85 percent of these individuals lived in families headed by a worker, and about half were full-time, full-year workers and their family members (Figure 3.1).

Lack of employment-based coverage is common for low-wage workers. Among civilian wage and salary workers with poverty-level incomes working on a full-time, full-year basis in 1990, only one-third had direct employ-

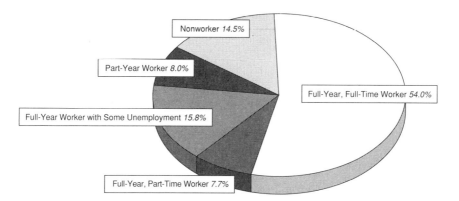

**FIGURE 3.1** Work status of the family head for the 35.7 million Americans under age 65 who were without health insurance, 1990. (See glossary for definition of work status categories.) SOURCE: Adapted from EBRI, 1992d. Reproduced with permission from EBRI Issue Brief Number 123, *Sources of Health Insurance and Characteristics of the Uninsured*, analysis of the March 1991 Current Population Survey.

ment-based coverage, compared with three-quarters of those with higher incomes (EBRI, 1992a). For all workers aged 18–64 earning less than $10,000 a year in 1991, about 30 percent had indirect employment-based coverage and 16 percent had direct coverage. This group includes many part-time workers (Long and Marquis, 1992). Decreases in employment-based coverage in the period 1988 to 1990 were concentrated among low-wage workers.

Young workers are also less likely to have coverage than older workers. An Urban Institute analyst working from March 1988 CPS data found that 42 percent of workers aged 18 to 24 were without employment-based coverage, compared with about 20 percent of those aged 35 to 44 (Swartz, 1992).

The numbers above are conservative because they include only those who were without insurance for all of 1990, not those who were uninsured for only a portion of the year. When Census Bureau analysts looked at their data for a 28-month period starting in 1987, they found that some 61 million people spent at least one month without insurance from any public or private source (Rich, 1992).

Workers or their family members may lack coverage for several reasons. A worker's employer (1) may not offer coverage at all, (2) may offer coverage only to selected categories of workers, such as those who work over some number of hours per week, (3) may require an employee contribution to the premium that the worker is unable or unwilling to pay, or (4) may exclude the worker or family member because of a preexisting health problem or because they have not completed a required waiting period (See Northwestern National Life Insurance Company, 1989, for examples of restrictions).

One analysis indicated that about 6 percent of workers are ineligible for the coverage offered by their employer, most because they worked less than full-time, some because they had not completed a required waiting period (Long and Marquis, 1992). That same analysis indicated that those individuals who declined employer-offered insurance but had no other coverage (only 2 percent of all those offered coverage) tended to earn less, work part-time, be younger, and have experienced more change in employment status than those who accepted coverage. They were, thus, similar to those who worked for firms that did not offer coverage at all. This means that voluntary strategies to extend employment-based coverage may need to include subsidies to stimulate employee ability and willingness to pay for coverage as well as incentives to encourage employers to offer insurance.

Encouraging employers who do not offer coverage to do so has not proved easy. Even when lower-cost, "bare bones" coverage is made available, many small employers still do not offer it. Employer participation rates in targeted demonstration projects aimed at uninsured workers in small groups have been quite low, generally 10 percent or less (Helms et al., 1992). Those assessing these projects argue that cost remains a barrier for many small employers. In addition, some employers do not believe that employers have any responsibility to offer coverage. Others argue that their workers have other sources of coverage, and some claim that their workers would rather have higher wages than health benefits (McLaughlin and Zellers, 1992). Other surveys show that the high cost of health insurance is cited by employers as a primary reason they do not offer coverage to their employees (HIAA, 1990, 1991a; Edwards et al., 1992).

## Retirees

Roughly one-third of those over age 65 have retained some employment-related health benefits, most of which are secondary to Medicare coverage but some of which serve—by law—as primary coverage for workers aged 65 to 69.[6] Although retirees aged 65 and over accounted for about 60

---

[6]Retiree coverage may be integrated with Medicare coverage in several ways. One consulting firm described three major options (Mercer-Meidinger-Hansen, 1989, p. 6). First is *coordination of benefits*, which "pays whichever is less: the regular benefit that the plan would pay if it were the sole provider, or the retiree's total covered expense, minus the Medicare payment. Under this arrangement, the retiree often pays no deductible or copayments." A second arrangement, an *expense carve-out* or *exclusion*, "determines the total expenses covered under the [employer] plan, reduces them by Medicare benefits and then applies the deductibles, coinsurance and other plan limits to the balance." The third approach, a *benefit carve-out*, "calculates the plan's payment as if there were no Medicare coverage and pays that amount

percent of retirees who received some coverage from a former employer, about 40 percent of covered retirees are under age 65 (GAO, 1990a,b). Of retirees under age 65, only about one-third have employment-based health benefits (EBRI, 1992c). Because most younger retirees are not eligible for Medicare, employment-based health benefits may be their only source of coverage. Some, however, may be covered under a spouse's plan or some other source. Men and higher-income workers are more likely to have retiree coverage than women and lower-income workers (EBRI, 1991d, 1992c).

According to DOL statistics for 1989, about 42 percent of employees who participate in health plans offered by medium and large private establishments work for organizations that offer some employer-financed coverage for retirees (DOL, 1990). In contrast, for small establishments (fewer than 100 workers), the comparable figure is only about 17 percent (DOL, 1991). According to the GAO (1990a), only 2 percent of firms with fewer than 25 employees provide retiree coverage, but many of these firms report that they have no retired employees.

A small percentage of employers cover only retirees under age 65 or only retirees aged 65 and over, but most employers that offer retiree coverage cover both groups (DOL, 1990). Generally, employees who leave a company before they retire are not eligible for retiree health benefits (Mercer-Meidinger-Hansen, 1989).

There is growing concern that employment-based coverage for retirees may decline as a result of two factors: cost pressures and a new accounting standard set by the Financial Accounting Standards Board (FASB) (GAO, 1990a; EBRI, 1992c; U.S. Senate 1992b). This standard, commonly called FAS 106, requires that future benefits promised to retirees be recognized as liabilities on a firm's financial statements.[7] By some estimates, complying with the standard may cause organizations' net worth—as measured on their balance sheets—to drop up to 15 percent across all companies and may lead to declines in pretax earnings—as measured on their current operating statements—of up to 10 percent for some employers (EBRI, 1992c). Individual companies are still analyzing what FAS 106 means for them and what legal and financial options they have for modifying or eliminating coverage for current and future retirees. Some are increasing the retiree share of the premium, some no longer promise coverage after retirement to newly hired workers, and some are phasing out coverage for current retirees (Woolsey, 1992f). Many are taking steps one way or another to reduce their future obligations to retirees.

---

minus what Medicare pays. Usually deductibles and copayments are the responsibility of the retiree." Other alternatives that employers may offer are plans that cover certain services not covered under Medicare (e.g., outpatient drugs), plans that cover Medicare coinsurance and deductibles, or plans that pay only the Medicare Part B premium (de Lissovoy et al., 1990).

[7]For more information on FAS, see EBRI, 1991d, 1992c.

## Sources of Variation in Employment-Based Coverage

The Current Population Survey, which uses the *individual* as the unit of analysis, shows that the prevalence of employment-based coverage is strongly associated with the size of the organization for which one works (EBRI, 1992d). For example, of wage and salary workers aged 18 to 64 who worked for employers with fewer than 25 employees, about 30 percent reported having coverage directly from their own employer, former employer, or union, and another 23 percent were covered under another's employment-based plan. In contrast, among those working for firms with 1000 or more employees, just over 70 percent had direct employer coverage, and only 13 percent had indirect employer coverage (Table 3.2).

Surveys that use the *firm*, not the individual, as the unit of analysis likewise show variations in coverage that are positively linked to firm size. A recent survey directed exclusively at small firms reported that health coverage for some or all workers was offered by half of firms with 2 to 5 workers, three-fourths of firms with 6 to 25 workers, and 90 percent of firms with 26 to 100 workers (Edwards et al., 1992). HIAA's broader survey, which used different categories, reported that 27 percent of firms with fewer than 10 employees offered benefits, compared with 73 percent of those with 10 to 24 workers and 87 percent of those with 25 to 99 workers (HIAA, 1991a; Sullivan and Rice, 1991). Overall, although only 42 percent of all firms surveyed by HIAA offered health coverage, an estimated 81 percent of employees worked for those firms.

HIAA data indicate that small firms with higher proportions of highly

**TABLE 3.2**   Variations by Size of Employer in Percentage of Wage and Salary Workers Aged 18 to 64 with Employer Health Coverage or No Coverage from Any Source, 1990

| Size of Firm | Percentage Workers with Employer Coverage | | | Percentage Workers with No Coverage from Any Source |
|---|---|---|---|---|
| | Total | Direct | Indirect | |
| <25 employees | 54 | 31 | 23 | 29 |
| 25–99 | 69 | 53 | 16 | 20 |
| 100–499 | 79 | 65 | 14 | 12 |
| 500–999 | 83 | 69 | 13 | 10 |
| 1,000+ | 84 | 71 | 13 | 9 |

NOTE: The remainder of workers had either other private or public health insurance.

SOURCE: EBRI, 1992d, Table 25. Based on EBRI analysis of the March 1991 Current Population Survey.

**TABLE 3.3** Variations by Industry in Percentage of Wage and Salary Workers Aged 18 to 64 with Employer Health Coverage or No Coverage from Any Source, 1990

| | Percentage of Workers with Employer Coverage | | | Percentage of Workers with No Coverage from Any Source |
|---|---|---|---|---|
| | Total | Direct | Indirect | |
| Agriculture | 39 | 24 | 15 | 39 |
| Personal services | 50 | 30 | 20 | 30 |
| Entertainment, recreation | 59 | 35 | 24 | 20 |
| Construction | 59 | 46 | 13 | 31 |
| Retail | 59 | 35 | 24 | 24 |
| Business, repair services | 64 | 46 | 18 | 23 |
| Professional | 77 | 55 | 22 | 11 |
| Wholesale | 80 | 68 | 13 | 12 |
| Transportation, utilities, communications | 82 | 75 | 8 | 11 |
| Finance, insurance, real estate | 84 | 67 | 17 | 8 |
| Manufacturing | 84 | 76 | 8 | 11 |
| Mining | 86 | 80 | —[a] | 10 |
| Government | 85 | 71 | 14 | 7 |

[a]Number of respondents is too small for percentage to be statistically significant.

SOURCE: Adapted from EBRI, 1992d, Table 23. Based on EBRI analysis of the March 1991 Current Population Survey.

paid workers are more likely to offer health benefits than are small firms with more low-paid workers. In general, firms that do not offer insurance employ higher proportions of low-wage and part-time workers and have higher rates of labor turnover than firms that do offer insurance (HIAA, 1990; Edwards et al., 1992).

Employment-based coverage also varies noticeably by type of industry. For example, Table 3.3 shows the striking variation in coverage across industries. Some of this variation reflects differences in the average size of firms in different sectors. Nevertheless, even in industries with low rates of offering coverage, firms with 25 or more employees were much more likely to offer coverage than smaller firms. According to HIAA data, in retail trade, 84 percent of larger firms but only 27 percent of smaller firms offered health coverage in 1990; for finance, the figures were 92 and 42 percent, respectively (HIAA, 1991a).

In addition to size and profit levels, another factor that may play a role in industry variations in coverage is what is variously called redlining or blacklisting. The terms refer to the practices of some insurers that refuse to sell coverage to certain groups, such as law firms, physician groups, hair salons, and restaurants (Zellers et al., 1992).

The level of employment-based health coverage also varies by region. The percent of the nonelderly with employment-based coverage ranges from just under 60 percent in the West South Central, Pacific, and East South Central regions to over 70 percent in the New England region. The lowest levels of employment-based coverage are reported for Mississippi (50.4 percent), the District of Columbia (51.6 percent), and New Mexico (51.9 percent). Some regional variation may reflect differences in the average size of firms in different parts of the country.

## WHAT TYPES OF COVERAGE ARE OFFERED?

### Types of Health Plans

If the typical health plan offering of 20 years ago could be described as a "plain vanilla" plan with some limited variations in ingredients, health plans today come in a multitude of flavors that are not easily categorized. The following discussion distinguishes simply between conventional and network plans on the basis of whether the plans impose restrictions on the participant's choice of health care provider.

Both conventional and network plans are evolving so rapidly that general characterizations and comparisons can become quickly outdated. In addition, behind this dichotomy lies much variability, particularly among network health plans. Moreover, because a network plan that is more restrictive on one variable (such as coverage for out-of-network services or the extent to which access to specialists and other care is controlled by a primary care "gatekeeper") may be less so on others, it is difficult to array different types of network plans along a simple continuum. These caveats notwithstanding, group and staff model health maintenance organizations (HMOs) are generally considered to be more restrictive than independent practice associations (IPAs), and the latter are assumed to be more restrictive than preferred provider organizations (PPOs) and point-of-service (POS) plans (see glossary for definitions).

### *Conventional Plans*

Conventional plans (which may also be called indemnity, fee-for-service, open panel, or freedom-of-choice plans) place few if any restrictions on the participant's choice of the health care practitioners and providers whose services are otherwise covered. They may and increasingly do incorporate managed care features such as prior review of proposed hospital care, but they continue to pay health care practitioners and providers largely or entirely on a fee-for-service basis.

Conventional plans have a long history in the United States, are familiar to most employees, and are often the only type of plan offered by employers. For purposes of this discussion, the category includes Blue Cross and Blue Shield plans that have very broad-based participating hospital and physician programs (see Chapter 2) that may include up to 100 percent of area providers. Depending on specific plan practices in contracting with and paying providers, some plans could be categorized as weak network plans. The border separating conventional and network plans thus contains a "gray area."

Among all employers offering coverage, HIAA (1990) found that 82 percent offered a conventional health benefit plan, either as the only plan or as one choice among others. As shown in Figure 3.2, larger firms were slightly less likely than smaller firms to offer such a plan. West Coast firms were also less likely to offer a conventional plan than firms in other regions. Currently, conventional plans enroll between three-fifths and three-quarters of all participants in employment-based health plans (DOL, 1990, 1991; Hoy et al., 1991).

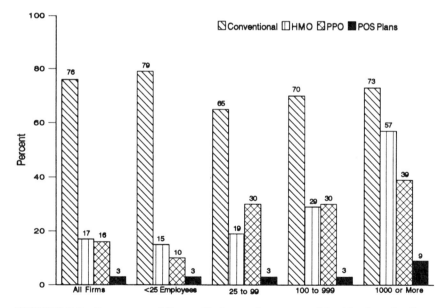

**FIGURE 3.2** Percentage of firms offering various types of health plans for firms offering a plan, by firm size, 1991. SOURCE: Unpublished data from HIAA Employer Survey.

*Network Plans*

Network plans, as the name implies, restrict coverage in whole or part to services provided by a specified network or group of physicians, hospitals, and other health care providers. Some network plans, such as various kinds of HMOs, limit nonemergency coverage entirely to network providers. Other plans, such as PPOs, POS plans, and open-ended HMOs, cover enrollees for some nonemergency services received from nonnetwork providers but typically impose higher deductibles, coinsurance, and other employee cost sharing for such care. In essence, employees can choose between network and nonnetwork services when they seek care rather than once a year when choices among health plans are made. A few employers have established their own networks, either by providing certain health services through company clinics and hospitals or by contracting directly with health care providers.

Network plans are sometimes termed *closed* or *exclusive provider panels* (if they exclude out-of-network coverage for nonemergency care), *alternative delivery systems*, or *managed care plans*, although each of these terms may be used in narrower, broader, or different ways. In particular, the term *managed care* may be applied to conventional plans that include certain utilization management strategies such as preadmission review and case management.

Network plans may pay physicians on a salaried, capitated, or modified fee-for-service basis. The modifications to fee-for-service payments may involve discounts to normal fees or acceptance by the provider of some risk for levels of use or expenses that are higher than planned. In addition to their payment arrangements, many network plans require members to designate a primary care physician who serves as "gatekeeper" for referrals to specialists and other services.

In the last decade, network-based health plans have grown greatly in numbers, enrollments, and variety (Table 3.4), partly because federal law required many employers to offer HMOs, partly because employers have seen these plans as vehicles for limiting increases in their health benefit costs, and partly because employers have considered choice of health plan attractive to employees. Across all firms surveyed by HIAA in 1990, 20 percent of covered employees were enrolled in HMOs, 13 percent in PPOs, and 5 percent in other network-based plans such as POS plans (HIAA, 1991a).[8] More recent data suggest that POS plans are growing rapidly (Moskowitz, 1992). Only 123 HMOs offered such plans in 1990, compared with 256 in 1991 (Marion Merrell Dow, 1992).

---

[8]DOL (1990, 1991) Bureau of Labor Statistics showed somewhat lower enrollments. Of health plan participants working for firms with 100 or more workers, 17 percent were enrolled in HMOs and 10 percent in PPOs; in small firms, the figures were 14 and 12 percent.

**TABLE 3.4**   Percentage Distribution of Employees Across Types of
Health Benefit Plans, 1987 to 1990

|  | 1987 | 1988 | 1989 | 1990 |
|---|---|---|---|---|
| Conventional without utilization management | 41 | 28 | 18 | 5 |
| Conventional with utilization management | 32 | 43 | 49 | 57 |
| Health maintenance organization | 16 | 18 | 17 | 20 |
| Preferred provider organization | 11 | 11 | 16 | 13 |
| Point-of-service plan | — | — | — | 5 |
| Total network-based managed care | 27 | 29 | 33 | 38 |
| Total nonnetwork plans | 73 | 71 | 67 | 62 |

SOURCE: Hoy et al., 1991, p. 19.   Based on Health Insurance Association of America
surveys, 1989 to 1991. Reprinted by permission of *Health Affairs*, Winter 1991.

Larger employers have been considerably more likely than smaller employers to offer HMOs and PPOs, but the differential is smaller for PPOs (HIAA, 1990).  Regional differences and urban-rural differences contribute to additional variation in employers' offerings.  These differences involve the availability of network plans (which can be difficult to establish in less populated areas), regional attitudes of physicians and others toward such plans, and state laws that may encourage or discourage such plans.

## Covered Services

As described in Chapter 2, the growth of employment-based health benefits started with the growth of plans covering inpatient hospital care. Inpatient physician care came next, followed by coverage for physician office visits.  In the 1970s, coverage for various other kinds of services, providers, and sites of care expanded, sometimes with a boost from state mandates.  Examples of state-mandated benefits are arrayed in Table 3.5, which shows the categories of providers, conditions and services, and eligible individuals for which coverage is mandated under various state laws.[9] In the face of charges that mandated benefits were increasing health care costs, encouraging more employers to self-insure, and benefiting providers more than patients, 25 states have since 1985 required that new mandates be subject to an objective evaluation of benefits and costs (Chollet, 1992b). Only one state with such a law has enacted any further mandates.

---

[9]Often these mandates do not apply to individually purchased insurance nor to HMOs (*Health Benefits Letter*, 1991).  Employers who self-insure may, in fact, provide most of the mandated benefits, but their decisions are voluntary rather than required.

**TABLE 3.5**   Selected Examples of State-Mandated Health Coverage

MANDATED PRACTITIONERS AND PROVIDERS

Acupuncturists, Chiropractors, Dentists, Licensed Health Professionals, Naturopaths, Nurses, Nurse Anesthetists, Nurse Midwives, Nurse Practitioners, Occupational Therapists, Optometrists, Oral Surgeons, Osteopaths, Physical Therapists, Podiatrists, Professional Counselors, Psychiatric Nurses, Psychologists, Social Workers, Speech/Hearing Therapists.

MANDATED CONDITIONS AND SERVICES

Alcoholism, Ambulance Transportation, Ambulatory Surgery, Breast Reconstruction, Cleft Palate, Diabetic Education, Drug Abuse Treatment, Home Health Care, Hospice Care, In-vitro Fertilization, Long-Term Care, Mammography Screening, Maternity, Mental Health Care, Orthotic/Prosthetic Devices, Pap Tests, Prescription Drugs, Prohibition of Abortion Coverage, Rehabilitation Services, Second Surgical Opinion, Temporomandibular Joint Disorder, Well Child Care.

MANDATED ELIGIBLES

Adopted Children, Dependent Students, Former Employees, Former Dependents of Active or Former Employees, Handicapped Dependents, Newborns, Noncustodial Children.

NOTE: Each of these mandates applies in at least two states. Mandates may require coverage or may require only that coverage be offered to groups (who may decline it). Mandates may be subject to various restrictions not identified here.

SOURCE: *Health Benefits Letter*, 1991. Based on data collected by the Blue Cross and Blue Shield Association.

Today, virtually all those covered by employment-based health plans are covered for inpatient hospital care (including prescription drugs), outpatient surgery, physician hospital and office services, and outpatient prescription drugs (DOL, 1990, 1991). In this last respect, most employment-based plans are more generous than Medicare, which does not cover outpatient drugs. A substantial majority of covered workers have some coverage for extended care facilities and home health services; fewer than half are covered for hospice care. Dental benefits are available to about two-thirds of health plan participants in medium and large private establishments but less than one-third of participants in small organizations.

Those covered by HMOs are more likely than those covered by fee-for-service plans to have benefits for home health care (99+ versus 72 percent) but less likely to have hospice benefits (30 versus 45 percent) (Burke, 1991). According to DOL (1990) data, nearly all those in HMOs are covered for routine preventive services, but only a small proportion of those in fee-for-service plans have such coverage, for example, 14 percent for immunizations and inoculations and 22 percent for well baby care. HIAA, however, reports conflicting numbers for well baby care, estimating that 50 percent of enrollees in conventional plans have such coverage (HIAA, 1990).

## Cost Sharing and Other Limits on Coverage

Aside from services or conditions that are categorically excluded from coverage, employees may face a variety of limits on the medical care expenses their health plan will cover. These limits may take the form of

• patient cost-sharing, such as deductibles and coinsurance (most common in conventional plans) and per-visit copayments (most common in HMOs);

• caps on the volume or frequency of services, for example, a limit on the number of physician visits that will be covered during a year or in a 30-day period;

• maximum amounts that a plan will pay for a specific service (e.g., $100 for a diagnostic test); or

• maximum amounts that a plan will pay over an episode of care, a period of time, or an individual's lifetime (e.g., $250,000 or $1,000,000).

In addition, coverage may be limited under the terms of some utilization management programs that reduce or deny benefits for care judged medically unnecessary or care not reviewed in advance for appropriateness. Conventional health plans typically make the enrollee responsible for any added costs, whereas many network plans make the health care practitioner or provider responsible.

A *deductible* is the amount of eligible health care expenses that an insured individual must pay before a health plan begins to pay benefits.[10] For health plan participants working for medium and large establishments, the *average* deductible in 1989 was about $160 for blue-collar workers and about $185 for white-collar workers (DOL, 1990); in 1990, the average deductible faced by workers participating in health plans offered by small establishments was just under $200 (DOL, 1991). In A. Foster Higgins's 1991 survey, firms reported a *median* deductible of $200, up from $150 in 1990. For family coverage, most health plans require that the individual deductible be met by each covered individual up to some maximum number of individuals (typically reached when three or four family members have met the individual deductible).

DOL (1990, 1991) reports that very few participants in employment-based health plans (under 2 percent) have deductibles (or premium contributions) that are linked to their earnings. To the extent that deductibles are intended to discourage use of medical care, the significance of a fixed dollar deductible is clearly less for higher-income workers. HMO members generally do not face deductibles but may have to pay defined dollar amounts

---

[10]Eligible expenses are expenses for covered services. In some plans, charges that exceed a level defined as reasonable may not be counted toward the deductible. Reasonableness may relate to what the provider normally charges for the services or what similar providers charge.

for specific services (e.g., $5 per office visit). Other network plans may have no or low deductibles for care received from network providers but may have deductibles for care outside the given network that are substantially higher than in a conventional health plan.

*Coinsurance* refers to coverage of eligible health care expenses that is split between the health plan and the enrollee. The most common split for coinsurance in conventional health plans is 80/20, meaning that 80 percent is paid by the health plan and 20 percent is paid by the employee (DOL, 1990, 1991). For individuals in PPOs who use network providers, about one-fifth have no coinsurance requirement, about one-third face a 90/10 split, and another one-fifth have an 80/20 division (Sullivan and Rice, 1991). When PPO enrollees go outside of the network, about half pay 20 percent coinsurance, about one-fifth pay 25 percent, and another one-fifth pay 30 percent. Forty percent coinsurance is required under some PPO contracts.

Cost sharing and coverage limits may be moderated by the caps that many employers place on out-of-pocket costs for employees. The size of such caps varies widely, with most workers covered by caps between $500 and $1,300 per individual (DOL, 1990, 1991). One-third of employees are in plans with no limit on the family out-of-pocket costs. Plans may not count the cost of some services against the out-of-pocket cap (for example, expenses for mental health services above the maximum coverage for those services). Plans that limit payments for physician services to a set fee or a reasonable charge may refuse to count enrollee payments in excess of these limits in determining whether a deductible or out-of-maximum is met. The result can be a substantial and to some degree unpredictable liability for health plan members.

Cost sharing and other limits on coverage may vary by type or place of service. For example, inpatient care may be covered more or less generously than outpatient care, and health plan members may pay more if they get brand name rather than generic drugs.

Mental health services are noteworthy for being covered less comprehensively than other services, a pattern that predates recent cutbacks in coverage (Shannon, 1992). Although over 95 percent of covered employees are in plans that cover services for mental illness, fewer than 20 percent are in programs that cover such illnesses to the same extent as other illnesses (DOL, 1990). For example, most plans place limits on the number of hospital days or visits covered, require higher levels of patient cost sharing, or set lower maximums on total plan payments; many do all three (Table 3.6). The explanations for these restrictions may lie in the stigma still attached to mental illness, the lack of evidence about the relative effectiveness of treatments of widely differing cost, and questions about the appropriateness of diagnoses and needs for starting and stopping care. A recent study conducted for the National Association of Psychiatric Hospitals indicated that costs for psychiatric care constitute about 8 percent of health plan

**TABLE 3.6** Selected Types of Limits on Mental Health Services Among Several Health Benefit Plans

| | Federal Employee Program | | Surveys of Private Firms | | | |
|---|---|---|---|---|---|---|
| Types of Limit | Blue Cross/ Blue Shield High Option | Typical Federal Plan | A. Foster Higgins | Hay/Huggins | DOL |
| Lifetime dollar maximum on adult inpatient mental health care | $75,000 a person | $43,500 a person | 58% of firms with this limit; $50,000 or less is most common | 18% of firms may have this limit; no data on most common | 33% of employees with this limit; no data on most common |
| Annual limit on adult inpatient mental health care | None specified | None specified | 46% of firms with this limit; 30 days is most common | 45% of firms with this limit; 30 days is most common | 38% of employees with this limit; no data on most common |
| Maximum number of mental health outpatient visits a year | 50 | 32 | 33% of firms have yearly limit on visits; no data on most common amount | 33% of firms have yearly limit on visits; 50 or fewer is most common | 34% of employees have yearly limit on visits; no data on most common amount |
| Yearly dollar maximum on outpatient mental health care | Based on the number of yearly visits and plan dollar copayments | 35% of the families in 8 of the 11 plans have stated yearly maximums; average maximum is $1,235 | 76% of firms with yearly dollar maximum; $2,000 or less is most common | 46% of firms with yearly dollar maximum; $2,000 or less is most common | 29% of employees with yearly dollar maximum; no data on most common amount |
| Copayment for inpatient room and board | 20% | 43% | 72% of firms require some copayment; 20% is most common | 86% of firms require some copayment; 20% is most common | 72% of employees pay copayments; 20% is most common |
| Copayment for inpatient professional services | 20% | 43% | 77% of firms require some copayment; 20% is most common | 20% copayment required by 53% of firms | 20% copayment required for 41% of employees |
| Copayment for outpatient mental health services | 30% | 44% | 50% copayment required by 78% of firms | 50% copayment required by 55% of firms | 50% copayment required for 43% of employees |

SOURCE: Adapted from GAO, 1991b.

costs, a figure that has remained fairly steady for two decades (Hay/Huggins, 1992).[11]

## WHAT DO EMPLOYMENT-BASED HEALTH BENEFITS COST?

### Premium Cost for Employer and Employee

In 1990, public and private employers paid $174.2 billion in premiums on behalf of their employees (Figure 3.3). In addition, private employers spent another $47.1 billion in Medicare contributions, workers' compensation and temporary disability insurance premiums, and in-plant health services (Levit and Cowan, 1991). Households collectively spent $42.6 billion on premiums for individually purchased policies and employment-based health benefits and $45.9 billion for Medicare contributions and premiums. They also spent $136.1 billion for out-of-pocket expenses for medical care.[12] Across all age groups, individual health spending as a share of adjusted personal income rose from 4.1 percent in 1980 to 4.7 percent in 1985 to 5.0 percent in 1990. As a share of income after taxes, the figure went from 4.8 percent in 1985 to 4.9 percent in 1989 (no data reported from 1980 or 1990) (Levit and Cowan, 1991).

According to DOL (1991) data, about three-fifths of workers participating in health plans offered by small private establishments had individual (self-only) coverage for which the premiums were fully paid by their employer. This compares to slightly less than half of workers in larger organizations. Approximately one-third of workers in both larger and smaller establishments received family coverage for which the employer paid the entire premium. More employers are requiring employees to pay a share of the premium cost than in the past (DOL, 1990). Nonetheless, the share of premiums paid by U.S. workers is not, on average, as high as it is for workers in countries such as Germany and the Netherlands (although cost sharing in the form of copayments or coinsurance is lower in these countries) (Kirkman-Liff, 1991).

---

[11]Both judicial and legislative challenges to disparities in coverage for mental illnesses with a physical or organic basis versus coverage for other physical illnesses have been raised in recent years with mixed results. Neither judicial nor state legislative requirements for "parity" reach self-insured employers. A recent proposal for a model mental health benefit in private health insurance noted that 10 of 26 health care reform bills introduced in the 102nd Congress did not explicitly require mental health coverage and most of the remainder provided special limits on such coverage (Frank, Goldman, and McGuire, 1992). At least one bill (S.2696) was introduced in 1992 that would provide for "health insurance protection for the costs of treating severe mental illnesses that is commensurate with protection provided for other illnesses" under any kind of health reform adopted in the future.

[12]This way of grouping expenditures differs from that used for Table 1.2 but is consistent with the grouping used to construct Figure 1.1.

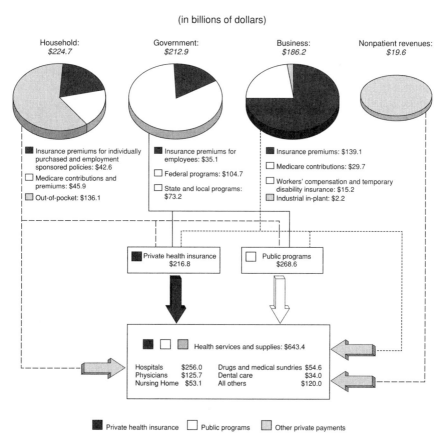

**FIGURE 3.3** Flow of funds from sponsors of health care into the health care system in the United States, 1990. Nonpatient revenues include revenues from philanthropy and income from the operation of gift shops, cafeterias, parking lots, and educational programs, as well as those received from assets such as interest, dividends, and rents. Under "health services and supplies," "all others" includes home health care, other professional services, durable medical equipment, other personal health care, administration and net costs of insurance, and government public health activities. SOURCE: Levit and Cowan, 1991. Data from the Health Care Financing Administration, Office of the Actuary: Data from the Office of National Health Statistics.

According to HIAA (1991c) data, the total monthly premium for individual employment-based health coverage in 1990 was $145 for conventional health plans ($1,740 per year). For family coverage the total premium was $316 per month ($3,792 per year). Data for 1989 indicated that the employer paid on average 86 percent of the cost for individual coverage and 74 percent of the cost for family coverage (HIAA, 1990). Note that even though the *percentage* of the premium paid by employers may be less for family coverage, the *absolute dollar amount* may be more because the premium for family coverage is higher than the premium for individual coverage.

As with other summary statistics, the premium figures cited above disguise an enormous amount of variation in what specific employers and employees pay. For example, a recent study of health benefits for state employees showed that total monthly premiums for 1991 ranged from $78 in Hawaii and $85 in Mississippi to $204 in California and $241 in Massachusetts (Segal Company, 1991). The percentage of premium contributed by the employer ranged from 50 percent in Louisiana and 60 percent in Hawaii to 100 percent in 26 states. Differences in premiums reflect a variety of factors, such as differences in coverage (e.g., Hawaii has a $250 individual deductible and Massachusetts's deductible is $50) and differences in area hospital and other input costs.

Although employment-based health benefit costs continue to increase more rapidly than general inflation, data from several sources suggest a modest slowing in the annual rate of increase in the last year or two (HIAA, 1991a,c; A. Foster Higgins, 1992). Figure 3.4 reports data from one survey on changes in average combined employee-employer spending on health benefits per worker from 1985 to 1991 (Geisel, 1992).[13] Table 3.7 shows HIAA data on rates of premium increases broken out for nonnetwork and network health plans for 1989, 1990, and 1991 (Hoy et al., 1991).

## Administrative Expenses

HCFA attributes 5.8 percent, or $38.7 billion, of total national health expenditures to the costs of administering publicly financed health programs and philanthropic organizations and to the cost of private insurance net of benefit payments (Levit et al., 1991). Almost one-fifth of this amount involves the administrative costs of government health programs such as Medicare and Medicaid, and almost all the rest is accounted for by private health insurance. The HCFA estimates do *not* include expenses for the

---

[13]These expenditure data do not include amounts paid by employees for noninsured health services and supplies unless they were paid with funds from employee spending accounts (see discussion under "Flexible Benefits" below).

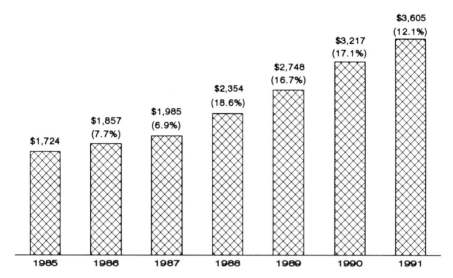

**FIGURE 3.4** Growth in health plan costs, expressed in total dollars per employee for 1985 to 1991 and percentage increase from previous year (includes employer and employee costs for indemnity plans, HMOs, dental plans, and vision and hearing plans). SOURCE: Geisel, 1992. Based on data from A. Foster Higgins, 1992.

employer's costs to administer health benefit and other health-related programs, expenses incurred by individuals, nor health care providers' administrative expenses (both insurance and not insurance related). Some administrative costs—for example, those expended in programs to deter fraud, detect and correct payment errors, and discourage inappropriate use of services—are intended to reduce overall payments for health services.

Total administrative costs for private insurance are typically broken

**TABLE 3.7** Employer-Reported Percentage Premium Increases, by Plan Type, 1989 to 1991

| Plan Type | 1989 | 1990 | 1991 |
|---|---|---|---|
| Conventional | 20 | 17 | 14 |
| Health maintenance organization | 16 | 16 | 13 |
| Preferred provider organization | 18 | 15 | 13 |
| All plans | 18 | 16 | 14 |

SOURCE: Hoy et al., 1991, p. 20. Based on Health Insurance Association of America surveys. Reprinted by permission of *Health Affairs*, Winter 1991.

down into such subcategories as general administration, claims administration, commissions, risk and profit charges, interest credit, and premium taxes. The percentage of costs attributed to the last two categories varies little or not at all by group size, but percentages for the other categories vary greatly. Overall, administrative expenses run a higher percentage of incurred claims expense for small employer groups than for large groups (CRS, 1988c). For example, administrative costs make up about 40 percent of claims expense among insured groups with 2 to 5 employees versus 16 percent for those with 100 to 499 employees and 5.5 percent for those with 10,000 or more employees. By way of comparison, administrative expenses for individually purchased health insurance make up approximately 40 percent of incurred claims expense but total approximately 2 percent for Medicare and 3 to 11 percent for Medicaid (Thorpe, 1992b).

Many factors contribute to the higher expenses associated with insuring small groups. For example, 100 groups of 20 employees generate higher marketing and service costs for insurers than does one group of 2000. In addition, small groups typically experience higher employee turnover than larger groups, and each added or dropped health plan member involves additional administrative expense. Also, because claims expense for small groups is less predictable (i.e., riskier), the risk charge increases.

Many believe that current administrative processes generate considerable inefficiency, that is, that the benefits of the procedures are not sufficient to justify the outlays. Estimates of the savings in hospital administrative and overhead costs if the United States adopted a Canadian-style single payer system range from $13 billion to $37 billion, and estimates of savings in insurance administrative and overhead costs range from $23 billion to $34 billion (Etheredge, 1992). This variability reflects the difficulties posed for national comparisons by differences in national health systems and health accounting practices (GAO, 1991a; Woolhandler and Himmelstein, 1991; Barer and Evans, 1992; Danzon, 1992; Poullier, 1992; Thorpe, 1992b). Estimates of additional expenditures that might result if certain administrative costs were eliminated also vary greatly, depending on what the estimates assume, for example, about the continued use of deductibles and coinsurance and utilization review. Government officials, insurers, and others have recently met to develop simpler, more standardized, and—it is hoped—less costly procedures for administering public and private health benefits, but it is too early to project the consequences.

## Tax Expenditures

Another important element in the financing of health care benefits is the exclusion of employer-paid health insurance premiums from the calculation of an employee's taxable income. For 1992 the federal "tax expenditure," that is, the tax revenue forgone as a result of this exclusion, is esti-mated to be $39.5 billion (Executive Office of the President, 1992). The deductibility of a portion of out-of-pocket expenditures by some individual taxpayers adds another $3 billion to the federal figure. Including estimates of revenues forgone by states that have similar or identical tax policies would further increase the total.

As is true for tax deductions, exemptions, and exclusions generally, higher-income individuals in higher tax brackets gain more in absolute dol-lars from the health benefit exclusion than do lower-income individuals. Were the exclusion to be eliminated or capped as called for in some health care reform proposals, the dollar burden would likewise be higher for the well-off. However, lower-income groups would likely find that the result-ing increase in taxes constituted a greater percentage of their taxable in-come. One estimate of the impact of capping the exclusion at $1,080 for individual and $2,940 for family coverage indicates the new taxes would constitute 1.94 percent of income for those earning $5,000 to $19,999 but 1.09 percent for those earning $50,000 to $99,999 (EBRI, 1992b).

## WHO BEARS THE RISK?

As noted in Chapter 1, insurance is a widely used mechanism for trans-ferring risk to another party, an insurer, for a fee. Although many employ-ers still use this mechanism, an increasing number bear all or most of the risk for employee health care expenses themselves; that is, they self-insure or self-fund their health benefits. The range of funding mechanisms avail-able to employers extends from fully insured plans to fully self-insured arrangements, and the details can be difficult to understand (CRS, 1988a; HIAA, 1992). According to one recent survey (A. Foster Higgins, 1992) directed at medium and large firms, 35 percent of surveyed employers pur-chased insurance and 65 percent self-insured (up from 46 percent in 1986). Of the self-insured group, fewer than one-fifth were totally self-insured; that is, they reported no stop-loss coverage as described below. Among state governments, 16 of 50 are insured, as is the federal government (Segal Company, 1991). Figure 3.5 shows that the use of self-insurance varies with firm size.

As noted in Chapter 2, self-insured employers can avoid a number of costs either by virtue of the device itself or by virtue of rulings under the Employee Retirement Income Security Act (ERISA) of 1974. Self-insured plans are exempt from state mandates that certain types of benefits be pro-vided; state limits on certain kinds of utilization management and provider contracting arrangements; solvency and prefunding requirements; defined claim settlement procedures; and mandatory participation in state risk pools or uncompensated care plans. Self-insured employers may also avoid risk

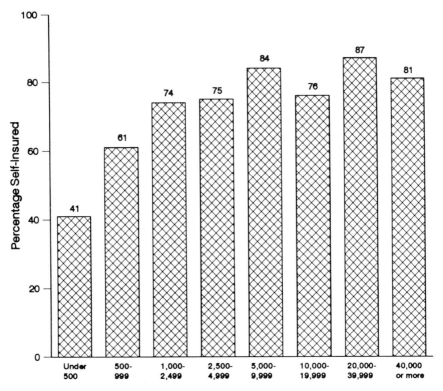

**FIGURE 3.5** Percentage of firms self-insured by total number of employees, 1991.
SOURCE: A. Foster Higgins, 1992.

charges, reduce cash flow demands, and earn interest on funds that would otherwise accrue to insurers. Except to the extent that they buy stop-loss insurance, they avoid state taxes on insurance premiums.

Employers who purchase insurance have premiums established in a variety of ways, some of which require significant sharing of risk with the insurer and other insured groups and some of which do not. For groups perceived as too small to have predictable claims experience, insurers generally set premiums using a manual that provides rates based on claims experience for different classes of employers. Manual rates reflect differences in experience related to industry, region, age, gender, and other factors. These rates may be modified by underwriters on the basis of the actual claims experience (or perceived risk) of specific small groups and marketing considerations. High-risk individuals may be screened out of the group before rates are set, or they may be charged a higher rate than others in the group.

For larger groups, which have more predictable claims expenses, insurers generally "experience rate" on the basis of the group's past claims experience or anticipated future experience. In a few areas, such as Rochester, New York, large employers have forgone experience rating and have shared risk more broadly with other employers and individuals in the community as part of a broader strategy to keep health care widely affordable throughout the community and to discourage cost control based on risk segmentation rather than on the more effective and efficient production and use of health services (see Chapters 5 and 6 for further discussion).

To attract employer clients who might otherwise self-insure, insurers have devised variants of experience rating that minimize the payments that actually flow from employer to insurer (see HIAA, 1992, especially the table on p. 61, Part C). For example, under what is called a minimum premium arrangement, the employer deposits money to cover a defined portion of its expected claims expense into a bank account or trust fund from which the insurer, acting as an administrative agent, pays claims. These amounts may be exempt from state premium taxes and can earn investment income that accrues to the employer, not the insurer. The portion of the premium that is actually paid to the insurer essentially provides for insurance should claims expenses exceed the defined amount that the employer has paid into the trust fund.

An employer may establish another type of partial self-insurance arrangement wherein it covers claims expense up to a defined level and purchases stop-loss insurance for expenses above that level. *Specific stop-loss* coverage applies when claims for a individual health plan member exceed a defined level, whereas *aggregate* coverage applies when total claims exceed a designated amount (e.g., 125 percent of total expected claims expense). Employers may purchase both kinds of coverage with different maximums. A self-insured employer may purchase stop-loss coverage from an insurer but purchase administrative services from either the insurer or a separate administrative agent. Fully self-insured plans may also purchase administrative services only (ASO) from either kind of organization. Some employers, however, administer their own claims.

Both minimum premium plans and self-insurance with stop-loss coverage involve relatively little transfer of risk to the insurer. Both may involve the creation of a special trust into which the employer pays to cover its defined level of claims expense. The most common approach is to establish a "501(c)(9)" trust (also called a voluntary employee beneficiary association, or VEBA).

A final point on funding is that most employers fund health benefits for both active workers and retirees on a pay-as-you-go basis rather than setting aside funds to cover obligations for future retirees. As noted earlier, recent changes in financial accounting standards require employers to recognize (but not prefund) promised retiree health benefits as liabilities on a firm's financial statements. When reported this way, liabilities may amount to 10 to 20 times the annual level of pay-as-you-go expenses (EBRI, 1992c). Over the long term the new accounting standards by themselves will have little impact on the organization's liabilities, expenses, or net worth, but this one-time "step up" in liabilities is prompting many employers to limit retiree health benefits in some way. Employers that plan to continue such benefits are becoming increasingly interested in tax-favored prefunding options. Current methods include setting aside assets in 501(c)(9) trusts, 401(h) accounts (defined benefit pension plans), and 401(k) plans.

## WHAT OTHER HEALTH-RELATED BENEFITS DO EMPLOYERS OFFER?

### Overview of Mandatory and Voluntary Programs

In addition to the medical expense coverage, employers may offer a variety of other health-related benefits. Some of these benefits are required by law; others are offered voluntarily.

Federal law imposes a payroll tax on employers (and employees) to help finance Medicare benefits and Social Security Disability Insurance. Workers' compensation benefits are required under a combination of federal and state laws. All but three states require employers to provide workers' compensation benefits, which are cash payments for workers killed, injured, or made ill in the course of work. The remaining three states give employers the choice between providing workers' compensation insurance or being subject to full liability for worker injuries as determined through litigation (EBRI, 1992a). In addition, federal and state governments have imposed on employers a variety of requirements intended to protect workers and others from occupational and environmental health hazards.

The array of benefits voluntarily provided by employers is considerably larger. These programs include

• paid sick leave (sometimes including leave to care for ill family members);

• short- or long-term disability insurance;

• employee assistance programs (EAPs), which may provide counseling, referral, and services related to certain health problems, such as alcoholism;

• health promotion programs, which may include on- and off-site screening services, exercise facilities, and other elements;

• worksite health clinics or infirmaries, which may treat worksite injuries and provide routine health services (such as allergy shots) as a convenience to workers; and

- worksite health and safety programs, which may involve strategies to eliminate or decrease general environmental and job-specific hazards associated with employment.

The rest of this discussion focuses on one mandatory health-related program—workers' compensation—and three voluntary programs involving health promotion, employee assistance, and flexible benefits. Each can interact with the design and operation of the basic program of health benefits in significant ways.

## Workers' Compensation

About 87 percent of civilian wage and salary workers are covered under mandatory workers' compensation programs that are fully financed by employers. In 1989, approximately 30 percent of the $46 billion paid by employers for workers' compensation premiums went for medical care (EBRI, 1992a). More recently, the proportion of workers' compensation spending attributed to medical care has risen to an estimated 40 percent (Freudenheim, 1992a). Over 45 percent of workers' compensation expenditures are accounted for by cash compensation payments and about one-quarter by administrative and other costs. While national spending on health care went up by 117 percent between 1980 and 1988, workers' compensation expenditures for medical care increased by 199 percent (Warren and Gerst, 1992). Some observers suggest that part of this rapid rise in workers' compensation expenditures is an indirect result of employers' attempts to contain costs in their regular health benefit programs.

Many public and private decisionmakers are growing increasingly concerned about the financial problems facing workers' compensation programs and are exploring ways to integrate workers' compensation, disability, and health benefit programs (Freudenheim, 1992a; Traska, 1992; Warren and Gerst, 1992). One objective is better management and coordination of health care provision and health plan features and, thereby, better control of health care and administrative costs. A related objective is to eliminate any incentive for workers facing increased cost sharing and limits on provider choice in their health benefit program to claim that their health problems are work-related and thus compensable under the sometimes less restrictive workers' compensation programs.[14]

The most expansive proposal for reforming workers' compensation is to establish a single benefits program to cover medical expenses for injury and illness whether incurred on or off the job. This integrated program would apply the same provider payment, health promotion, and managed

---

[14]In addition, deductibles, coinsurance, and other patient cost sharing do not apply in workers' compensation programs.

care concepts to either sort of medical expense (Cannon, 1992; Fletcher, 1992; Garamendi, 1992). More limited proposals would not integrate the programs but would allow states to channel those with workplace injuries to HMOs or to physicians who agreed to cooperate with special fee schedules and utilization management programs. As part of overall efforts to control fraud, some states are comparing treatment and charge information for workers' compensation patients with data for patients covered under Blue Cross or other health benefit programs (Kerr, 1991). They are also instituting some of the same auditing and antifraud measures that Medicare, Blue Cross, and other health insurers use.

Proposals for integrating workers' compensation and health benefit programs raise many complex legal issues and are controversial. To be adopted and implemented, many would require changes in state laws and perhaps in ERISA as well as renegotiation of existing union contracts.

## Health Promotion and Employee Assistance Programs

Rising health benefit costs and accumulating research on the correlations between health status and health care expenditures, absenteeism, and other associated business costs have combined with broad public interest in health promotion to increase employers' interests in strategies for achieving a healthier and less costly work force (Warner, 1990; Becker, 1991; EBRI, 1991b; Muchnick-Baku and McNeil, 1991; Muchnick-Baku and Orrick, 1991; Weiss et al., 1991; Conrad and Walsh, 1992). Because employers' costs for health benefits are not a fixed percentage of payroll (as are Social Security taxes) but are affected by the age, health status, and other characteristics of each employer's work force, employers may have an incentive for adopting more aggressive health promotion programs than would exist on grounds of worker productivity and employee relations alone.

Worksite health promotion and safety programs, which often overlap, may involve (1) health and safety activities specifically related to workplace hazards; (2) health promotion and education intended to promote healthful behavior, improved health status, and informed decisions about health care services; (3) appraisals of individual health status and behavior and feedback of information from such risk assessments to employees and others; and (4) positive or negative financial incentives related to health behavior or health status.[15] Of the 300 quantitative objectives developed as part of the *Healthy People 2000* plan to improve the health of Americans (U.S. Public Health Service, 1990), 17 focus on occupational health and safety and 3 focus on general workplace health promotion.

---

[15]Some discussions of health promotion through benefit design extend to a variety of "family support" policies including parental leave, on-site day care services, financial assistance for dependent care, and flexible working hours (Muchnick-Baku and McNeil, 1991).

DOL (1990, 1991) statistics indicate that structured corporate wellness programs were offered to 23 percent of employees of medium and large firms but only 2 percent of those in small firms. Surveys that use the firm as the level of analysis indicate that at least one-third of employers report specific health promotion programs, such as smoking cessation, weight control, cholesterol screening, stress management, and exercise programs (EBRI, 1991b; A. Foster Higgins, 1992). Some of these programs may be managed through the employee assistance programs described below.

The actual or perceived link between health promotion programs and employment-based health benefits varies by program and employer. Some employers reinforce their health promotion messages with changes in their health benefit programs. For example, health plan coverage may be extended to preventive and wellness services that were previously not covered. Benefits for smoking cessation programs may take effect when workplace smoking bans go into effect. Departing from these more positive approaches, a few employers have sought to reduce or eliminate health plan coverage for illness or injury attributed to drugs, alcohol, or sexually transmitted disease (Kramon, 1989; Dowell, 1992).

Instead of focusing on coverage for specific kinds of medical services, some employers focus on the characteristics of the individual. Large employers have traditionally not engaged in "risk rating" (i.e., making higher-risk individuals and groups pay more for coverage or refusing coverage in part or whole), but some are now departing from this policy, and more are expressing interest in doing so (NYBGH, 1990; Frieden, 1991; Miller and Bradburn, 1991; Rowland, 1992; Woolsey, 1992b,c,d,e,g). Employers may link employees' premium contributions to behavior (e.g., smoking), health status (e.g., blood pressure), or claims expense (e.g., claims during a six-month period). Some reward the healthy with discounted premiums or rebates; others add surcharges for the less healthy. Alternative financial incentives include cash awards, credits for use in purchasing other benefits (e.g., life insurance), and credits or coupons for health examinations, exercise gear, and similar health-related items. Some programs waive penalties or make positive incentives available for those under a physician's care for a problem or attempting to improve their health. Most financial incentives appear to cost between $10 and $35 per month ($120 to $420 per year).

The most drastic actions that employers may take to avoid high-risk employees or change high-risk behavior come in the form of hiring bans and dismissal policies. The news media have paid considerable attention to these policies, particularly as they affect off-the-job behavior (Schiller et al., 1991; Sipress, 1991, Span, 1991; Woolsey, 1992d).[16] The Americans

---

[16] The following examples, which are taken from the references just cited, illustrate what a few employers are on record as doing or attempting to do. The city of North Miami requires new employees to sign a document stating that they have not smoked in the preceding 12

with Disabilities Act of 1990 may constrain some of this behavior, depending on how the act's definition of disabilities is interpreted by the courts and administrative agencies (see Chapter 5). Even before this act took effect, some courts were discouraging some kinds of discrimination.[17] For example, Xerox was successfully sued several years ago for refusing to hire an obese individual on grounds that the person would likely increase the company's disability and life insurance costs. In addition, some states have also acted to protect some off-the-job behaviors, especially smoking, that have not been correlated with job performance.

Although EAPs are sometimes described as a type of health promotion program (DOL, 1990), they may involve fairly broad-based efforts to identify and help workers to resolve a variety of family and other personal problems that can affect job performance. In fact, many EAPs do focus on mental health and substance abuse problems of employees or their family members, and companies may need to resolve overlaps and inconsistencies among their EAP, health benefit, and managed mental health care programs. Employers may operate EAPs using company personnel, or they may contract for services from outside organizations. About half of the employees in medium and large establishments but fewer than 10 percent of those in small firms are eligible for EAPs (DOL, 1990, 1991).

A particular concern of workers has been that employers' actions to influence individual health behavior (1) not be substitutes for efforts to make the workplace safer, (2) not be used to shift blame to workers for problems associated with the work environment, and (3) not discriminate against workers by virtue of age, health status, and related characteristics (AFL-CIO, 1986). Some see corporate health promotion programs as potential means to "select or shape workers in the name of health, bypassing modern discrimination laws that have limited the employer's degrees of freedom to select and fire employees" (Conrad and Walsh, 1992, p. 104). Concern is increasing about some employers' interest in genetic screening to identify workers thought to be at higher risk of incurring an occupational illness or injury or generating health insurance expenses (Office of Technol-

---

months; those who will not sign are not hired—one such prospective employee is suing the city. Ford Meter Box, which also has stringent prohibitions on hiring smokers, is being sued by an offending employee detected through random urinalysis. The city of Athens, Georgia, attempted to bar the hiring of anyone with high cholesterol, but the threat of litigation from the American Civil Liberties Union dissuaded the city from instituting the policy. Best Lock Corporation is on record for firing a social drinker, and Multi-Developers will not hire motorcycle riders, mountain climbers, and those with similar leisure time activities.

[17]The Americans with Disabilities Act permits conventional forms of medical underwriting, whether by insurers or employers. Some employers have used risk appraisals to provide the information base for reward or penalty programs. The act appears to preclude or limit the use of these appraisals for this purpose.

ogy Assessment, 1990; Rothstein, 1992). This issue is being studied by another Institute of Medicine committee, which plans to issue a report in 1993.

## Flexible Benefits

Although not a health benefit program per se, various kinds of flexible benefit programs established by employers may significantly alter employment-based health benefits. Under provisions of the Internal Revenue Code, these programs allow individual employees some choice in the way benefit dollars are allocated and taxed (EBRI, 1991a). One arrangement, the flexible spending account, permits employees to set aside pretax dollars for dependent care or certain medical expenses; some include a contribution from the employer, and some do not. More broadly, flexible benefit plans may offer employees a choice between certain nontaxable and taxable benefits or even cash.

According to DOL statistics for 1989 and 1990, flexible benefits in some form were offered to nearly one-quarter of the employees in medium and large establishments but only 8 percent of those in small organizations (DOL, 1990, 1991; see also U.S. Chamber of Commerce Research Center, 1991 for other data). White-collar workers were more likely to have a flexible benefit program available than blue-collar workers. The DOL data do not provide information on the detailed features of such programs.

One reason organizations may introduce flexible benefit arrangements is to accommodate the diversity of today's work force. Another and often more important objective for employers may be to introduce a cap on increases in the cost of employee benefits—health benefits, in particular—and shift more of the burden of those increases to employees. Some employers have seen choice among more and less restrictive health plan options as a strategy for eliminating the plans that are most attractive to higher-risk or higher-cost individuals by allowing biased risk selection to make them unaffordable. Overall, for employees, flexible benefit programs may bring both advantages and disadvantages.

## CONCLUSION

That most nonelderly Americans have reasonable health coverage through the workplace is clear. That certain kinds of employees and employers are more likely than others not to participate in this system is also clear. Those who work in low-wage jobs for small employers, those who willingly or unwillingly retire early, and those with seasonal or part-time jobs—and the families of these workers—are particularly vulnerable.

To supplement the general, often statistical portrait presented in this chapter, the next chapter examines in more detail what employer sponsorship of health benefits may involve for employers, employees, and health care providers. It stresses the array of decisions and tasks that employers may take on and the factors that affect their decisions.

# 4

# What Does Employer Management of Health Benefits Involve? Overview and Case Study

*"Debugging" is not something done on the rare occasions when things go wrong but is an expected part of making a program work.*

Jeffrey Pressman and Aaron Wildavsky, 1973

## OVERVIEW

American employers—in varying degrees—have voluntarily undertaken responsibilities for making health insurance work that are unknown to most of their counterparts in other advanced industrial countries. Moreover, in each decade since employers first began to get significantly involved with health benefits over 50 years ago, the diversity of their options and the complexity of actually implementing them have grown. Accelerating innovation in biomedical science and medical specialization have interacted with rapidly growing costs, an increasing pluralism in health care delivery and financing, and diverse regulatory mechanisms to create an increasing array of matters that require judgment by health plan sponsors and an enlarged range of options for exercising that judgment. Increasing costs have, in particular, motivated many employers to increase their oversight of employee health plans and expand their participation in plan management.

Matching this diversity of responsibilities and opportunities is the diversity of employer circumstances, capabilities, and preferences, which leads to further variability in employee health benefit programs and their management. By choice or necessity, many smaller employers delegate virtually all tasks to the insurer for their health benefit program. For the very smallest employers, "the glove compartment in their pickup truck may be the file drawer for their employee health benefits program" (Polk, 1992). At the other extreme, a few large employers take on almost all insurance and administrative functions themselves, shouldering risk, directly paying claims, negotiating with health care providers, and auditing payments and utilization.  Most employers fall at various points in between these extremes, although the general trend has been toward more involvement or at least more active oversight.  Neither employers nor their environments are static, so a report such as this one necessarily provides only a snapshot of the proverbial moving target.

This section reviews some of the decisions, tasks, and options faced by those responsible for the design and maintenance of employers' health benefit programs, considers sources of diversity in the actions taken, and briefly describes some of the organizations that supply various kinds of services to employment-based programs.  The next section presents a partly real, partly hypothetical case study that attempts to provide a more vivid sense of the policy, technical, and interpersonal challenges that can be involved in offering employees a health benefit program.  A subsequent section selectively contrasts this core case with the situations faced by one much smaller organization and one much larger organization in order to illustrate further the diversity of employer and employee situations and the tangled issues of equity that employers and employees confront in considering various options.  The final two sections examine how the roles of employees and health care providers in health benefit management are particularly affected by the link between employment and health benefits.

## Types of Decisions, Tasks, and Options

In considering the advantages and disadvantages of employment-based health benefits, it is important to understand what responsibilities and tasks may be assumed when an organization decides to offer employee health benefits.  Building from the discussion in Chapter 3, Table 4.1 depicts major categories of decisions and options that employers may face once they make the fundamental decision to offer health benefits.  As will be made clearer shortly, not all items are relevant for all employers.

## Sources of Diversity in Program Design and Management

What information, organizational characteristics (e.g., demographic structure of the work force and site[s] of operations), and principles guide employers' decisions about the design and operation of health benefit programs?  How much do employers rely on consultants, brokers, and other outsiders?  How are day-to-day matters managed, for example, the monitoring of plan utilization and expenses and handling employee complaints or problems?  What tax, antidiscrimination, insurance, liability, and other legal constraints or concerns must be considered?  What is involved in changing a health benefit program?

Answers to these questions are far from straightforward—as might be

**TABLE 4.1**   Selected Types of Decisions, Tasks, and Options Faced by Organizations That Choose to Offer Employment-Based Health Benefits

*Identification and Analysis of Alternatives*
- Employer's staff
- Agents and brokers
- Outside consultants

*Definition of Eligible Participants in Health Plan*
- Employees, full-time or part-time
- Dependents of employees
- Retirees, under or over age 65

*Decisions About Health Plan Options*
- Single plan
- Multiple plans, multiple carriers
- Multiple plans, consolidated carrier(s)
- Conventional and/or network plans
- Care directly provided by employer
- Flexible benefit plan
- Other health-related benefits

*Determination of Scope and Depth of Coverage*
- Generally covered services, providers, sites of care
- Specific technologies (experimental, established, obsolete)
- Amount of individual cost sharing
- Incentives and disincentives for use of particular services or providers

*Decisions About Payment and Oversight*
- Care reimbursed under auspices of conventional or network health plan(s)
- Care reimbursed under direct contracts with providers
- Method and level of paying providers (may be determined by health plan)
- Utilization review, delegated or internally administered
- Claims auditing, delegated or internally administered
- Analysis of health care financial and utilization data

*Choice of Risk Bearing/Funding Mechanism*
- Insured, fully or partly
- Self-insured, fully or partly

*Options for Claims Administration*
- Delegated to one or more insurers or third-party administrators
- Self-administered, fully or partly

*Other Tasks*
- Enrollment of health plan members
- Payroll deduction of employee share of premium
- Electronic submission of data to carrier

*Community Role*
- Complying with government regulations (e.g., ERISA, COBRA)
- Participation in communitywide or business-specific activities
- Lobbying for policy change at state or national level

**TABLE 4.2**   Sources of Variation in Employment-Based Health Benefits

---

*Corporate Philosophy on Fringe Benefits*

*Size of Organization*

*Single State or Multistate Sites*

*Demographic Structure of Active Work Force and Retirees*

*Location of Headquarters and Other Major Operations*
- Region
- Size, demographics, and other features of community
- Characteristics of local health care delivery system and health insurance market

*Nature of Business*
- Prevailing benefits and traditions in key lines of business
- Competitiveness in these lines of business
- Competitiveness and other characteristics of relevant labor markets
- Unionization and other work force characteristics (e.g., education, turnover, and age)
- Profitability, stability
- Health care services or supplies as a line of business, or health care organizations as major customers

*Legal Environment*
- State and federal statutes, regulations, and enforcement
- State and federal case law

---

expected given the variability of employment-based benefits related to employer size, location, corporate philosophy, and business sector. Table 4.2 summarizes some of the factors that contribute to diversity in employment-based health benefits.

Table 4.3 suggests how just one factor—organizational size—may affect employer options and involvement in managing health benefits. The simplest function is to enroll employees in a health benefit plan; virtually all employers can do this. Even quite small organizations often have automated payroll systems that allow health plan enrollment, premium deductions, and other information to be entered, updated, and conveyed to others with relative ease—although the smaller the organization and the higher its employee turnover, the more of a problem these tasks become. More complex than these simple administrative activities are those that involve analysis of claims data, active oversight of insurers and administrative agents, offering choices among health plans, and direct negotiations with providers.

Larger employers are likely to have specialized staff responsible for health benefits. They are also more likely to work with outside consultants who offer a variety of technical services, such as audit or analysis of health claims data, advice on benefit plan design, development of requests for proposals from insurers or others interested in competing for the account,

**TABLE 4.3** How Size May Affect How Employers Manage Health Benefits

| Options and Tasks for Employers | <25 employees | 25–200 employees | 201–999 employees | 1,000–4,999 employees | 5,000–9,999 employees | 10,000+ employees |
|---|---|---|---|---|---|---|
| Offers health benefits | P | L | Y | Y | Y | Y |
| Has dedicated health benefit staff | N | N | N | P-L | Y | Y |
| Relies on agents or brokers | Y | Y | P | N | N | N |
| Uses outside consultants | N | N | P-L | Y | Y | Y |
| Enrolls health plan members | Y | Y | Y | Y | Y | Y |
| Uses automated payroll system | P | L | Y | Y | Y | Y |
| Submits data to carriers electronically | N | N | P | L | Y | Y |
| Conducts independent audits of claims | N | N | P | P-L | Y | Y |
| Analyzes detailed financial and utilization data | N | N | P | L | Y | Y |
| Offers choice among health plans | N | P | P-L | Y | Y | Y |
| Manages risk selection or risk adjustments among health plan options | NA | N | P | L | Y | Y |
| Negotiates individually with health care providers | N | N | N | P | P | P |
| Joins community coalitions to influence health care costs and delivery | N | N | P | P | L-Y | Y |
| Fully or partly self-insures | N | N | P | Y | Y | Y |

NOTE: Y indicates usually yes; L indicates likely; P indicates possibly; N indicates not likely; and NA indicates not applicable.

financial and other evaluation of proposals received, and advice on design of health promotion and other specialized programs. Some larger employers want to get deeply involved in the details of program design and management, whereas others want, by and large, to hand off the tasks to consultants and others.

Owners or office managers of smaller organizations are likely to rely on insurance agents or brokers for advice and assistance.[1] Depending on the health status and claims expense profiles presented by the organization, its financial strength, and its geographic location, finding an insurer may range from simple to impossible.

### Suppliers of Health Insurance, Administrative, and Other Services

Even the largest employers rarely carry out internally all the tasks necessary to operate a health benefit program. For the most basic function of claims administration, 9 out of 10 self-insured firms contract with one of the hundreds of independent or insurer-owned third-party administrators (TPAs) (Woolsey, 1992a). Many of the well over 1,000 commercial insurance companies and the 73 Blue Cross and Blue Shield plans offer a broad range of claims and benefit management services in conjunction with or independently of their insurance functions. Businesses in some communities have formed coalitions to provide some of the same services.

In addition to conventional insurers and TPAs, there are approximately 60 staff model health maintenance organizations (HMOs), 75 group model HMOs, 80 network model HMOs, and 360 independent practice associations (IPAs) (GHAA, 1991; Marion Merrell Dow, Inc., 1992). Over 40 percent of HMOs are sponsored by Blue Cross and Blue Shield plans or commercial insurers, but these plans account for just under 30 percent of total HMO enrollments. In addition, specialized networks have been created to cover dental, podiatric, vision, mental health care, and other services.

Employers may purchase services from other organizations, which vary in scope from broad to narrow. They include utilization management organizations that review the necessity or appropriateness of health services; organizations that review the performance of utilization management organizations; case management firms that help manage services and costs for very expensive patients; accounting firms that audit claims and provide consulting and other services; firms that specialize in data analysis; and firms that specialize in health promotion and health risk appraisal.

---

[1]An agent acts on behalf of an insurer to sell its products to individuals and groups. A broker, in theory, acts on behalf of an employer or other group in placing business with an insurer.

## Cooperative Efforts

Business groups in several dozen communities have cooperated to establish coalitions to help inform employers about health care delivery and financing and, in some cases, provide utilization review, data analysis, and other services. In a few locations, public or private organizations have been created especially to assist employers, especially small employers, with the administrative side of insurance purchasing (Helms, 1992; Sailors, 1992). A frequently cited—and probably the best developed—example is the Council of Smaller Enterprises (COSE) established by Cleveland's Chamber of Commerce. Using the TPA subsidiary of its primary insurer, COSE collects premiums from member firms, makes lump sum payments to health plans on a monthly basis, handles changes in enrollment and questions from enrollees, analyzes utilization data, negotiates with insurers, and takes on the responsibility for marketing its services and products to small businesses (Alpha Center, undated; National Health Policy Forum, 1992). COSE's participating insurers (with the exception of three HMOs) medically underwrite group applicants and reject about 20 percent of business applications on that basis.[2] Within groups, individual premiums are adjusted for age but not health status. Chapter 5 discusses this general purchasing concept further.

A fundamentally different and apparently unique kind of employer cooperative action is found in Rochester, New York, where the largest employers in the community have maintained a 50-year commitment to community rating that has allowed small businesses and the self-employed to receive the same Blue Cross and Blue Shield and HMO premiums as such local giants as Eastman Kodak and Xerox (Taylor, 1987; Freudenheim, 1992b; Taylor et al., 1992). In addition, the large employers have supported communitywide health planning since the early 1960s, HMO development since the early 1970s, and innovations in provider payment. Many credit this support as a major reason that Rochester has a low percentage of uninsured individuals, a lower-than-average supply of hospital beds, a higher-than-average hospital occupancy ratio, and relatively low insurance premiums and per capita health care costs.

---

[2]During its early years of operation in the 1970s, when there was no medical underwriting, COSE attracted older and sicker groups disproportionately. This essentially nullified the discount that had been negotiated with the local Blue Cross and Blue Shield plan. This led the organization to allow medical underwriting. The local Kaiser plan does not medically underwrite, and it expected to suffer from adverse selection. In analyzing its business, however, Kaiser found that it was getting less-risky small groups through COSE than it was securing through its own efforts—perhaps because the other plans were using such strict underwriting that many of the rejected applicants who turned to Kaiser were relatively low risk (National Health Policy Forum, 1992).

## CORE CASE STUDY

The following case study is included here for two reasons. First, the diversity of employer activities in health benefit management makes orderly and comprehensive discussion of the topic difficult; the case study is a simplifying device. Second, the case study is intended to make more vivid the demands of responsibly managing an employment-based health benefit program. The case is also designed to illustrate the impact on individual employers and their employees of developments in the larger health care environment such as rising costs, debates about equity and risk sharing, and innovations in health plan design. Although many of the data are adapted from real organizations, the case itself cannot be read as a true or even average story, as an illustration of a perfect process, or as a process or outcome that the committee necessarily endorses. For an organization of the size depicted in the case study, the degree of internal analysis and employee involvement is probably atypical.

### The Organization and Its Environment

The organization has about 1500 nonunionized employees, about half professional and half administrative and clerical. Turnover is moderate. The average age of employees is about 40, and the organization has approximately 5 active employees for every retiree. Employees reside over a wide urban, suburban, and rural geographic area surrounding the organization's offices. The organization has a small clinic that provides some routine medical care, such as allergy shots.

The metropolitan area is plentifully supplied with primary care and specialist physicians, hospital beds, tertiary care services, and other health care providers. Several dozen insurers market coverage in the area, and most of the major ones have organized HMOs, PPOs, and other kinds of network health plans that compete with several locally created plans. The business community is not particularly active in health care issues, although there is a nascent purchasing coalition for small and medium-sized firms.

The state has the usual array of mandated benefits but no rate-setting commission, anti-managed-care laws, or state insurance pool for high-risk individuals. Health care providers complain about Medicare and Medicaid payment levels. Nevertheless, the reimbursement formulas for these government programs have left providers better off than their counterparts in many other areas and less likely to seek offsetting revenues from private purchasers of medical services.

### History

As with most organizations, the health benefit program has evolved through a combination of marginal year-to-year adjustments punctuated by a few more substantial shifts as costs rose or as the program needed to adapt to changing health care delivery and financing arrangements. The original program was adopted in the 1950s, quite early for an employer whose employees were not represented by a union. It was designed to cover full-time workers, part-time workers working 20 hours or more, spouses and children of these workers, and retirees. Employees were initially required to pay 60 percent of the premium, a contribution that came to $1.50 per month for individual coverage and $3.50 for family coverage; retirees with more than 25 years service paid no premium, and other retirees paid the same share as active employees. Inpatient hospital and physician services were fully covered in the original plan, but outpatient care was more limited. A separate plan to cover catastrophic expenses was added after the first few years. After 10 years (in the early 1960s), the employee contribution to the premium for the basic plan had risen to $2.50 and $5.90 per month for individual and family coverage, respectively.

By the mid-1970s the organization was paying 75 percent of the premium to stay competitive in the local labor market. It added a large staff model HMO as an option for employees and established a yearly open enrollment process. During the first open enrollment, 15 percent of employees opted for the HMO, which cost them $12.50 a month for individual coverage, compared with $5 for the original plan. Shortly thereafter, the organization, which had grown increasingly unhappy with the claims service and the benefit structure provided by the original insurer, switched to a competitor for its indemnity plan. Program changes were communicated to employees through memos and plan booklets.

During the 1980s the organization added four more HMOs as options for employees, all independent practice association (IPA) plans. Four plans were needed to provide sufficient geographic coverage.

Five years earlier, the organization had made substantial changes in some aspects of its health benefit programs, mainly in response to the rapidly rising cost of the indemnity program, especially the cost for retirees. (All the retirees not eligible for Medicare were in the indemnity plan, and 95 percent of the rest had Medicare supplemental coverage under the indemnity plan.) Taking the advice of an outside consultant, the organization changed coverage for Medicare-eligible retirees so that the combination of Medicare and organization benefits would not exceed the benefits available to active employees. It also instituted the same premium cost-sharing requirements for retirees as applied to active workers. For all enrollees in the indemnity plan, the deductible was doubled; first-dollar coverage was eliminated for hospitalization costs but provided for preadmission testing, outpatient laboratory and X-ray services, and outpatient surgery. Hospice benefits and provisions for preadmission and continued stay review and case management were instituted. The organization also established a limited program of flexible benefits that either provided $500 in taxable extra income or provided for a nontaxable reimbursement account for medical care or dependent care.

## Considering New Options

In the late 1980s the organization's management became concerned about the continued viability of the indemnity option. That plan's premiums had jumped by increments of 25 percent and more per year, and it was losing younger people to the HMOs while retaining the older and more costly employees. The premiums for the original HMO also were going up about 15 to 20 percent each year, as the average age of its members increased and the IPAs enrolled more new, young employees.

Concerned that the indemnity plan might become prohibitively expensive and that the insurer might on short notice decide to withdraw, the organization's top management took action. It decided that a comprehensive look at the health benefits program was in order and that new ways of structuring the program and stabilizing its costs should be examined. It established several provisional objectives for a new program. The program should

• continue to be attractive for recruiting high-quality professional and other staff (i.e., be reasonably competitive with the health benefits offered by similar organizations);
• include at least one network plan and one plan that does not lock employees into a closed provider network;
• substantially reduce the degree to which higher- and lower-risk employees are segmented into separate risk pools;
• offer some real potential for limiting future escalation in total costs; and
• conform with applicable state and federal laws.

The provisional strategy was to consider two major options: (1) a complete replacement program from a single carrier that provided employees with choices among a fee-for-service plan, an HMO, and a PPO; (2) a program that retained the staff model HMO, eliminated the four IPAs, and replaced the indemnity plan with a point-of-service (POS) plan. Another provisional decision was that the mental health benefits offered in the existing indemnity plan should be scaled back. The human resources staff had been advised that the existing benefits were more generous than was typical in the area and might be attracting higher-risk individuals to the organization and the indemnity plan. (A summary of the indemnity plan is included as part of Addendum at the end of this chapter.)

*Further Data Analysis*

To better understand what had happened with their health benefit program and to inform their evaluation of alternatives, the human resources staff concluded that they needed more data on the current situation. They decided that they needed to examine

- the profile of enrollments and premiums for the six health plans over the period from 1980 to 1990;
- the variation in enrollee demographics and utilization of services in the different health plans;
- the turnover in enrollment experienced by the different plans; and
- the distribution of very high cost employees and dependents across the plans.

Some of this information was in the organization's files and required no special effort to array, at least for those data collected since personnel records were computerized in 1980. Putting together other information required more effort, and certain data were not available. In particular, the organization did not know the number of dependents covered under each plan, their age or income, and whether they were also covered under another organization's health plan. Even for employee enrollees, the organization had no information on individual health status or satisfaction with the selected health plan. It had some claims data only for the indemnity plan, but those data were difficult to interpret for several reasons. First, the full enrollment of both employees and dependents was not known (thus, the true denominator to calculate utilization and other rates was unavailable); second, the composition of its enrollment had almost certainly changed through selective loss of lower-risk enrollees from the indemnity plan (thus comparisons of utilization and payment rates over time would be distorted); and third, only certain limited inferences were possible for a group of this size.[3]

Table 4.4 shows some of the results of the analysis of available data. Overall, the indemnity plan had less than 50 percent of all enrollees, down from 70 percent less than a decade earlier. The average age in the indemnity plan was considerably older than for any of the network plans. The analysis showed no appreciable difference in the percentage of female and male employees enrolling in the indemnity plan, about half of each group.

---

[3]In one respect, however, they had more data than they felt comfortable with. The carrier reported employee names with its monthly listing of claims, so personnel staff knew who the high-use enrollees were and what general types of services they or their family members were using. Given company policies regarding leave for illness and employee requests for some kind of information or assistance, staff were aware of some of these situations, but the claims data made the costs much more visible.

**TABLE 4.4**   Selected Comparisons of Existing Health Plans in Case
Study Organization

| | Share of Total Employee Coverage, % | Average Age of Enrollee, years | Monthly Premium Paid by Employee, $ | | Enrollment Turnover at Last Open Season | |
| | | | Individual | Family | % From Other Plans | % To Other Plans |
|---|---|---|---|---|---|---|
| Indemnity | 48 | 45 | 56 | 140 | 3 | 4 |
| HMO 1 | 17 | 38 | 39 | 97 | 3 | 3 |
| IPA 1 | 11 | 34 | 35 | 90 | 10 | 11 |
| IPA 2 | 12 | 33 | 28 | 75 | 14 | 13 |
| IPA 3 | 7 | 35 | 31 | 85 | 12 | 11 |
| IPA 4 | 5 | 32 | 30 | 95 | 18 | 18 |

However, 58 percent of all male employees selecting family coverage were
in the indemnity plan, compared with only 36 percent of women with such
coverage; for individual coverage, the figures were almost the reverse (54
percent for women and 36 percent for men). These latter differences seemed
interesting, but no one was exactly sure what to make of them. Perhaps the
women selecting family coverage were lower-paid single parents who were
choosing the plans with the lowest out-of-pocket costs. Turnover (the number of plan enrollees in the preceding year who left for another health plan
or joined from another plan at the year-end open enrollment as a percentage
of total plan enrollees in the preceding year) was fairly low for the two
oldest plans but considerably higher for the newer plans. On the basis of
their informal log of complaints about each plan, staff identified only one
plan as a significant source of complaints and difficulties in resolving them.
That plan was the one with the 36 percent turnover rate (see Table 4.4).

The human resources staff wanted to know more about the extent to
which the differences in premiums across the health plans reflected differences in benefits, in enrollee characteristics, and in plan efficiency. It knew
the HMOs had more generous benefits for the most part (e.g., no deductible,
no or low copayments, and more coverage of preventive services). On the
other hand, the indemnity plan covered all the physicians and hospitals in
the community (and outside the community for that matter), including the
tertiary care hospital with the best reputation for heart surgery. Overall, the
indemnity plan also had substantially more extensive and more flexible
coverage for inpatient and outpatient mental health services.

The HMOs did not provide data on high-cost cases that could be compared with data from the indemnity plan. On the basis of employee requests
for advice, short-term disability benefits, unpaid leave to care for ill family
members, and similar matters, the human resources staff believed that the

indemnity plan had most of the high-cost employees, dependents, and early retirees—including several seriously ill with different kinds of cancer, three with AIDS, one with a heart transplant, one very-low-birth-weight baby, several who had undergone coronary artery bypass grafts, and a father and daughter severely injured in an automobile accident. The indemnity plan reported that 1 percent of its enrollees generated 39 percent of all claims expenses in the preceding year.

## Financial and Legal Questions

The vice president for human resources and the chief financial officer also wanted to look at the organization's financial arrangements with the different health plans and consider whether they might be changed to the organization's advantage. The HMO options were all insured and charged the same premium to all groups in the community. The HMOs received premiums on a monthly basis and kept any excess over their costs but also absorbed any losses (at least for the year in question).

One question was whether to ask the HMOs to quote premiums by age class because the younger employees were concentrated in the HMOs. This would be legal. It would not, however, have been legal for these plans, which were all federally qualified HMOs, to base their rates on the claims experience of any single employer group (that is, to fully experience rate the group).

The financing arrangement for the indemnity plan was more complicated. The plan was experience rated, so that last year's claims expenses determined next year's premium adjusted for the estimated trend (always upward) in medical care costs. In addition to claims expenses, the premium included a "retention" factor (primarily to cover administrative costs and profit) plus a premium for stop-loss coverage for any individual whose claims reached $80,000 in one year. Premiums were paid on a monthly basis. The insurer had a substantial reserve accumulated over several earlier periods of favorable claims experience.

The vice president and chief financial officer of the organization knew that many organizations its size were self-insured, that its state's premium tax was costing it an extra 1.5 percent of premium costs per year (not paid by self-insured organizations), and that any carrier it chose could probably provide the necessary administrative services for a self-insured program. On the other hand, a self-insurance arrangement would have its own burdens and risks. In particular, the organization would have to manage the financial reserves such an arrangement would require. Overall, the case for self-insurance was not as strong for this organization as it might have been for one with multiple sites and multiple sets of state-mandated benefits with which to contend.

A final concern of legal counsel related to the potential tort liability that might arise from the organization's adoption of a health benefit program that limited employee choice of provider and applied utilization management techniques to control health care utilization. The counsel's concern was not acute, but she urged that the organization make a point of examining—and documenting—how candidate health plans selected and monitored providers, how they arrived at and applied judgments of medical necessity, and what processes they used to determine when to cover experimental procedures. The chief financial officer pointed out that such an examination would also give the organization a firmer sense of how effective and efficient the plans might be at managing costs.

### Preliminary Discussion of Alternatives

Because the organization had a basically good relationship with its indemnity carrier, the staff called the service representative to arrange a meeting to discuss the organization's concerns and plans and the carrier's assessment of problems and possible solutions. The service representative acknowledged the undesirable premium trends and openly recommended that the organization should aggressively explore options to the current indemnity plan, in particular, a POS plan. At the same time, staff began to contact the service representatives of their HMOs to explain what was happening and to ask what options those plans might be able to offer. On the basis of informal consultation with colleagues in other organizations in the community, they also asked for meetings with three large insurers not currently represented in the organization's health benefit program. They wanted to get acquainted with the different insurers and their programs before arranging for any formal consulting services.

Over a period of three months, staff scheduled meetings with seven insurers, all of whom had POS or similar replacement options to discuss. Their conclusions based on these meetings were as follows:

• All of the options being proposed by the carriers were new or very recently developed products (e.g., PPOs or POS plans), so that none had much of a history in the community.

• The companies were thought to be making excessive and sometimes misleading claims for their plans.

• Some carriers appeared much more flexible in their underwriting policies, in particular, their tolerance for other HMOs continuing as options and their lack of insistence on preexisting condition clauses for new employees.

One major issue that needed careful thought was what to do for participants in existing HMOs that would no longer be available to employees.

Their alternatives would be to enroll in a staff model HMO or in the new POS plan, both of which would almost certainly be more expensive than the least expensive of the existing HMOs.

The group decided to formalize its planning in several respects. First, it would create an employee advisory group. Second, it would develop an explicit request for proposals (RFP) from various carriers. Third, it would bring in its own benefit consultants to review the draft RFP and to help evaluate responses. Fourth, each carrier would be asked to provide a list of references from community organizations that have had experience with the carrier.

*Employee Advisory Group*

The employee advisory group was constructed to serve two purposes. One was to represent the range of employee interests within the various departments within the organization. The other was to take advantage of employee expertise in two areas: communications strategies and information evaluation. The advisory group had no formal decisionmaking power. Putting the advisory group together, arranging a meeting, and preparing background materials on the current health benefit program, organization objectives, terminology, and alternative programs took several weeks.

During the first meeting, the group broke into three work teams: one to draft key features of the RFP (with final preparation by the benefit consultant), one to consider carrier selection, and one to develop a plan for ongoing communication with employees. The entire advisory group would participate in a series of meetings with the six insurance organizations that would be invited to bid on the new health program.

The first work team started with information about the existing health plan benefits plus the materials that potential bidders presented about their POS, PPO, or similar products. They divided their task into four parts or questions: (1) how many options of what type should employees be offered; (2) what level of cost sharing should be required for in-network services and what level for use of out-of-network providers; (3) what kinds of providers and services should be covered; and (4) what other limits or features should be included? They presented two major alternatives to the rest of the advisory group plus a number of points for further discussion. The alternatives reflected their concern about the overall levels of benefits as they related to the plan premium and the relationship between the new plan premium and the premiums of the HMOs that would be canceled.

In discussing options and alternatives, the advisory group got into a number of questions about equity. For example, some members expressed concern that if all the stand-alone IPA options were dropped as tentatively recommended, monthly premiums for some employees would go up. Others countered that these people appeared to be the youngest and probably the healthiest employees and that their choice of the most inexpensive IPA plans fractured the sharing of risk among well and ill. This point, in turn, was countered by the argument that the younger employees probably earn less and they would be subsidizing older, richer employees in a combined risk pool. The debate prompted one employee to ask whether premiums or deductibles could be varied by employee income. This encouraged another employee to complain that she as a single mother with one child paid the same premium as a married coworker with four children. A worker with no dependents then asked why the total pool of benefit dollars subsidized family coverage in general and thus provided others like himself with lower total compensation. Someone else then returned to the question of dropping the stand-alone IPAs and argued that some people in those options would have to change their physicians and pay more to boot. After some discussion, the group concluded that such changes probably would not be a major problem because the relatively young IPA members (in these relatively young IPAs) probably did not have strong physician relationships. Furthermore, many of the IPA physicians probably took patients on a fee-for-service basis, so—at worst—a patient might have to pay somewhat more to avoid changing physicians.

Someone observed that with a PPO or POS plan, most enrollees in the current indemnity plan would either have to switch doctors or pay more. Clearly, gains and losses would not be distributed uniformly among all employees, but no single group would be getting all the benefit or all the loss.

Related but somewhat different questions arose about specific benefits, particularly the reduced coverage for mental health care. Staff knew that one advisory group member was worried about her adolescent son who had undergone expensive inpatient, outpatient, and drug therapy for depression. Other questions were relayed by the advisory group from other employees. They involved requests that Christian Science healers, acupuncture, and herbal medicine be covered. The discussion dealt in part with whether such services are effective and whether the new health plan should have to offer them when the HMO option did not.

Yet another question was raised about technology assessment. An employee said he had read in the newspaper that one of the plans that would likely submit a bid on the organization's health program had been sued to force it to cover a bone marrow transplant for a breast cancer patient. Shouldn't that plan be rejected out of hand as denying care to the very ill even if the care was still experimental? Another employee said that he read the newspapers, too, and thought medical technology and costs were out of control and the plan was right not to pay for unproven new procedures. The issue in his mind was how good the plan was at assessing new medical technologies and identifying effective medical practices.

A final point of some debate was whether the organization should start setting higher premiums for smokers. One employee said because smoking was no longer permitted at work many people were trying to quit; why put more stress on these individuals? Someone else pointed out that verification of information about individual health behavior could be a problem, either tempting employees to lie if there were no verification process or embroiling the organization in blood testing and other intrusive activities if they did seek to verify information.

The discussion of all these issues of fairness was not acrimonious, but all participants came away with a new understanding of how complicated and potentially divisive are arguments over risk sharing, subsidies, and coverage options. The work team on communications realized that it must deal with these issues carefully and in some depth.

The advisory group accepted the recommendations of the benefit design work team with a few changes. The organization's senior management also accepted the recommendations.

*Request for Proposals*

The next step was to bring the benefit consultant into the process to review the proposed program design and draft an RFP. The consultant's primary recommendations were that the prescription drug coverage should include a network of preferred pharmacies, a mail-order service, reduced cost sharing for generic drugs, and a program of drug utilization review to promote both cost containment and quality. Legal counsel had already said that the initially proposed mental health benefit had to be raised to be consistent with state laws.

Excerpts from the RFP are reproduced in Addendum 4. Because the advisory group still had a lot of questions remaining from its preliminary discussions with the carriers, the consultant recommended that it should formulate a set of questions for bidders. Most of the financial questions came from the consultant. Carriers were told they should assume in their bids that the group would continue to offer one staff model HMO as an enrollment option. They were given six weeks to respond.

*Evaluating Responses and References*

When the responses to the RFP arrived, the consultant began to analyze them, concentrating in particular on the rates quoted for individual and family premiums. On the basis of the detailed information accompanying the rates, the consultant came to the following conclusions: the lowest rates for individual and family coverage, which came from the carrier for the old indemnity plan, may have been underbid and probably assumed that some of the excess reserves in the old plan could be applied to reduce initial rates; the second-lowest rates looked sound and apparently reflected some optimism that this network plan could attract a lot of the younger employees and thereby achieve a less adverse risk pool than that of the current indemnity plan; and the highest premiums (which were 50 percent higher than the lowest premiums) were quoted for a program that had more restricted benefits and apparently reflected a conservative strategy on the part of that carrier.

The work team focusing on carrier selection developed a list of questions to ask the references submitted by each carrier. That list focused on specific plan features (e.g., coinsurance for out-of-network care), employee reactions, quality of plan administration, and similar matters. As soon as the carriers' responses to the RFP arrived, two members of this team began to contact the references.

By the time the consultant reported, the carrier selection group had contacted all the references. It found the exercise useful not only in assessing the bidders but also in learning about possible employee reactions and helpful strategies for implementing a new program. At that stage the major remaining challenge was how to evaluate the networks of physicians, hospitals, and other health care providers offered by each health plan. As part of the RFP, the bidders were asked to submit information on the characteristics of their panels (e.g., geographic coverage by zip code of the employer's work force, board certification) and their procedures for evaluating and improving provider performance.

The advisory group's assessment of the responses produced mixed findings. The most expensive plan appeared to have the best program for selecting participating providers and monitoring and improving their performance, but it also had the smallest numbers of network physicians and hospitals and was particularly short on coverage of the central city. The second least expensive plan had a much larger panel of participating providers and covered the geographic area much better, but it appeared to be less far along in its network management and quality assurance procedures. The other bidders had relatively small networks, geographic coverage problems, middling network management procedures, and, for three out of four bids, higher premiums.

The group discerned a trade-off between better access and tight panel management, but it noted that the smaller, more tightly managed panel still was the most expensive and offered less extensive benefits. The vice president felt that a significant convergence in group attitudes had occurred as the proposals came in and were evaluated. It helped that one proposal offered a higher level of benefits at a lower prospective cost than expected. Members of the advisory group who had previously seemed skeptical appeared to be "buying in" more fully to the switch from an indemnity to a

**TABLE 4.5** Summary Evaluation of Responses to RFP

| | Total Monthly Premium | | Size of Physician Panel | Geographic Coverage | Benefits as Specified in RFP | References |
|---|---|---|---|---|---|---|
| | Individual | Family | | | | |
| Bid 1 | 160 | 410 | 450 | – | = | + |
| Bid 2 | 185 | 465 | 1,000 | + | + | ++ |
| Bid 3 | 215 | 550 | 600 | – | = | + |
| Bid 4 | 225 | 565 | 400 | – | – | + |
| Bid 5 | 210 | 530 | 500 | – | = | – |
| Bid 6 | 206 | 520 | 450 | – | – | ++ |

NOTE: + indicates proposal is more attractive than other proposals; = indicates proposal is acceptable; and – indicates proposal is deficient on this dimension.

POS health plan. On the basis of the references and other analysis (e.g., geographic coverage), the group identified two bidders with particularly favorable reports and proposals, three with acceptable proposals and reports, and one that was essentially unsatisfactory (Table 4.5).

These results were discussed with senior management, which expressed satisfaction with the progress that had been made and with the way the options were being evaluated. It looked as if a new health benefit program could be instituted in conjunction with the next open enrollment, although it would be a squeeze to undertake an adequate employee communication program and to complete all the administrative steps.

The final step was to go back to the bidders with questions about various details of their responses and with a request for a best and final offer to be delivered within 10 days. Each bidder had submitted an original response that was in some way unacceptable to the working group, but the vice president for human resources and the consultant expected that most or all could be successfully negotiated. The organization, in particular, challenged requirements that the organization drop all other plans and impose preexisting condition limitations on new employees.

### The Final Decision and Its Implementation

*Weighing Alternatives*

After the final bids arrived, the advisory group met to hear the consultant's appraisal and to decide what to recommend to senior management. It felt that no option was free from defects and worrisome uncertainties, but, nonetheless, one option was substantially more attractive than the others. The determining factors were that (1) one proposal offered the second-lowest premium and the lowest one that the consultant considered reasonably sound; (2) the rate for that proposal included more benefits than did most of the more costly alternatives; (3) the plan also offered the broadest panel of participating providers with the best geographic coverage; (4) the references consulted spoke highly of the plan's service capacity and ability to deal effectively with problems as they arose and reported high employee satisfaction; and (5) the carrier backed off all of its underwriting restrictions (thus, for example, permitting the organization to continue to offer one staff model HMO), dropped a preexisting condition provision for new employees, and adjusted its original premium very modestly upward to reflect the greater risk it expected to assume as a result.

The major worries about the option were twofold. First, did the rate—despite the consultant's statement that the carrier had reasonably estimated prospective claims—represent a "low ball" estimate, making the organization vulnerable to a big rate increase the next year? Second, was the plan's program to evaluate and manage provider performance as strong as it should be? In many respects, the specific capacities of the health plan remained a black box despite the advisory group's best efforts to evaluate it.

Another crucial question was how attractive the POS plan would be to employees generally and how its benefits would be perceived in relation to its higher premium for the 25 percent of all employees whose current health plans would be canceled. The vice president had received estimates of renewal rates from all of the current HMO options. The news was generally encouraging. Of the four plans to be canceled, two were very close in premium to the new option; however, the other plan would have remained a substantially cheaper option. In the new year, an employee switching from that particular option to the staff model HMO would have to pay $4 (individual) or $12 (family) more per month; switching to the new POS plan would cost such an employee $9 (individual) or $20 (family) more in monthly premiums. Would this be a burden on the lower-paid staff? Which option would the participants in the canceled plans pick? Would the results help ease the adverse selection problems?

After considering these issues, the advisory group stayed with its preliminary evaluation and recommended that that option be adopted. The organization's senior management agreed.

*Implementation*

Once the decision was made, both the organization's staff and the staff of the selected health plan went to work to meet the tight time table for informing employees, conducting the yearly open enrollment period, processing the results, and delivering membership identification cards and other necessary materials needed to make sure benefits would be available January 1. In developing information for employees about the new program, the communications work team posed all the hard questions they could imagine. Human resources staff then drafted answers. The work team also came up with the initial format for the main communications document. When it had produced a complete draft, the team convened a focus group to critique the document. The revised document was reviewed by the new carrier, revised again, and distributed to employees.

Over 30 employee education sessions were scheduled after employees had a chance to read the information on the new program. Approximately 75 percent of the total employee group attended one or another of the sessions. The questions they asked were generally straightforward. The most frequent questions were about how the primary care gatekeeper arrangement really worked, what the extra cost sharing for out-of-network services would be in various cases, and how the preventive dental benefits and mail-order prescription drug program worked.

In general, employee response was more positive than expected. Most sessions produced one or two "loaded" questions that individuals clearly expected to be awkward but that were, in fact, based on misunderstandings of the new plan and were easily addressed. However, in one session, several participants were openly hostile and prepared to be disruptive with questions about coverage restrictions that particularly affected them. Even that session concluded smoothly enough because the justification for the coverage restrictions had been carefully considered early in the planning process and could be clearly explained. Following the education sessions, the human resources and insurer staff thought employees understood the basics of the program but would undoubtedly be calling with many further questions as the program was implemented.

The results of the open enrollment were encouraging given the objective of reconstructing the risk pool. The new POS plan attracted about 75 percent of employees who chose coverage (18 percent declined coverage, about the same as previously), with the remaining 25 percent in the staff model HMO. Analysis of the decisions by the former IPA members showed that 90 percent elected the new option instead of switching to the somewhat less costly staff model HMO or to a family member's plan.

One of the first major challenges the organization faced once the enrollment process was completed involved individuals hospitalized when the change in health benefits occurred. The new insurer and the organization's human resources staff had agreed in advance to negotiate benefits for these individuals so that they received the benefits that would have applied under their old plan. The new plan was surprisingly accommodating, and a total of 11 cases were handled in this way. All the affected employees were satisfied with the decisions.

During the first three months after the new plan went into effect, the human resources staff fielded a lot of questions, most of which they referred to the health plan's service representatives. Only a few employees complained that the responses to their questions or complaints were not satisfactory.

The most serious early problem resulted from changes in the network of primary care physicians that occurred after the directory of participating physicians had been published. Twelve employees had designated physicians who were not accepting new patients or had dropped out of the network entirely. Even worse, some of the latter physicians or their staffs made disparaging comments about the network, apparently as their "parting shots." Other early complaints involved slow claims payment, the complexity of the prescription drug program (which was administered separately), and the fact that enrollees did not get their own copies of the list of participating specialists to consult if they wanted to approach their primary care physician for referral to a specific specialist.

Informal feedback on the new plan is now generally good, with more positive than negative comments. The new plan is also proving attractive to new staff. Having passed the initial shakedown period, the organization is waiting for its first reports on plan utilization and claims expenses. For the first year the switch to the new health benefit program has meant a slightly lower yearly increase in the organization's health benefit costs than would have occurred if the previous plans had been retained. Whether the program will stabilize rates over the long term (and keep them lower than they were in the late 1980s) is more a question than a clear expectation.

The human resources staff has not undertaken an explicit analysis of the costs involved in revising the health benefit program but has estimated that other organization staff had contributed about 100 hours of their time and that the greatest demand on their own time came during the 30 employee education sessions. If the new program proves satisfactory and stable, these costs will not be soon repeated.

## CONTRASTING CASES

For contrast with the case just presented, two very short cases are presented below. One describes the experience and circumstances of a small employer; the other, the experience and circumstances of a large, multistate employer. Both are based on a combination of news stories, personal experiences, and analyses in health policy journals. Again, the cases are illustrative but not in any sense statistically representative of the variety of environments and challenges facing different kinds of employers and employees.

## A Small Employer

In marked contrast to the case of the preceding organization is the case of a small business in an adjacent state. It employs 13 people, experiences little turnover, has no retirees, and relies primarily on its office manager to deal with all of its employee benefits. Four years ago, the company's previous insurer—citing changes in its business strategy—declined to renew coverage for the group. Other insurers said they would cover the group only if it excluded one employee's daughter, who was born with serious birth defects. Her care had cost the previous insurer over $400,000 the previous year. Fortunately, with a considerable amount of time and effort, the firm's owner and office manager were able to arrange for the child to be covered under the state's high-risk pool and thus were able to obtain coverage for the rest of the group. Insurer rejection of particular individuals in a group is a problem rarely if ever faced by large insured groups such as the one described in the preceding case.

Over the past five years, the health benefit costs for the small business have increased by 40 percent overall even though it has markedly reduced benefits, shifted the high-risk child to a state pool, and substantially increased employee contributions to premiums, deductibles, coinsurance, and other cost sharing. In addition, employees have been encouraged to seek coverage under a spouse's health plan if possible, but none have been able to do so. No employee—not even the youngest and lowest paid—has dropped out of the health plan, even though the out-of-pocket costs are high in relation to wages.

The time and emotional energy spent on efforts to arrange and maintain the new health plan have constituted a significant drain on the small organization. Particularly given the paucity of alternatives, it has been infeasible to invest more time to investigate whether the organization's insurer was doing anything (beyond recommending higher employee cost sharing and avoiding sick individuals) to contain health care costs, much less monitor quality of care. Likewise, except for trying to answer employees' most basic questions about their health coverage, the office manager has had neither the time nor the skills to help employees become more informed users of health care services.

Some competitors in the area do not offer health benefits and think this business is foolish for doing so. Moreover, there is the worry that health benefit costs might make the difference between surviving and failing if the recession persists or worsens. Nonetheless, after balancing the advantages and disadvantages of offering health benefits, the owner has concluded once again that these benefits have helped to attract and keep the productive and committed employees who have maintained the firm's reputation for quality. She has resolved to continue her efforts to maintain employee health coverage.

## A Large, Multistate Employer

Yet another contrast can be found in the experience of a large and mature manufacturing company with headquarters in an adjoining county. It has 71,000 employees and worksites in 17 states with from 6 to 6,000 workers at each site. The ratio of active workers to retirees is about 2.5 to 1, which makes the cost of retiree benefits a major issue, particularly compared to more recently established competitors who have few retirees.

The company is completely self-insured—primarily for financial reasons, but partly to avoid the complexities of dealing with 17 different sets of state-mandated benefits and providers and other requirements. Thirty percent of the work force is unionized, and the company has separate health plans for its union and nonunion work forces. Across all its worksites, it has 51 HMOs, down from 67 two years ago, and the company has been interested in consolidating the number and management of the remaining plans insofar as possible. The company operates on-site clinics at six sites that provide routine physical examinations and care for some injuries and illnesses. It has considered expanding the clinics' role but has put that question aside for now.

The company has several full-time staff involved in managing the company's program, and various senior executives also must devote some of their time to program review and decisionmaking. Staff rely heavily on outside consultants for a wide range of advice and analytic services. Company executives or union leaders participate in business coalitions in seven communities or states. Bargaining with unionized employees over characteristics of the last major health program changes took 11 months, and the changes provoked considerable contention. The company's unionized competitors in its major line of business were offering comparable benefits, but its nonunionized competitors had plans with much more employee cost sharing.

In locales where the company has several thousand employees, its utilization and cost data can be more extensively and reliably analyzed than in locales with a few dozen or a few hundred employees. One characteristic of its work force is clear: the average age of employees has risen because of layoffs that hit harder among younger workers. Age also figures in another finding: the company's indemnity plan has a higher average age at all work sites than do the available HMOs.

The company's interest in programs tailored to its complex characteristics was reflected in the size of the RFP for the health program just instituted. The RFP was four times the thickness of the document for the organization described in the core case study. The RFP went into great detail on the data reports the company wanted. In addition, the request asked for a nurse hotline, centers of excellence for heart transplants, a high-risk pregnancy program, and a mail-order prescription drug benefit as well as other special programs. The RFP also described how the new indemnity plan would have to relate to several programs that were contracted for separately, in particular, a separate mental health PPO. Although staff believe they may be able to document the cost and some other consequences of the new drug and pregnancy programs, they suspect that many of the strategies they have adopted have redistributed rather than saved expenditures. Some programs have, they believe, cut inappropriate hospital care, but they wonder whether that reduction, too, has been offset by more inappropriate out-of-hospital care.

The company has not yet formally considered comprehensively revamping its offerings of HMOs and other network-based health plans, but it plans to assess various options, including a reduction in the number of HMOs, contracts with one or more HMO networks that could cover most company locations, and conversion of the basic indemnity plan into a POS plan. Such changes would, however, involve another set of negotiations with the unions and would also require coordination with the companywide plan just instituted.

The company's human resources staff sees its current activities as part of a continuing process of evaluation, action, reassessment, and adjustment—a process that has grown decidedly more complex and demanding over the last decade and promises to become more so. When these activities periodically come to the attention of the chief executive officer he usually expresses dismay, complaining that "widget builders shouldn't try to be health care managers" and that other employers—and his staff—are "fooling themselves if they think they can contain health care costs." Still, for the time being, he is not willing to join the business leaders who have endorsed one or another of the health care reforms that would limit or eliminate the employer role in health benefit management.

## CONSEQUENCES FOR EMPLOYEES

As is obvious from the above discussion, the role of the employee in health benefit management is shaped by employers' decisions about the overall design of health benefit programs. Still, employees often have an array of important decisions to make and responsibilities to manage. They may need to adhere to managed care requirements, understand complex coverage rules, and choose among competing health plans with different features and rules.

Such tasks, of course, are not limited to health coverage that is employment based, although they can be made more variable by employers' decisions. To cite a foreign case in point, the Netherlands is adopting a "managed competition" program that would provide Dutch citizens with structured choices among health plans but would require little if any involvement from employers. To illustrate with a domestic example, Medicare coverage policy is far from simple, and claims filing can be a tedious and complex chore, particularly because the elderly use more services than the nonelderly and therefore have more details to track. Also, Medicare beneficiaries in many areas can choose to enroll in selected network health plans (mainly HMOs) and thus may face the same benefits and burdens of choice as do those covered by employment-based benefits.

If employees can choose among health plans, they, in principle, would evaluate which option appears the most financially advantageous given their expected need for health care in the coming year. From year to year, employees can take strategic advantage of health plan differences, for example, selecting a plan with good vision benefits one year and a plan with restorative as well as preventive dental services the next year. A planned baby or the onset of a serious illness could change the calculus considerably. Chapter 5 discusses the consequences of such choices for health plan risk pools.

Table 4.6 lists tasks, responsibilities, and decisions that commonly face U.S. workers who receive health benefits through their employment. Again, none is unique to an employment-based system, but the overall complexity and variability are almost certainly greater than what faces workers in other advanced industrial nations. That variability can have positive or negative consequences.

The case studies in this chapter suggest the kinds of experiences that distinguish employment-based health benefits from most health benefit systems. For example, all employees working for the organization featured in the core case study except those enrolled in the staff model HMO had to switch from one of four different health plans to a new plan with coverage, procedures, and responsibilities either entirely new to them or similar but not identical to rules under their previous plan. Some had to look for new physicians and to cope with a plan change in the midst of an illness. If any of the case study organizations hired someone from one of the other organizations, that employee would find some—maybe a great many—changes in his or her health benefit program. One of the advantages of some union plans covering multiple employers is that they maintain common as well as continuous benefits for members switching from one participating employer to another.

To facilitate informed decisionmaking by employees and to assist them with questions and problems, employers such as the one described in the core case study may invest considerable resources in explaining health plan features and intervening with health plans when workers run into difficulties with claims and other matters. To the degree they do this, they serve as a kind of support and advocacy mechanism for health plan enrollees that Medicare beneficiaries and individual purchasers of insurance typically lack.

**TABLE 4.6**   Possible Tasks, Responsibilities, and Decisions for Employees

*Understanding Health Benefit Program Offered by Employer*
  • Before making an employment decision
  • After starting work
  • Before using health care services
  • Keeping track of program changes

*Evaluating Health Plan Options If Employer Offers a Choice*
  • Reading plan descriptions
  • Identifying differences and trade-offs related to scope and depth of coverage, restrictions on access to health care providers, quality of network health plan providers, premium and out-of-pocket costs, convenience
  • Weighing the value of choice of provider in light of individual and family circumstances (e.g., health status, residence, other family coverage, tolerance for risk, existing physician relationships)
  • Determining whether to change plans at next opportunity based on satisfaction with the quality of service, need for care, and other factors

*Using Health Services in Accord with Plan Requirements*
  • Understanding restrictions on choice of physician or other provider
  • Selecting primary care or gatekeeper physician, if required
  • Obtaining referrals or approval for selected services, through primary care or gatekeeper physician or through direct contact with plan utilization review entity
  • Negotiating with gatekeeper or plan in event of disagreement or error
  • Seeking employer assistance with problems, providing feedback

*Filing Claims If Required by Health Plan*
  • Determining what services are covered under what conditions
  • Tracking expenses and services
  • Completing and submitting claims forms with required documentation
  • Monitoring plan payments for submitted claims
  • Following up on denied claims, problems, or questions
  • Seeking employer assistance with problems, providing feedback

---

The willingness and capacity of employers to provide such assistance vary considerably.

For many workers a positive consequence of employment-based benefits may be health plans that are better tailored to fit variations in work force characteristics and community resources than would be likely under a simpler, more uniform system. Some plans are undoubtedly more generous and others less generous than a national plan would likely be.[4]

The link between health benefits and employment also extends—for

---

[4]It should be noted that virtually all employment-based plans, unlike Medicare, cover outpatient prescription drugs.

good and ill—the potential scope of employer interest and involvement in the personal lives and health status of employees, potential employees, and employees' family members. On the positive side, employers may be motivated to take constructive steps to influence worker health status because they believe the result will be lower health benefit costs as well as improved productivity, reduced workers' compensation claims, and advantages in retaining and recruiting workers. As summarized in Chapter 3, the steps they take may include health education, screening, fitness, nutrition, and other programs.

Less positively, employees may worry that employers might misuse information about their health status (or that of their family members) in making layoff decisions or by otherwise discriminating against them because of the economic burden they pose to the company health plan. Employees may, in some cases, be reluctant to seek needed health services for fear of such misuse or may pressure physicians to list nonthreatening diagnoses on insurance records. The Americans with Disabilities Act is supposed to protect workers with disabilities from discrimination, but how the act will be interpreted and enforced is not yet clear. In addition, proving that health benefit costs were a factor in, say, a layoff could be difficult. Chapter 5 discusses this legislation further.

Although not directed narrowly at employment-based health benefits, the survey designed by the committee and the Employee Benefit Research Institute to explore questions of interest in this study provides some useful perspectives on individual experiences with and attitudes about health benefits generally and the employers' role specifically. Key points are summarized below, and a fuller report is provided in Appendix A.

• People rated their current health benefits positively, with 27 percent describing them as excellent, 46 percent good, 20 percent fair, and 6 percent poor. Only 7 percent said they would rather have more cash and fewer health benefits, whereas 20 percent would prefer more benefits to cash.

• For 60 percent of those surveyed, their health benefits had not changed in the preceding few years. For 24 percent, they had gotten worse, but for 16 percent they had improved.

• Of those who had access to employment-based benefits (nearly three-quarters of respondents), about half had a choice among health plans and half did not.

• A substantial majority expressed confidence that their employer was contracting with the best available health plan.

• One in 10 respondents thought that the employer is in the best position to influence the cost of care or make decisions about quality of care. Over half thought individuals could best make such quality decisions, with one-third citing government. In contrast, 28 percent thought government is in the best position to influence costs, 23 percent cited doctors, 20 percent nominated insurers, and only 14 percent mentioned individuals.

• Eleven percent of respondents said that they or a family member had foregone a job opportunity or stayed in a job because of health benefits. Those reporting such "job lock" said that another employer either did not offer health benefits, provided less generous benefits, offered a plan that would be too costly, or restricted coverage for preexisting conditions. The young, less educated, and middle class were the most likely to be affected.

• A minority of respondents reported one or more negative experiences with cost management programs. Seventeen percent thought they had experienced unreasonable hassles or delays, 16 percent said they had to receive care from a physician they would not have chosen, and 9 percent thought they had been denied needed care.

• About 1 respondent in 10 said most of their health plan was hard to understand, over one-third said some of it was hard to understand, and half said it was easy.

A system that links health benefits and employment clearly adds an additional layer of complexity and variability for both employer and employee over that which would exist with a unified national health insurance system. In comparison with the current market for individually purchased insurance, the employment-based system increases the burden on employers. However, it almost certainly reduces the decisionmaking and monitoring burden on most employees, although it can increase complexity or pose problems under some circumstances (e.g., part-time work and change of employment). The consequences for employees of employment-based health benefits may be both positive and negative, depending on the circumstances, philosophies, and choices of specific employers and on the leverage employees have within different organizations.

## CONSEQUENCES FOR PRACTITIONERS AND PROVIDERS

Twenty years ago, or even 10 years ago, most physicians, hospitals, and other health care providers might have kept track of Medicare, Medicaid, and Blue Cross and Blue Shield plan requirements, filed information on the specific health benefit plans of dominant local employers (e.g., steel or auto companies), and—less commonly—contracted with one or two network health plans. These arrangements were not necessarily simple. They might involve complicated cost reimbursement or usual, customary, and prevailing reimbursement methodologies, auditing requirements, variations in coverage, and utilization review requirements. In 1959, even before Medicare, an official with the Kaiser Foundation Health Plan could note that "'it may be fashionable in some quarters to speak of the third party in medical care as if it were a social disease'" (Weissman, quoted in Somers and Somers, 1961, p. 218).

Now, however, the rapid growth of network health plans, managed care indemnity plans, community coalitions, and employer-specific programs means that a health care practitioner or provider may have to deal with hundreds of different health plans and related organizations with different requirements and administrative procedures (IOM, 1989, 1992a). In addition, as large, multistate employers seek benefit uniformity for their employees, they may unintentionally disrupt uniformity within particular communities and complicate the administration of local medical practice and the relationships between patient and practitioner.

No other nation appears to have a system that is as complex for health care providers as that of the United States. Although many features of employment-based health benefits have been significantly shaped by insurers, public programs, and other factors, pressure from employers for action—particularly for cost containment—has been an important stimulus with respect to the intensity of effort, the pursuit of new strategies, and their tailoring to fit employers' preferences and circumstances. What the distinctive pluralism of the U.S. health care financing and delivery system appears to do is to

• multiply both the number and the variety of parties with which providers have to deal;

• expand the diversity of (1) payment procedures and levels, (2) criteria for assessing appropriate care, and (3) information demands and formats for providing that information;

• increase the probability that the office and other staff of physicians will be confused about different plan requirements and that they will encounter health plan, review organization, or other staff who do not interpret or apply these requirements appropriately;

• add further pressure for detailed oversight and questioning of practitioners' judgment and increase the opportunity for friction between patients and health care practitioners or providers;

• complicate efforts to maintain continuity of care for chronically ill and other patients; and

• intensify practitioners' concerns about the confidentiality of patients' medical information and the consequences of breaches in confidentiality.

The following set of complaints from an internist is typical, although not as colorfully phrased as the earlier quote from the Kaiser executive:

> Almost every day, our office receives missives from several of [the 450 plans they deal with], dictating new regulations, guidelines or procedures. We're expected to digest and follow them immediately. . . . At 8:00 a.m., I asked our office manager to obtain urgent referrals for [two managed care

patients with arm fractures requiring orthopedic referrals]. She made 20 calls to the HMO, the patients, and several orthopedists before finding one with the requisite affiliation who could see the patients that day. . . . Pacific HMO patients with hyperlipidemia will be treated one way; PruNet hyperlipidemics, another. And if those same patients switch to Blue Cross CaliforniaCare HMO, they'll get plugged into yet a third protocol. (Bodenheimer, 1992, pp. 29, 30)

Their bitter and understandable complaints notwithstanding, most U.S. medical organizations do not favor adoption of such simpler systems as those found in England and Canada, where network health plans and managed care requirements have not proliferated. One fear is that any system dominated by a single payer will be able to more effectively limit the resources going to the health sector, thus reducing incomes, investments in new technology, opportunities for specialized practice, and other advantages experienced by U.S. health care practitioners and providers. The ever-increasing level of complexity, growing restrictions on consumer choice, and the decreasing reliance on professional judgment may, however, be causing many practitioners to change their outlook. On balance, complexity and diversity may be viewed by others as a lesser burden—and one more susceptible to provider influence—than uniform government dictates about payment methodologies, appropriate care, and similar matters.

Public and private insurers have periodically been pressed by health care providers to agree on simpler and more uniform administrative procedures. In addition, some supporters of health care reform have argued vigorously that the nonuniformity of the current system wastes as much as $100 billion per year that could be saved under a single public program (Woolhandler and Himmelstein, 1991), although others have questioned these assumptions (Danzon, 1992, but see also Barer and Evans, 1992, and the discussion in Chapter 3 of this report). The most recent simplification initiative involved a summit called by the Secretary of the U.S. Department of Health and Human Services. Agreements were reached among some large payers, and legislation was proposed to reduce paperwork and increase consistency of claims administration rules (McIlrath, 1992).

Furthermore, an increasing number of physicians are simplifying their practice by abandoning fee-for-service medical practice and contracts with multiple health plans and going to work for prepaid group practices and other integrated systems. By virtue of their recruitment processes, their use of salaried or similar reimbursement methods, peer influence, and other characteristics, these organizations may use less intrusive means of constraining discretion and costs.

In any event, an end to employment-based health benefits in the United States would almost certainly not mean an end to all oversight. This seems ensured by the public interest in accountability, performance and outcome assessment, and cost containment. Depending on the particular course taken, however, health care reform might greatly reduce the volume and variability of demands made on practitioners.

## A NOTE ON EMPLOYERS' LEGAL LIABILITY
## FOR MANAGED CARE

When employers adopt programs to review the necessity and appropriateness of medical services provided to specific patients or to direct employees to specific health care providers, they may expose themselves to claims that their programs have caused medical harm to individuals (APPWP, 1991; Holoweiko, 1992; Kent, 1992a). To date, the claims of medical harm or negligence that have been raised against insurers, utilization management organizations, HMOs, and similar arrangements have not yet directly involved employers, but as the degree of direct employer involvement in managing health benefits increases so does the potential for litigation.

Although case law is limited, it seems reasonably clear that a utilization review firm, an HMO, or even an employer—depending on applicability and interpretation of the Employee Retirement Income Security Act of 1974 (ERISA)—could be "held legally accountable when medically inappropriate decisions result from defects in the design or implementation of cost containment mechanisms" (*Wickline* v. *California*, 228 Cal. Rptr. 661 [1986], p. 670). For a particular party involved in a utilization management program to be held liable for medical harm to a patient, legal experts say that four questions must be answered positively (Miller, 1991). Does the party have a duty of care to patients? Has that duty been breached? Was there injury? Was the breach of duty a proximate cause of the injury? Litigation has, to date, raised more questions than answers about how the second and fourth questions will be evaluated and answered (Gosfield, 1991; Miller, 1991; IOM, 1992a).

An employer that purchases utilization management services from an insurer or independent vendor would seem to be less directly linked to individual medical care decisions than one that engages in such activities directly. Conversely, an employer that directly evaluates and contracts with health care providers for services to employees may be viewed as more proximately involved than one that contracts with an HMO. In any case, the more directly involved employers become in influencing patient care and choice of provider, the more they risk liability if they fail to exercise "good management, good judgment, good faith, and good documentation" (IOM, 1989).

ERISA, however, is a major barrier to legal claims of corporate negligence even if the criteria for negligence described above are met (Costich, 1990-1991; Holoweiko, 1992; Moses, 1992; and Appendix B to this report).

This legislation has discouraged suits arising from retrospective denial of claims because it precludes the award of punitive damages and limits compensation to the amount of benefits denied, which tends to be relatively small compared with amounts typically sought for punitive damages or physical harm.

Recently, a federal circuit court held that ERISA preempted a negligence claim against a utilization review company on grounds that the firm's activities related to an ERISA-covered employee benefit plan (*Corcoran* v. *United Healthcare, Inc. and Blue Cross and Blue Shield of Alabama, Inc.*, 1992 U.S. App. LEXIS 14621). The court noted, however, that it was troubled by the result, which involved a fatal case of fetal distress. The court went on to suggest that congressional review of ERISA was warranted to see whether it continued to safeguard the interests of employees in this area.

In the event that an employer is sued for financial losses (e.g., loss of income) resulting from medical harm attributable to employer imprudence, it is possible that a court could be persuaded that certain employer actions might be treated as a breach of fiduciary responsibility for which some compensation for the financial losses would be possible. A federal appellate court affirmed that a self-insured employer's decision to terminate benefits for hospital care (following a judgment by an outside utilization management firm) constituted an abuse of its discretion as a fiduciary because the case review was inadequate (*Salley* v. *E.I. DuPont de Nemours & Co.*, 966 F.2d 1011, 1992 U.S. App. LEXIS 16850). In this case, the patient's parents kept the child in the hospital until proper alternative care could be arranged and sued only to recover the cost of the hospital stay. No medical harm or costs for care resulting from such harm were involved. If they had been, a precedent for recovery of these costs might be found in an earlier decision by a federal appeals court to uphold monetary damages under ERISA for an individual who suffered financial losses after his pension fund trustee had ignored an order regarding the treatment of certain assets (*Warren* v. *Society National Bank*, 905 F.2d 9975 [6th Cir. 1990]).

The Department of Labor has sued the fiduciaries of a pension plan for not investigating the soundness of the company it selected to provide annuities for plan participants (Moses, 1992). This action suggests that it is prudent for self-insured organizations to investigate the soundness of firms they use to administer their health benefit program. Both the utilization management and HMO industries are moving toward standard-setting procedures and structures that should be useful to employers in such investigations.

## CONCLUSION

In the United States, diversity is a fundamental feature of employment-based health benefits and health insurance markets, one that brings a mix of benefits and burdens to employers, employees, and health care providers. Within broadly typical patterns, differences in region, industry, philosophy, and other factors can contribute to significant variation in the number and types of health plans offered, the extent of coverage, the role of employees in decisionmaking, and other factors. The three hypothetical organizations featured in this chapter illustrate what can be involved in managing health benefits and highlight the importance of company size as a variable affecting needs, resources, and options for health benefit management.

Certain proposals for health care reform would undoubtedly reduce diversity by establishing a single national health plan, creating highly regulated competitive systems with fewer approved health plans, or moving decisionmaking responsibilities from the employer to the individual. Most proposals retain a financing role for employers, and some would permit employers a supplemental or facilitating role. In examining how individual and organizational decisions in a market-based system can create problems of biased risk selection and risk segmentation, the next chapter provides further perspective on diversity in health benefits and its consequences.

# ADDENDUM

### Excerpt from the Request for Proposal,
### "Contract for Managed Health Care Plan," Issued by the
### Office of Human Resources

Issuance Date: August 09, 199-
Closing Date: August 30, 199-

(The organization) is seeking proposals from qualified firms interested in providing the services detailed in the attached solicitation. The objective of this solicitation is to replace the current comprehensive medical plan maintained by (the organization) with a new high-quality, cost-effective managed health care program for its employees and their dependents. The solicitation consists of this cover letter and the following documents:

| Section No. | Title |
|---|---|
| I | RFP Instructions and Conditions [omitted here] |
| II | Current Health Plan Coverage/Rate and Claims History [second part omitted here] |
| III | Proposed Plan Design |
| IV | Questionnaire |
| V | Selection Criteria |
| Attachment A | Appendix [omitted here] |
| Attachment B | Representations and Certifications [omitted here] |

If a proposal is submitted by your organization, it must be presented in accordance with the attached solicitation and received no later than 4:00 p.m. local time on the closing date indicated above. All proposals must be submitted in sealed envelopes and addressed as follows: (organization address).

The material presented in this solicitation represents the complete set of proposal specifications that will be needed by your company to underwrite and administer the benefit program for (the organization). Included is information that describes the current and proposed plan design, historical claims data, rate history, and census information. Also included are a zip code listing, specific questions regarding your provider network, and complete instructions for responding to this proposal request.

Issuance of this solicitation does not constitute an award commitment, nor does it obligate (the organization) to pay for costs incurred in the preparation and submission of a proposal. Any award resulting from this solicitation shall be construed under the laws of (state). Offerors should retain for their records one copy of any and all enclosures that accompany their proposals. If there are any questions concerning this solicitation, please call (staff contacts) at (phone number).

## Section II
## Current Health Plan Coverage

I. A census of plan participants with zip codes is included in the appendix of this RFP [not included in this excerpt]. In general, coverage in the various plans is as follows:

|  | Individual | Family | Total |
|---|---|---|---|
| Indemnity | 375 | 250 | 625 |
| All HMOs | 410 | 265 | 675 |
| Waived | NA | NA | 200 |
| Total Active |  |  | 1500 |
| Indemnity Retirees |  |  |  |
| Under 65 | 10 | 15 | 25 |
| 65 and over | 150 | 95 | 245 |

### Current Indemnity Plan Design

*Carrier*                     Company Z

*Funding*                     Fully insured—dividend experience rated

*Eligible Classes*            Salaried employees regularly scheduled to work half-time or more for at least 6 months

*Eligibility Date*            Immediate

*Deductible*
  Individual                  $200
  Family                      $400

*Coinsurance*
  Inpatient Hospital Charges  80% (after deductible)
  Inpatient Physician Charges 80% (after deductible)
  Second Surgical Opinions;   100% (no deductible)
    Preoperative Testing;
    Outpatient Surgery;
    Birthing Center Charges
  Emergency Accident          100% (no deductible) for outpatient expenses incurred due to an accident

| | |
|---|---|
| Convalescent Facility | 100% (no deductible) |
| Inpatient Surgical | 80% (after deductible) |
| Lab and X-ray | 100% (no deductible) |
| Home Health Care | 100% (no deductible) |
| Other Medical Expenses | 80% (after deductible) |
| Mental/Nervous & Substance Abuse* | |
|   Inpatient | Same as covered medical expense |
|   Outpatient | 50% (after deductible); $50,000 lifetime maximum |

| | |
|---|---|
| *Out-of-Pocket Maximum* (including the deductible) | |
|   Individual | $1,000 |
|   Family | $1,500 |
| | |
| *Lifetime Maximum* | None |

## Section III
## Proposed Plan Design

| | ALTERNATIVE: | |
|---|---|---|
| | I | II |
| *In Network* | | |
| Copay (office visits) | $10 | $5 |
| Coinsurance (outpatient surgery, hospital inpatient, X-ray & lab) | 90% | 100% |
| Out-of-Pocket Maximum | $1,000/$2,000 | $750/$1,500 |
| Coinsurance (mental and nervous/ substance abuse)** | 90% (50% for outpatient)** | 100% (50% for outpatient)** |
| Prescription Drug Card | | |
|   Generic | $5 | $5 |
|   Brand name | $8 | $8 |
| *Out of Network* | | |
| Deductible | $400/$800 | $350/$700 |
| Coinsurance | 70% (50% for outpatient mental and nervous/ substance abuse)** | 75% (50% for outpatient mental and nervous/ substance abuse)** |

---

*Expenses do not count toward out-of-pocket maximum.

**No expenses for mental and nervous/substance abuse count toward the out-of-pocket. Outpatient mental and nervous/substance abuse subject to a $50,000 lifetime maximum.

|                                                |                                                              |                                                              |
| ---------------------------------------------- | ------------------------------------------------------------ | ------------------------------------------------------------ |
| Out-of-Pocket Maximum (including deductible)   | $2,500/$5,000                                                | $2,000/$4,000                                                |
| *Outside Service Area*                         |                                                              |                                                              |
| Deductible                                     | $200/$400                                                    | $200/$400                                                    |
| Coinsurance                                    | 80% (50% for outpatient mental and nervous/ substance abuse)* | 80% (50% for outpatient mental and nervous/ substance abuse)* |
| Out-of-Pocket Maximum (including deductible)   | $1,000/$2,000                                                | $1,000/$2,000                                                |

In preparing your proposal, please note/provide the following:

• Only a point-of-service PPO will be considered; (the organization) wants employees to choose in-network versus out-of-network benefits at the time health services are needed as opposed to choosing one or the other at open enrollment.

• Retiree coverage is on a Medicare carve-out basis.

• Current pregnant IPA participants will be allowed to continue receiving care from their IPA obstetrician.

• For alternative I, provide the cost impact of decreasing the in-network out-of-pocket maximum to $750/$1,500.

• For each alternative, provide the cost impact of changing the prescription drug benefit to

— $8 generic/$10 brand name co-pays with card.

— a card with a $100 deductible and 80 percent coinsurance.

— no prescription drug card; benefits will be paid at the coinsurance level after a $100 deductible has been satisfied (this counts against the out-of-network deductible).

• For each alternative and for all plan designs (in-network, out-of-network, outside service area), provide the cost impact of limiting the mental and nervous inpatient benefit to 30 days per confinement and the outpatient benefit to $2,600 per year. Will either of these alternatives be in conflict with your interpretation of the (state) law?

• State which, if any, preventive dental services (routine cleanings and exams once every 6 months) are offered through your standard network benefits. If preventive dental services are not standard, provide the cost to add this coverage and outline the design.

---

*No expenses for mental and nervous/substance abuse count toward the out-of-pocket. Outpatient mental and nervous/substance abuse subject to a $50,000 lifetime maximum.

## Assumptions and Exhibits

Please note that the attached exhibits [omitted here] are to be completed for each of the following funding approaches and alternatives below:

1. Fully insured—dividend experience rated.
2. Minimum premium.

The assumptions to be used:

1. Cash flow exhibits are to be completed for each line of coverage separately.

2. Rate all options on a zero dividend basis, net of commissions.

3. Quote fully insured dividend experience-rated coverages with IBNR reserves. Minimum premium should be quoted with (the organization) holding the reserves and alternatively with your company holding the reserves.

4. Provide costs for $85,000, $100,000, and $115,000 specific stop-loss levels with 110 percent and 120 percent aggregate stop-loss. Also provide costs for aggregate stop-loss only.

5. Assume that the effective date of coverage is January 1, 199-, and that the existing carrier will administer IBNR liability.

6. Use the present enrollment from the census as the average number of employees for the bid.

7. Assume that there will be direct claims administration and certification of eligibility.

8. A separate zip code listing of employees is included in the census, which must be matched to determine the viability of your provider network. Provide a comparison chart showing where your network(s) matches our population.

9. Quote *two*-tier medical rates.

10. Indicate any start-up costs, network access fees, and capitation fees separately.

[exhibits omitted]


# Section IV
# Questionnaire

Although your proposal may contain much of the following information, please prepare answers to the following questions, in the order in which they are asked. Please restate the question when providing your response.

*General*

1. Describe any variation in the proposed benefits that *you* would require. Please give the reason(s) for any variations.

2. From what office(s) will the general administration of this case be handled? Who would be assigned to service the account? Would a dedicated claims payor be assigned to the group? Provide names, titles, addresses, and phone numbers.

3. Please confirm in writing that no employee or covered dependent will lose benefits in switching to your program and that the actively-at-work requirement will be waived for all participants covered under the prior plan, including HMO participants and COBRAs. Also, please indicate how you would propose to handle "deductible credits" during the implementation phase if the change in carrier were made off anniversary.

4. What are the applicable conversion privileges for medical benefits? What is the cost to the policyholder for each conversion? Describe the provisions of the proposed conversion coverage.

5. How much advance notice would you require before taking over this account? Describe how you would handle implementation, and detail any additional expenses involved and indicate whether these expenses are included on your bid sheets. It is expected that individuals from your company will be available to aid in implementing the program.

6. (The organization) must have the plan booklets by (date). If you are notified of your selection by (date), can you meet this deadline?

7. Please provide a detailed list of your standard coverage exclusions (e.g., injuries sustained while committing a felony) and limitations (e.g., number of home health visits, number of days for hospice). Specifically identify your standard coverage for

- transplant benefits (heart, kidney, cornea)
- hospice and home health care
- durable medical equipment.

*Financial*

8. How long will you guarantee your proposal rates before implementation? The first renewal will be January 1, 199-.

9. What is the maximum period for which you guarantee rates?

10. In the event of a master policy termination, either on or off anniversary, what are the penalties (if any) to the policyholder?

*Claims Administration*

11. From what office(s) will claims be paid? How many processors would be involved in servicing this account? Is a toll-free phone number available for claims questions? What is the average wait time for the month of June at the proposed claims office?

12. Please provide a sample of the statistical claims data that are normally provided as part of the "standard fee." What additional types of management reports are available and at what cost?

13. What is your turnaround time in the claims office(s) that would be used by this client for non-coordination of benefits (COB) or otherwise "clean" claims? What percentage of claims would you expect to fall into this category?

14. What are your companywide COB and subrogation savings as a percentage of incurred claims? Detail these savings by type of coverage, i.e., Medicare, workers compensation, other carrier liability, etc.

15. Please list those services provided as part of your "standard fee." Do you provide complete Form 5500 information, as well as assistance with other governmental forms?

16. To what extent is your claims payment system computerized? How long has the current system been in operation?

17. Does your database maintain eligibility records and family history files?

18. What levels of payment authority have been established for claims examiners? Can an examiner override the claims payment system? If so, is there a review by a second claims examiner (or supervisor)?

19. What methods do you have to ensure that payments are being made to "legitimate providers"? What security safeguards do you have to prevent "in-house" or "out-of-house" fraud?

20. Who is assigned to handle quality control procedures?

21. What percentage of claims are reviewed for accuracy, both before and after payment? Does the dollar level of the claim affect the review process?

22. What types of external audits do you use to check large hospital and medical bills? Do you charge the client for the use of outside audit services? If so, how much do you charge?

23. We may be required to have an outside auditor review your claims-paying procedures. Will this present any problems?

24. Please furnish a copy of the payment explanation form and claims form used by the claimant. Does your adjudication system produce free-form memos requesting additional information? What special procedures are followed when a claim is denied in whole or in part?

25. Will you accept financial responsibility for errors and overpayments made by company personnel in processing claims? Is there a separate charge for this? If so, how much?

26. If employees identify erroneous charges in hospital bills, we would like to share some percentage of the savings with employees. Will this present a problem under the dividend funding arrangement?

*Managed Care Features*

27. Indicate the total number of individuals enrolled in your network in the metropolitan area. Provide information on all your networks nationally.

28. How do you determine your service area (distance from residence zip code?)? Do you allow employees residing outside the service area to use network physicians and hospitals?

29. Please explain your gatekeeper procedures, particularly in light of in-network versus out-of-network plan usage. Are any specific services not included in the network? What benefits are paid if the gatekeeper refers an employee to a specialist who is not in the network?

30. How do you measure patient satisfaction with your providers? How do you handle inquiries and complaints?

31. What goals have you established for the turnaround time from when information reaches you from the provider until a check is cut? What percent of the time do you achieve these goals? Would you consider guaranteeing this service level?

32. How often do you provide employees with updated lists of network providers?

33. What communication materials are available for employees?

34. Are there separate fees for the hospital and/or physician network (network access fee)? Do the access fees vary by size of employer?

35. Is there a charge for utilization review services?

36. In the event of the termination of the plan contract, (the organization) would require access to and the right of ownership of all records. Will this requirement pose a problem for you? If so, how would you propose to resolve that problem?

37. Please include the following documents with your proposal and a brief summary of each:

- sample of the contract that you would want (the organization) to sign
- standard contract with a hospital
- standard contract with a physician
- standard contract (if any) with other health care providers, such as skilled nursing facilities, podiatrists, chiropractors, and urgent care facilities
- physician application form
- samples of standard reports prepared for employers
- samples of custom reports that you have been able to produce for other employers and would be willing to produce for (the organization)
- samples of any feedback reports that you routinely send to your providers

- samples of material that you will use to communicate with your network
- a copy of your most recent financial statement.

*Provider*

38. Is your network hospital or physician based or both? On average, how long are your contracts with each provider (i.e., hospital and physician differentiated)? Are there inflation caps?

39. How many physicians do you have under contract? What is your plan's definition of a primary care physician (general practice, family practice, internal medicine, gynecology, and pediatrics)? How many PCPs do you currently have? How many in your network are specialists? How many are Board certified? Board eligible?

40. What criteria are used to select physicians?

- Board certification
- Board eligible
- Licensed
- Graduate of U.S. medical school
- Credentialing done by practicing physicians in community
- Hospital admitting privileges
- Other

41. Are the physicians (segregate primary care and specialists) paid on a discounted fee-for-service basis, negotiated fees based on a specific diagnosis or service, or on a capitated basis? How often do these levels change? Be specific.

42. What other health care providers do you have under contract? How are these other health care providers reimbursed?

43. Please provide a current directory of all hospitals and physicians under contract.

44. In which additional areas do you expect to have hospitals and physicians under contract by January 1, 199-?

45. What criteria are used to select hospitals? What is the average discount available? How is it determined? Indicate the reimbursement system(s) under which you contract with physicians, specialists, and hospitals to provide services to the covered network population. For each hospital, indicate specific payment arrangement; and for each, estimate percentage reduction from charges:

- full charges only
- discounted charges (specify percentage)
- per diem (specify dollar amount)
- DRGs (specify weights and the dollar amount to be applied to each case)

- capitated rate (specify monthly per individual dollar amount)
- other (please specify method and rate).

In addition, if you propose special consideration for "outlier" patients, show how you propose to define an outlier under each payment system checked and specify the payment amounts proposed.

46. How are lab, X-ray, and mental health services provided by your network?

47. Do you agree not to bill any network patient or his individual guarantor for amounts deemed inappropriate by your plan?

48. What is the average length of participation of your physicians (separately identify PCPs and specialists)? What percent of physicians have left your plan in the last three calendar years? Please complete the following chart:

| | PCPs | | |
|---|---|---|---|
| | 1988 | 1989 | 1990 |
| New | | | |
| Left | | | |
| Net | | | |

49. What are the criteria that hospitals and physicians must meet to continue in your network?

50. What risk (i.e., financial liability) do the providers assume in contracting with your network? Is there a "withhold" provision, and, if so, how does this arrangement work?

51. How much advance notice must the physician or hospital give you if they wish to cancel their contract with you?

52. Do your physician and hospital contracts have a "continuation of care" clause that says that if a physician or hospital cancels or fails to renew their contract, care begun while a network provider will continue to be provided and reimbursed as if a network provider?

53. Provide dollar equivalent reimbursements, in and out of network, for the following CPT codes, assuming zip code (xxxxx):

CPT-4

| | |
|---|---|
| 90020 | Office Visit—Complete |
| 90060 | Office Visit—Initial |
| 70450 | Computerized Axial Tomography—Head |
| 10121 | Incision and Removal of Foreign Body—Complicated |
| 12013 | Repair of Superficial Facial Wounds |
| 25600 | Radial Fracture |
| 31625 | Bronchoscopy |

| 42820 | Tonsillectomy/Adenoidectomy |
| 44950 | Appendectomy |
| 49505 | Inguinal Hernia |
| 71270 | Computerized Axial Tomography—Thorax |
| 71550 | Magnetic Resonance Imaging (MRI)—Chest |

54. Please describe your utilization review (UR) process, including hospital precertification, concurrent review, and large-case management. Do any of these procedures differ for in-network claimants versus out-of-network claimants; for example, who is responsible for handling the precertification in each situation—the physician or the patient?

55. How do you set your criteria to ensure quality of care?

56. What UR procedures do you apply to outpatient care, particularly outpatient surgery and office visits?

57. Describe the effectiveness of your utilization review program including

- average days/1,000 admissions for medical, surgical, maternity, and mental/nervous admissions
- demographics of the book of business supporting these data
- statistical effectiveness of your outpatient review programs.

58. How long do you store utilization data?

59. What normative factors do you use when evaluating a hospital admission or length of stay?

60. How do you control the number of referrals made by your physicians, and how do you encourage them to refer to other network providers?

61. How do you identify providers that are overutilizers or underutilizers, and what do you do once you have identified them?

62. Do providers bear any risk for overutilization? Does the network bear any risk for overutilization?

63. Do you have any programs that specifically address mental health or substance abuse utilization? Please describe these programs.

64. What percent of participating physicians *do not* accept new patients?

65. What do you do to manage prescription drug charges?

## Section V
## Selection Criteria

Information relevant to these criteria may be presented within the normal format of your proposal in response to this RFP. The criteria will be uniformly applied in the evaluation of the proposals.

- availability of a comprehensive range of managed care services providing value, access, quality, and accountability to (the organization)
- ability and efficiency of the administrator to provide quality administrative and claims-processing services
- net cost (cost of services, management of claim cost, retention)
- maximum cost liability
- overall response to the specifications as presented
- the character, reputation, financial condition, and experience of the bidding company.

*Determination of Competitive Range and Contractor Selection*

The competitive range will be determined on the basis of the above evaluation factors and will be made up of all offerors whose proposal has a reasonable chance of being selected for award considering such factors. Award will be made to the responsible offeror whose proposal, conforming to the solicitation, is most advantageous to (the organization), the above factors considered.

# 5

# Risk Selection, Risk Sharing, and Policy

*Some of the . . . controversy reduces to a mundane debate about who will pay for whom and how much.*

Douglas M. MacIntyre, 1962

Biased risk selection is always possible when individuals, employers, or other groups can choose whether or not to buy health coverage or whether to select one health plan instead of another. Unfortunately, this continual exercise of choice—a valued feature of individual liberty and of markets generally—can create both philosophical and practical problems in the health care arena. In particular, it can seriously diminish the degree to which the burden of health care expenses is shared among the well and the ill.

In addition, risk selection can lead health plans to compete for lower-cost enrollees and to avoid higher-cost individuals because the price and profit advantages from such tactics can outweigh the gains to be achieved by cost-effective management of health care and administrative services. Health care costs are highly skewed in their distribution. In any year, perhaps 5 percent of a population will account for 50 percent of expenditures, and 20 percent will account for 80 percent. Thus, any health plan (or employer) that is more successful at avoiding those who are likely to be in the small-group of higher utilizers will have a significant competitive advantage of a particular sort, but not the principal one desired by advocates of market-based strategies for health care reform.

The evolution and current structure of employment-based health benefits and proposals for change are difficult to understand and evaluate without a careful analysis of risk selection. This chapter reviews basic concepts, examines factors contributing to risk selection, considers evidence about its extent, and discusses key policy issues and proposals for managing the unwanted effects of risk selection. The focus is on employer groups, not individual purchasers of health coverage, and on choices among health plans, not the choice to purchase or not purchase coverage.

## BASIC CONCEPTS

As defined in Chapter 1, *biased risk selection* exists (1) when individuals or groups that purchase health coverage differ from nonpurchasers in their likelihood of incurring health care expenses or (2) when those who enroll in competing health plans differ in the level of risk they present to specific plans. The first kind of risk selection primarily involves the market for individual and small-group coverage in which those with higher risks are thought to be more likely than those with lower risks to purchase insurance.[1] The individual and small-group market also suffers from the second form of biased risk selection when higher-risk purchasers seek more generous or flexible coverage than lower-risk purchasers.

In general, because large employers almost universally provide health benefits and have more predictable costs, large groups present fewer problems with risk selection than either individuals or small groups. However, problems can arise in larger groups when they create an internal market by offering employees a choice among health plans and their higher-risk and lower-risk individuals select different plans.

One result of risk selection is risk segmentation, the clustering of individuals at higher and lower risk of incurring health care expenses in different health plans or insurance pools. As noted in Chapter 1, risk segmentation can also occur when insurers experience rate groups on the basis of their claims (cost) history and when larger, less risky employers depart the group insurance market—as most have—in favor of self-insurance.[2]

---

[1]Some suggestive information on differences between enrollees with individual coverage (who must seek out coverage for themselves) and those with group coverage (who have it offered to them as a matter of routine) is available from an insurer who has not used medical underwriting to screen individual purchasers. Independence Blue Cross (Philadelphia), which offers individual coverage without medical underwriting on an open enrollment basis throughout the calendar year for its five-county service area, reports information on both its individual and its group enrollment. For 1987, its individual subscribers were 6 years older on average than its group subscribers, had a 46 percent higher hospital admission rate, and incurred costs that were 60 percent higher (Independence Blue Cross and Pennsylvania Blue Shield, 1988). Fifty-five percent of the individual subscribers were age 50 or over, compared with 35 percent of the group subscribers.

[2]Risk segmentation also can occur when individual choice is quite limited. As noted in Chapter 1, risk segmentation among the German sickness funds occurs because plans draw or are assigned their membership from occupational and other groups that differ in age, income, and other risk factors (Wysong and Abel, 1990).

When a health plan, insurer, or employer attracts a less risky and less costly group than the average (or than its competitors), it has experienced *favorable selection*. A plan that attracts a more risky and costly membership has *unfavorable* or *adverse selection*. If the cost of health coverage is linked to the risk level of the pool of covered individuals, premiums for those who find themselves in groups with unfavorable selection will be higher, even if their own risk of medical care expense is low. The financial incentive then is for these lower-risk individuals to exit, making the remaining pool even more expensive, perhaps so expensive that even those most in need of the coverage cannot pay the premium and the plan fails.

Some argue that the solution to adverse selection is better information, so that everyone pays his or her exact risk-rated premium based on detailed personal information about health status, health behavior, work environments, and other factors affecting the risk of medical care expenses. This approach reflects a value judgment that the young and the healthy should not have to subsidize the old and the unhealthy (i.e., that risk segmentation is fair and desirable), a judgment with which the majority of this committee disagrees. For technical and practical reasons, perfect risk rating is unlikely if not impossible, so adverse selection related to information imperfections would still exist. (As described later in this chapter, technical problems also affect strategies to compensate for or discourage selection by risk adjusting employers' or governments' [not individuals'] payments to health plans.)

The policy problem with risk selection is not that it can put adversely affected health plans out of business. Rather, risk selection is a concern because it encourages socially unproductive competition based on risk selection rather than on cost-effective management of care for the ill and injured (GAO, 1991e; Hall, 1992; Light, 1992).[3] Any strategy of health care reform that is based on competition and choices about health coverage should address these problems, and several options are discussed later in this chapter. Design of an appropriate strategy depends on an understanding of some of the factors that produce selection and the degree to which the insurers, the insured, and policymakers can manipulate them to exacerbate or control risk selection (Feldman and Dowd, 1991; GAO, 1991e; Light, 1992).

---

[3]The charge that competition in accident and health insurance tends to focus on marketing rather than product quality is hardly new. For example, the following statement dates back to 1928: "[The] outstanding characteristics [of commercial accident and health insurance] are the heterogeneity of its policy forms and the non-scientific nature of its premiums . . . [Each is] a direct consequence of competition, which unlike competition in life and many casualty covers, devotes itself to the devising of new forms rather than to the emphasis of security and service on standard, or practically standard policies" (Kulp, cited in Faulkner, 1940, p. 1).

## FACTORS CONTRIBUTING TO RISK SELECTION

Many factors have been identified by anecdote, theory, survey data, and other research as sources of favorable or unfavorable selection (see, generally, Pauly, 1974; Berki and Ashcraft, 1980; Berki et al., 1980; Luft et al., 1985; Neipp and Zeckhauser, 1985; Wilensky and Rossiter, 1986; Luft, 1987, 1991; Luft and Miller, 1988; Mechanic et al., 1990; Anderson, 1991b). These factors relate to the characteristics and choices of individuals, employers, and health plans.

### Individual Factors

Individuals' choices about health plans are affected by a variety of characteristics that may not be easy to measure directly but that are correlated to more easily measured characteristics, such as age, gender, occupation, and income. The underlying characteristics that affect choice include

* individuals' actual and perceived health status (and that of their spouses and children);
* the knowledge and preferences individuals have about using and paying for health services and their willingness and ability to accept risk; and
* their willingness and ability to engage in informed decisionmaking about joining, leaving, or continuing in a health plan.

The dynamics of individual choice among multiple health plans have not been studied in much detail, but one pilot effort suggests that individuals (1) examine only a few options, (2) are aware of coverage differences for their special needs (e.g., mental health care and pregnancy care), and (3) tend to understand traditional plans better than newer plans with their gatekeeper and other managed care features (Mechanic et al., 1990). Freedom to choose one's physician appears to be particularly important to those choosing conventional plans. Individuals with a significant ongoing relationship with a physician will tend to stay with the health plan that includes or covers that physician rather than switch to another plan.

Unpublished research on the Federal Employees Health Benefits Plan (discussed below) indicates that expected out-of-pocket costs (employee-paid premium and other cost sharing) is the single most important factor in decisionmaking for low-risk individuals. High-risk individuals focus first on plan benefits.

### Employer Factors

Among small employers, some of the same factors that influence individuals' choices may likewise influence the decisions made by employers to purchase health coverage or to seek a particular kind of insurance. Virtually all large employers provide broad health benefits, but smaller, more economically marginal employers may be particularly motivated to seek insurance if they have employees with health problems and may be especially sensitive to price in making the buy or no-buy decision.

As noted earlier, the major factor affecting risk selection for larger employers is the offering to employees of a choice of health plans (Luft, 1991). A multiple-choice health benefit program allows the individual risk factors identified above to operate within the employment group. In attempting to make individuals more cost conscious or to accommodate the varied personal circumstances of employees, employers may unintentionally—but sometimes deliberately—influence risk selection in a number of other ways, such as

- requiring that individuals pay part of the premium;
- limiting the employer contribution to the premium to a portion of the premium for the least expensive plan or otherwise structuring the premium contribution to favor a particular kind of plan;
- offering a choice of more and less generous (high and low option) health plans and requiring employees to pay more for the more generous coverage;
- including preexisting condition limitations or requiring specific kinds of coverage in some but not all health plans;
- offering a flexible benefit program that encourages employees to select benefits on the basis of individuals' needs and preferences;
- allowing employees to opt out of coverage entirely;
- combining active employees and non-Medicare-eligible retirees in the same risk pool for purposes of setting the active employees' contribution to premium; and
- frequently adding new health plans or major new features to existing plans.

The first seven of these employer actions make it attractive for healthier individuals to minimize their purchase of health coverage and to segregate themselves in different risk pools from less healthy individuals (Luft et al., 1985; Luft, 1991). The eighth action sets up a situation in which the sponsors of a new health plan with moderate benefits can "low ball" premiums (set them lower than the benefits and employee population might seem to warrant) to encourage enrollment by low-risk individuals who are willing to "take a chance" because they are not currently using health services and do not anticipate the need for any. The selection advantage a health plan gains by this strategy may take years to fade.

Employers may also deliberately attempt to make specific types of health plans more or less attractive to high-risk individuals. For example, to encourage higher-risk individuals to enroll in plans thought to manage health care more efficiently, coverage may be restricted or cost sharing greatly increased for specific services in conventional self-insured plans but not in health maintenance organizations (HMOs). Alternatively, employers may treat their conventional plan as the insurer of last resort for individuals with costly problems, in particular, mental illness.

To the extent that some employers offer health benefits and others do not or some offer more generous or flexible coverage, these employers may attract higher-risk employees (either the workers themselves or their families) and also thus suffer from unfavorable risk selection. Employers—like insurers—may respond by reducing coverage for specific medical conditions, strengthening exclusions for preexisting conditions, making higher-risk individuals pay more for health benefits, and other practices. One major airline now permanently excludes coverage for preexisting conditions for new employees (Seeman, 1992). Although evidence of employers' efforts to protect themselves in these ways is limited, the rationale for protective strategies is strong enough to raise concerns not only about further segmentation of access to health benefits but also about the resulting distortions in labor markets.

The most drastic actions that employers may take to avoid high-risk employees come in the form of the explicit hiring bans and dismissal policies involving smokers, social drinkers, mountain climbers, and others that were described in Chapter 3. The current extent of such overt policies and similar covert practices is unknown.

## Health Plan and Insurer Factors

Of much current interest to policymakers are the characteristics and strategies of health plans and insurers that may affect individuals' choices. These include

- underwriting and pricing practices;
- plan benefit design;
- incentives for use of a network of practitioners and providers;
- administrative procedures;
- marketing strategies; and
- general reputation.

As discussed below, health plans can manipulate their features and practices to varying degrees. Much of the controversy over risk selection relates to charges that some health plans deliberately "skim," "cream," or "cherry pick" good risks or "blacklist," "redline," "churn," or otherwise avoid poor risks (GAO, 1991e; Chollet, 1992a; Hall, 1992; Zellers et al., 1992). This behavior is particularly associated with the small-group insurance market.

The most powerful tool that health plans have to limit or channel risk selection is medical underwriting, which allows them to classify risks, price them, and accept, reject, or limit coverage for individuals and groups. The most extreme form of underwriting is to exclude altogether from coverage individuals with certain characteristics, such as HIV infection, and entire categories of employers or occupations, such as hairdressers and lawyers— the latter for higher perceived risk of litigation. Coverage for a preexisting condition can also be barred temporarily or permanently. In addition, premiums for individual and small-group coverage are commonly based on individual risk factors, including both demographic characteristics and health status. Figure 5.1 shows how age and gender can affect premiums (CRS, 1988b). A health plan that does not use medical underwriting makes itself vulnerable to unfavorable risk selection if its competitors do engage in risk rating and similar practices.

Benefit design can crucially affect a health plan's potential for unfavorable or favorable risk selection. The range of relevant design features is broad and includes the types of services, providers, and sites of care cov-

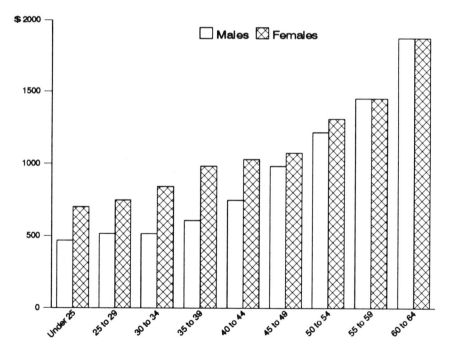

**FIGURE 5.1** Variation in average annual plan premiums for the typical health plan, by age and gender, 1986. SOURCE: Adapted from CRS, 1988b, Vol. 1, p. 41; original data from Hay/Huggins.

ered; the requirements for patient cost sharing; and caps on the volume, frequency, or duration of a covered service. Some benefits, in particular more extensive inpatient and outpatient mental health benefits, are thought to attract higher-cost patients. Other benefits, for example, fitness and other health promotion programs, may attract healthier individuals. A health plan that chooses (or is required by courts or legislatures) to cover expensive services, such as transplants, hospice care, or certain experimental treatments, when other plans can exclude such services will likely have both a more costly benefit package and a more costly membership.

Another characteristic that may contribute to risk selection is whether a health plan limits coverage to a specified network of physicians, hospitals, and other health care practitioners and providers. As defined in Chapter 3, conventional health plans place no or few limits on choice of provider, whereas network plans (e.g., HMOs, preferred provider organizations [PPOs], and point-of-service [POS] plans) reduce or exclude coverage for nonnetwork providers. Plans that limit coverage to a defined panel of practitioners and providers may be unattractive to individuals with chronic health problems who want flexibility in choosing medical specialists and who have established a relationship with a physician that they do not want to disrupt. In addition, individuals such as retirees who travel a lot outside the plan's service area may find a network plan difficult.

Network plans may also be vulnerable to risk selection. Independent practice associations (IPAs), PPOs, and other health plans whose physicians also see patients in other plans may attract some higher-risk individuals who would have to switch physicians if they changed to a staff model HMO. Similarly, mature HMOs will likely have a core of older patients with established physician relationships who are not interested in switching to a new HMO. The latter thereby gains a selection advantage. In addition, because plans with maximum choice of provider generally cost more, network plans with nominal copayments may incur adverse selection for some conditions, such as routine pregnancies.

The composition of a particular limited or closed provider panel is also relevant. For example, a network plan that includes a university hospital known for its care of a particularly costly medical problem is more likely to attract patients with this problem than a plan that excludes this hospital. A plan that includes more subspecialists is similarly vulnerable. In general, the potential for risk selection is one more factor (in addition to cost, quality, reputation, and geographic coverage) to be weighed when network plans consider the composition of their provider panels.

The lore of health plan efforts to avoid poorer risks also includes a variety of imaginative administrative practices (Luft and Miller, 1988). These include requiring individuals to visit health plan offices in order to enroll, permitting long appointment queues to develop for certain kinds of services, requiring new female enrollees to change gynecologists and obstetricians regardless of whether their existing physician is part of the plan, and counseling sicker members to switch to other plans where they will have better coverage.

Marketing and sales strategies are particularly sensitive to risk selection issues. A health plan is more likely to seek or accept an advertising spot during a sports telecast than a spot during a program on the latest strategies for treating HIV infection. A health plan for the elderly that markets in senior centers is less vulnerable to unfavorable risk selection than one that markets in nursing homes.

## A Case in Point

To illuminate the impact of individual, employer, and health plan factors, the experience of the Federal Employees Health Benefits Program (FEHBP), the oldest consumer-choice employer health program in the country, is instructive (Towers, Perrin, Forster & Crosby, Inc., 1988; CRS, 1989; Enthoven, 1989; Jones, 1989; U.S. House of Representatives, 1989; Welch, 1989; Wiener, 1990; GAO, 1992c; *Washington Post*, 1992; see also Chapter 2 of this report). Established in 1959 and operational in 1960, FEHBP has always offered numerous choices among fee-for-service plans and among HMOs. There is an annual "open season" during which any subscriber can switch from any plan to any other plan available in its geographic area. FEHBP has never allowed medical underwriting. It includes retirees as well as active employees and thus covers a very wide age range. It has always required premium cost sharing by the subscribers. A statutory formula sets the government contribution to any plan at 60 percent of the average premium of the six largest plans' high-option offerings. This contribution cannot, however, exceed 75 percent of the chosen plan's premium costs.

According to internal studies conducted by the Blue Cross and Blue Shield Association, a large majority of the 4 million contract-holders (or subscribers) in this program annually review their own health care plan and two or three others and consider making a change (though usually fewer than 10 percent actually make a change). The primary factors considered are out-of-pocket costs, perceived need for specific benefits, and sometimes the quality of plan services, such as claims processing. The weight assigned by individuals to each factor varies from year to year, depending on changes in individual circumstances.

The FEHBP has in fact suffered from serious risk selection problems, even for the plans with very large enrollments. Table 5.1 illustrates the impact of risk selection on premiums for three conventional health benefit plans in the federal program. An analysis of high-option and low- (or

**TABLE 5.1**   Estimated Impact of Biased Risk Selection on Premiums in a Multiple-Choice Program, Individual (self-only) Coverage, Federal Employees Health Benefits Program, 1989

| | Individual (self-only) Premium | |
| --- | --- | --- |
| Plan | Standardized Premium (actuarial value) | Total Actual Premium |
| Low-coverage plan | $1,422 | $ 833 |
| Median-coverage plan | 1,700 | 1,502 |
| High-coverage plan | 2,016 | 3,032 |
| % Difference between low and high plans | 42% | 264% |

Discussion:   The first column reports the standardized premium or actuarial value of the benefits in three FEHBP fee-for-service plans assuming a standardized or comparable group of enrollees in each.   The actuarial value is based on the differences in covered services (for example, whether hospice services are covered) and patient cost sharing (for example, level of deductible and coinsurance).   The plan with the most extensive benefits is worth 42% more in coverage than the low-coverage plan.

The second column reports the actual premium for each plan, which reflects past utilization of health services.   The premium for the high-coverage plan is 264% higher.   The difference in the range of actual premiums is substantially greater than the difference in actuarial value.   This shows how characteristics of enrollees choosing different plans (risk selection) affect premiums.

SOURCE:   Adapted from CRS, 1989, p. 123.

standard) option plans managed by one insurer that were estimated to have the same actuarial value (despite their labels) found the actual (experience-related) premium for the high-option plan was 79 percent above that for the low-option plan (Welch, 1989).   Adverse selection problems contributed significantly to the decision by several fee-for-service plans and dozens of HMOs to withdraw from the program during the late 1980s.   For example, it was the major factor in the departure of Aetna, which was one of the original FEHBP participants and which had nearly 200,000 contracts in 1988 before it withdrew from the market.   In general, there has been a market "shake-out," due in large part to risk selection.

Some efforts have been made to control or limit the extent of risk selection in FEHBP, and some changes made for other reasons may also have been helpful.   First, benefit packages among the competing carriers have become more similar (for example, through changes in mental health benefits and dental benefits), and all are moving to incorporate more managed care features.   Such correspondence reduces the differences in health plans that might attract or deflect high-risk individuals and encourage frequent switching among health plans. Second, the government's Office of Personnel Management has not allowed new fee-for-service carriers to enter the program and has set community rating rules for newly participating HMOs that discourage "low ball" pricing to attract low-risk individuals. Third, because the government caps its contribution at 75 percent of any health plan's premium rather than paying a fixed dollar amount (which might cover all the premium for a low-cost plan), it mitigates somewhat the reward for enrolling in plans with particularly favorable selection.[4] Finally, legislation made federal retirees over age 65 who retired after 1982 eligible for Medicare. When Medicare became the primary payer for this group, it significantly reduced the cost to FEHBP carriers and HMOs of their highest-cost enrollees.

## EVIDENCE OF RISK SELECTION

Several researchers have presented or reviewed the evidence of risk selection (Berki and Ashcraft, 1980; Jackson-Beeck and Kleinman, 1983; Neipp and Zeckhauser, 1985; Price and Mays, 1985; Welch, 1985; Wilensky and Rossiter, 1986; Hellinger, 1987; Luft, 1987; Luft and Miller, 1988; Newhouse et al., 1989; Lichtenstein et al., 1991; Robinson et al., 1991). Although this evidence is not conclusive and the dynamics of the health insurance market are changing rapidly, the evidence taken as a whole does suggest that selection is fairly common and is related to the factors identified above. Nonetheless, it is important to note that (1) the health plans studied are not random or even representative of all plans and communities; (2) most studies have small "sample" sizes; (3) variations related to local delivery systems and cultures may be insufficiently identified; and (4) measures of risk (e.g., average age or average functional status) may inadequately capture important differences among groups.

Despite the shortcomings of the data, several policy-relevant findings are suggested by accumulated evidence, the direct experience of the committee members, and the perspective of experts consulted by the committee. First, risk selection is not confined to one type of health plan or benefit design. Both indemnity health plans and HMOs have been found to suffer from unfavorable selection. However, in competition with indemnity plans, HMOs overall are more likely to have experienced favorable selection than indemnity plans.

This difference between HMOs and conventional plans is clearest in studies comparing the utilization of those enrolling in HMOs ("leavers")

---

[4]However, it could also reduce somewhat the financial incentive for individuals to enroll in health plans that have gained their premium advantage through efficient management of medical care and medical resources.

versus those remaining with conventional fee-for-service (FFS) health plans ("stayers"). It is less commonly identified when the comparisons of "leavers" and "stayers" involve measures of health status (e.g., patient perceptions, reported chronic conditions, and functional status) (Wilensky and Rossiter, 1986; Hellinger, 1987; Robinson et al., 1991; but see Lichtenstein et al., 1991). However, when existing enrollees in HMOs and FFS plans are compared (which is preferable to studying just "leavers" and "stayers"), the health status measures tend to be more favorable for the HMO members. This finding could also be interpreted as demonstrating the impact of better preventive and curative care, although this has not been studied explicitly (Luft and Miller, 1988).

Second, the age of a health plan or its tenure in a particular health benefit program may affect its risk profile (Neipp and Zeckhauser, 1985; Grazier et al., 1986). New health plans, particularly network-based plans, are more likely to attract individuals who are younger and less likely to have an established relationship with a physician, although specifics of their benefit design can counter this selection advantage (Sorensen et al., 1980).

Third, enrollment, continuation, and disenrollment decisions all contribute to selection dynamics. Risk pools can be dramatically affected by who joins, who stays, and who leaves during various periods (Luft et al., 1989). Those who depart one plan voluntarily for another may differ from those whose departure from a plan is involuntary.

Fourth, classifications such as "low user of care" and "high user of care" are not permanent categories (Welch, 1985). Much utilization in any given period flows from acute events for which individuals do not usually require ongoing care in subsequent years. Both high and low users of care in one year are likely to "regress" toward the mean level of use over time, with most of the effect occurring in the second year (Newhouse et al., 1989). If health plan participants remain in their original pools, the benefit from attracting an individual who has used little care is likely to diminish somewhat.

In the small-group insurance market, the response of many underwriters to this phenomenon is "durational" rating. This practice sets low initial premiums for low-risk groups and then sharply increases rates at renewal time (Hall, 1992). (The literature does not mention an equivalent use of durational rating to lower rates for high-risk groups.) In contrast, in the large-group market in which employers offer multiple health plans, the effects of regression toward the mean may be offset by continued risk selection at each year's open enrollment.

Fifth, "stay or move" decisions by very high risk individuals may be particularly important. The impact on health plan costs of members who require very high levels of care has been repeatedly documented. Between 1 and 10 percent of a group will typically account for 30 to 70 percent of its claim expense in a given year (Rosenbloom and Gertman, 1984; Alexandre, 1988; Berk et al., 1988). For example, a report on one large University of California indemnity health plan showed that just 227 individuals accounted for 42 percent of all reimbursable hospital charges for the 1982/83 contract year (Prudential Insurance Company, 1984 cited in Luft et al., 1985). In another university health plan, 0.4 percent of the Blue Cross enrollees filing claims accounted for 21 percent of reimbursements (Luft et al., 1985). How these individuals choose among health plans can have a marked effect on a plan's costs.[5] Such selection is not easy to predict using the usual demographic measures of risk.

Sixth, if health status comparisons focus only on averages and not on what happens to the most or least healthy, they may be insensitive to some forms of risk selection. For example, one recent study of Medicare beneficiary enrollment in 23 HMOs (Lichtenstein et al., 1991) found that 9 HMOs showed favorable selection and 14 showed neutral selection when the comparisons were based on *mean* health status for each plan. In contrast, when the extremes were compared (i.e., proportions of the *most* disabled and the *least* disabled enrolled in each plan), 10 additional HMOs showed favorable selection. None of the 23 HMOs experienced unfavorable selection on either measure, and 4 showed neutral selection on both.

Seventh, even if the extent of risk selection is considered modest as reflected in the current data, health plans' actions may still be influenced by a strong fear of adverse selection or a strong conviction that the benefits of favorable selection are significant. The consequence may be the same protective strategies that would result from documented evidence of serious selection effects.

## POLICY QUESTIONS

Risk selection and risk segmentation raise both philosophical and practical questions for employers, health plans, and public policymakers. These questions involve the fundamental, interrelated issues of equity, access, cost, and quality. This section considers how risk selection may affect each issue and concludes by discussing the implications of the Americans with Disabilities Act of 1990.

### Equity

Americans are still debating a basic ethical question in health care, that is, whether all people should be guaranteed some appropriate level of health

---

[5]Likewise, movement by the 20 to 30 percent of individuals who never file a claim in a year could be critical. Schemes for marketing health insurance along with fitness club and spa memberships target this group.

coverage as a matter of public policy. This fundamental question aside, there remain in dispute other questions of equity or fairness. The basic issue is: should those who are good risks help finance health benefits and health care for bad risks or should individuals bear directly some or all of the cost associated with the level of risk they pose? Some differentiate between two kinds of risk—that based on factors beyond individual control (e.g., developing multiple sclerosis) versus that associated with factors at least partly within individual control (e.g., smoking and obesity, both of which appear to have a genetic as well as a behavioral component).

Conventional insurance theory, following the principle of "actuarial fairness," concludes that higher-risk individuals should pay more regardless of the type of risk in question (MacIntyre, 1962; Arrow, 1963; Fuchs, 1991; Intindola, 1991; Jose, 1991; Chollet, 1992a). Advocates of "actuarial fairness" go beyond the arguments of business necessity and economic efficiency to argue as a matter of principle that the cost of and access to coverage must be linked to an insured's risk class. They draw analogies to homeowners, life, and other forms of insurance. People cannot get homeowners insurance when their house is on fire or life insurance when they are dying. People with bad driving records pay more for auto insurance as do young people, who, as a group, have more accidents than older people. Why should insurance for medical expenses be different? Why should it be priced the same for the young and the old, the well and the ill, and other individuals or groups whose risk of health care expense differs? The concept of actuarial fairness has been applied most extensively to individual health coverage, to a lesser extent to small groups, and to a very limited degree to larger groups.[6] However, some large employers have imposed premium differentials based on so-called life-style factors, such as smoking or high blood pressure (Frieden, 1991; Woolsey, 1992c,d).

An efficiency-related argument for premium differentials is based on two propositions: (1) not all people need, want, or can afford as much medical care and coverage as most health plans now provide and (2) those individuals should have the opportunity to contract for a lower level of benefit or standard of care in return for a lower premium (Havighurst, 1991). Concomitantly, those who need or want a higher standard of care should pay for it and should not be subsidized by those who need or want less.

Some accept the actuarial perspective on fairness as long as the pre-

---

[6]Large employers, however, generally do establish different premiums for employees purchasing insurance for themselves only and those purchasing it for themselves and their families. Some employers distinguish between two-person families and larger families; others do not. The basic distinction here is not related to individual risk of incurring expenses but to the number of individuals who may generate expenses.

mium differences across risk classes are not extreme and subsidies are available to low-income groups (Pauly et al., 1991). Others (Feldman and Dowd, 1991) focus less on the unfairness of low-risk individuals subsidizing high-risk individuals than on the unfairness of younger and often lower-income workers subsidizing older and often higher-income workers, as they may in large employment groups or other plans that do not use some form of risk rating. To correct this perceived inequity, premiums, deductibles, and other insurance cost sharing can be pegged to income, although such modifications are not feasible under some circumstances and do involve additional administrative cost.[7]

In contrast to the perspective of actuarial fairness is the principle underlying community rating and social insurance, a principle accepted by most members of this committee. The principle here is that the risk of medical care expenses should be shared very broadly and that broad risk sharing across a community can help keep rates within reach of both higher-risk and modest-income individuals. Because most people move from lower-risk to higher-risk status over time, community rating achieves a rough actuarial fairness if the time perspective is long enough.[8] However, because low-income, low-risk individuals will find it difficult to divert income from food and shelter to health insurance whether or not their premiums are risk rated, subsidies will still be required to make insurance broadly available across income classes. Principles aside, community rating in this country's private insurance market has, for the most part, proved unsustainable in the face of competition based on experience rating for larger groups and medical underwriting for individuals and small groups.

Following the social insurance principle, policymakers in other countries have singled out health coverage or its equivalent as a social good that differs from auto, life, homeowners, and other forms of insurance. They have largely rejected the perspective of actuarial fairness as it relates to medical underwriting and risk rating.

In this country, federal and state policies vary in the degree to which they sanction differences in the cost and availability of health coverage

---

[7]A second rationale for income-adjusted cost sharing involves a pragmatic behavioral equity: $200 deductibles or $1,000 limits on out-of-pocket expenses are unlikely to have the same impact on the use of care for higher- and lower-income workers. Income-adjusted cost sharing is relatively uncommon, in part because it can be burdensome to design and implement (e.g., from a policy and practical perspective, how would one treat two-income families?) and may cause employee relations problems.

[8]Time may be factored into arguments for community rating in another way. In Rochester, New York, community rating still prevails, in part because the large employers that would normally self-insure believe that their participation in a system that emphasizes risk sharing and collective strategies to contain costs results in a system that is keeping costs lower over the long term than they would be in a segmented, risk-rated competitive market.

based on the risk presented by an individual or group. For example, almost all state insurance regulations permit risk-based premium differences, but they vary greatly in the limits they place on underwriting practices. Several states have attempted to preserve a degree of community rating and open enrollment through their regulation of Blue Cross and Blue Shield plans. However, the success of medically underwritten individual and small-group coverage and the spread of self-insurance for large groups have undermined these state policies. The federal Americans with Disabilities Act permits most medical underwriting, and the Employee Retirement Income Security Act of 1974 (ERISA) is silent on the issue.

As a consequence of the deterioration and fragmentation in community risk pools, states are increasingly looking for new risk-spreading strategies. A few have recently adopted limits on medical underwriting along the lines discussed later in this chapter (Freudenheim, 1992c). In addition, some have imposed taxes on insured health plans, health care providers, and other sources to support state-subsidized programs for high-cost and low-income individuals. One problem with such subsidy strategies is that, as noted in Chapter 2, ERISA generally protects employee health benefit plans from state-imposed premium or claims-based taxes and from other state regulations.

## Access to Health Care

Risk selection can affect access to health care in at least four ways. First, to the extent that fear of unfavorable risk selection leads insurers to refuse coverage—in whole or part—to higher-risk individuals, those individuals may face barriers in obtaining needed health care. Second, if health plans fear that covering, providing, or improving specific services will attract higher risks, they may limit coverage of those services even more than they might simply in pursuit of cost containment. Third, to the extent that some individuals are discouraged from selecting a health plan that fits their particular needs because the plan's premiums have been raised by unfavorable selection, the result may again be reduced access to appropriate health care. Fourth, if people worry that their use of health services may disqualify them from future insurance coverage, they may limit their use of needed services, fail to submit claims for covered expenses, or pressure physicians to record diagnoses that are less likely to attract an underwriter's attention. The last two actions add error to the data bases used for health care research and monitoring.

Strategies to control or compensate for risk selection may make health coverage more affordable and accessible for many high-risk individuals in the short run, but they will not by themselves make coverage more affordable in general. In fact, by limiting the degree to which low-risk individuals can segregate themselves in separate risk pools, such strategies may increase costs for those individuals by pooling them with higher-risk groups, including groups that previously could not obtain insurance (GAO, 1991d). This broader pooling could price health benefits out of reach for some lower-income people. On the other hand, decreasing the incentive for health plans to compete on the basis of risk selection should encourage competition based on efficient management and other practices, and such competition could limit the overall cost of health benefits.

In any case, lack of health coverage does not inevitably mean complete lack of health care, although it is associated with lower use of both outpatient and inpatient services (Davis and Rowland, 1983; Lewin/ICF, 1990; Hadley et al., 1991; Stern et al., 1991). Conversely, having health coverage does not remove all barriers to care (Long and Settle, 1984; PPRC, 1992b). For example, physical, cultural, geographic, and linguistic factors may limit access (Davis, 1991). Moreover, greater use of health care is not perfectly correlated with better health outcomes, presumably in part because some medical services have little or no benefit and in part because the palliative and other benefits of care may be difficult to measure. Nonetheless, evidence does suggest that being uninsured can be harmful to one's health (Hadley, 1982; Lurie et al., 1984; Pauly, 1992).

## Cost

As noted earlier in this chapter, risk selection may make it easier for health plans to compete on the basis of who they enroll rather than on the basis of true cost containment. Without means of identifying or controlling such selection, purchasers of health plans may be unable to distinguish between premium differences based on risk selection and differences based on benefit design or management efficiency. One result is that competition among health plans may not serve the most important long-term objectives intended by its advocates.

Efforts to control or compensate for risk selection will not eliminate cost differences between larger and smaller groups because many other factors affect these costs. For example, health care use and costs are less predictable for small groups. Fixed administrative costs are spread across fewer individuals, and nonpayment of premiums is more likely among small groups. As pointed out in Chapter 3, working with 100 groups of 20 is more expensive than working with one group of 2,000. Further, to the extent that cost containment programs depend on employers to educate employees, monitor program operations, or apply economic leverage to influence provider behavior and prices, small size can also be a disadvantage.

As noted earlier, steps to control or compensate for risk selection may make health coverage more affordable for high-risk groups but may increase costs for low-risk groups. Such steps may also affect the level and distribution of costs in other ways. For example, because reform in underwriting practices is intended to make insurance more available and because the presence of insurance tends to increase the use of care, reforms may increase health care costs. On the other hand, because those without insurance do not necessarily go without any care, even when they cannot pay for it out-of-pocket, the care they now receive must show up as costs to someone else.[9]

Hospitals, in particular, have emphasized the financial burden of the uninsured, or "uncompensated," care that they provide (by law, principle, or inadvertence) to ill and injured individuals. Private employers and insurers have complained about the shares of these costs that are shifted to them in the form of higher prices. In addition to this kind of "cost shifting," hospitals presumably absorb some of the marginal costs of this care through reduced employee compensation, cover some of it through philanthropic sources, and sometimes secure additional state and local tax appropriations.[10] Controversy continues about (1) the existence and magnitude of the cost shift due to uncompensated care, (2) the degree to which some third-party payers can insulate themselves from it *or* add to it through "inadequate" reimbursement to providers, and (3) the extent to which cost shifting should be regarded as inequitable (Coulam and Gaumer, 1991; National Association of Manufacturers, 1991; Blendon et al., 1992). Chapter 6 discusses this issue further.

## Quality of Care

A recent Institute of Medicine study defined quality of care as "the degree to which health services for individuals and populations increase the likelihood of desired health outcomes and are consistent with current professional knowledge" (IOM, 1990b, p. 4). To the extent that fear of risk selection discourages health plans from covering certain kinds of appropriate medical services or deters more effective and efficient management of health services, it may diminish the quality of health care. To the extent that methods for controlling risk selection allow better assessment of differ-

---

[9]Interestingly, one study has suggested that the employed uninsured may be more likely to generate uncompensated care (i.e., not pay their bills) than the unemployed uninsured (Campbell, 1992). If true, this might mean that the costs for mandated and subsidized employment-based coverage would produce more offsetting savings from reduced costs for uncompensated care than would expansion of care for the unemployed.

[10]For example, New Jersey established a formal cost-shifting arrangement that helped cover uncompensated care in hospitals through surcharges on third-party payers. As noted in Chapter 2, a federal court recently ruled that this system violated ERISA.

ences in the health status of health plan members and channel health plan energies away from risk selection and toward management of health services and resources, they should improve quality of care. To date, most proposals for health care reform (regardless of what they would do about risk selection) focus on health care access and costs. Although they often lack specifics on these issues (e.g., how a global budget would work), they tend to be even less informative about quality assurance.

## Implications of the Americans with Disabilities Act

One question for the future is how the Americans with Disabilities Act (ADA) may affect employers' efforts to limit health benefits for those with health problems. ADA prohibits discrimination in the conditions and privileges of employment (Feldblum, 1991; Jones, 1991; Rothstein, 1992). Disability is defined as it is under section 504 of the Rehabilitation Act of 1973, that is, "(A) a physical or mental impairment that substantially limits one or more of the major life activities of such individual; (B) a record of such an impairment; or (C) being regarded as having such an impairment." ADA took effect in 1992 for employers with 25 or more employees and goes into effect in 1994 for employers with 15 to 24 employees.

Under the act, employers cannot refuse to hire the disabled because company health benefit costs would increase. They also cannot question job applicants about disabilities except with respect to job-related functions. Medical examinations of job applicants are permitted only following a conditional offer of employment, must apply to all entrants, and must generate confidential records that are separate from other records. The law forbids compulsory non-job-related medical examinations once an employee is hired. In addition, employers may not deny all coverage under a health benefit plan for an individual with disabilities.

However, the act explicitly permits most health insurance underwriting practices based on or consistent with state law unless such practices are a "subterfuge" for discrimination. Either the statute itself or associated committee language indicates that insurers and employers may limit coverage for preexisting conditions, restrict or exclude coverage for certain procedures and treatments, and charge higher premiums for higher risks. It would also appear that medical examinations or questionnaires may be legal if their only purpose is to establish, classify, or underwrite risks for a company health benefit plan. The act says nothing about the confidentiality of this information—or the information provided on claims forms, underwriting questionnaires, or medical records submitted during utilization review. Although it would be illegal to discriminate against a disabled individual on the basis of information from these records, access to personal medical information still provides the opportunity and perhaps the stimulus to attempt covert discrimination (e.g., when layoffs are being planned).

Many uncertainties about the applicability of the law to health benefits will probably be resolved through litigation (Council on Ethical and Judicial Affairs, 1991; Feldblum, 1991; Juengst, 1991; Rothstein, 1992). At this time, major remaining questions include the following:

- How are routine uses of medical underwriting, revisions of health benefit programs, and similar actions that have a disparate impact on individuals with a particular health condition to be distinguished from such actions employed as a subterfuge with the intention of discriminating? For example, how would one make the distinction in the case of an employer who singles out AIDS-related treatment for reduced coverage after an employee begins to file claims?[11]
- How broadly might the courts interpret the prohibition on discrimination against those regarded as impaired? For example, could an employer refuse to hire an individual who was without any functional impairment but had a high cholesterol level or a genetic predisposition to disease (but no expressed illness)?
- Does the law protect partly volitional conditions or behaviors such as obesity or tobacco use that also appear to have a genetic component?

The Equal Employment Opportunities Commission may yet issue further regulations to clarify some matters. Also, legislation has been introduced to extend the definition of disability to include a "genetic or medically identified potential of, or predisposition toward, a physical or mental impairment that substantially limits a major life activity" (Gostin and Roper, 1992, p. 249).

Although ADA may or may not be interpreted to protect certain workers, for example, smokers, some states have taken the initiative to prohibit employers from refusing to hire or continue to employ off-the-job smokers (Schiller et al., 1991; Sipress, 1991).[12] The tobacco industry has successfully lobbied for these laws, but protection for other individual behavior or characteristics does not appear at this time to have much financial or other backing. Nonetheless, the more employers attempt to regulate this and other off-the-job employee behavior that does not affect job performance,

---

[11]In a case decided before the disability law took effect (*McGann* v. *H&H Music Co.*, 946 F.2d 401 [5th Cir. 1991]), a federal appeals court ruled that it was not illegal for a company to reduce coverage for AIDS-related care, regardless of the impact of the policy (Rothstein, 1992).

[12]At least 34 states limit smoking in government offices, and 16 also limit smoking at private worksites (EBRI, 1991b).

the more pressure is likely to grow for states to restrict what has been called "life-style discrimination" in hiring and benefits. Such state initiatives will not, however, apply to the benefit programs of self-insured employers as long as ERISA remains unchanged.

## STRATEGIES FOR RESPONDING TO RISK SELECTION AND RISK SEGMENTATION

A variety of policies and techniques have been suggested to limit or adjust for risk selection. Some proposals deal primarily with problems in the small-group market. Others focus on problems experienced by larger groups. The broad options are summarized in Table 5.2.

With respect to these options, the committee believes that risk selection—both as a real phenomenon and as a threat perceived by health plans—is a serious enough problem to warrant strategies to discourage or compensate for it. Therefore, it rejects the first option (i.e., simply tolerating risk selection).

The second option, which would eliminate risk selection among health plans by eliminating choice among health plans, is noted here but not discussed at length because it is more politically than technically challenging. However, depending on the methods used to pay health care practitioners and institutions, this option might still permit or encourage health care providers to "skim" good risks. It thus would warrant attention to some of the issues discussed in this chapter.

The third option, single purchasers acting on their own, is one already open to employers, particularly larger employers. In contrast, implementing the components of the fourth option—a multifaceted, collective strategy—would require significant changes in current public policies and employer preferences and practices. It would also depend on extensive analysis and sophisticated answers to some difficult technical questions.

### Limiting Underwriting Practices

Most proposals for limiting insurers' underwriting practices focus explicitly or implicitly on smaller employer groups (Blue Cross and Blue Shield Association, 1991a; GAO, 1991d, 1992b; HIAA, 1991a; National Association of Insurance Commissioners, 1991; National Health Policy Forum, 1991; Snook, 1991; Hall, 1992). Most would not apply to larger groups and self-insured groups at all. Table 5.3 highlights some key features on which proposals may vary.

The general objectives of underwriting reforms are to make health insurance more accessible to high-risk groups and individuals within these groups, to place uniform legal limits on the underwriting practices of all

**TABLE 5.2** Some Possible Strategies for Responding to Biased Risk Selection

---

*Tolerance*
- Accept risk selection and all but its most extreme consequences as an acceptable and fair outcome of relying on competitive markets, freedom of choice, and traditional underwriting principles.

*Elimination*
- Eliminate risk selection by eliminating competition among health plans and establishing a single health plan for the entire country.

*Single-Purchaser Action*
- Reduce or eliminate risk selection within an employer's health program by reducing the number of health plans offered or providing all options through a single insurer or equivalent mechanism.

*Collective Action*
- Reduce or compensate for risk selection through one or more of the following:
    (1) restrict underwriting practices (e.g., preexisting condition clauses and risk rating individual premiums) that limit the availability of coverage or set individual premiums on the basis of the risk posed by the individual or group;
    (2) manipulate or regulate the terms of health plan competition to limit the number of health plans, standardize benefit packages, create purchasing arrangements, and control other factors that may lead to adverse selection in a competitive market;
    (3) adjust employers' or governments' (but not individuals') payments to health plans to reflect the risk level of their membership; and
    (4) establish special mechanisms (e.g., reinsurance) for handling high-risk individuals.

---

small-group insurers, and to reduce premium variations across groups.[13] Beyond these broad objectives and underlying the differences in the details of proposals are several basic differences in perspective:

- One difference involves competing perspectives on equity. Some proposals answer the equity questions posed in this chapter by affirming that premium differences based on certain risk factors (e.g., age and health history) and within certain fairly broad limits are fair, whereas others essentially reject that view.
- Another and often related difference involves the degree to which the proposals recognize that unfavorable selection is a legitimate worry of

---

[13]These proposals would still permit substantial differences across groups, particularly once geographic differences in health care costs are factored in. For example, Hall (1992) has estimated that under reforms proposed by the Health Insurance Association of America and the National Association of Insurance Commissioners "a group of three healthy, 28-year old[s] . . . in North Carolina might pay only $1,865 a year [for a health plan with an average annual rate of $1,500 per enrollee for single coverage] whereas a group of three sickly, 58-year olds . . . in Boston might pay $30,555" (p. 568).

insurers and, accordingly, propose explicit mechanisms to deal with selection problems as they threaten health plans.

• A third difference lies in the exceptions the proposals make to accommodate the special characteristics of various health plans (e.g., HMOs that lack needed data, insurers with a small market share, and Blue Cross and Blue Shield plans that want to bear a broader range of risk).

• One further difference is that some reform proposals envision change through federal legislation, whereas others depend on voluntary state-by-state change.

As noted earlier, most small-group reforms would probably increase premiums for many employer groups now judged to be low risk according to current underwriting practices (GAO, 1991d; Hall, 1992). These groups would move from narrow low-risk pools to broader and more costly risk pools. If employers that now finance these premiums in whole or part responded by withdrawing from the small-group market (e.g., by dropping coverage, giving employees cash to purchase insurance on their own, or self-insuring), then premiums for the remaining employers could rise even more. Over the last decade, smaller and smaller groups have opted for self-insurance, a phenomenon that raises additional questions about plan solvency.

Some reform proposals go beyond underwriting regulations to recognize the price sensitivity of small-group and low-income purchasers in a

**TABLE 5.3** Major Provisions on Which Proposals for Reform in Underwriting Practices May Differ

---

*Access to Coverage (not including subsidies)*
• Definition of circumstances under which insurers must issue coverage to a group and all of its members (sometimes labeled "guaranteed availability" or "guaranteed issue").
• Restrictions on preexisting condition limitations.

*Continuation of Coverage*
• Conditions under which insurers must renew existing insurance contracts (sometimes labeled "guaranteed renewability").
• Provisions for continuing individual coverage without interruption and without new waiting periods for coverage following change of employment or employer's change of insurer.

*Consumer Information*
• Disclosure of information about rating practices to consumers and regulators.

*Premium Variations*
• Definition of permissible bases for varying premiums across groups and limits on the magnitude of these variations (sometimes described under the headings of rating bands and classes of business).
• Delineation of permissible bases for increasing premiums over time and limits on the magnitude of these increases.

---

voluntary system.  One response is to subsidize the voluntary purchase of health insurance by employers, employees, or both.  Another response is to mandate coverage.  Such a policy would necessarily eliminate risk selection as it arises from the decisions of groups or individuals to purchase or not purchase insurance but would not affect selection effects related to choices among health plans.  Both approaches have been questioned on grounds of political feasibility, the latter in the short term, the former in both the short and the long term (Brown, 1992).[14]

A third possible response to the affordability problem is to reduce the rate of increase in health care costs, which would, over the long term, help to make insurance more affordable for both individuals and society.  Unfortunately, as Chapter 6 discusses, many doubts exist about the potential long-term effectiveness of both current and proposed cost containment strategies.

One question that needs more analysis is how different proposals would affect insurers with unfavorable selection (e.g., those that have covered higher-risk groups).  If these insurers find that permissible premiums are insufficient to cover their risk and are introduced without an adequate period for adjustment, they might withdraw from the market.  The remaining available alternatives might be less satisfactory or possibly nonexistent. The issue here is not whether reform would lead to a reduction in the total number of companies operating in the small-group market but whether it would permit a sufficient cadre of responsible insurers to survive over the long term.  Some committee members believe a reduction in the number of health insurers—now numbering well over 1,000—would actually promote a more manageable and accountable market for purchasers, providers, and regulators.

Finally, whether small-group reform should be undertaken on a state-by-state basis or mandated on a uniform federal basis is partly a strategic issue and partly an issue of power.  State governments may move on insurance reform even if the federal government does nothing more than debate. On the other hand, if one believes that certain underwriting practices are unacceptable and that a number of states will not act to eliminate them, then the argument favors uniform national policy (Light, 1992).

## Managing or Regulating Competition

### Consolidating Choices or Risk at the Employer Level

Some employers have responded to concerns about risk selection by reducing or consolidating choices among health plans (Darling, 1991; Gold,

---

[14]Conceivably, such subsidies would not have to be as high to discourage the dropping of coverage as to encourage new purchases, but this distinction might have little practical policy relevance (see Chapter 3).

1991).  In particular, they have reduced the number of HMOs they offer. This strategy also may simplify the analysis of risk selection among the remaining plans as well as reduce the complexity of plan administration and employee decisionmaking.

Others have sought to preserve choice by bringing risk under a single umbrella through a "total replacement" package.  One approach under this option is to find a single insurer that will underwrite (in full or part) two or more health plan choices, for example, an HMO and an indemnity plan, or those options plus a PPO.  Under such dual- or triple-option arrangements, employees still chose among the two or three plan options on a periodic basis and face separate premiums for each option.  The theory is that this approach will eliminate the incentive for health plan competition based on risk selection within the employer group because the same insurer fully or partially underwrites all options within the employer group.  It would leave untouched the incentives for insurers to compete to attract low-risk employer groups.

A simpler approach—at least descriptively—is the point-of-service health plan, which (1) does not require that a yearly choice be made between network and nonnetwork enrollment and (2) does not establish different premiums for those choosing in-network versus out-of-network services. Instead, employees may choose at the point of service whether they want to use nonnetwork services and pay more for that choice (usually up to some limit).  POS plans may be part of a replacement strategy or a consolidation strategy, as in the core case study presented in Chapter 4.  Depending on the payment arrangements for network providers, these plans may shift some of the selection problem to the network providers.  If the provider network is not attractive to individuals with chronic illnesses, then the plans may shift the burden to these individuals.

Replacement and consolidation strategies have been criticized for restricting employee choice among health plans and potentially discouraging innovation.  In addition, if an employer becomes dissatisfied with the POS plan or the "umbrella" carrier for dual- or triple-option programs and switches to another plan or carrier, the switch may disrupt patient-physician relationships and interfere with continuity of care.  Overall, because consolidation strategies are relatively new and subject to little or no independent evaluation, their impact on employer or employee costs, quality of care, and employee relations has yet to be demonstrated.

*Regulating the Terms of Competition at the Community Level*

Other approaches to consolidation would operate at the community level, not at the level of the individual employer.  They would create a system of health plan certification and purchasing cooperatives to streamline the purchase of health benefits on a state or regional basis.  Some proposals are aimed at the small-group market; others would cover large groups as well. Proposals that have the control of risk selection as a major objective generally would not allow multiple cooperatives to operate in the same area and would discourage or prohibit coverage through noncertified health plans.

Purchasing cooperatives would consolidate the role of purchasing agent for small employers and would operate somewhat like large employers now do when they screen, select, and monitor a choice of health plans for their employees. They could also administer a policy of risk adjusting employer (or employer and government) contributions to health plans. Depending on the certification criteria and their enforcement, the certification mechanism could shrink the number of insurers and health plans and thus result in further consolidation of the risk pool. Still, for the individual who had previously been offered a single health plan by a small employer, some choice of plans would become available.

The consolidation of the purchaser role is part of a broader concept of "managed competition." Some comprehensive managed competition strategies propose to regulate various kinds of health plan practices that encourage risk selection and complicate comparisons of health plan performance (Enthoven, 1988a,b; Ellwood, 1991; Enthoven and Kronick, 1991; Kronick, 1991a,b, 1992). Table 5.4 lists some of the targets of these proposals.

**TABLE 5.4**   Some Steps Proposed to Manage or Limit Health Plan Competition Based on Risk Selection

*Health Plan Features*
 • Definition of standard benefit package(s) to limit features intended to discourage enrollment by high-risk individuals.
 • Requirements for health plans to contract with certain types of providers (e.g., tertiary care centers) so as not to discourage membership by high-risk individuals.

*Consumer Protection Processes*
 • Regulation and monitoring of enrollment and disenrollment processes and results and surveys of membership satisfaction to limit and detect deliberate risk selection and discrimination.
 • Regulation and monitoring of marketing practices to limit selective or discriminatory marketing.
 • Specification of information to be made available to consumers and regulators and of complaint-handling mechanisms.
 • Limits on medical underwriting.
 • Risk adjustment of employer or government payments to health plans.

*Oversight and Management Structures*
 • Creation of one or more official bodies to implement the program and certify health plan compliance.
 • Creation of regional purchasing cooperatives to select and oversee health plans that small (or all) employers would be required to offer.

Some proposals include a variety of other features that are not aimed at risk selection but are instead concerned with providing coverage for low-income individuals (e.g., through some kind of subsidy) or increasing cost-conscious behavior.

The first of the elements in Table 5.4—standardized benefit packages—is included in a wide array of proposals for health care reform (including those that would deal with risk selection by establishing a single national health insurance system). The definition of a standard benefit package poses a number of practical and theoretical challenges (Chollet, 1992b; IOM, 1992a). What principles will be applied in defining basic benefits? How will they reflect consumer, provider, payer, and other perspectives? Will they be sensitive to differences among patients with the same medical condition? What procedures will be followed to determine and update coverage features? There are a variety of ways of answering these questions, and considerable disagreement and uncertainty have been provoked by the approaches that have actually been tried. (Chapter 7 suggests these issues should be part of the government's research agenda.) The debate over the Oregon strategy for defining basic benefits, which was part of its Medicaid reform strategy, is a vivid case in point.[15]

Standardizing benefits will limit the choices available to individuals and possibly constrain desirable innovations in benefit design. However, the strategic use of benefit design to attract good risks and discourage bad risks appears to be so appealing that it will—if not limited—almost certainly undermine other steps to control risk selection and limit the advantages to be gained from such control.

Monitoring health plan enrollment, disenrollment, and marketing strategies has been tried in the Medicare program to control abuses that might arise as the government encouraged beneficiaries to enroll in HMOs. These efforts have had some successes, but reviews have, in general, been mixed (GAO, 1991d; Welch, 1991). Obviously, the larger the number of insurers that choose to or are able to persist in a highly regulated market, the larger the number of separate entities that would have to be monitored.

Most proposals that go under the "managed competition" label envision the creation of a quasi-public body or bodies to oversee the creation and maintenance of a regulated market and to serve as a purchasing agent for the self-employed, small employers, and perhaps others (see, for example,

---

[15]A major objective of Oregon's proposed restructuring of its Medicaid program was to extend basic health care services to all needy citizens and to deemphasize expensive services of minimal benefit. The state initiated an extensive process to define priorities for coverage of treatments for various medical conditions based on their social importance, clinical effectiveness, and other factors. Of the 709 condition-treatment pairs initially ranked, the state appropriation would have covered the top 587 (Wiener, 1992). Implementation of the program will require a waiver of certain federal regulations (Firshein, 1992a).

Enthoven, 1988a; Etheredge, 1990; Resnick, 1992). Depending on the specifics of the proposal, there might be (1) one or more purchasing agents; (2) relatively open or highly selective procedures to select or qualify participating health plans; (3) voluntary or mandatory participation by employers and others; and (4) requirements that employers offer at least one qualified plan, only qualified plans, or all qualified plans. To the extent that proposals provide for multiple purchasing agencies, voluntary participation by employers, and limited standardization of coverage, they would almost certainly create their own problems of risk selection.

One critical question is whether the oversight and management entity (or entities) called for by proposals for managed competition can be made sufficiently accountable for its exercise of power. The converse question is whether any governmental or quasi-governmental entity can withstand the pressures that historically have led to constant expansions in coverage without regard to cost-effectiveness and budget constraints. Another issue is how vulnerable the protections offered by such a body would be to changing partisan tides regarding regulation and deregulation.

### Risk Adjusting Payments to Health Plans

Fundamental to a number of proposals for health care reform, especially those based on "managed competition," are methods to adjust how employers, governments, purchasing cooperatives, or other entities pay health plans based on the risk presented by their enrollees. Unlike medical underwriting, the idea is not to adjust the premium paid by the individual health plan member but rather to adjust the premium contribution from the employer, government, or other entity.[16] The focus of risk-adjusted payment is on group insurance rather than on individually purchased coverage. The objectives are to reduce the financial advantage obtained from strategies to attract low-risk individuals and avoid high-risk individuals and to reduce the extent to which individuals are penalized for being members of a plan that has attracted higher-risk individuals.

*Policy and Strategic Issues*

Several criteria for risk adjustment schemes have been suggested (Welch, 1985; Newhouse et al., 1989; Anderson et al., 1990; Anderson, 1991b; Bowen

---

[16]For example, a 30-year-old employee, a 50-year-old employee, an employee with diabetes, and an employee with no significant health problem would pay the same individual premium to any given health plan—unless the individual's contribution was linked to his or her income. The employer (perhaps with some kind of government contribution or subsidy) would contribute more to the health plan for the older employee and the employee with diabetes and less for the others.

and Slavin, 1991; Luft, 1991; Robinson et al., 1991). Commonly mentioned criteria specify that a method should be

- based on characteristics of plan enrollees, not characteristics of the delivery system (e.g., inefficient management of health problems);
- related to individual need for health care rather than taste for more or less care;
- resistant to individual or organizational manipulation or "gaming" (e.g., misreporting health status);
- feasible to administer for many types of employers and health plans (e.g., HMOs, fee-for-service plans, and large and small groups); and
- compatible with other policy objectives (e.g., encouraging responsible use of medical care).

In general, the strategies for risk adjustment attempted to date have not met one or more of the above criteria. A strategy need not be perfect to be helpful, but the most feasible of existing methods have not yet demonstrated enough power and practicality to serve their intended policy purposes. Several types of risk adjustment strategies are discussed below.

Beyond the question of what kind of data should be and can be used to assess and adjust for risk is the question whether the adjustment should be prospective or retrospective or some combination of the two. Prospective adjustments permit health plans to budget and manage expected revenue and allow the adjusted premium contributions for individuals to be used during open enrollment periods. Retrospective adjustments are less administratively demanding and allow collection of some information (and therefore permit adjustments) that would not otherwise be feasible. Retrospective adjustments may also be helpful in monitoring health plans for selectively encouraging disenrollment of high-cost individuals. However, they may create problems should a health plan have to "refund" payments after its fiscal year has ended. This problem would be lessened by a system that was primarily prospective in administration with retrospective adjustments for specifically defined situations.

Another issue related to risk adjustment strategies involves the definition and stability of the entire population to which the adjustments would be applied. If groups and individuals can easily join or leave the pool or if multiple, competing pools (e.g., competing purchasing cooperatives) are possible, then the problem of risk selection is unlikely to be resolved. Some kind of required pooling arrangement, such as the mandatory purchasing entities proposed in some "managed competition" legislation, may be necessary as part of an effective strategy to control risk selection.

Improved risk assessment methods have value beyond the applications discussed above. For example, one concern about Medicare's method of paying for care provided to patients with end-stage renal disease is whether it adequately adjusts for differences in the severity of illness of patients across time or different providers (IOM, 1991). The same concern has been raised about Medicare's prospective payment system for hospitals (Gertman and Lowenstein, 1984; Iezzoni, 1989; Iezzoni et al., 1991; McGuire, 1991; Schwartz et al., 1991). In addition, efforts to compare the performance of health care providers are complicated by uncertainties about differences in their patient populations, especially when claims-based administrative data are used (Chassin et al., 1987; Greenfield, 1988; IOM, 1990b; Park et al., 1990; PPRC, 1992b). Similarly, although the IOM and others have argued that assessments of the effectiveness of different medical treatments need to move beyond highly controlled and artificial clinical trials to real-world settings, this move is made more difficult by the absence of inexpensive, practical methods of relating differences in outcomes to differences in patient risk (IOM, 1992a). Thus, improved risk adjustment methodologies may have multiple uses.

### Techniques for Risk Adjusting
### Payments to Health Plans

Assessments of risk adjustment techniques involve both policy and technical challenges (Welch, 1985; Newhouse et al., 1989; Anderson et al., 1990; Anderson, 1991b; Bowen and Slavin, 1991; Luft, 1991; Robinson et al., 1991). The policy challenge is to determine whether adjusting government or employer contributions for a particular individual risk factor (e.g., use of over $50,000 in medical services) is consistent with other policy objectives (e.g., avoiding incentives for inefficient use of resources). The technical challenge is to devise appropriate measures of health risk that use readily available or easily collectible data and that are valid predictors. Specific risk adjustment techniques may use (1) demographic information, (2) data on health service utilization, (3) measures of health status, or some combination of these.

*Demographic Measures*

In some respects, the demographic approach to risk adjusting the health plan contributions of employers and governments parallels insurers' use of such variables to establish premiums for individually purchased insurance. The most familiar demographic risk adjusters are age and gender. The Medicare formula for paying HMOs (the average adjusted per capita cost, or AAPCC) includes these variables plus Social Security disability status, welfare status, and institutional status (e.g., nursing home residence). (The complete calculation is more complex and takes other factors such as geographic location into account.) Risk adjusters have also included education, income, occupation or job classification, length of employment, and marital status (Robinson et al., 1991).

A major advantage of demographic data such as age and gender is that they tend to be more available than data on health care utilization or health status. The disadvantage is that demographic factors are relatively crude indicators of risk; for example, variations in health status, utilization, and cost within demographic categories can be quite substantial. One study of the Medicare AAPCC found that it could explain less than 1 percent of the variation in Medicare spending for the elderly (Lubitz et al., 1985). Few observers regard demographic data as sufficient elements of a successful risk adjustment strategy.

## Prior Use and Cost Measures

Some risk assessment strategies have turned to measures of health care utilization or expense to improve the strength of their estimates. In doing so, they again parallel to some degree a strategy long used by insurers for employer groups, that is, experience rating. Adjustment based on prior utilization of health services may use past claims expense alone or also factor in information about types of utilization (e.g., days of hospital care, surgical care, and number of physician visits).

Prior use and cost data are a much stronger predictor of expenditures than demographic factors (Newhouse et al., 1989). Even so, such data have been criticized as a basis for risk adjustment on several grounds (Luft and Miller, 1988; Anderson, 1991b). First, they may reflect inefficiencies in health care provision rather than differences in individual risk. Second, they may reflect individual tastes for consumption of health services. Third, they may reflect individual decisions to defer or advance medical care in conjunction with a planned switch in health plans. Fourth, certain measures may be susceptible to provider or patient manipulation.

These problems have prompted efforts to develop utilization measures based on relatively nondiscretionary services or diagnoses. The objective of most of this work has been to improve the way Medicare pays HMOs that enroll Medicare beneficiaries. In one approach (Ellis and Ash, 1988; Ash et al., 1989), researchers developed diagnostic cost groups (DCGs) that involve diagnoses thought to entail less patient or physician discretion in the use of services. These less-discretionary diagnoses are weighted and grouped according to expenses projected for the year following hospitalization. In pilot projects testing the use of DCGs to risk adjust payments to HMOs for enrolled Medicare beneficiaries, "many of the HMOs have found that the current . . . method [the AAPCC] provides higher payment rates than does the [DCG]" (Anderson, 1991b, p. 22). Not surprisingly, these projects have suffered considerable attrition of participating HMOs.

Another approach developed for Medicare (Anderson et al., 1990) also uses information about previous hospital admissions (e.g., major diagnostic category as used in Medicare prospective payment and chronicity of the condition) but adds information on whether the individual exceeded the Part B deductible. The rationale for adding this latter factor is that it will identify individuals who may not have been hospitalized but have used outpatient services. The criticism is that providers might be prompted to encourage patients to use enough care to meet the relatively low ($100) Part B deductible. Under this adjustment strategy, the utilization measures are then factored into a larger payment adjustment formula (the payment amount for capitated systems, or PACS) that also includes data on three other individual characteristics—age, gender, and Social Security disability status— as well as adjustments for provider input costs and urban/rural location.

### Health Status Measures

The third major approach to risk adjusting payments attempts to measure health status using indicators such as mortality data, measures of functional status, self-reported health status, clinical diagnosis, and physiological indicators (Anderson, 1991b). Each measure or index of health status or health-related quality of life has strengths and weaknesses (see, generally, McDowell and Newell, 1987; Lohr, 1989, 1992; Spilker, 1990). Mortality data have been widely criticized as a limited indicator of health status, whether the purpose is to evaluate the performance of a health care system, practitioner, or procedure or to adjust per case or capitated payments for care to reflect the severity of illness of a patient population. More valid, stable, and direct are various multifactor measures of health status such as the Quality of Well-being Scale (Kaplan et al., 1989), the Sickness Impact Profile (Bergner et al., 1981; Temkin et al., 1989), and the Medical Outcomes Study 36-Item Short Form Health Survey (SF-36) (Stewart and Ware, 1992; Ware and Sherbourne, 1992).

Although health status measures are becoming more useful for clinicians and quality improvement programs, they have not yet proved practically useful in predicting health care expenses for purposes of risk adjusting health plan payments. One problem is that health status measures generally involve data not easily available to those who would use them to risk adjust contributions to health plans. They require either direct access to medical records, direct questioning of individuals about their perceptions, activities of daily living, and other matters, or both. In addition, health status measures may be poor predictors of cost if they do not differentiate between people whose health status is good because a health problem is being successfully treated (at a cost) and people whose health status is less good because they are not being treated but who are not suffering costly adverse effects in the short term.

Some studies have suggested that subjective generic measures of health status may be less useful than measures related to specific physical conditions in explaining variations in health care expenditures, although both may improve on explanations that rely only on demographic and prior use measures (Beebe et al., 1985; Howland et al., 1987; Newhouse et al., 1989). Although progress is being made in developing less costly and more useful measures of health status, such measurement will still be expensive. Its introduction outside the research setting is best justified as part of a broader strategy aimed at assessing the quality of health care, the performance of specific health care providers, and the effectiveness of alternative medical services.

### Reinsuring, Allocating, and Pooling High Risk Individuals

Many advocates of underwriting reforms, risk-adjusted premiums, and managed competition concede that very high risk or high cost individuals may pose adverse selection problems beyond the reach of their approaches (Blue Cross and Blue Shield Association, 1991a; HIAA, 1991a; National Association of Insurance Commissioners, 1991). Thus, they have offered several strategies for spreading risk for these individuals, including

• reinsurance mechanisms to cover all or a portion of medical care expenses above a certain level for individuals or entire groups;
• assignment of high-risk individuals or groups to individual insurers on an unbiased basis;
• grouping of high-risk individuals in a single "pool" subsidized by contributions from private insurers, taxpayers, or others; and
• channeling of high-risk individuals to case management programs.

Some of these strategies could be used together. For example, reinsurance arrangements might focus on groups with higher than average costs because of a higher incidence of relatively common, relatively expensive problems such as coronary artery disease or mental illness. The separate risk pool might be restricted to extraordinarily high cost individuals.

One major question about all these mechanisms is whether the funding arrangements would be sufficient and fair, particularly in the context of a broader effort to extend coverage to the currently underinsured and uninsured. Costs for state risk pools are notorious for being underestimated, for reflecting severe adverse selection, and for burdening state budgets with higher-than-expected expenses (Bovbjerg, 1992). Risk pools also are criticized for relieving primary insurers of too much of the responsibility for managing costs and sharing risk. Current proposals for reform in the small-group market that include reinsurance provisions leave open the possibility of state funding if the reinsurance premiums paid by insured plans are insufficient, a likely prospect as long as self-insured groups remain outside the funding stream for any reinsurance or similar mechanism. Whether such funding would be forthcoming in amounts adequate to achieve policy objectives is far from clear.

Another question is whether high-risk pools or other options would encourage continuity of care and effective management of high-risk individuals by mainstream health plans. Would they instead segregate these individuals in plans that are ill-equipped to provide state-of-the-art management of complex and difficult medical problems?

Although not intended as a high-risk pool per se, the public plan component of "play or pay" reform proposals also appears vulnerable to selection by higher risks. Employers with higher-than-average risk groups and premiums above the level required for the pay option (typically 7 to 9 percent) might find it financially attractive to drop their health plan so that their employees would be covered by the public plan. The likely impact would be higher-than-anticipated costs for the public program.

## CONCLUSION

To a considerable extent, the history of health insurance in the United States is a history of efforts to overcome, exploit, or manage risk selection. Today, the debate over risk selection has many dimensions—empirical, normative, strategic, and technical. Opinions vary about how much selection occurs and why, which kinds of health benefit plans tend to have favorable or unfavorable selection, what the consequences generally are, whether these consequences create inequities or other problems in need of correction, and what corrections are feasible.

This committee concludes that risk selection does occur, that it harms individuals and distorts competition, and that it can be difficult to detect and overcome. The fundamental issues for policymakers are these: First, can the deterioration in the insurance market be reversed and the market be made to work? Second, can high-risk individuals be reasonably protected against overt or covert discrimination in insurance or employment? Third, in a highly fragmented insurance market, can effective monitoring of marketing and underwriting be reasonably expected? Fourth, how good does a risk adjustment need to be in predicting or compensating for risk selection to be a useful policy tool?

Managing risk selection has proved a difficult task in part because of technical difficulties (e.g., availability of information) and in part because the solutions may conflict with other objectives such as promoting a competitive health care market. There are several strategies to improve market functioning by reducing or compensating for risk selection. These involve (1) narrowing or eliminating differences in individual or group premiums based on age, gender, health status, or other risk factors, (2) limiting health plan discretion in benefit design, regulating marketing practices, and otherwise closely managing the terms of competition among health plans, (3) risk adjusting employers' or governments' (not individuals') payments to health plans to reflect differences in risk level of their membership, and (4) establishing special mechanisms for handling high-risk individuals.

The committee recognizes that these policies and techniques will not directly attack the problems of increasing health care costs and may in fact increase costs for some while lowering them for others. However, some improvements in techniques for risk adjustment may help researchers better assess the performance of health care providers and better evaluate the value of specific medical services. The next chapter examines health care costs and considers further the question of value.

# 6

# Health Care Costs:
# More Questions than Answers

*Optimum "stress" results when the carrot is just a little way ahead of the donkey—when aspirations exceed achievement by a small amount.*

James March and Herbert Simon, 1958

Given the gap between aspirations and achievements in controlling health care costs, Americans clearly are experiencing more than optimum stress—and have been for some time. Surveys of employers and the population at large consistently show that high costs are the number one health care concern. For example, in the EBRI-IOM poll conducted by the Gallup organization in late 1991, half the respondents cited cost as the biggest health care concern facing families (see Appendix A). Four-fifths cited cost as the biggest health care concern for society as a whole. Surveys also indicate that people tend to greatly underestimate national health care spending and to greatly overestimate the portion of total spending accounted for by their out-of-pocket spending rather than by direct government or business financing (Immerwahr, 1992).

Among small employers, costs are often a determining factor in decisions about whether to offer health benefits. Among large employers, the increasing share of employee compensation and after-tax income consumed by health care costs has stimulated a shift from relatively passive monitoring to more active involvement in health benefit management.

For more than two decades, concerns about high and escalating medical care expenditures and strategies to control those costs have been a major focus of health policy. The continuation of the former and the ineffectiveness of the latter not only have made it more difficult to extend health coverage to those now uninsured and underinsured but also have been partly responsible for the growth of this pool. Further, inexorably rising costs threaten—it is claimed—the solvency of federal, state, and local governments, the competitiveness of U.S. industry, the productivity and health of the U.S. work force, and the health and financial security of tens of millions of Americans. In one analysis or another, all parties—government, employers, insurers, health care providers, and consumers—have been held responsible in varying degrees for creating "the cost problem" and have been assigned some role in solving—or, more realistically—mitigating it. The structure of health care financing and delivery and its consequences now rank among the most examined aspects of U.S. social policy.

Although two decades of public and private cost containment initiatives have produced considerable institutional, administrative, and regulatory innovation and some successes, the rapid growth persists in real expenditures for medical care relative to spending for most other goods and services. Both public and private decisionmakers have viewed this result with intense frustration and a shaken faith in medical professionals and nonprofit providers of health care and health benefits as reliable agents to keep costs at "reasonable" levels. Judgments now abound that health care costs are out of control.

It must be remembered, however, that concern about rising health care costs is shared by countries with quite different health care financing and delivery systems. This suggests that the forces behind increased spending may be less related to institutional structures than to other factors such as advances in biomedical science and medical technology and changing perceptions about what medical care is appropriate.

This chapter analyzes key trend data, examines the rather different cost containment paths taken by the public and private sectors, reflects on the nature of markets in health care and health insurance, and presents a reformulation of the questions that should be asked about health care costs. This reformulation recognizes that the health and well-being of the population is the yardstick against which the cost and provision of medical care must be assessed. The key issue is the value received for health care spending compared with the value that could be expected from other investments in population well-being.

Fortunately, U.S. employers, government decisionmakers, clinicians, and others have become more interested in the question of value and are supporting efforts to improve its measurement. Unfortunately, there are at this time insufficient data to reach clear conclusions about the overall value associated with this country's high level of spending or the value added by current increases in health care spending. Many efforts to evaluate the impact of various cost containment strategies focus on dollars, not health outcomes. Some data suggest that certain strategies may reduce particular kinds of spending, in particular, spending for hospital care. Evidence is, however, sparse about successful methods to cut overall spending or control the rate of increase in health care spending. There are also inadequate data to support straightforward judgments about the relative effects on costs and value of granting or precluding a major role for employers or of emphasizing regulation or competition to control costs.

## HEALTH CARE SPENDING:
## TRENDS AND EXPLANATIONS

Americans are reminded almost daily that total health care expenditures are high and increasing. In 1991, total health care spending exceeded $666 billion and made up over 12 percent of the gross national product, up from 9.2 percent in 1980 and double the level of the 1960s. No other nation devotes such a large fraction of its resources to health care.

For the past three decades, personal health care spending has exhibited double-digit rates of annual growth in the United States, as it has in many other economically advanced nations (see Table 1.3 in Chapter 1). In real terms (adjusted for economywide inflation), U.S. spending grew at a rate of 4.4 percent during the 1980s, compared with 5.4 percent in the 1970s and 6.9 percent in the 1960s (Levit et al., 1991). Adjusted for inflation, personal health care spending has risen 143 percent in the last two decades, while real disposable income rose only 74 percent (Economic Report of the President, 1992). Inpatient hospital spending grew at a somewhat slower rate than overall spending, whereas spending for outpatient hospital services and physician services grew more quickly (CBO, 1992d).

The standard analyses of health care spending identify three broad sources of increased expenditures—population growth, economywide price inflation, and excess medical price inflation—plus a fourth residual category that includes changes in such factors as the intensity and volume of medical services (Jencks and Schieber, 1991; Levit et al., 1991; ProPAC, 1992; Thorpe, 1992a). Figure 6.1 breaks down spending increases for each of the last 10 years using these categories. Overall, about 45 percent of growth in personal health care spending over the last decade is accounted for by general price inflation. Another 10 percent of the increase reflects population growth. Over one-fifth of the growth is attributed to increases in medical care prices in excess of general inflation, and the residual fifth is attributed to increases in the volume and intensity of services and other unidentified variables.

Unfortunately, measurement problems make it difficult to distinguish the effects of increased medical care prices and increased medical care quality on increased total spending and to judge trends in productivity appropriately (Cleeton et al., 1992; CBO, 1992a; Newhouse, 1992). The primary measure of medical care prices, the medical care component of the consumer price index, suffers from several weaknesses. First, it does not adjust for changes in the quality of the medical care product, such as when

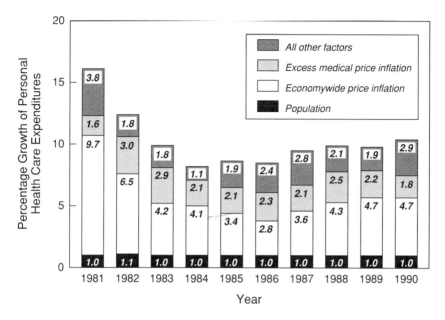

**FIGURE 6.1**   Reasons for growth in personal health care expenditures, 1981 to 1990. SOURCE: ProPAC, 1992. Based on data from Health Care Financing Administration, Office of the Actuary.

a new drug, test, or procedure has fewer adverse side effects than its predecessor. Second, the medical care price index focuses on hospital days and physician visits rather than the episode of treatment for a medical problem. Thus, a new surgical strategy that allows quicker hospital discharges and reduced total costs may be perversely registered as increasing costs on a per diem basis (because the early days of a surgical stay are usually the most expensive). Third, the components of the index (i.e., hospital, physician, dental, and drug prices) are weighted on the basis of out-of-pocket rather than total (including insured) expenditures; this means the index is probably not a good deflator for overall national health care spending. Fourth, the index uses providers' charges for services rather than what purchasers actually pay, which is often less—especially in today's world of discounted, negotiated, and per case payments. Given these problems, it might be more appropriate to combine Figure 6.1's medical price inflation category with the residual category.

Only a modest portion of increased health care spending has been attributed to the aging of the population, increased insurance, or rising administrative costs (Fuchs, 1990; CBO, 1992a,d; Newhouse, 1992). On the other hand, most observers assume that new, advanced medical technologies—

from organ transplants to magnetic resonance imaging—have contributed significantly to health care cost escalation, although this assumption is difficult to document explicitly (Altman and Wallack, 1979; Garrison, 1991; Weisbrod, 1991; CBO, 1992a; Newhouse, 1992). In most analyses of the factors contributing to cost increases, changes in technology are not examined directly. Rather, they tend to be both intermingled with price effects (e.g., when an expensive CAT scan substitutes for an X-ray) and treated as part of a residual category to the extent that they add to the volume of medical procedures and services (e.g., when both an expensive CAT scan and an expensive MRI are substituted for or added to a less costly and generally less useful X-ray). Nevertheless, several recent analyses suggest that the development and use of new technologies—more than the increasing use of existing technologies—constitute a major source of cost increases (Schwartz, 1987; Weisbrod, 1991; Berenson and Holahan, 1992; CBO, 1992a; Newhouse, 1992).

Public and private financing and management practices are also cited as major contributors to the "cost problem," although these factors may more easily explain high levels of health care spending than the recent escalation in the rate of health care expenditures. The practices commonly mentioned in this regard include provider payment systems that do not encourage the efficient use of resources (e.g., open-ended retrospective third-party reimbursement), insurance coverage and tax subsidies that may encourage excessive consumption, increasing malpractice litigation, excess capacity in hospital beds and in certain medical specialties, nonprice competition among providers, the ability of practitioners and providers to generate demand for an even broader set of medical services, and the difficulty of conditioning the spread of new technologies on demonstration of their cost-effectiveness. The public views such explanations of high costs as implying greed and waste on the part of physicians, drug companies, and insurers, and this viewpoint tends to limit the public's support for cost-cutting strategies that focus on any other target (Immerwahr, 1992).

## PUBLIC AND PRIVATE RESPONSES
## TO ESCALATING HEALTH CARE COSTS

The current policy preoccupation with medical care costs is primarily a product of the last quarter century.[1] Before the late 1960s, both public and private sector decisionmakers concentrated on expanding the supply of medical services (both physicians and hospitals) and widening access to these ser-

---

[1]Much of the discussion in this section follows that presented in IOM (1989). Chapter 2 of this report describes early strategies to contain health benefit costs.

vices. Concerns about rising health care costs were relatively muted, perhaps because everyone was satisfied with the results: more readily available services, more effective treatments for many specific medical problems, and better protection against medical care expenses. A rapidly growing economy also helped by providing new resources for a wide range of private and social needs.

As noted above, all this has changed dramatically. At least three major developments differentiate the periods before and after 1965. The first is the entry of government as a powerful force for both cost escalation and cost control following the adoption of Medicare and Medicaid in 1965. Federal and state spending for health care services and supplies rose from just under 25 percent of total public and private spending on health care in 1960 to over 40 percent by 1990 (Levit et al., 1991). The nation's governments, which also provide health benefits for their own employees and direct medical services to various special populations (e.g., veterans), have become the largest purchasers of medical care. An understanding of government cost control activities has become especially important because governments have a central role both as purchasers in their own right and as regulators of social transactions. Intentionally or not, their policies and programs can have positive or negative effects on private purchasers. The most widely cited example of a negative effect is so-called provider cost shifting, which is discussed below. A positive example is the development of tools or models for cost containment that private payers can use, for example, research on the effectiveness of alternative ways of treating specific health problems.

The second development was the beginning of serious efforts by private employers to control their expenditures for employee health benefits. Excluding public employers' premiums for employee health benefits and private employers' contributions to Medicare, private employers accounted for about one-quarter of total spending for health care services and supplies in 1990.

A third development was that forceful arguments began to be made that market competition—not government or community-oriented private programs—should be the primary vehicle for making health care effective, efficient, and affordable (see IOM, 1975, for several early formulations of the regulation versus competition debate). Community and regulatory strategies have by no means disappeared, but they have undoubtedly lost ground in recent years. On the other hand, proponents of market-based strategies generally argue that their approaches have been the subject of much talk but little real action.

The following sections examine a broad array government and employment-based initiatives to contain health care costs. Researchers' conclusions about the impacts of these programs are briefly summarized.

## Government Initiatives

In the words of one historian, "Medicare gave hospitals a license to spend" (Stevens, 1989, p. 284). Government efforts to limit that license have proceeded along various fronts with mixed results.

### Attempts to Control the Use, Price, and Supply of Medical Services

The preamble to the Medicare legislation prohibited federal "supervision or control over the practice of medicine or the manner in which medical services are provided" (P.L. 89-97). Consistent with this preamble, the government required and initially relied on hospitals and extended care facilities to operate utilization review committees to ensure the medical necessity and quality of care "without involving government in day-to-day hospital operations" (Mills, 1968). Rather quickly, however, policymakers came to view delegated utilization review as ineffective, "more form than substance," and moved to require Medicare's fiscal agents to undertake utilization review (U.S. Senate, 1970; Law, 1974; Blum et al., 1977). Medical and consumer groups were soon complaining, however, because this latter review process sometimes resulted in denial of payment after care had been rendered.

Before these complaints about utilization and quality review were addressed, the government acted on another front: medical care prices. August 1971 saw the start of the Economic Stabilization Program (ESP), a three-month federal freeze on all prices and wages. In the health sector, ESP controls applied in one form or another until April 1974, affecting provider charges to private as well as public payers. The end result of wage-price controls, in one evaluator's assessment, was considerable effectiveness in "reducing rates of increase in hospital employees' wages but [little impact] . . . on hospital costs" (Ginsburg, 1978). Although wage-price controls were a distinctively governmental strategy imposed on the private sector, they still left private health care providers and health insurers with substantial discretion about what services would be provided and covered.

In the middle of the wage-price control program, Congress enacted the Social Security Amendments of 1972 (P.L. 92-603), a multipronged effort at health care cost containment (U.S. Department of Health, Education and Welfare, 1976). The legislation included provisions for

• regulation of capital expenditures through Section 1122, which provided that health care facilities would not be reimbursed by Medicare for certain expenses associated with capital expenditures that were inconsistent with state or community health planning criteria,

• state initiatives under Section 222 to establish hospital rate-setting programs,

• community- rather than hospital-based utilization and quality review mechanisms to be applied by Professional Standards Review Organizations (PSROs) to care received by Medicare beneficiaries, and

• a Medicare economic index designed to limit the rate of increase in Medicare payments for physician services.

The capital expenditure provisions of the 1972 act were reenforced by the Health Planning and Resources Development Act of 1974 (P.L. 93-641), which attempted to strengthen state and community capacity to plan and control major capital investments in health care (Cain and Darling, 1979; IOM, 1981; Bice, 1988). This law viewed health care rather like a public utility or at least a service vested with a special community interest. The community, with the involvement and support of employers, insurers, unions, providers, and other local interests, would agree on the basic shape of the health care system and would influence the flow of available resources into areas of need, using its authority to grant certificates of need (CON) for certain major capital investments. Employers, employees, and the community generally—not just government as a purchaser—would benefit by better distribution of resources and restraint on the contribution of increased supply of resources to increased demand for services.

In the late 1970s and early 1980s, faith waned that this type of community-based planning and capital control—given its limited authority and the economic and other community incentives for resource expansion—could ever constrain costs (Salkever and Bice, 1978; Steinwald and Sloan, 1981). Much of the federal and state legal framework for health planning was abandoned as incompatible with newly popular market-oriented proposals for cost control. Nonetheless, about three-quarters of states still have some kind of CON legislation (Garrison, 1991). One recent analysis suggests that CON laws did affect the spending for inpatient hospital care and had mixed effects on the proliferation of certain advanced technologies (Lewin/ICF and Alpha Center, 1991).

Like health planning and wage-price controls, the Section 222 rate-setting provisions were, to a considerable degree, aimed at communitywide cost containment. They helped prompt more than 30 states to adopt some kind of hospital rate-setting program (Anderson, 1991a). Only a few of these programs were mandatory, and fewer still received waivers from HCFA to operate programs that applied to all payers within the state, including Medicare and Medicaid. Only one of the all-payer programs, that in Maryland, remains in place. Several studies have concluded that mandatory rate-setting programs can limit hospital cost increases, although program results are less consistent across states when the measure is the rate of increase in hospital costs per capita rather than per admission or per day (see Rosko, 1989; Anderson, 1991a; and Garrison, 1991, for summaries and citations of the research literature). The 1980s emphasis on Medicare prospective payment for hospitals (and on competition as the preferred vehicle for communitywide cost containment) reduced federal government support for state rate-setting programs.

At about the same time that the above regulatory strategies were being formulated, what was to become a dominant federal argument for market-oriented strategies began to manifest itself in the promotion of health maintenance organizations (HMOs). The term HMO was coined in 1970 when Paul Ellwood argued—with great impact—that prepaid comprehensive health care could restructure incentives to reward health care practitioners for keeping people from getting ill or returning them to health as quickly as possible (Ellwood et al., 1971; Ellwood, 1975; Starr, 1982). It was an alternative to existing fee-for-service medicine and a way of avoiding a government-based health plan. The government first encouraged HMO enrollment options for Medicare beneficiaries, then, in 1973, it established administrative, financial, coverage, and other requirements that organizations had to meet to become federally qualified and it provided grants, loans, and training programs to encourage the growth of HMOs. More important, the government required that employers with more than 25 employees offer an HMO option if the employer was approached by a local, federally qualified HMO (a requirement that under more recent legislation will expire in 1995). It also acted to supersede state laws that had limited the growth of prepaid group health plans.

For a variety of reasons, employees have proved to be a more amenable target for enrollment in HMOs than have Medicare beneficiaries. In 1991, only about 7 percent of Medicare beneficiaries were enrolled in an HMO or other coordinated care plan (to use the currently preferred term), compared with over 15 percent of the entire population and perhaps 30 percent of employees (GHAA, 1991; Hoy et al., 1991; Wilensky and Rossiter, 1991). Overall, government regulations and other activities have almost certainly been a major factor behind the growth in employment-based enrollment in HMOs and other network health plans. Evidence about the impact of these plans on costs is discussed in the next section of this chapter.

In 1982, Congress, once again dissatisfied with the track record of Medicare utilization review programs, replaced PSROs with statewide "utilization and quality control peer review organizations," PROs for short (P.L. 97-248) (IOM, 1976; Congressional Budget Office, 1979, 1981; Gosfield, 1989). These new organizations built in many ways on the PSROs, which had refined many of the data collection and analysis techniques used later by both public and private purchasers (Gosfield, 1975; Blum et al., 1977; Nelson, 1984; Ermann, 1988; IOM, 1990b). As their full title suggests, PROs have an explicit quality assurance mission as well as a cost containment role. Although PROs do sell services to private employers (and Medicaid), they generally are not major actors in this arena. In contrast to the private sector utilization review programs described below, PROs have been subject to little evaluation of their effectiveness.

*The Move to Prospective Payment*

Quality and utilization review by PROs was intended to supplement and monitor another legislative reform of 1982 that most observers viewed as much more important: the initial shift away from cost-based reimbursement of hospitals toward prospective payment. A year later in 1983, P.L. 98-21 established a prospective per case payment system (PPS) for hospitals that became fully effective in 1986. Limited data suggest that perhaps one-third of private network health plans make some use of a diagnosis-related group (DRG)-based payment method (ProPAC, 1992).

In addition, in 1989, Congress adopted a new physician payment methodology for Medicare (P.L. 101-239), a fee schedule set according to a resource-based relative value scale (RBRVS) with certain geographic and other adjustments (PPRC, 1990). It became effective in 1992.

Although the physician payment changes are too recent to be evaluated, several evaluations of the hospital payment system are available (Russell, 1989; Coulam and Gaumer, 1991; ProPac, 1992). One recent summary of these evaluations concluded that PPS "appears to have been successful in controlling its own benefit costs, without shifting the burden to beneficiaries" but to have had "little ultimate success in controlling the overall growth in U.S. health care expenditures" (Coulam and Gaumer, 1991, p. 62). Similar but less consistent findings are reported for the hospital rate-setting programs established by states before the adoption of PPS. A limited amount of research related to Medicare prospective payment suggests it might help constrain selected cost-adding technologies (e.g., cochlear implants, for which HCFA declined to provide a device-specific DRG) and encourage certain cost-cutting technologies (e.g., reusing disposable medical supplies) (OTA, 1984; Kane and Manoukian, 1989; IOM, 1991; Weisbrod, 1991).

*Payment Adequacy and Cost Shifting*

As noted in Chapter 5, some observers worry that the hospital prospective payment system does not adequately consider differences in patient severity within DRG payment categories. The result may be underpayments to institutions that care for disproportionate numbers of these patients and associated hospital efforts to avoid or dump such patients. A related concern about government programs has been that they are generally reducing payments to health care providers below cost and inducing providers to shift some of the cost burden to other employer and individual purchasers of health care.

A recent analysis for the Prospective Payment Assessment Commission (ProPAC, 1992) indicated some of the dimensions of the so-called cost shifting problem. It showed that Medicare covered only about 90 percent of Medicare patients' hospital costs, whereas Medicaid covered only 80 percent of its patients' hospital costs. Across the various state Medicaid programs, the same analysis showed wide discrepancies. Medicaid payments covered 56 percent of Medicaid patients' hospital costs in Illinois and 59 percent in Oregon but 104 and 102 percent in Maryland and New Jersey, respectively. Moreover, the study indicated that most hospitals with a greater need to shift costs to (that is, to secure additional revenues from) other payers were more able to do so than those with less need, but about 8 percent of hospitals with a moderate or great need to shift costs were unable to do so successfully. How long hospitals will be able to shift the cost burden to others is an open question. In any case, the ability of health care providers to get other purchasers of medical care to "make up" the losses they may experience from treating public program beneficiaries reflects— once again—the particular characteristics of the U.S. health care financing and delivery system.

## Private Purchasers

The continued rise in health care spending by employers gradually led them to become more prudent and aggressive buyers of health benefits for their employees. Indicative of the low profile of employers in the 1960s was a National Conference on Medical Costs, convened at the request of President Johnson to consider the general problem of rising costs. This 1967 conference had no corporate members on its advisory committee from outside the health industry, listed no business associations among the groups that were consulted, and included only one corporate representative on its agenda (U.S. Department of Health, Education and Welfare, 1968). As one employee benefits manager put it later: "In the past, many of us in the business community . . . unknowingly . . . contributed to the continuation of many abuses in the medical care system by simply signing the check and looking the other way" (Chinsky, 1986).

The oil embargo in 1973 and subsequent jumps in oil prices, rising interest rates, stiffer foreign competition, and other economic shocks combined with even sharper increases in health benefit costs to overcome employer passivity. The extended wage-price controls in the health sector and other public sector actions also focused attention on alternative cost containment strategies. As described in Chapters 2 and 3, the passage of the Employee Retirement Income Security Act of 1974 (ERISA) increased employer interest in self-insurance and more direct involvement in benefit cost management.

The surge in employer actions intended to limit the rate of increase in their health benefit costs dates primarily from the 1980s. Some initiatives have been collectively bargained and developed with labor union participation, whereas others have been unilaterally adopted by employers. Some communities have seen collective efforts by employers and others to tackle various cost problems. Like governments, employers may limit their own costs without necessarily affecting costs overall, particularly if their efforts merely shift the cost burden to others.

## Strategies

The portfolio of employer cost containment strategies includes six major kinds of approaches, some of which represent an intensification of older methods and some of which are largely new. These approaches, which have been described in more general terms in Chapter 3, include

• increased employee cost sharing and limits on some covered services, such as mental health care, although the range of covered services has also expanded in several areas such as outpatient, home, hospice, and preventive care;[2]

• utilization management programs intended to limit the volume of health care services through case-by-case review of their appropriateness;

• network health plans that typically combine various kinds of direct utilization management tools with provider payment and selective contracting methods intended to control the volume of services or the price of services or both;

• health promotion, which is often seen as a contributor to good employee relations and employee productivity as well as a possible means to lower health care costs through better health practices;

• flexible benefits, which has as one objective the capping of the employer contribution to health benefits so that employees absorb an increasing share of increasing health care costs, either directly or through sacrifice of other benefits; and

• self-insurance, which is aimed in part at avoiding the cost of state-mandated benefits and in part at cutting premium taxes and other costs associated with the purchase of insurance.

Tables 6.1 and 6.2 provide summary information on some employer activities in this arena. As with most other aspects of employment-based

---

[2]New benefits may be added for a variety of reasons: to improve employee relations and recruitment, to reflect changing medical practices, and to encourage a shift from more-expensive inpatient care to less-expensive outpatient care, the latter with the expectation that the result would be net cost savings.

**TABLE 6.1**   Percentage of Surveyed Employers Reporting Selected Utilization Management Features, 1987 to 1991

| Type of Program | 1987 | 1988 | 1989 | 1990 | 1991 |
|---|---|---|---|---|---|
| Preadmission certification | 61 | 68 | 73 | 81 | 81 |
| Concurrent review | 49 | 49 | 52 | 65 | 65 |
| Catastrophic case management | 51 | 50 | 55 | 65 | 67 |
| Second surgical opinion | —[a] | 73 | —[a] | —[a] | —[a] |
| Mandatory[b] | —[a] | —[a] | 59 | 55 | 49 |
| Voluntary[c] | —[a] | —[a] | 30 | 33 | 33 |

NOTE: The scope of the survey varies with the different years represented here. The range is from 1,600 employers covering more than 10 million employees to 2,016 employers covering 13 million employees from all 50 states and including all sizes and types of industry.

[a]Data not available.
[b]For specific procedures.
[c]For all procedures.

SOURCE: A. Foster Higgins & Co., Inc., 1992, as summarized in EBRI, 1992a.

health benefits, employers' practices vary substantially, both in the kinds of cost containment strategies they pursue and in the intensity of their involvement. Most larger businesses can take advantage of the approaches described above. Small businesses, however, often lack the resources and interest needed to evaluate options and implement many of these cost containment strategies and even to participate in community coalitions. In addition, insurers, utilization management firms, network health plans, and other organizations have aimed their products at large employers and have been less interested in marketing to small groups. As noted in Chapter 3, small employers are less likely to offer HMOs.[3] Many small employers see cutting or eliminating health benefits as their key cost containment option. Another option used by large as well as small employers is to hire greater proportions of part-time and contract workers who are not eligible for company health benefits.

Because many individual employers—even large ones—in big cities

---

[3]Some of the reasons for this have been that (1) offering a network health plan as the only option may be viewed as too restrictive by employees, (2) managers of smaller organizations may feel that they can judge better among indemnity plans than among plans with restricted panels of health care providers, (3) offering a choice of plans and splitting enrollment from an already small group will likely increase insurer risk and charges and internal administrative costs, and (4) some HMOs try to limit adverse selection by not marketing to small groups or by imposing medical underwriting or other restrictions that limit access by many small groups. Also, the HMO Act of 1973 did not require groups with fewer than 25 employees to offer an HMO.

lack leverage on their own, business coalitions in a number of communities are attempting to combine employer purchasing power. Data from the American Hospital Association's database on 130 coalitions indicated that their overwhelming emphasis is on member education and information collection. About one-quarter, however, describe themselves as actively involved in some kind of health care purchasing activity (*Business and Health*, 1991). The experience of one of the most active of these coalitions, Cleveland's Council of Smaller Enterprises, was described in Chapter 4, which also described a quite different, communitywide strategy promoted by employers in Rochester, New York.

Not only do employers differ in their ability to experiment with cost containment strategies, they also vary greatly with respect to the level and nature of their concern about health care costs. Understandably, most employers, especially if they self-insure, identify the health care cost issue with their own firm's experience. This experience, however, differs for employers, depending on their geographic location, industry, employee characteristics (e.g., proportions of older and younger workers, full-time and part-time, and active and retired), and sense that they can affect health care costs. As a result, although employers in some areas have formed coalitions and other vehicles for collective action, both the motivation to act collectively and the degree of consensus on specific strategies are often limited.

**TABLE 6.2** Percentage of Full-time Participants in Employment-Based Fee-for-Service Health Plans Subject to Selected Cost Containment Features

| | Small Establishments, 1990 | Medium and Large Establishments, 1989 |
|---|---|---|
| Incentive for use of generic prescription drugs | 15 | 15 |
| Mail-order drug program | 6 | 10 |
| No or limited reimbursement for nonemergency weekend admission to hospital | 14 | 14 |
| Prehospital admission certification requirement | 59 | 50 |
| Incentive to use birthing centers for delivery | 21 | 22 |
| Incentive for participants to audit hospital statement | 7 | 7 |

SOURCES: Adapted from Department of Labor, 1990, Table 52 and 1991, Table 51.

Some large employers are directly involved in administering cost management programs, for example, negotiating reductions in "excessive" provider charges. Many, however, rely on insurers, third-party administrators, or others to negotiate and contract with providers, develop and administer payment methodologies, design and operate utilization review programs, and otherwise implement selected strategies. In this latter situation, individual employers may still demand programs tailored to their preferences or circumstances and thus may influence third-party strategies.

*Impact of Private Cost Containment Strategies*

Most proposals for health care reform that mandate employer-provided coverage (including those that allow the option of employer payments for public program coverage) and otherwise retain a significant role for employers envision expanded use of the cost containment strategies described above. In particular, they rely on utilization management and regulated competition among network health plans (as described in Chapter 5). Some proposals, however, would also reinvigorate government rate-setting and capital investment controls, discussed earlier in this chapter, and some would try to superimpose some kind of global budgeting mechanism (not just rate-setting) on the private sector. The evidence that any of the designated strategies would actually limit the rate of increase in health care costs temporarily or over the long term is, at best, quite modest, although certain techniques appear to have reduced some unnecessary or inappropriate spending and some have shifted a portion of the cost burden from employers to employees. (Some of the suggested strategies have not really been implemented either in the United States or elsewhere.) Chapter 4 noted that the proliferation of employer cost containment initiatives has increased the administrative and psychological burdens on employers, employees, and health care providers.

Many researchers have tried to assess the impact of private sector cost containment programs over the last two decades (for overviews, see Luft et al., 1985; Eisenberg, 1986; Russell, 1986, 1990; Merrill and McLaughlin, 1986; Luft, 1987; Scheffler et al., 1988; Warner et al., 1988; Hadley and Swartz, 1989; IOM, 1989; Brown and McLaughlin, 1990; Merlis, 1990; Warner, 1990; Wickizer, 1990; Anderson, 1991a; Bailit and Sennett, 1991; EBRI, 1991c; Fielding, 1991a,b; Jencks and Schieber, 1991; Scheffler et al., 1991; CBO, 1992b; Newhouse, 1992; Pauly, 1992; Steinwachs, 1992; Thorpe, 1992a). Such assessments necessarily face three serious problems: the insufficient availability and quality of relevant data; the lack of statistical or physical control over environmental or other variables that might affect results; and the difficulty of disentangling the impact of multiple interventions that overlap both chronologically and geographically and that may have so-called lagged or delayed effects.[4]

The literature emphasizes possible effects on costs rather than effects on quality of care, access, or patient and provider satisfaction. Most analyses do not examine effects on communitywide costs, although some initiatives might be expected to have spillover effects if broadly enough implemented. The only techniques discussed here that depend particularly on employment-based health benefits as they are structured in the United States are self-insurance and flexible benefits.[5] The following six points are summarized from the literature and reflect the emphasis on effects on costs.

First, employee cost sharing does reduce employer costs both by transferring some costs to employees and by reducing episodes of care, but it does not appear to reduce costs per episode of care nor the underlying rate of increase in costs. Reductions in care do not appear to be restricted to care judged unnecessary or ineffective but also extend to effective services (Lohr et al., 1986). Depending on the measures used (i.e., overall use of hospital or other services versus use of specific services such as Pap smears), cost sharing may or may not reduce utilization more for lower- than for higher-income groups (Newhouse et al., 1981; Lohr et al., 1986). Some negative outcomes associated with cost sharing have been reported for poor children, but the impact of being uninsured altogether appears to have far more serious effects (Brook et al., 1984; Lurie et al., 1984).

Second, private sector utilization management appears to have reduced utilization of inpatient hospital care and to have constrained spending for firms adopting these programs, but some, perhaps most, of this reduction has been offset by increases in out-of-hospital care. Reductions are more likely for firms with high baseline utilization rates and tend to level off over time as easy targets are exhausted. The effect of utilization management programs on access to care or communitywide costs has not been systematically studied. Like cost sharing, utilization management appears not to have a long-term effect on the rate of increase in health care costs.

Third, the ability of network health plans to achieve cost savings for

---

[4]The analysis within this report makes little or no use of simple before-after comparisons of single employer experiences. Although flawed as a basis for drawing conclusions, such "one-shot" case studies may be helpful in formulating hypotheses about the impact of cost containment programs and instructive regarding the practical challenges involved in implementing particular cost containment strategies.

[5]Whether employers affect cost containment strategies elsewhere is largely undocumented. For example, it is not clear whether German employers made any special contribution (whether as sickness fund board members or fund managers) in stimulating or designing the 1987 revisions in the fees paid to physicians by principal statutory funds (Brenner and Rublee, 1991).

employers—compared with conventional health insurance plans—is related to plan characteristics and is complicated by difficulties in identifying and controlling for biased risk selection. The evidence of cost savings is clearest for staff model HMOs, weaker for IPAs, limited and mixed for PPOs, and essentially nonexistent for newer "open-ended" or point-of-service plans. Unfortunately, for areas not now served by staff model HMOs, these plans are the most time-consuming to establish and may not be feasible for many smaller metropolitan and nonurban areas. Lower levels of hospital use have accounted for most of the differences in costs for network versus conventional health plans. Limited evidence suggests that the rate of increase in costs for HMOs is comparable with that of conventional plans and that higher HMO market shares do not have much effect on communitywide health care costs.

Fourth, systematic evaluations of workplace health promotion programs are few in number, and some analyses suggest that net cost savings are limited and frequently overstated. However, evidence indicates that some health promotion efforts may still be relatively more cost-effective than many of the medical treatments commonly paid for by company health plans.

Fifth, although self-insurance and flexible benefits appear to offer some financial benefits to larger employers, there is no documentation that either reduces the longer-term rate of increase in health care costs. Whether flexible benefit programs will over the long term allow employers to cap the overall rate of increase in employee benefit costs (regardless of what happens to employer- and employee-paid health care costs) remains to be seen.

Sixth, real "one-time" reductions in costs—particularly if they involve gains or at least little or no sacrifice in access, equity, or outcomes—should not be downplayed. In particular, continued public-private efforts to identify and eliminate care that is not clinically appropriate and to limit the introduction of expensive technologies of limited benefit are warranted on grounds of both quality of care and cost.

To summarize, continued innovation by employers and third-party carriers in benefit plan design may help some employers lower the level of their health benefit costs and may, in some cases, encourage more effective utilization of health care services. It is, however, discouraging to find little evidence that private sector cost containment strategies affect the long-term rate of increase in health care costs and virtually no evidence that suggests whether employer efforts to contain costs have positive, neutral, or negative communitywide or societal impacts.

If any community may be viewed as an exception to this last generalization, it is Rochester, New York. It has a distinctive history of active, long-term employer support for community rating and other programs by the community's dominant insurer (a Blue Cross and Blue Shield plan), communitywide health planning, HMO development, and restraint in hospital pricing. Without this support, it is doubtful that the area would have such low health insurance costs for both individual and employer group coverage (Taylor, 1987; Freudenheim, 1992b; Taylor et al., 1992). In 1991, per enrollee health benefit costs for Blue Cross in Rochester were $2,378, compared with the overall national figure of $3,605 reported in Chapter 3. Only 6 percent of the adult population reported they were uninsured, less than half the national rate. In addition, major Rochester employers, such as Eastman Kodak, have chosen not to self-insure, believing that any short-term savings would be outweighed by higher longer-term costs from the destruction of their cooperative strategy for health care financing and delivery.

Hawaii, which has among the nation's lowest costs for health care despite its pattern of higher prices for most services and goods, might also be cited as a place where employers have made a difference in overall health care costs (GAO, 1992a; Kent, 1992b; Priest, 1992).[6] It is not clear, however, whether their role has been one of direct involvement in cost containment strategies or one of more passive support for state- and insurer-initiated programs. The state is unusual in having won the only ERISA waiver to date, for its 1974 Prepaid Health Care Act.[7] This legislation requires employers to provide, and employees to accept, coverage unless coverage is provided under another plan, sets a maximum level of employee contribution, and defines a required benefit package. Most employers voluntarily cover dependents even though they are not required to do so. Reports on cost control strategies in Hawaii focus not on employers but on the state, the Hawaii Medical Service Association (a Blue Shield plan that covers 53 percent of the population), and the Kaiser Foundation Health Plan, which covers 20 percent. These plans voluntarily use a modified form of community rating for employers with fewer than 100 employees.

By and large, private sector innovation in cost containment has been designed to attract large employers rather than small employers or individual purchasers. If market reforms essentially removed the large employer from the purchasing role in favor of the individual, the cost containment strategies adopted by health plans might change. The nature of any such changes would be affected by the extent to which reforms also required basic benefits, standardized utilization review, regulated payments to

---

[6]Like the railroad, lumber, and mining industries on the mainland, Hawaii's sugar and pineapple plantations have a long history of providing health services to workers.
[7]After one large employer, Standard Oil, successfully challenged the state legislation, the state's congressional delegation quickly sought a statutory waiver of ERISA's preemption of such state regulation of employee benefits. Because the waiver applies only to the 1974 Prepaid Health Care Act, the state has been seeking another waiver under ERISA that would allow it to make further changes.

hospitals and physicians, and otherwise constrained private initiative. Health plan strategies would also be affected by the degree to which reforms strengthened or weakened traditional insurance regulations to discourage competition based on risk selection, assure financial solvency, and generally police the market for deceptive practices.

## FUNCTIONING OF THE HEALTH CARE MARKET

In an economy such as that of the United States, questions about the appropriateness and effectiveness of various price signals and resource allocations are often most easily settled by reference to the workings of well-functioning markets. In many circumstances, markets can be expected to generate highly effective price signals that help ensure the efficient use of resources. Unfortunately, the market for health care services—as it is currently structured—cannot make such claims. Leading issues in the debate over health care reform are whether major changes in public policy can create an effectively functioning market, whether the employer should have a major role in a market-oriented approach, and whether, on balance, the projected effects of one or another kind of reformed market would be better or worse than the major alternatives. The major alternatives are incremental changes in the current system, mandatory employer coverage (similar to the Hawaii plan or with a public plan option), and a uniform, universal public plan.

To understand the debate over market reforms, it is useful to review what economists described as the basic requirements for an effectively functioning, competitive market (see, for example, Fuchs, 1988; Aaron, 1991; Weisbrod, 1991; CBO, 1992a). These requirements include easy entry into the market by buyers and sellers; freedom from government supply or price regulation and from buyer or seller collusion to fix prices or supplies; absence of dominant buyers or sellers; buyers and sellers with reasonable and relatively equal information about price and quality; and no subsidies that distort prices and price consciousness.

In health care, however, one finds large government and private payers; organized groups of providers; some regulation of prices and substantial regulation of market entry, particularly through licensing and accreditation requirements for health care practitioners and providers; considerable doubts about the independence of supply and demand; substantial imbalances in provider and consumer information but lack of significant information about outcomes—even on the part of providers; and market agents insulated by third-party insurance practices from full price sensitivity or cost minimization pressures. In many cases, the physician, not the patient, effectively decides what quantity and quality of care will be provided, and the incentives affecting physician choices, thus, need to be understood. As noted in

Chapters 1 and 5, although the tendency of insured individuals to use (and have provided for them) more services than uninsured individuals is a partly intended and partly unwanted consequence of health insurance, such a "utilization effect" is not a desirable feature of competitive markets.

Aaron (1991) notes that "health insurance and health care pose special problems [for economic analysis because] health insurance typically is purchased by healthy people, while most health care is consumed by sick people. Society normally has little interest when people gamble and lose. But when the gamble concerns events that change basic preferences and that affect the life and health of oneself and one's family, it is not clear why past consumer decisions deserve priority over new preferences" (p. 17). Moreover, many of the most expensive decisions involve individuals whose ability to weigh expected benefits and risks of treatment alternatives are stressed by pain and fear, time pressures, and lack of information and technical understanding of specific options and the possible consequences. The more drastic the consequences of the choices people make about health care, the more compelling are the questions and arguments about the role of government in intensifying or limiting market-based incentives for individual choice and responsibility. Similar issues arise in debates over the need for government constraints on the use and interpretation of living wills and advance directives about the use of life support in cases of terminal illness or injury.

Markets that are characterized by poorly informed consumers are unlikely to yield appropriate prices and quantities. Although the information imbalance between providers and employer purchasers may be less than for the individual patient, the complexity of the medical care product and the difficulty of assessing outcomes remain obstacles to informed purchasing. (Employer interest in outcome assessment is discussed shortly.) In addition, biased risk selection can encourage competitors to focus on competition for good risks rather than on competition based on effective and efficient management of health care.

High and rising costs, gaps in coverage, and unequal access to health coverage and health care are not surprising consequences of the current structure and operation of health care markets. The committee's view is that this structure encourages the proliferation of medical technologies and services without evidence of effectiveness and that neither the producer nor the consumer side of the health care transaction faces sufficiently the real costs of its actions. Because the current incentive and market structure is widely viewed as inefficient, cost containment has become a central objective of decisionmakers even though it is not inevitably a sensible goal if high costs are producing appropriately high value. A major question for decisionmakers is whether the health care market can and should be reformed or whether the nation would be better off with a single national health plan.

Those who believe that policy changes can make market forces an effective constraint on health care use and prices propose several specific steps. They include capping the tax exclusion for employer-paid health benefits; increasing the employee's contributions for health benefit premiums; requiring multiple choice of health plans; limiting or financially rewarding individual choice of certain kinds of health plans; capitating provider payment; standardizing benefit packages; and developing better performance monitoring techniques.

Some argue that market forces would work better if the individual, not the employer, were the key decisionmaker in health insurance purchases. They would adapt the proposals just mentioned to eliminate employer discretion in the design, selection, or operation of health plans (Garamendi, 1992). Most but not all proposed market strategies would be supported by a fairly extensive regulatory structure, regardless of whether these approaches envision any role for the employer beyond certain nondiscretionary financing and administrative tasks.

Proposals for market reform generally would shift more of the direct burden for health care spending—at the margin—away from the government or employer to the individual. They would then mitigate—to varying degrees—the burden of this shift through income-related subsidies intended to make health insurance more affordable for low-income individuals. Proposed changes in federal tax and other policies to make the choice of certain health plans more costly to individuals might also work to produce more one-time reductions in the level of health care expenditures. Whether such market strategies would selectively affect inappropriate spending, slow the development and introduction of expensive medical technologies, or reduce the underlying rate of growth in health care costs is unclear. Most of the formal economic analyses of markets and health insurance focus on efficiency and spending at a particular time rather than on effects across time (Newhouse, 1992).

Tax, regulatory, and other reforms that introduce more marketlike mechanisms of one type or another into health care delivery and financing probably can mobilize health care resources more efficiently in some areas. Given, however, the current distribution of income and the desired distribution of health care services and improved health outcomes (to note only one particular concern), such reforms, unaided by significant public subsidies for the purchase of insurance and improved mechanisms for monitoring health plan performance, are unlikely to generate appropriate responses.

Some aspects of managed competition or market reform proposals have been considered in Chapter 5. This discussion noted the uncertainties surrounding the methods and principles for defining basic benefits, controlling or adjusting for risk selection, monitoring health plan practices for abuses, and ensuring accountability on the part of whatever oversight entity is created. Some of these issues are raised as topics for continued research in Chapter 7. Many of the basic assumptions of market reform models have never been tested, whereas real examples of single national health plans exist as a basis for analyzing the pluses and minuses of such a strategy and evaluating its relevance to the United States.

## THE QUESTION OF VALUE

Whether or not the real expenditures on health care in the United States negatively affect the country's standard of living depends more critically on the return on this investment rather than on its level. If health care expenditures were viewed as productive enough in terms of their impact on work force quality, morale, and performance (e.g., through reduced levels of injury, absenteeism, or behavior impaired by chronic illness), perhaps concern about overall resource commitments would diminish. In short, the dividends would be worth the investment. If, however, health care expenditures divert resources from more productive expenditures or if health expenditure increases cannot, in the short-term, be offset by reductions in wages or other components of total compensation, then some specific companies and industries may suffer a competitive disadvantage.

Clearly, concern is widespread that the high level of resources devoted to the U.S. health sector is not being matched by a sufficiently high return in overall health status and individual well-being. This conclusion is controversial but is kindled by (1) studies showing that the per capita use of many medical practices varies greatly depending on geographic location, insurance status, supply of health resources, and other factors,[8] (2) evidence that a significant amount of care is not medically appropriate or effective, and (3) the lack of an obvious health status advantage for the United States compared with other advanced nations that commit fewer resources to health care and yet still cover virtually of their populations (Wennberg, 1984, 1990, 1991; Brook et al., 1986; Chassin et al., 1987; Eddy and Billings, 1988; Starfield, 1991; Schieber and Poullier, 1991; Fuchs, 1992).

Increased health care expenditures have, nonetheless, coincided with some improvements in overall health status as measured, for example, by infant mortality, average life expectancy, and age-adjusted death rates from heart disease and stroke (U.S. Department of Health and Human Services, 1991). Although changed behaviors in diet, exercise, and smoking probably have played a role in these developments, there is little question that new

---

[8]Researchers emphasize that studies showing variable utilization do not, in themselves, demonstrate that higher rates are either better or worse than lower rates of use for a particular service.

drugs, new types of surgery, and other medical advances have also made important contributions. Significant differentials remain, however, between more and less advantaged segments of the population. For example, the infant mortality rate for African Americans is twice that of whites in the United States. Even for infants born to college-educated women, a notable gap between the races remains (Schoendorf et al., 1992). The reasons for such differentials are not well understood but almost certainly include a mix of socioeconomic and biological factors that increased health care spending by itself could leave largely unaffected (Davidson and Fukushima, 1992; Kempe et al., 1992).

Recent decades have seen spectacular developments in biomedical science, medical technology, and medical education that hold considerable promise for future improvements in health status. In general, the American health care system produces an enormous amount of innovation; at its best, medical care in this country has no rival. Moreover, much of the innovation and trained personnel produced by or for the U.S. health care sector is available to people in many other countries, so others, too, have a stake in the innovative and educational developments induced by the complex set of existing arrangements in the U.S. health care sector. Policymakers assessing options for reform should think carefully about the impact of new policies on the country's continued capacity for innovation and education and the expected impact of this capacity on health status and well-being.

From a public policy viewpoint, it would be highly desirable to understand to what extent the high and rapidly rising health care costs stem from cultural and scientific influences (e.g., higher standards of living, higher expectations, and advances in basic science) and to what extent they derive from the way the health care system is currently organized and financed (e.g., relying heavily on employment-based health benefits rather than a single public program or an individual insurance market). Similarly, it would be highly desirable for policymakers to know whether the spending gap between this country and others is caused by greater availability and consumption of effective health services (a good idea), the greater use of ineffective health services (a bad idea), unnecessarily high payments to providers (a bad idea), or simply the slower growth of the U.S. economy (an unfortunate development)?

Policymakers can also ask more specific questions. For example, if medical training and payment were substantially reoriented to increase the proportion of generalists relative to specialists (as many recommend), would the health care system become more effective overall in reducing ill health and poor functioning? If some resources were shifted away from certain kinds of high-technology care for adults toward primary and preventive care for children and pregnant women, especially in poor and minority communities, could gains in health and well-being for the latter group be achieved, and what would be the effect on the former group? If physician fees were decreased or increased by 20 percent, would this have any significant impact on the supply of quality medical services in the short or long run? If pharmaceutical prices were cut or increased by 20 percent, would this have any appreciable bearing on the level of introduction of useful new medical compounds? Is the administrative overhead associated with the current multipayer system matched by appropriate benefits related to the diversity of purchaser circumstances?

Answers to the above questions are not easy to pin down because the variables cited are interdependent, and the data are incomplete and sometimes misleading. The measurement problems associated with medical care prices (discussed earlier) are matched by problems in measuring medical care outputs, that is, their effect on health and well-being in the aggregate and for specific population subgroups. Aggregate measures of health are still relatively crude; most analyses rely on mortality statistics with occasional use of other measures such as proportion of infants with low birth weights (Schieber et al., 1991).

On the other hand, some important advances in measuring health status and well-being at the individual level are being achieved using both generic and disease- or problem-specific measures of functioning and of health-related quality of life that go well beyond traditional measures of mortality and morbidity (Lohr, 1989, 1992). These advances have not yet had much utility for general comparisons of population health status over time and across geographic units. This is in part because these measurement tools are not well known outside certain research settings and in part because they require information reported by individuals that is not routinely and widely enough available from such sources as birth and death records, health insurance claims, national health surveys, and disease reporting systems.

With varying degrees of sensitivity to the complexities involved, policymakers, providers, employers, unions, and consumers have begun to focus increasingly on the question of value and to demand comparisons of the cost-effectiveness of individual practitioners, providers, and both new and existing medical services (Roper et al., 1988; Lohr, 1989, 1992; Eddy, 1990a,b,c, 1991a,b; IOM, 1990a,b; Couch, 1991; Fox and Leichter, 1991; Buck, 1992; Mulley, 1992). The results may be used (and possibly misused) to help determine what services health plans should cover, set payments for medical care, select providers for network health plans, and develop clinical practice guidelines for practitioners, payers, and patients (IOM, 1985, 1991, 1992a,b; ProPAC, 1986, 1992; PPRC, 1988, 1989; Rettig, 1991).

Most efforts to assess the effectiveness of medical services and technologies, especially new technologies, are publicly supported, although some private organizations, such as the Blue Cross and Blue Shield Association, have become involved in technology assessment. Initiatives by private payers, however, are limited partly because of the expense and complexity of technology assessment and partly because they cannot fully capture the benefit of their work, the results of which can be used by their competitors (the "free rider" problem). Reflecting the growing perception that the federal government needed to bolster its involvement in effectiveness research, Congress created the Agency for Health Care Policy and Research in the Department of Health and Human Services in 1989 and gave it broad responsibilities to develop practice guidelines and conduct research on the effectiveness of alternative forms of care for specific clinical conditions.

Although much of the interest in health status and outcome measures has come from either national policymakers or clinicians, employers and unions in a number of communities are becoming involved in pragmatic efforts to apply these measures, often with the support of private groups such as the John A. Hartford and Robert Wood Johnson foundations. Employers and unions are working with researchers, providers, and public officials to find practical ways to gather better data on outcomes and then use this information to improve the quality and efficiency of care (Borbas et al., 1990; Geigel and Jones, 1990; Madlin, 1991a; Stern, 1991; Buck, 1992; Mulley, 1992). Such efforts are under way in communities in Iowa, Minnesota, Ohio, Tennessee, and elsewhere.

The United States is clearly a leader in the arena of effectiveness research and technology assessment. Whether employers are, at the margin, providing any extra stimulus to effectiveness research and methodology development (beyond what government, private foundations, and some insurers would provide) is hard to say. Undoubtedly, many employers focus on costs and little else. Arguably, however, some large employers and employer coalitions may be encouraging a speedier movement from the research to the application stage for effectiveness assessments. Furthermore, a greater level of interest in local, communitywide assessments of provider performance may exist now than would be the case were employers uninvolved in health benefits.

Nonetheless, the challenges in devising good measures of outcomes and effectiveness, collecting accurate data, making fair comparisons, and doing it all at a cost perceived as reasonable are enormous. Given the complexity of medical care processes and the problem of controlling for the impact of economic, ethnic, and other variables on health, difficulties will surely continue for efforts to link many health care services—and expenditures—to specific outcomes. In addition, better measurement of health care outcomes and performance and programs to judge and improve the appropriate use of new or existing technologies may add to the cost—broadly defined—of administering health benefits. Like any other costs, these should be judged by whether and how much they help improve the value of health spending, for example, by reducing spending for inappropriate care or achieving better outcomes for the same amount of spending.

Overall, policymakers, researchers, employers, unions, and health care providers must be committed for the long term to asking the right questions and seeking their answers. Whether initiatives such as those described above will produce information and responses that are convincing and timely enough to persuade purchasers—including government purchasers—to look beyond the unit price of services, the "premium" for an insured or self-insured health plan, or the appeal of cost shifting remains to be seen.

## CONCLUSION

Startling as they may be, high levels and rates of increase in health care spending may by themselves provide little reason for anxiety. The crucial issue for policymakers is not whether the ratio of health care spending to GNP is high and rising, but whether the level, distribution, and rate of increase in health care spending produce appropriate value compared with alternative kinds of spending within the constraint of available resources. In times of economic difficulties, when many important needs may not be satisfied, concerns about the relative value perceived for health care spending may intensify.

Although individuals and employers in the United States can and must make resource-related trade-offs about spending for health care versus spending for other purposes, it is at the level of national policy that the most complex balancing must occur. It is there that competing interests, short-term and longer-term objectives, and calls for major restructuring of the health care system are most explicitly weighed.

Should policymakers expect that incremental changes in existing institutional arrangements and public policies can improve the distribution and deployment of resources in the medical sector to achieve acceptable health outcomes at a reasonable cost? Most of the committee members believe the answer to this question is no. Without major restructuring of the current system of voluntary employment-based health benefits, certain problems, such as cost shifting, inadequate access to appropriate care for many of the uninsured, competition based on risk selection, and rapid diffusion of new technologies without evidence of cost-effectiveness, are unlikely to diminish.

In its quest for a more cost-effective health care system, would the nation be better off removing the employer from any active decision-making role and leaving the field mainly to government policies and programs or mainly to the operation of some reconfigured individual market for health care services or—more likely—some combination of the two? The committee could not agree on an answer to this question. Although committee members agreed that employers' capacities and incentives to manage health benefit programs effectively are quite uneven and narrowly focused on their own employee groups, they disagreed about the theoretical and empirical case for different strategies for controlling health care costs and the philosophies underlying these strategies. The next chapter, however, outlines some areas in which the committee did generally agree on steps that could improve the performance of the current system of voluntary employment-based health benefits.

# 7

# Findings and Recommendations

*In some ways the public interest resides in the no man's land between government and business.*

E.E. Schattschneider, 1960

*Yes, I favor national health insurance as long as you don't have the government too involved.*

Focus group participant, 1992

*If we are going to govern ourselves without inflating our governments more and more, the nongovernments in our society will have to think of themselves quite self-consciously as part of governance.*

Harlan Cleveland, 1937

The United States can make more constructive use of its mixed structure of public and private health coverage. Doing so will require, at a minimum, a new self-consciousness about the role of the employer and significant changes in the relationship between the public and the private sectors in the governance of the nation's arrangements for financing and delivering health care.

Precedents for such change exist. Beginning in the 1930s and 1940s, voluntary private initiative combined with some indirect regulatory stimulus helped produce for millions of Americans a remarkable breadth, quality, and depth of medical care and medical expense protection. In the mid-1960s, the nation reached a consensus that public programs were necessary to finance appropriate coverage for the elderly (through Medicare) and some of the poor and near-poor (through Medicaid), although the latter program has failed to reach many low-income individuals and families. Now, at the end of the century, renewed creativity and public-spiritedness are required to devise and negotiate public and private initiatives to protect more Ameri-

229

cans against the costs of ill health, to achieve health outcomes commensurate with the resources expended for health services, and to encourage broad risk sharing among the well and the ill.

Reform that maintains a major role for employment-based health benefits is certainly not the only option for the United States, as witnessed by proposals for a single government program, on the one hand, or for a market based on the individual purchase of insurance, on the other. Some members of the Institute of Medicine study committee believe that improving the employment base has more pragmatic and philosophical appeal than abandoning it. Other committee members disagree and believe this base is too structurally flawed to ever meet basic access, quality, and cost objectives. In any case, no one should expect that a significantly more equitable and cost-effective system of employment-based health benefits can be obtained without major adjustments in current arrangements.

In examining today's structure of employment-based health benefits, the committee had two basic tasks, one empirical, the other evaluative. The first task—to understand and describe the current system—provided the focus of the preceding chapters. This task was a challenge given the system's variability, its bent for change, and the limited evidence to distinguish the consequences of employment-based health benefits from those of third-party payment in general or from other features of health care financing and delivery in this country.

The committee's second task gives rise to this concluding chapter, which presents the committee's assessments and findings. What follows is (1) a brief recapitulation of themes to this point, (2) a characterization and assessment of key features of this country's system of voluntary employment-based health benefits, (3) a set of findings and recommendations about how this system might be improved, (4) a few comments on practical and technical challenges, and (5) a number of suggestions for future research.

The findings reported here do not constitute a blueprint for health care reform, even for reform that seeks to build on voluntary employment-based health benefits. In particular, the findings do not address the most effective means to limit the rapid escalation in health care costs and define the appropriate role of advanced technologies, two issues that trouble all economically developed countries, regardless of their system of medical expense protection. In addition, the discussion here does not touch directly on the problems facing Medicare, Medicaid, and other public programs, although the committee recognizes that efforts to resolve these problems cannot go forward in isolation from the system examined here.

Instead, this chapter sets forth some steps that government, business, individuals, and health care practitioners and providers could take to alleviate certain problems related to the link between the workplace and health benefits. These steps are grouped into two divisions: one that assumes the preservation of a voluntary system of employment-based health benefits and a second that assumes that a move beyond a voluntary system is required if the nation is to extend access significantly and use resources more effectively to improve health status. These steps do not constitute a general committee endorsement or rejection of either a voluntary or a compulsory system of employment-based health benefits.

## RECAPITULATION

The preceding chapters have examined the evolution of employment-based health benefits in the United States, described basic coverage and management features of the current system, and identified several sources of variation across workplaces. They have depicted some of the practical implications for employers, employees, and health care providers of employer involvement in managing health benefits. The troublesome problems of biased risk selection and risk segmentation have been examined, along with some proposed responses to these problems. Finally, concerns about the level and rate of increase in health care costs and the means of controlling costs have been explored. The focus has not been on costs as such but rather on the value achieved for health care spending compared to alternative uses of limited resources.

Clearly, this nation's continued reliance on voluntary employment-based health benefits to cover most workers and their families reflects a distinctive American history. One facet of this history is the result of the creative private efforts of employees, trade unions, employers, health care providers, and others to develop mechanisms to spread and budget the risk of medical expenses for many workers and their families. Another facet of this history involves a cultural predilection for private rather than public action, which has contributed to the repeated failure of proposals to extend social insurance programs to cover medical care expenses for the entire population. Instead, the public interest has been reflected in tax, collective bargaining, and other policies that have directly and indirectly shaped and stimulated a voluntary system of employment-based coverage for workers and their families. The adoption of Medicare and Medicaid in 1965 and Medicare's expansion to include the disabled in 1972 brought public insurance to many of those for whom private insurance was ill-suited.

In 1974, under the Employee Retirement Income Security Act (ERISA), the national government assumed sole authority to regulate employee benefits. It has not, however, exercised much regulatory oversight in the health benefits arena. The states still have some indirect influence when employers transfer financial risk for their health benefit programs to insurance companies, which states may regulate under the McCarran-Ferguson Act of 1945. The impact of state regulation has, however, diminished as more and more employers have opted for self-insurance arrangements that are exempt from state oversight and as the courts have broadened the interpretation of ERISA's preemption of state statutory and common law in matters "related to" employee benefits.

Overall, for most Americans with a strong connection to the workplace, the system provides very reasonable access to the benefits of biomedical science and technology at a relatively modest direct personal cost in the form of premium contributions and other cost sharing. When people are asked to rate the most important employee benefit, a substantial majority select health benefits. Surveys also indicate that more Americans think employers rather than government should be the most responsible for providing health benefits for full-time employees and their dependents, although no specific plan design or policy commands the unequivocal support of the majority.

The offering of employment-based health benefits is virtually universal in large and medium-sized organizations. These organizations generally cover a large portion of the cost or premium for employee coverage but vary considerably in their contributions for family coverage. They often help employees understand their health coverage and resolve problems with specific health plans. Employers have become increasingly active in the management of health benefits by offering employees choices among competing health benefit plans that limit employee choice of health care practitioner, adding managed care features to indemnity health plans, and developing workplace health promotion programs. At the same time, some larger employers are focusing—more than ever before—on how they can have employees pay a larger share of costs directly, how they can avoid sharing the risk for medical care and benefit costs for anyone other than their employees and, perhaps, their dependents, and how they can get the best possible rates from health care providers regardless of the impact on others in the community. In this latter regard, they join Medicare, Medicaid, and some network health plans in contributing to concerns about cost shifting, that is, the attempt by health care providers to make up for certain payers' discounts and underpayments through higher charges to less powerful groups and individuals.

Table 7.1 depicts some of the important functions assumed by employers and their relative difficulty or complexity. In general, the participation by employers in these functions falls off sharply between the first and second functions (particularly among small employers) and the second and third functions represented on the left side of the table. The table does not attempt to rate employer performance or to portray the positive and negative effects on employees or the community that may follow from specific steps taken by employers in carrying out these functions.

Only about half of all workers are employed by the large and medium-

**TABLE 7.1** Broad Functions or Activities That May Be Undertaken by Employers Providing Health Benefits, Arrayed by Approximate Level of Administrative Difficulty or Complexity

| LEAST DIFFICULT OR COMPLEX | | MOST DIFFICULT OR COMPLEX |
|---|---|---|
| | | Direct Contracting with Health Care Providers or Direct Provision of Health Care Services |
| | Direct Administration of Claims, Utilization Review, and Other Management Functions | |
| | Extensive Tailoring and Detailed Oversight of Health Benefit Program | |
| Contributing to Plan Premium, Monitoring Basic Aspects of Health Plan Performance, Assisting Employees with Problems | | |
| Facilitating Participation in Health Plan: Enrollment, Information Distribution, Payroll Deduction | | |

sized organizations in which health benefits are virtually universal, and this fraction is declining. Among organizations with fewer than 10 employees, one survey suggests that only one quarter offer health benefits, although another survey suggests that proportion may be nearer to half. Moreover, efforts to reach employees of small firms through "bare bones" insurance and other relatively inexpensive products have had limited success. The reasons are diverse: many small employers feel that even limited coverage is still too expensive; others believe their employees do not need or want it; and some do not see its provision as an employer's responsibility. In general, the problems and options regarding health coverage faced by small organizations differ in significant ways from those faced by larger organizations. Many proposals for health care reform are particularly targeted at small employers.

High health care costs are frequently portrayed as the nation's number one health policy problem, but the problem is more complex. That is, the country is spending a greater share of national resources on medical care and making it less affordable for many without being confident that it is achieving better health outcomes, greater labor productivity, or other equivalent value for its increased investment. Efforts to accumulate evidence on outcomes and to evaluate and compare the costs and benefits of alternative medical practices are increasing in number and sophistication. Nonetheless, the resources devoted to these efforts are minuscule compared with those devoted to new medical treatments and technologies, and—as noted later—this is an area in which further research is a priority.

In considering the current system of voluntary employment-based health coverage and various proposals for change, it is important to remember that coverage is not the same as access. Some who have coverage still face access problems by virtue of their location, their race or other personal characteristics, or specific characteristics of their coverage, such as low rates of payment for physician services. Likewise, even those who lack health insurance have some access to care on an emergency basis for serious illness or injury, although the financial burden of this uncompensated care is very unevenly borne across communities. Access to preventive and primary care services is much more difficult for the uninsured, although public and private outpatient programs and charity care offered by individual practitioners do help some needy individuals who lack health coverage.

Extending health insurance to the currently uninsured population would not guarantee adequate access to appropriate health services, but it almost certainly would assist them in obtaining preventive and primary care that could improve their health status and quality of life. Whether some of the currently uninsured—and some who are now insured—would be better served by direct care arrangements (such as the U.S. veterans hospitals or publicly funded preventive and primary care clinics) or some other alternative or supplement to individual health insurance is a serious question, one that is not much discussed in the current debate over health care reform.

## FEATURES, STRENGTHS, AND LIMITATIONS
## OF THE CURRENT SYSTEM

Any concise statement of key features of the U.S. system of health care coverage and the role of employment-based health benefits must simplify and generalize from a world that is neither simple nor uniform nor static. Nonetheless, based on the descriptions and analyses presented in the first six chapters of this report, the following nine characteristics stand out:

- Voluntary group purchase
- Lack of universal coverage
- Dispersed power and accountability
- Diversity

- Innovativeness
- Discontinuity
- Risk selection and discrimination
- Barriers to cost management
- Complexity.

Most of these characteristics distinguish the system in the United States from systems in other advanced industrial nations and from what is envisioned by proposals for a fully public system of health insurance. They are not, however, purely a function of voluntary employment-based health coverage. If the link between employment and health benefits were abandoned or retained only as a conduit for financing health benefits, some of the features discussed below would likely disappear, but others might persist—or even become more prominent—depending on the specific changes made. Reforms that retained a significant role for employers might bring significant or only marginal changes, again depending on their specifics.

## Voluntary Group Purchase

The very subject of this report is a defining, indeed unique, feature of the U.S. health care system: reliance on health benefits voluntarily sponsored by employers—or collectively bargained between employers and unions—to cover the majority of nonelderly individuals. The use of the employee group (more specifically, the larger employee group) as a basis for health insurance has mitigated the problems of risk selection that plagued initial private efforts to insure individual expenses for medical care. It has offered an alternative to government mandates but still created purchasers with more leverage than single individuals can normally bring to bear in buying health insurance, identifying and resolving problems, and securing efficiencies in program administration.

Once an employer opts to offer health benefits, some governmental limits on its discretion may apply. For example, employers are generally required to provide employees with certain summary information about their health plan, offer continued coverage to former workers and others under certain circumstances, and cover workers aged 65 to 69.

In assuming the purchaser role, the main question for employers has been what, if anything, do they need to offer as health benefits to attract and maintain a productive work force and to compete or otherwise function effectively. The collection of employer—and employee—responses to this question have in large measure defined the current system (both its public and its private aspects) and directly affected both the definition and the realization of broader societal objectives. Most proposals to eliminate the voluntary character of the current system through mandatory public, employer, or individual coverage are a response to the following characteristics of this system.

## Lack of Universal Coverage

Group purchasing voluntarily supported by employers helps make health coverage possible for many who would likely go without it in the current market for individually purchased insurance. Nearly two-thirds of Americans under age 65, almost 140 million individuals, are covered by employment-based health benefits. Another 10 million of those aged 65 and over have Medicare supplemental benefits provided by a former employer. Compared with the previous system in which neither government nor employers assisted individuals in covering medical care expenses, this system has undoubtedly expanded health coverage.

On the other hand, more than 35 million Americans lack insurance, and the great majority of those without health benefits are workers or their family members. Virtually every other advanced industrial nation covers all, or all but a very small fraction of, its population. Most either require employers to help finance coverage for workers or strongly encourage them to do so through positive incentives or subsidies aimed at the employer or employee or both, and most have special provisions for those with limited links to the work place. In contrast, many U.S. employers choose not to offer health benefits to all or some of their employees. Such employees are especially likely to work part-time, on a seasonal basis, or in low-wage jobs for small employers. Some, if offered a choice of health benefits versus higher wages or the opportunity to work full-time, might decline the former— as do some workers today.

## Risk Selection and Discrimination

Employment-based health insurance was initially a powerful vehicle for spreading risk among the well and the ill, and it still offers distinct advantages over the current market for individually purchased coverage. In recent years, however, some of the advantages associated with employment-based coverage have been diminishing, most notably for employees of small organizations but increasingly for those who work or seek to work for larger organizations. For employers as well as insurers, the selection of low-risk workers or enrollees or the use of rules regarding preexisting conditions to exclude high-risk workers from health plans can be a more attractive strategy for limiting costs and increasing profits than trying to manage health care utilization or prices more effectively. Although federal law limits the use by employers of medical examinations and questionnaires, employers can generally obtain from their health plans extensive medical information about employees and their families. They have the potential to use that information to make overt or covert decisions about workers' continuing employment, a particularly troublesome form of risk selection. Rapid advances in genetic technologies for identifying individual risk for various diseases is making information available that could be used by insurers or employers to limit coverage for an ever-larger proportion of the population.

## Dispersed Power and Accountability

It is in the nature of both voluntarism (as a mechanism for decisionmaking) and federalism (as a form of government) to disperse power, although the degree and nature of this dispersion can be quite variable. For example, the current structure of voluntarism in the health sector concentrates a great deal of discretion with the employer. It also leaves employers free to require employees to select insurance or show evidence of another source of coverage, and many employers do so in order to discourage adverse selection in the organization's health benefit program. Although the structure may not give as much discretion to the employee as to the employer, the employer may be in a better position than the individual to use its purchasing power to secure better prices, services, and disclosure of information from health plans. At their best, employers are available—and have a direct financial incentive—to act as ombudsmen for their employees and to support them in making informed decisions and resolving problems. Such assistance is less readily available to those with Medicare, Medicaid, or individually purchased private insurance.

On the other hand, with power dispersed to organizations of vastly different sizes and resources, large purchasers have had much more leverage than small employers to negotiate with health care providers for discounts and other favorable payment arrangements. One consequence of this heterogeneity is a considerable amount of cost shifting, which occurs when providers are able to offset discounts or other reduced payments from some purchasers by increasing charges for smaller, weaker, less aware, or less concerned purchasers.

Among governments, the power to regulate employee benefits is no longer delegated to the states but reserved for the federal government through ERISA. Because the federal government has, in practice, chosen to leave many important aspects of employee health benefits unregulated, the power to provide, negotiate, and restrict such benefits devolves to thousands of self-insured employers of widely differing competence, outlook, and accountability.

## Diversity

Virtually every employer's program of health benefits differs from every other employer's program in some aspect (e.g., who is eligible for coverage, through what kinds of health plans, for which kinds of services, with what level of employee cost sharing and other cost containment features, and at what overall cost). Although other nations vary substantially in the uniformity of their systems of health care, none appears to permit the degree of coverage, eligibility, and other variability seen in this country. Nonetheless, even amidst the microlevel diversity of the U.S. system of employment-based and public health coverage, specific patterns have developed that are associated with variations in employer size, region, industry, and other factors. In addition, voluntary efforts and government regulations have over time reduced some of the variability inherent in the U.S. system.

Behind these patterns and trends, however, and certainly behind the broader generalizations offered in this report, lie substantial differences in the cost and quality of health benefits that may be quite important for individuals in need of care and for those who share in its financing. A change in employer policies or a change of job may bring better coverage, poorer coverage, or no coverage at all. It may bring more choice among health plans or less and more freedom or less to select or continue with a health care practitioner of one's own choosing.

Although employers—especially smaller employers—do not necessarily provide choices for employees and some provide choices only because the HMO Act of 1973 mandated it, the interaction of employer and worker interests has certainly given Americans more health plan options than citizens in most or all other countries. On the provider side, the multiplication of health plan options and features has promoted diversity in the prices paid by different purchasers and, as described below, in the administrative practices with which providers have to comply.

## Innovativeness

In addition to their diversity at a given point in time (and in part because of it), the design of employment-based health benefit plans is quite dynamic, inventive, and changeable over time. Compared to other nations, the United States has witnessed great innovation and entrepreneurship in the creation and marketing of health plans and coverage options and in the design or modification of cost containment and quality assurance strategies.

For a variety of reasons, including generous government support, a large pool of talented researchers, and leadership from academic health centers and voluntary organizations, the United States is also a leader in clinical and health services research. Although their specific influence cannot be easily identified, the country's largest employers and unions have helped encourage certain fields of research, in particular, the devising of practical methods to measure health status and quality of care, to assess the benefits and costs associated with specific medical services, and to compare the performance of health care providers.

Innovativeness is widely viewed as positive, but the ultimate value of many health care innovations may be difficult to assess, particularly when individual and collective interests diverge. Some—such as flexible benefits, choice among health plans, expanded coverage of preventive services, and case management—are viewed positively by many employers and employees. A number of techniques and strategies developed in these areas are being carefully studied by other countries for possible implementation to help overcome their own problems with rising costs and ensuring good quality care. On the other hand, some innovations, such as health plan tactics to attract low-risk and avoid high-risk individuals, may have negative effects for many and for society as a whole. Some observers consider many innovations to be merely "Band-Aids" for a flawed system or counterproductive steps for a society that should be concentrating on fundamental reforms.

## Discontinuity

Although many of the above characteristics produce positive social products, they can also promote discontinuity of health coverage and health care. They are thus a mixed blessing. From one year to the next, an employer may add or drop health plans, increase or decrease the types of services covered, increase (but rarely cut) the level of employee cost sharing, change provider networks, or make other major and minor changes in the health benefits offered to employees. Some individuals lose some or all coverage when they voluntarily or involuntarily change jobs or move from welfare to working status. Others suffer "job lock" or "welfare lock" rather than voluntarily give up medical coverage. Sometimes financial protection is continuous, but the continuity of medical care may still be disrupted because a new job's health plan may require a change of health care practitioner. Such discontinuity of care for those with serious health problems is likely to become an increasingly urgent issue as more employers and health plans attempt to restrict individuals to defined networks of health care practitioners and providers, especially if they periodically drop and add networks. Through both their general commitment to universal coverage for basic health services and their national health plans or regulatory standards for sickness funds and similar organizations, other economically advanced countries generally limit the opportunity for changes in job status or employers' policies to interrupt care or coverage.

## Barriers to Cost Management

Whether the measure is health spending as a percentage of the gross national product or spending per capita, the United States is noted for spending considerably more on health care than other nations. However, virtually all economically advanced countries—regardless of how they finance and deliver care—are concerned that their health care costs are too high or at least increasing too quickly. Furthermore, given the nation's wealth, commitment to medical research and technological development, and other factors, it is quite possible that the United States would lead the world in the proportion of national resources devoted to health care even if 20 or 40 years ago it had adopted the social insurance model for health coverage that is commonplace elsewhere.

Overall, employers' capacities and incentives to manage health benefit programs effectively are quite uneven and likely will remain so. For most employers, managing health benefits remains a secondary issue. At their best, employer skills in health benefit management can be quite sophisticated, but Chapter 4 makes clear that the deployment of these skills depends on a significant commitment of resources and that such commitment is mostly limited to some larger employers.

Although the net effect is a matter of controversy, using the workplace as the base for health benefits for most people under age 65 and granting employers extensive discretion to design and manage their health benefits almost certainly add to systemwide administrative costs.[1] A competitive system based on individual purchase of insurance (through vouchers or other means) could have high marketing and other administrative costs, depending on the degree of regulation and uniformity imposed. It is generally assumed that a single national health insurance scheme similar to Medicare would generate lower administrative costs.

Today, whether a government program or a more competitive market would better control the *total* future cost of health care is a central question in the debate over health care reform. Some criticize this nation's decentralized employment-based system as lacking the clout to control prices and allocate resources that they say a single-payer or all-payer system would have. Others criticize both public and private payers for failing to adopt the kind of market-based incentives that they believe would result in more efficient and effective use of health care services. The evidence and arguments reviewed by members of this committee led them to no definitive conclusions, although various members had strong (and conflicting) views on desirable future strategies.

### Complexity in Coverage, Administration, and Regulation

Several of the features singled out above—diversity, innovativeness, risk segmentation—contribute to another distinctive feature of the U.S. health

---

[1]The controversy involves how administrative costs are to be counted (particularly those seen as indirect or hidden), what effect they have on total spending, and what value is obtained for that spending.

care system: the immense complexity of its public and private methods for providing and managing health benefits. The combination leads to a great array of differing coverage features and administrative procedures that have been devised by insurers, claims administrators, and others in response to different employer priorities, employee values, and government policies. Individually purchased insurance, while certainly not simple for consumers to evaluate, is less administratively complex in some respects—if only because individuals lack the leverage and the desire to obtain the customized cost management, data collection and reporting, and other health plan features that many employers successfully demand from insurers and providers.

On the other hand, it cannot be denied that Medicare has created a complex maze of accountabilities and administrative procedures that dismays both beneficiaries and health care providers and that equals or exceeds the complexity of individual employer programs. Nonetheless, employer actions to tailor their health benefit programs to their own circumstances and values have clearly multiplied the number of mazes to be negotiated, especially for health care providers. Although individual employers may weigh the virtues of more complicated programs against the complexity of administering them, no comparable process exists to weigh advantages and disadvantages for the health care system as a whole.

## Strengths and Limitations

The above discussion portrays a system with both positive and negative features that appear to be related at least in part to this nation's distinctive reliance on voluntary employment-based health benefits. Many of the negatives are experienced most acutely by small employers and their employees, and certain of the positives may accrue mainly to larger employers and their employees. As noted, the system has made coverage possible for many who would find it difficult to secure coverage in the current market for individually purchased insurance.

Some or most of the negative features of the U.S. system are nonexistent or less serious in other economically advanced countries. As discussed in the section following this one, some weaknesses might be completely or partly resolved by certain reforms in the U.S. health care system, including some reforms that would retain a significant role for employers. Depending on their specifics, however, reforms (including those that dispense with employment-based coverage) might leave other negative features untouched, make some problems worse, or weaken certain positive features of the current system.

Certainly, individuals who have employment-based health benefits are by and large satisfied with them, although satisfaction with the health care system overall is relatively low. Moreover, even though larger employers generally report that they are very worried about the cost of health benefits and pessimistic about their ability to control these costs, most seem reluctant to give up their sponsorship of these benefits, particularly if the alternative is a government-based system.

The committee found it impossible to characterize several of the features described above as simply strengths or simply limitations. It did, however, place lack of universal coverage, discontinuity of coverage and care, risk segmentation, barriers to cost management, and complexity on the negative side.

Each of these negative features may be viewed, to some degree, as a generally unwanted but necessary consequence of efforts to achieve some more positively viewed objective. Few would argue that public or private decisionmakers have deliberately sought these ends or viewed them positively. The exception may be risk segmentation, which is viewed by many insurers and some economists as both fair and efficient. Many employers reject that view as it applies within their employee group but support it as it applies to outside individuals and groups. This committee rejects the argument for risk segmentation on both philosophical grounds (i.e., the least vulnerable should share risk with the most vulnerable) and practical grounds (i.e., competition based on risk selection should be discouraged in favor of competition based on effectiveness and efficiency in managing health care and health benefits).

Most of the other characteristics discussed above have both positive and negative aspects. Americans tend to value voluntary initiative and distributed power as barriers to overweening government control of individual and business life. Diversity is one face of this country's generally treasured pluralism, and innovation is regarded as a source of wider choice and improved medical care. However, there are negative sides to each of these features, for example, when innovation focuses on ways to avoid insuring the ill or high-risk individual. This kind of innovation is unproductive and distracts from more socially productive creativity to improve the efficiency and effectiveness of health services.

In sum, today's system of voluntary employment-based health benefits earns both high and low marks. It is a dynamic one that continues to change in both positive and negative ways. This committee believes that the negatives are becoming more significant and need to be confronted through both public and private action if the nation wants to preserve a constructive role for voluntary employment-based health benefits.

## FUTURE DIRECTIONS

In response to the limitations identified above, what changes might be undertaken in employment-based health benefits that would not do appreciable damage to the system's strengths? The committee's findings and recommendations are presented in two parts. The first part assumes the continuation of a voluntary system. The second part sets aside this assumption and briefly examines the options for some form of compulsory coverage. Both make only limited reference to Medicare and Medicaid, quality improvement, data systems, and other areas in which policy changes have been recommended by the IOM and others. Neither significantly addresses the fundamental technological and social trends that are troubling the health care delivery and financing systems of all economically advanced countries, regardless of their system of medical expense protection.

Nearly all members of this committee[2] believe that without the first set of changes described below, the system of voluntary employment-based health benefits will significantly deteriorate and even collapse in some sectors. They also believe that even with these changes, a voluntary system will be unable to either significantly expand and subsidize access to health benefits for those in need or manage the problems of risk selection that so undermine the current system. Indeed, piecemeal change could further destabilize rather than strengthen the small-group market. Thus, although committee members are not united on a single specific strategy that either involves or excludes employers, nearly all believe some form of universal, compulsory coverage accompanied by major financing reforms is essential.

The committee agreed that what follows should not be interpreted as either an endorsement or a rejection of employment-based health benefits. On the one hand, a substantial minority of the committee believes employment-based health coverage is, on balance, not socially desirable, except perhaps as a financing vehicle and a supplement to a national health plan. In contrast, other committee members believe that an employment-based system can—if significantly restructured—serve the country as well or better than the likely alternatives and that such restructuring is the most workable strategy for securing reforms that move the nation toward universal coverage.

### To Improve a Voluntary System

Table 7.2 summarizes the committee findings and recommendations that are discussed in this section and the next. It also links the findings to the weaknesses in the current system identified earlier. The emphasis in the first subsection is on the problems created by risk selection and risk segmentation in both large and small employee groups. The final four subsections emphasize the committee's concerns about the affordability of coverage, its continuity, and its stability.

---

[2]See the supplementary statement at the end of this chapter for one member's dissenting views.

**TABLE 7.2**   Summary of Committee Findings and Recommendations on Steps to Respond to Certain Current Limitations of Voluntary Employment-Based Health Benefits

| Current Limitation | Responses that Continue a Voluntary System |
|---|---|
| • Risk Segmentation<br>• Lack of Coverage | Risk selection should be controlled as it affects individuals in large and small employee groups through steps that<br>• prohibit insurance companies from denying coverage to groups and individuals within groups based on their past or expected health status or claims experience;<br>• price coverage to individuals without regard to medical risk or claims experience;<br>• amend the Employee Retirement Income Security Act (ERISA) to prohibit medical underwriting practices in employee health benefits;<br>• amend ERISA (through provisions analogous to those contained in the Americans with Disabilities Act) to regulate employer access to individual medical information collected in connection with employment-based health benefits;<br>• devise methods and mechanisms (such as purchasing cooperatives) for risk adjusting employer and government contributions to health plans to reflect the risk level of enrollees; and<br>• extend public subsidies to help employers, employees, or both purchase health coverage for workers and their families. |
| • Discontinuity<br>• Complexity | National (ERISA) regulations or national standards for state regulation should be adopted to fill selected gaps and achieve more uniformity in the oversight of employee health benefits (e.g., solvency regulations, medical expense payments as percentage of total health plan expense, definition of basic benefits, coverage for workers changing jobs, and data collection protocols). |
| Current Limitation | Responses that Go Beyond a Voluntary System |
| • Lack of Coverage<br>• Risk Segmentation | The above responses will not significantly extend access or control risk segmentation and thus should be augmented by policies that<br>• require that all individuals have coverage through a mandated employer program, mandatory individual purchase, public provision, or some combination of these approaches; and<br>• minimize the financial burden of such coverage on low-income individuals and low-wage organizations. |

## Reducing or Compensating for Risk Selection

As a first priority, if a system of voluntary employment-based health benefits is to be maintained and improved, risk selection and risk segmentation must be significantly reduced as they affect both large and small employee groups. Movement in this direction will require a set of interrelated actions affecting (1) underwriting practices, (2) employers' access to medical information, and (3) methods and mechanisms for risk adjusting employer or government contributions to health plans and for monitoring health plan behavior. Because these changes will do little to make health benefits more affordable and will likely increase costs for some, new subsidies to help lower-income groups (or their employers) purchase health benefits will be necessary. Even then, some will choose not to purchase coverage.

*Medical underwriting in the small-group market.* To reduce risk selection and segmentation in the insurance market for small groups, one step that policymakers can take is to prohibit insurance companies from denying coverage to groups and individuals within groups on the basis of their past or expected health status or claims experience. In addition, what an individual pays for health coverage also should not, in principle, be based on her or his health status, past medical expenses, or similar factors, although the initial stages of policy change and implementation may concentrate on the narrowing of price differentials. The committee recognizes that these steps by themselves could encourage some insurers or health plans to be even more energetic in their efforts to attract the well and avoid the ill and could encourage some low-risk individuals to drop coverage if their premiums increased. Some of the steps discussed below address these problems.

Although the committee sees some merit in the argument that individual prudence may be encouraged by relating health status or health behavior to individual payments for health benefits, most members believe that such risk rating of health coverage is, on balance, neither fair nor productive. Genetic, economic, cultural, and other factors determine individual health and limit individual self-determination in ways that are not well understood and that in the end serve to undermine the prudence argument. In addition, identifying a risk factor is not the same as identifying a reliable and successful strategy for reducing the risk and its health consequences. Those who support positive health promotion strategies and incentives for healthful behavior in the workplace must also recognize these uncertainties and exercise care in their promises and programs.

*Medical underwriting among larger employers.* Steps to modify the small-group insurance market would not affect risk selection as it is practiced among larger, self-insured employers, where the committee sees disturbing signs that the concepts of medical underwriting and risk segmentation are becoming more attractive to financially pressed employers. To prohibit medical underwriting within self-insured groups would require federal action to amend ERISA. If action on the small-group insurance market were undertaken at the federal level, then provisions related to medical underwriting affecting both small and large groups could be explicitly coordinated.

*Protection of personal medical information.* Even if explicit medical underwriting disappears, the health benefit costs of experience-rated and self-insured employers will be affected by the health status, age structure, and other characteristics of the work force. Thus, some may still be tempted to reduce their exposure to high health care costs by using information obtained through their health benefit plans to discriminate against high-cost and high-risk workers.

To discourage this form of risk selection, employer access to certain kinds of information collected in connection with employment-based health benefits should be limited through provisions analogous to those contained in the Americans with Disabilities Act of 1990 (ADA). Although ADA prohibits certain employer-required physical examinations and questions about employee or family health status and restricts access to permitted sources of information, it does *not* restrict access to information available from claims data, medical underwriting questionnaires, or other sources of data associated with employment-based health benefits. This information, which involves covered family members as well as workers, can be as revealing and potentially damaging as that covered by ADA.

Information restrictions that are analogous to those in ADA might define what kind of individual-specific information insurers, claims administrators, or similar entities may share with employers; what employer uses of the information are permissible (e.g., detecting fraud or developing programs to target specific health problems, such as premature births); which staff may have access to the information; and how shared information is to be stored. They might also have to define more specifically the rules for employers who choose to self-administer claims and who thus have the greatest access to personal information about employees.

As long as employers' payments for employee health benefits vary depending on the health status of their workers, employers will still have an incentive to avoid high-risk or high-cost workers or dependents above and beyond that related to their concerns about workers compensation, absenteeism, and similar costs. Bringing self-insured and experience-rated employers back into a broader community risk pool would lessen the motivation for discrimination. Absent movement in that direction, regulatory, educational, and other efforts to discourage discrimination have an important role, although covert discrimination is difficult to detect and eliminate.

*Risk-adjusted employer contributions to health plans.* An end to medical underwriting may diminish one source of risk segmentation, but it would leave other sources unaffected. As long as health plans can reap sizable financial advantages from favorable risk selection, they will have an incentive to devise creative and difficult-to-regulate tactics to do so. To discourage these tactics and encourage stability, some protection is needed for health plans that have existing high-risk enrollments, services, features that attract sicker individuals, or other characteristics that do not warrant marketplace penalties. One protection is risk-adjusted contributions from employers or governments, although additional protections involving very high cost individuals will still be needed.

Unfortunately, the methods to assess relative risk or determine appropriate payment adjustments are still in their infancy. They are relatively weak, often require data not readily available when needed, and may incorporate unwanted incentives for inefficient behavior. Several employers are using different methods to make risk-adjusted payments to health plans, and a number of public and private research projects are under way to build better methods. Slow progress in risk-adjustment methodologies is probably the single greatest barrier to making competition a more positive force in the health care arena.

*Purchasing cooperatives.* The mechanisms as well as the methods needed to make risk-adjusted payments are inadequate in significant respects. Small employers, in particular, lack the resources to manage risk-adjusted contributions for the plans they offer to employees. Some kind of external mechanism is needed to handle the process, for example, as the government does in its administration of capitated payment for HMOs enrolling Medicare beneficiaries. Purchasing cooperatives have been suggested as one such mechanism. Such cooperatives might also reduce marketing and other costs and allow employees of small employers a choice among health plans. However, if multiple, competitive purchasing cooperatives were created, rather than the single entity envisioned by most managed competition proposals, then problems of risk selection across cooperatives would likely arise and savings in marketing and other costs would diminish.

Taken together, the above steps should provide individuals with new protection from restrictions on their access to health coverage related to their past, present, or expected future health status. However, they are unlikely to eliminate completely the advantages health plans receive from favorable risk selection and the incentives for plans to engage in the selection strategies described in Chapter 5. To further discourage discrimination against higher risk individuals or "skimming" of lower risk individuals, it will probably be necessary to monitor health plan enrollment and disenrollment patterns and their marketing, management and other strategies, although the design and implementation of practical and reasonably effective policies will be a challenge.

## Subsidizing Coverage and Controlling Cost Shifting

As noted above, eliminating or significantly reducing medical underwriting and risk segmentation will in the short term do little to make health benefits more affordable for many employers and employees, especially those in low-wage industries. Costs might even increase for some groups and individuals now in low-risk pools, and some low-risk individuals might avoid buying insurance until they thought they needed it.

In the absence of some financial assistance to some employees or employers or both, access to health benefits is not likely to improve. The committee therefore concludes that some public subsidies are necessary to extend coverage to more workers and their families. The policy dilemma this creates in the current fiscal environment is discussed further below.

Several committee members also argue that steps need to be taken to ensure that governments, very large employers, and network health plans do not command excessive discounts from the fees charged by health care providers, thereby leading the latter to offset losses by shifting costs to others. Further, they argue that self-insured employers should be subject to hospital surcharges and other schemes to fund care for the uninsured or to maintain special risk pools for high-risk individuals. Proponents of this approach generally concede that increased individual income taxes or broad-based corporate taxes that affect conventionally insured, self-insured, and uninsured employers are preferable revenue-raising strategies, but they argue that hospital surcharges or similar strategies are better than nothing. These latter approaches would, however, in most if not all cases require further amendments to ERISA.

## Other Regulatory Issues

If the above actions were taken, they would go some distance toward making health benefits "portable," alleviating the phenomenon of "job lock," and discouraging efforts by some employers to gain a competitive advantage by restricting or not offering health benefits. However, further action would be necessary—probably through amendments to ERISA—to limit the use of waiting periods and other health plan provisions that may interrupt coverage and thereby discourage labor mobility and permit some continued degree of risk selection by employers and health plans.

*ERISA.* The above findings taken together point to the need for amendments to ERISA or other legislation that would limit medical underwriting, restrict employer access to sensitive health plan information, reduce barriers to labor mobility, and monitor certain health plan practices. In addition, most members of this committee believe that the system of voluntary employment-based health benefits could be further strengthened by more coherent, uniform, and protective regulatory oversight of employee health benefits, whether they are conventionally insured or self-insured and whether they involve a single employer or a multiple employer benefit plan. The current regulatory vacuum, wherein states cannot regulate employee health benefits and the federal government largely refrains from doing so, needs at a minimum to be filled in selected areas such as plan solvency and data collection protocols. Oversight could be extended either as part of a policy of uniform national regulation or as part of a policy that permits some state discretion within national guidelines or standards.

*Defining basic benefits.* The committee would not favor a proliferation of federal or state mandates for coverage of individual treatments, providers, or sites of care. Such movement could be curtailed by a government commitment to define a basic benefit package developed through processes that weigh the advantages expected from coverage against its costs and risks. Ideally, this package should apply to public and private programs. If the value of the basic benefit package is to be constrained by some kind of cap on its expected actuarial cost, the problems in defining the package become particularly acute, as Oregon's recent experience in trying to set coverage priorities demonstrates. Because the committee does not agree that current methods and definitions are sufficient for this formidable and sensitive task, particularly given the variability in individual patients and the extra decisionmaking burdens imposed by a budget constraint, the research agenda discussed below returns to this issue.

## State Experimentation

The committee recognizes that many states would like to take action beyond that described above but are constrained by ERISA. Some state strategies for substantial changes in health care financing and delivery may very well provide useful lessons should federal policymakers be willing to take more substantial steps. To make such experimentation and learning possible, ERISA would need to be amended either to provide authority for specific state experiments or to create a process by which the Department of Labor could grant waivers for experiments meeting certain criteria. In the committee's view, a waiver should be available only for comprehensive state-level experiments intended to extend access to effective health services, control risk selection, and improve the value obtained for health care spending. State experimentation in the development of anti-managed-care laws (e.g., requirements that physician reviewers for out-of-state utilization management firms be licensed within the state) would not be encouraged.

One major source of opposition to state programs is multistate, self-insured employers, which do not want to be burdened by coverage mandates such as those described in Chapter 3. Statutory criteria for the granting of an ERISA waiver should be considered that would exempt such employers from state-defined benefit packages. If the major objective of a state experiment were to extend and subsidize coverage for the uninsured and underinsured, this kind of exemption would not preclude a requirement that self-insured employers help finance coverage for high-risk, high-cost, or low-income individuals. If the major objective of a state experiment were, however, to establish a statewide health insurance program with no role for the employer except financing (as has been proposed in California), then the exemption for multistate employers described above would stand in the way.

For many members of the committee, state experimentation of the kind described above is preferred only as an alternative to inaction. These members would prefer, on balance, relatively uniform federal policy to define and govern the basic terms on which health care coverage is provided, priced, financed, and administered. For some the basic terms would be those generally proposed by advocates of managed competition; for others the terms would involve a single national health plan.

## The Financing Dilemma

Some of the steps described above would involve gains or losses for specific interests (e.g., low-risk small businesses and some or most health insurance companies) but would not make major new demands on federal or state budgets nor impose major new financial obligations on employers or workers overall. Other steps, however, could add significant financial burdens. In particular, the committee realizes that any broad new policy of subsidized voluntary coverage that is substantial enough to induce more employers and employees to purchase insurance will be costly, probably cannot be financed primarily at the state level, and will therefore have to compete with other demands in a federal budget process that is already severely stressed.

New subsidies to employers or employees could be financed by increasing taxes in some fashion, by cutting health care spending, by shifting resources from other areas, or all three. In principle, as described in Chapter 6, costs may be reduced in many ways, for example, by controlling prices, eliminating inappropriate use of services, controlling the introduction and use of new technologies of untested cost-effectiveness, and reducing administrative costs. In practice, most members of the committee believe it is unrealistic to expect such good performance in these areas that all the costs of extending coverage could be offset. The magnitude of theoretical savings is even disputed. One step several committee members believe is both fair and budgetarily necessary is to limit the amount of an employer's premium contribution that can be excluded from an employee's income for tax purposes. Others oppose the removal of this specific subsidy, particularly as long as other subsidies they view as less socially constructive remain.

These observations notwithstanding, the committee did not have the resources or charge to evaluate financing options in depth. It also saw the issues in this area as so intertwined with the broader health care reform agenda that detailed recommendations would go beyond the committee's charge. The committee, however, acknowledges that the changes discussed in this section—and the next—are unlikely as long as policymakers lack a realistic financing strategy that they feel is feasible politically.

Furthermore, it may be important to consider employer reactions to health care reforms that limited employers' involvement in managing employee health benefits and assigned them only a voluntary or nonvoluntary financing role (e.g., a direct premium contribution or payroll tax). Employers might more vigorously oppose increases in their financial obligations for a health benefits program over which they had no control, and some might withdraw altogether from a voluntary role.

### Beyond Voluntary Coverage

The above steps could encourage some employers that do not offer coverage to begin to do so and could help some workers afford coverage that is now beyond their reach. Some employers and workers, however, would still choose not to offer, purchase, or accept health coverage, even if substantial (but not total) subsidies were provided to assist vulnerable small employers and lower-income workers. For a majority of the committee members, therefore, an important finding is that these steps alone—difficult as they may be to achieve in today's environment—cannot significantly extend access or control biased risk selection. To do so, in the view of the majority of the committee, will almost certainly require that some form of compulsory and subsidized coverage be imposed on the employer, the employee, or both. In fact, without universal participation, the problems facing the small-group market could get even worse.

One reason lies in a major limitation of a voluntary system that eliminates medical underwriting. That is, some individuals or groups would choose not to purchase coverage until faced with a health problem. Such behavior is like buying fire insurance while one's house is burning down or life insurance once terminal illness has been diagnosed. This hazard can be controlled by waiting periods and other medical underwriting, but the majority of this committee believes, on balance, that leaving individuals and families without coverage is not a desirable strategy, especially since low-income groups—absent near-total subsidies—are likely to be overrepresented in the excluded class.

Furthermore, this report has already noted that those without coverage can generally obtain health care once a problem has become an emergency. Such care tends, however, to come late in the course of medical problems, many of which could have been prevented or treated more effectively with more timely care. It also tends not to be coordinated to meet other important but less immediately pressing health care needs. Moreover, because much care for the uninsured is written off as charity service or bad debt, health care providers seek to finance it by shifting the cost to other parties, particularly those who lack market leverage. Although some states have created special schemes (e.g., earmarked taxes on hospital services and regulated hospital rates) to help cover uncompensated care in hospitals and have established limited programs to provide primary and preventive care to the uninsured, this is a second-best strategy in the view of this committee— especially given the vulnerability of these schemes to ERISA challenges. Again, most members of this committee believe that extending health benefits is preferable on grounds of health and equity.

Greatly different approaches are possible to implement compulsory and subsidized coverage, and calls for some form of mandated coverage are embedded in reform proposals that span the political spectrum. Not all would continue a significant role for the employers. For example, some strong advocates of market-oriented strategies urge a move toward mandatory individual purchase of insurance, some government subsidy for lower-income individuals, and an optional and limited role for employers. Others who advocate a strong government role favor a unified social insurance program that would make health coverage near-universal and compulsory and would largely restrict employers to a financing role.

Both these approaches would resolve many of the complexities associated with mandated employer coverage, for example, treatment of different categories of workers (e.g., part-time, seasonal, free-lance) and discontinuity of specific benefits or sources of health care prompted by changes in job status. Depending on its specific features, an individual mandate could make universal the problems of risk selection now found in the individual purchase of insurance or it could attempt to control them through the kinds of features described in the preceding section. A unified national system following the Canadian model would eliminate risk selection by eliminating choice among health plans (but not choice among individual practitioners or providers). A national nonemployment-based program that allowed for choice among health plans would, however, require some mechanisms for controlling or compensating for selection.

Among the proposals that continue employment-based health benefits on some kind of mandated basis, specific approaches vary. Some would require employers to offer health benefits. Others would offer employers the option of providing coverage or contributing to some kind of public or quasi-public insurance program. Employer-based proposals vary in their attention to expanded coverage for those without a connection to the workplace or with a limited or episodic connection.

The primary appeal of the proposals that provide a significant role for employment-based health benefits is that they would continue a familiar structure that is, in general, viewed favorably by most Americans. This structure provides many employees with an accessible source of information and assistance in making health plan choices and resolving problems. It encourages employer interest in the link between health care and worker productivity and well-being and the link between health spending and health outcomes.

The major criticisms of employer mandates are that they would (1) impose too heavy an economic burden on businesses, particularly smaller businesses, (2) still leave uncovered many part-time, seasonal, or free-lance workers and their family members, (3) generally leave untouched the problems of complexity and discontinuity in specific benefits and sources of care that now arise during changes in individual job status, and (4) substitute the heavy hand of government regulation for the more efficient operation of competitive markets. An additional criticism is directed at one particular form of employer mandate, the so-called "play or pay" proposal, which would give employers the choice of providing health coverage or paying a fixed amount (generally between 5 and 9 percent of payroll) to cover their employees under a public program. This "pay" feature would allow employers to cap their liability for health benefits. Depending on the size of the payroll contribution and other specific policy decisions, it could, however, leave the public program vulnerable to adverse selection and financing shortfalls if employers with more healthy employees choose to play (i.e., provide benefits) and employers with less healthy employees choose to pay (i.e., let the public program take over).

Again, this committee does not take a specific position about broad options for health care reform. A form of mandatory employment-based health benefits is not the only option for extending coverage to more workers and their families, and committee members vary in their views about the feasibility and desirability of this option compared with others. This committee does, however, agree that the strengths of the current system should be appreciated and the potential for preserving these strengths while reducing the system's weaknesses should be thoughtfully considered.

Although the combination of the steps described in this and the preceding section would address important weaknesses in the current system, they would do nothing to control the rate of increase in health care spending or better ensure the value received in return for such spending. Committee members have quite different views on what cost containment strategies show potential for being effective, equitable, and compatible with good quality care and on whether these strategies should include an important role for employers. Because the committee could not undertake an evaluation of the cost containment potential of the many proposals for fundamental health care reform, this report must remain silent on a central issue in the debate over reform. As policymakers and others make judgments and define policies to influence health care costs, they should be guided by informed understanding of the systemic factors behind rapidly rising expenditures and a realistic sense that their proposed reforms can affect at least some of these factors and give the nation more confidence in the value received for its health care spending.

Facing problems and trade-offs squarely will be an immense challenge for the policy process. Data analysis is helpful but limited and, in any case, not conclusive given that powerful interests and values are at stake. The nation's inability to decide whether access to basic health care and medical expense protection is a collective obligation or a private responsibility encourages impasse rather than action and rhetoric rather than reasoned problem solving. Surveys indicate considerable public misunderstanding of health care cost and access problems, and this misunderstanding could be a significant obstacle to change if not successfully addressed by a careful public education strategy. These constraints are reinforced by the oppressive persistence of large federal budget deficits, slow economic growth, and the view that effective cost controls must precede expanded access. The committee grants these difficulties, but it is, in general, a group of optimists who believe that this nation's policymakers and its citizens have met equal challenges in the past and can do so again.

## A FEW COMMENTS ON PRACTICAL
## AND TECHNICAL CHALLENGES

As noted early in this chapter, the committee's findings and recommendations do not constitute a blueprint for reform but are rather a statement of some basic steps that appear necessary if employment-based health benefits are to play a more constructive social role. However, to be helpful to those not already involved in the "nuts and bolts" of drafting specific legislation, this section lists some practical questions that may need to be faced by state and federal policymakers and those who seek to advise or influence them.

For any major changes, drafting specific legislative language and implementing regulations require that a great array of technical issues be resolved and matched to the objectives and scope of a particular proposal. Table 7.3

**TABLE 7.3**  Examples of Practical and Technical Issues in Drafting State or Federal Legislation and Regulations to Implement Major Changes in Employment-Based Health Benefits

*Definitions*
• What is the definition of an employer of record for part-time, seasonal, temporary workers? of workers with multiple jobs? of workers under age 65 who have retired from another job that provides post-retirement health benefits?
• Should employers below a specific size (e.g., 500 lives) or employers operating in only one state be subject to state insurance regulation even if larger and multistate employers are not?
• How are employer responsibilities for covering family members to be allocated when both spouses work and have similar or quite different coverage available?
• How should employer fiduciary responsibilities be defined with respect to plan solvency? adequacy of coverage? continuity of coverage for specific services or conditions? mandated contributions to state reinsurance or high-risk pools?

*Underwriting[a]*
• Are waiting periods permissible before newly hired employees and their dependents become eligible for coverage?
• If the provisions of the Consolidated Omnibus Budget Reconciliation Act of 1985 for continued benefits to certain former employees and dependents are generally retained, should former employees be required to accept coverage if it is available when they accept a new job?
• Should employers be permitted to adopt restrictions on coverage for a certain condition after an employee has developed that condition?

*Premium Contribution*
• Should a minimum contribution level be established for conventionally insured or self-insured employers? How should it relate to any public subsidy available for either the employer or the employee?
• Should the employer contribution be the same for the employee and covered dependents? Should it vary by family size? by individual or family income?
• What will be the basis for determining any minimum contribution (e.g., local, state, regional, or national medical care costs)?
• Should a cap on administrative costs for individual health plans be established?
• Should all or some of the employer contribution be taxed as income to the employee? If the current tax subsidy is capped, should the cap be expressed as a percentage of premium, a fixed dollar amount, or some portion of the cheapest plan's premium?

*Benefit Design*
• Should a basic benefit package be established? or a minimum and a standard package? If so, how?
• Should deductibles and coinsurance rates be higher or lower than they generally are now or about the same?
• What special characteristics of group or network health plans must be considered (e.g., cost sharing and coverage for in-network versus out-of-network care)? Should closed panel plans (only in-network coverage for nonemergency care) be more or less strongly encouraged?

*continued on next page*

**TABLE 7.3**  *Continued*

*Data Collection and Outcomes Measurement*
• Should uniform standards for data collection be defined for insured and self-insured health plans? for determining health outcomes?
• If employer access to claims and related information is restricted, is monitoring of compliance feasible? How will employee privacy be protected as electronic storage and transmission of medical records become commonplace?

*Relationship to Public Programs*
• Should coverage for employees with incomes that would otherwise make them eligible for Medicaid coverage be linked to the employer or to Medicaid? Can coverage responsibilities be shared?
• Should self-insured employers be exempt from comprehensive state programs to restructure the health system and extend health benefits for most residents?

*a*This assumes that many underwriting practices are eliminated, as described in the findings presented in Table 7.2.

lists a selection of these issues or questions as background for those not already immersed in the intricacies of proposal drafting.

Definitions or rules may be easy to draft for the great majority of people or situations to be covered by a proposal. For a minority of situations, rules may be highly contentious or their consequences uncertain. One such question involves coverage of domestic partners. A question that is almost as contentious and even more difficult technically involves how to allocate coverage responsibilities for families with children and both spouses working.

The committee has already noted a number of areas in which amendments to ERISA would be helpful. With respect to Table 7.2, the committee further notes that ERISA is silent on most of these questions and yet precludes states from answering them. As states grapple with problems that have immediate and visible ramifications for their budgets and their citizens, this situation will become increasingly unsatisfactory.

## AGENDA FOR RESEARCH AND EVALUATION

Implied or stated in the committee's findings are several important research questions, which are listed below. Some are already the subject of much attention, whereas others have, as yet, been little emphasized. Although not singled out below, other IOM reports (IOM 1989, 1990a, 1990b, 1992a) have identified other important priorities including, in particular, the need for continued research on (1) reliable and valid measurement of health status and well-being at both the individual and the aggregate level, (2) evaluation of the relative effectiveness and costliness of alternative strategies for treating medical problems, and (3) development of clinical research strategies that better identify the effectiveness of services under real-world conditions, not just in highly controlled clinical trials. Progress in these areas will support research and policy in most if not all of the following areas.

## Methodologies for Risk Adjusting Payments to Health Plans

A first priority is to continue public and private efforts to develop, refine, and pilot test risk measurement and payment adjustment techniques. These tests need to reflect the real-world environments in which the methods would be applied (e.g., government programs and small-group purchasing cooperatives). Committee members disagree about how good a risk adjuster must be (that is, how much variation in plan costs it can explain or predict), but all believe that existing techniques are insufficient. Some of the more robust adjusters (e.g., past use of health services and certain health status measures) may create undesirable incentives for health plans or be impractical to implement on a routine basis. Further refinements in these approaches may mitigate some of these problems. In general, a uniform approach to data collection and analysis is needed that meets actuarial and statistical standards and also serves quality improvement purposes. Methods that purport to risk adjust with a proprietary "black box" would not qualify unless their models were revealed.

## Consequences of Underwriting Reforms

Plans should be developed to monitor the consequences of state or national reform in the small-group market and to simulate possible consequences of alternative reforms to guide eventual policy decisions. Underwriting reforms and community rating policies should not inadvertently undermine those insurers who have been willing to insure higher-risk individuals and who thereby have accumulated a risk pool that is more expensive than the community average. Although the reform proposals of the National Association of Insurance Commissioners are intended to deal with this problem, policymakers may benefit from monitoring of their adoption to detect possible unintended and unwanted consequences of particular policies.

In addition, in-depth case studies of those few communities where some form of community rating is still significant might be useful. One objective would be to examine the conditions under which this practice has survived despite the presence of competing health plans and the absence of risk adjusted employer payments. Another would be to assess, if a plausible analytic strategy could be devised, whether overall health care costs and costs for low-risk and high-risk individuals or groups would have been lower or higher over the long term had community rating not existed.

## Basic Benefits

As noted in the preceding section, the committee endorses more research and analysis to support the definition of basic, standard, or minimum benefits. Such standardization, which is a feature of most health care reform proposals, could help discourage risk selection, reduce certain kinds of complexity, and better relate the cost of care to its value. At this time, however, proposals for reform vary substantially in the processes explicitly or implicitly envisioned for defining basic benefits, and different conceptualizations of the term are likewise evident. Some proposals emphasize preventive and primary care services that have relatively low unit prices and simple technology. Other discussions suggest that a basic benefit package is an "urgent care" package aimed primarily at the kinds of illness or injury that produce significant expenditures (a few days of hospital care) but not necessarily catastrophic expenditures (more than 30 or 60 days). Some proposals appear to start with the relatively broad range of services now covered by most health plans but then apply notions of appropriateness (medical benefit exceeds medical risk), relative cost-effectiveness (coverage to some cutoff point), importance as perceived by patients, potential patients, or physicians, and decency (lack of coverage would offend human decency).

These issues are complex and could benefit from a careful and structured effort to outline and analyze the conceptual issues and the procedural issues raised by alternative approaches. The dimensions of the issues include consumer and patient preferences and capacities for decisionmaking; practitioner attitudes, behaviors, and capacities for decisionmaking; the state of technology assessment and the knowledge base concerning effectiveness and outcomes, including measures of health status; cost-effectiveness analysis; the state of the art in actuarial modeling to project the implications of alternative benefit packages; ethical perspectives; legal considerations; and administrative feasibility. Therefore, another research priority is an assessment of the evidence base and methodologies specified or implied by different proposals for standardizing health plan benefits, their potential to limit or exacerbate biased risk selection, and their likely impact on health care costs, health outcomes, and patient/consumer satisfaction.

## Employer Assistance with Employee Decisionmaking and Problem Resolution

Employers can provide useful assistance to employees in making decisions among health plans, understanding and conforming to their requirements, and resolving problems. In assessing future policy choices, it would be helpful to know the extent to which employers do, in fact, assist employees in ways that might be difficult to recreate under other models (such as those that now exist for individual purchasers of health insurance, including Medicare supplemental benefits). Such models include consumer watchdog groups and senior citizen advisory services. Whether the purchasing cooperatives suggested for small employers could act as an advocate for employees needs further exploration. In general, the differences between the capacities of different-sized employers to manage benefits have not been adequately explored.

## Continuity of Care

Individual choice of health care practitioner is becoming an increasingly important issue with respect to limited groups or networks of providers that may encourage continuity of care within the network but may disrupt care when individuals must move from one network to another. Such disruption may occur when a job change is made and the new and former employers offer different networks or when the same employer adds and drops networks over time. The incidence and clinical consequences of such disruption need investigation, particularly for the chronically ill and others at higher risk of problems.

Assuming that discontinuity in the patient-physician relationship does create significant problems for some patients, mechanisms to avoid or compensate for such problems also need to be tested. The open-ended HMO or point-of-service plan is one mechanism that might allow continuation of patient-physician relationships across separate networks, but the extent to which such plans actually facilitate continuity of care is untested. It is reasonable to expect that such systems might affect low- and high-income individuals differently and that their impacts would vary depending on the required extra cost sharing, particularly the maximum out-of-pocket spending.

Another approach that might foster continuity of care is included in some reform proposals that would establish a certification system for health plans and require that employers offer all approved plans to their employees. If employers may offer only a subset of approved plans, then some continuity of care problems would likely continue. The amount of discretion that employers might retain concerning their health benefit program under the "offer all" approach is not clear.

Currently, when employers drop and add network health plans, they may work with the plans to ease the transition for some patients, such as those who are pregnant and whose obstetrician is not part of the new network. Such arrangements would be considerably more difficult to arrange and maintain for those with long-term, expensive problems, but research on the design and financing of such arrangements should be considered.

## FINAL THOUGHTS

As noted throughout this report, the United States is unique in its reliance on employers to provide voluntarily health benefits for workers and their family members. This constantly evolving arrangement has its pluses and minuses, although the limitations of the system are becoming considerably more visible and worrisome. In particular, the dynamics of risk segmentation, the potential for increased discrimination, the persistence of millions of uncovered individuals through economic upturns and downturns alike, and the increasing complexity generated by employer—and government—cost containment efforts have led to many proposals for health care reform. Some retain a central role for employment-based health benefits—voluntary or mandatory—whereas others eliminate them (or relegate them to a minor position) in favor of a government health plan or a market for individually purchased insurance. As the details of specific proposals are emerging and being subjected to increasing critique and analysis, the arguments about their particular characteristics, expected consequences, and apparent trade-offs are growing more specific.

Do employment-based health benefits offer sufficient "value added" that reforms in the U.S. health care system should continue—indeed mandate—them even if some important limitations of the system cannot be fully corrected by such reforms? Each member of the committee has a somewhat different answer to this question, one affected to varying degrees by the practical reality that this system is what is in place and is familiar and valuable to most Americans. Nonetheless, most foresee a continued deterioration in the quality and scope of health coverage unless major steps are taken to reduce or correct serious weaknesses in the system. Most believe it unlikely that more small employers could voluntarily and independently provide the coverage and assistance offered by large employers.

Overall, policymakers and reform proponents of all stripes may both overstate and understate the advantages and disadvantages of current arrangements, a circumstance made easy by the diversity of these arrangements. Despite the diversity of its views on specific directions for health care reform and the role of the employer, the committee would not like to see lost the assistance that employers can bring to employees facing problems with their health coverage. Because neither a single national system nor a competitive market based on individual (not employer) choice would be perfect, employers might—given either scheme—very well see advantages in a new kind of "employee assistance program" or fringe benefit that would provide employees with assistance and explanation of their health plan coverage or help in resolving problems with denied claims, bureaucratic inertia, or whatever similar difficulties a reformed system might present. Furthermore, the committee would not like to see employers unconcerned about the link between health coverage, health status, and worker well-being and uninterested in efforts to improve assessments of the cost-effectiveness of specific medical services and health care providers. Because workplace and community health promotion programs, local health care initiatives and institutions, and other health-related activities have attracted employees' and employers' support for reasons beyond any specific tie to their health benefit programs, continued support can be expected and fostered.

Given the creativity shown by both public and private sectors in the past and the considerable accomplishments of employment-based health benefits, there is reason to be optimistic that decisionmakers—if they can agree on a basic framework for reform—can find a positive role for employers. That role may be larger or smaller than it is today, but in either case it should be designed to support the country's broad objective of securing broader and more equitable access to more appropriate health care at a more reasonable cost.

# SUPPLEMENTARY STATEMENT OF A COMMITTEE MEMBER

### John K. Roberts, Jr.

Health insurance is based on the concept of risk sharing. If individuals are allowed to wait until they get sick or injured to purchase insurance, then there is no risk sharing and the insurance mechanism breaks down. This is a concern, particularly in the individual and small group markets, where the insurance buying decision is more likely to be based on current needs for medical care. Individual underwriting and pre-existing condition limitations serve as incentives for individuals to purchase insurance while they are still healthy. If these tools are to be eliminated, they must be replaced by other means of assuring a broad spread of risk. Further, the result of the recommendations as outlined would be to increase the cost of insurance protection for many. This, in turn, will likely result in fewer people—not more—being able to afford insurance coverage, producing a result exactly opposite that intended by the recommendations.

# References

Aaron, H.J. *Serious and Unstable Condition: Financing America's Health Care.* Washington, D.C.: The Brookings Institution, 1991.

A. Foster Higgins & Co., Inc. *Foster Higgins Health Care Benefits Survey, 1991: Report 1, Indemnity Plans: Cost, Design and Funding.* Princeton, N.J.: A. Foster Higgins & Co., Inc., 1992.

AHCPR (Agency for Health Care Policy and Research). *Program Note. Medical Treatment Effectiveness Research.* Rockville, Md.: U.S. Department of Health and Human Services, Agency for Health Care Policy and Research, March 1990.

Alexandre, L.M. Who Are the High Cost Cases in a Health Benefits Plan? *Medical Benefits,* September 15, 1988, p. 7.

Alpha Center. COSE: A Health Insurance Purchasing Group for Small Businesses. Washington, D.C.: undated.

Altman, S., and Wallack, S. Technology on Trial—Is It the Culprit Behind Rising Health Costs? The Case For and Against. In: *Medical Technology: The Culprit Behind Health Care Costs?* S. Altman and R. Blendon, eds. Proceedings of the 1977 Sun Valley Forum on National Health. Washington, D.C.: U.S. Department of Health, Education and Welfare, 1979, pp. 24-38.

American Federation of Labor and Congress of Industrial Organizations (AFL-CIO). Statement by the AFL-CIO Executive Committee on Smoking and the Workplace. Unpublished statement presented at Bal Harbour, Fla., February 19, 1986.

Anderson, G. All-Payer Ratesetting: Down but Not Out. *Health Care Financing Review* 1991 Annual Supplement:35-41, 1991a.

Anderson, G. Health Status Adjustments as the Response to Adverse Selection. Paper prepared for Society of Actuaries 1991 Health Care Symposium, Washington, D.C., June 5, 1991b.

Anderson, G., Steinberg, E., Powe, N., et al. Setting Payment Rates for Capitated Systems: A Comparison of Various Alternatives. *Inquiry* 27(3):225-233, 1990.

Anderson, O. *The Uneasy Equilibrium: Private and Public Financing of Health Services in the United States 1875-1965.* New Haven, Conn.: College and University Press, 1968.

Anderson, O. *Health Care: Can There be Equity? The United States, Sweden, and England.* New York, N.Y.: John Wiley & Sons, 1972.

Anderson, O. *Blue Cross Since 1929: Accountability and the Public Trust.* Cambridge, Mass.: Ballinger Publishing Company, 1975.

APPWP (Association of Private Pension and Welfare Plans). *Managed Care and the Courts: An Overview.* Washington, D.C., November 1991.

Arnott, R.J., and Stiglitz, J.E. *The Basic Analytics of Moral Hazard.* Working Papers Reprint No. 1350. Cambridge, Mass.: National Bureau of Economic Research, January 1988.

Arnott, R.J., and Stiglitz, J.E. *The Welfare Economics of Moral Hazard.* Working Papers Reprint No. 1552. Cambridge, Mass.: National Bureau of Economic Research, 1990.

Arrow, K. Uncertainty and the Welfare Economics of Medical Care. *American Economic Review* 53(5):205-206, 1963.

Ash, A., Porell, F., Gruenberg, L., et al., Adjusting Medicare Capitation Payments Using Prior Hospitalization Data. *Health Care Financing Review* 10(4):17-29, 1989.

Association of American Medical Colleges. *Avenues to Access: A Resource Guide to Health Care Reform.* I. Baer and A. Evans, eds. Washington, D.C.: Association of American Medical Colleges, 1992.

Bailit, H.L., and Sennett, C. Utilization Management as a Cost-Containment Strategy. *Health Care Financing Review* 1991 Annual Supplement:87-94, 1991.

Barer, M.L., and Evans, R.G. Interpreting Canada: Models, Mind-Sets, and Myths. *Health Affairs* 11(1):44-61, 1992.

Becker, M. In Hot Pursuit of Health Promotion: Some Admonitions. In: *Health at Work.* S. Weiss, J. Fielding, and A. Baum, eds. Hillsdale, N.J.: Lawrence Erlbaum Associates, Publishers, 1991, pp. 178-188.

Beebe, J., Lubitz, J., and Eggers, P. Using Prior Utilization to Determine Payments for Medicare Enrollees in Health Maintenance Organizations. *Health Care Financing Review* 6(3):27-39, 1985.

Berenson, R., and Holahan, J. Sources of the Growth in Medicare Physician Expenditures. *Journal of the American Medical Association* 267:687-691, 1992.

Bergner, M., Bobbitt, R.A., Carter, W.B., and Gilson, B.S. The Sickness Impact Profile: Development and Final Revision of a Health Status Measure. *Medical Care* 19:787-805, 1981.

Berk, M.L., Monheit, A.C., and Hagen, M.H. How the U.S. Spent Its Health Care Dollar: 1929-1980. *Health Affairs* 7(4):46-60, 1988.

Berki, S.E., and Ashcraft, M.L. HMO Enrollment: Who Joins What and Why: A Review of the Literature. *Milbank Memorial Fund Quarterly* 58:588-632, 1980.

Berki, S.E., Penchansksy, R., Fortus, R.S., and Ashcraft, M.L. Enrollment Choices in Different Types of HMOs: A Multivariate Analysis. *Medical Care* 16:682-697, 1980.

Bice, T.W. Health Services Planning and Regulation. In: *Introduction to Health*

*Services.* S.J. Williams and P.R. Torrens, eds. New York, N.Y.: Wiley Publishing Co., 1988.

Blendon, R.J., and Edwards, J.N. Caring for the Uninsured: Choices for Reform. *Journal of the American Medical Association* 265(19):2563-2565, 1991.

Blendon, R.J., Edwards, J.N., and Hyams, A.L. Making the Critical Choices. *Journal of the American Medical Association* 267(18):2509-2520, 1992.

Block, L. Companies Eye New Approach to Coverage for Working Dependents. *Business Insurance,* February 17, 1992, pp. 1, 19.

Blue Cross and Blue Shield Association. *Health Care in America: Reforming the Small Group Health Insurance Market.* Washington, D.C., March 1991a.

Blue Cross and Blue Shield Association. *National Health Care Reform: Organizing the Solutions.* Chicago, Ill., 1991b.

Blum, J., Gertman, P.M., and Rabinow, J. *PSROs and the Law.* Germantown, Md.: Aspen Systems Corporation, 1977.

Bodenheimer, T. Insurance Clerks Are the Real Gatekeepers. *Medical Economics,* June 1, 1992, pp. 29-33.

Borbas, C., Stump, M., Dedeker, K., et al. The Minnesota Clinical Comparison and Assessment Project. *Quality Review Bulletin* 16:87-92, 1990.

Bovbjerg, R. Reform of Financing for Health Coverage: What Can Reinsurance Accomplish? *Inquiry* 29(2):158-175, 1992.

Bowen, B., and Slavin, E. Adjusting Contributions to Address Selection Bias: Three Models for Employers. In: *Advances in Health Economics and Health Services Research,* Vol 12. M. Hornbrook, ed. Greenwich, Conn.: Jai Press, Inc., 1991, pp. 77-96.

Brandes, S. *American Welfare Capitalism: 1880-1940.* Chicago, Ill.: University of Chicago Press, 1976.

Brenner, G., and Rublee, D. The 1987 Revision of Physician Fees in Germany. *Health Affairs* 10(3):147-171, 1991.

Brook, R., Ware, J., Keeler, E., et al. *The Effect of Coinsurance on the Health of Adults.* Santa Monica, Calif.: Rand Corporation, 1984.

Brook, R., Chassin, M., Park, R., et al. A Method for Detailed Assessment of the Appropriateness of Medical Technologies. *International Journal of Technology Assessment in Health Care* 2:53-63, 1986.

Brown, L. *Politics and Health Care Organization: HMOs as Federal Policy.* Washington, D.C.: The Brookings Institution, 1983.

Brown, L., and McLaughlin, C. Constraining Costs at the Community Level. *Health Affairs* 9(4):5-28, 1990. See also pp. 29-46 in the same volume.

Brown, L.D. Policy Reform as Creative Destruction: Political and Administrative Challenges in Preserving the Public-Private Mix. *Inquiry* 29(2):188-202, 1992.

Buck, C. The Question of Value: An Employer Perspective. Presented at Symposium on American Employers and Health Care: Roles, Responsibilities, and Risk, sponsored by the Academy Industry Program of the National Research Council and the Institute of Medicine's Committee on Employer-Based Health Benefits, Washington, D.C., May 19-20, 1992.

Burke, T.P. Alternatives to Hospital Care Under Employee Benefit Plans. *Monthly Labor Review* 114(12):9-15, December 1991.

*Business and Health.* The 1990 National Executive Poll on Health Care Costs and Benefits. *Business and Health* 8(4):24-38, 1990.

*Business and Health.* Data Watch: Coalitions Across the Country. *Business and Health* 9(10):6-7, 1991.

Cain, H. II, and Darling, H. Health Planning in the United States: Where We Stand Today. *Health Policy and Education,* Vol. 1, 1979, p. 10.

Campbell, E.S. Unpaid Hospital Bills: Evidence from Florida. *Inquiry* 29(1):92-98, 1992.

Cannon, L. California Official Offers Health Plan. *Washington Post,* February 13, 1992, p. A4.

Cantor, J.C., Barrand, N.L., Desonia, R.A., et al. Business Leaders' Views on American Health Care. *Health Affairs* 10(1):98-105, 1991.

CBO (Congressional Budget Office). *The Effects of PSROs on Health Care Costs: Current Findings and Future Evaluations.* Washington D.C.: U.S. Government Printing Office, 1979.

CBO. *The Impact of PSROs on Health Care Costs: Update of CBO's 1979 Evaluation.* Washington, D.C.: U.S. Government Printing Office, 1981.

CBO. *Selected Options for Expanding Health Insurance Coverage.* Washington, D.C.: U.S. Government Printing Office, 1991a.

CBO. *Trends in Health Expenditures by Medicare and the Nation.* Washington, D.C.: U.S. Government Printing Office, October 1991b.

CBO. *Economic Implications of Rising Health Care Costs.* Washington, D.C.: U.S. Government Printing Office, October 1992a.

CBO. *The Effects of Managed Care on Use and Costs of Health Services.* Washington, D.C.: U.S. Government Printing Office, 1992b.

CBO. *Factors Contributing to the Growth of the Medicaid Program.* Washington, D.C.: U.S. Government Printing Office, 1992c.

CBO. *Projections of National Health Expenditures.* Washington, D.C.: U.S. Government Printing Office, 1992d.

Chassin, M., Kosecoff, J., Park, R., et al. Does Inappropriate Use Explain Geographic Variations in the Use of Health Care Services? A Study of Three Procedures. *Journal of the American Medical Association* 258:2533-2537, 1987.

Chinsky, D. Employee Insurance Division, Ford Motor Company, Speech, February 19, 1986.

Chollet, D. Building a Private-Public Partnership That Works. *Inquiry* 29(2):116-119, 1992a.

Chollet, D. Minimum Health Insurance Benefits. In: *Improving Health Policy and Management: Nine Critical Research Issues for the 1990s.* S.M. Shortell and U.E. Reinhardt, eds. Ann Arbor, Mich.: Health Administration Press, 1992b, pp. 37-74.

Cleeton, D., Goepfrich, V., and Weisbrod, B. What Does the Consumer Price Index for Prescription Drugs Really Measure? *Health Care Financing Review* 13(3):45-51, 1992.

Colman, J. An Analysis of the Components of Rising Costs. In: U.S. Department of Health, Education and Welfare, *Report of the National Conference on Medical Costs,* June 27-28, 1967. Washington, D.C.: U.S. Government Printing Office, 1968, pp. 91-133.

Committee on the Costs of Medical Care. *Medical Care for the American People.* Chicago, Ill.: University of Chicago Press, 1932. (Reprinted by U.S. Department of Health, Education and Welfare, 1972.)

Conrad, P., and Walsh, D. The New Corporate Health Ethic: Lifestyle and the Social Control of Work. *International Journal of Health Services* 22:89-111, 1992.

Costich, J. Denial of Coverage for "Experimental" Medical Procedures: The Problem of De Novo Review Under ERISA. *Kentucky Law Journal* 79(4):801-827, 1990-1991.

Couch, J., ed. *Health Care Quality Management for the 21st Century.* Tampa, Fla.: American College of Physicians, 1991.

Coulam, R.F., and Gaumer, G.L. Medicare's Prospective Payment System: A Critical Appraisal. *Health Care Financing Review* 1991 Annual Supplement:45-77, 1991.

Council on Ethical and Judicial Affairs, American Medical Association. Use of Genetic Testing by Employers. *Journal of the American Medical Association* 266:1827-1830, 1991.

CRS (Congressional Research Service). *Health Insurance and the Uninsured: Background Data and Analysis.* Washington, D.C.: U.S. Government Printing Office, June 1988a.

CRS. *Insuring the Uninsured: Options and Analysis.* Washington, D.C.: U.S. Government Printing Office, October 1988b.

CRS. *Cost and Effects of Extending Health Insurance Coverage.* Washington, D.C.: U.S. Government Printing Office, October 1988c.

CRS. *The Federal Employees Health Benefits Program: Possible Strategies for Reform.* Washington, D.C., May 24, 1989.

Danzon, P. Hidden Overhead Costs: Is Canada's System Less Expensive? *Health Affairs* 11(1):21-43, 1992.

Darling, H. Employers and Managed Care: What Are the Early Returns? *Health Affairs* 10(4):147-160, 1991.

Davidson, E., and Fukushima, T. The Racial Disparity in Infant Mortality. *New England Journal of Medicine* 327:1022-1024, 1992.

Davis, K. Respondent: What Can Europeans Learn from Americans? *Health Care Financing Review* 1989 Annual Supplement:102-107, 1989.

Davis, K. Inequality and Access to Health Care. *Milbank Quarterly* 69(2):253-273, 1991.

Davis, K., and Rowland, D. Uninsured and Underserved: Inequities in Health Care in the United States. *Milbank Memorial Fund Quarterly/Health and Society* 61(2):149-176, 1983.

Davis, L. *Fellowship of Surgeons.* Chicago, Ill.: American College of Surgeons, 1988.

de Lissovoy, G., Kasper, J., DiCarlo, S., et al. Changes in Retiree Health Benefits: Results of a National Survey. *Inquiry* 27(3):289-293, 1990.

DiCarlo, S., and Gabel, J. Conventional Health Insurance: A Decade Later. *Health Care Financing Review* 10(3):77-89, 1989.

DOL (Department of Labor). Bureau of Labor Statistics. *Employee Benefits in*

*Medium and Large Firms, 1989.* Washington, D.C.: U.S. Government Printing Office, 1990.

DOL. Bureau of Labor Statistics. *Employee Benefits in Small Private Establishments, 1990.* Washington, D.C.: U.S. Government Printing Office, 1991.

Donabedian, A. *Benefits in Medical Care Programs.* Cambridge, Mass.: Harvard University Press, 1976.

Dowell, M. Disability Act Clouds AIDS-Coverage Issue. *Business and Health.* 10(2):69, 1992.

Ebert, R. The Medical School. In: *Life and Death and Medicine.* San Francisco, Calif.: W.H. Freeman and Company, 1973, pp. 103-109.

EBRI (Employee Benefit Research Institute). *Flexible Benefits Plans and Changing Demographics.* Washington, D.C. Issue Brief Number 113, 1991a.

EBRI. *Health Promotion: Its Role in Health Care.* Washington, D.C. Issue Brief Number 120, 1991b.

EBRI. *Issues in Health Care Cost Management.* Washington, D.C. Issue Brief Number 118, 1991c.

EBRI. *Retiree Health Benefits: Issues of Structure, Financing, and Coverage.* Washington, D.C. Issue Brief Number 112, 1991d.

EBRI. *Databook on Employee Benefits.* 2nd ed. Washington, D.C., 1992a.

EBRI. *Health Care Reform: Tradeoffs and Implications.* Washington, D.C. Issue Brief Number 125, 1992b.

EBRI. *Retirement Security in a Post-FASB Environment.* Washington, D.C. Issue Brief Number 124, 1992c.

EBRI. *Sources of Health Insurance and Characteristics of the Uninsured.* Washington, D.C. Issue Brief Number 123, 1992d.

*Economic Report of the President.* Washington, D.C.: U.S. Government Printing Office, 1992.

Eddy, D. Comparing Benefits and Harms: The Balance Sheet. *Journal of the American Medical Association* 263:2493-2505, 1990a.

Eddy, D. Connecting Value and Costs: Whom Do We Ask, and What Do We Ask Them? *Journal of the American Medical Association* 264:1737-1739, 1990b.

Eddy, D. What Do We Do About Costs? *Journal of the American Medical Association* 264:1161-1170, 1990c.

Eddy, D., ed. *Common Screening Tests.* Philadelphia, Pa.: American College of Physicians, 1991a.

Eddy, D. Rationing by Patient Choice. *Journal of the American Medical Association* 265:105-108, 1991b.

Eddy, D., and Billings, J. The Quality of Medical Evidence: Implications for Quality of Care. *Health Affairs* 7(1):19-32, 1988.

Edwards, J., Blendon, R., Leitman, R., et al. Small Business and the National Health Care Reform Debate. *Health Affairs* 11(1)164-173, 1992.

Egdahl, R. Foundations for Medical Care. *New England Journal of Medicine* 288(10):491-498, 1973.

Eisenberg, J. *Doctors' Decisions and the Cost of Medical Care: The Reasons for Doctors' Practice Patterns and the Ways to Change Them.* Ann Arbor, Mich.: Health Administration Press Perspectives, 1986.

Ellis, R., and Ash, A. *Refining the Diagnostic Cost Group Model: A Proposed Modification to the AAPCC for HMO Reimbursement.* Grant No. 18-C-98526/1-03-HCFA. Prepared for Health Care Financing Administration. University Health Policy Consortium, Brandeis/Boston University. Waltham, Mass., February 1988.

Ellwood, P.M., Jr. Alternatives to Regulation: Improving the Market. In: *Controls on Health Care.* Papers of the Conference on Regulation in the Health Industry, January 7-9, 1974. Washington, D.C.: National Academy of Sciences, 1975, pp. 49-72.

Ellwood, P.M., Jr. Uniform Effective Health Benefits. Policy Document No. 3 (of four). Unpublished paper prepared for the Jackson Hole Group, Jackson Hole, Wyo., August 30, 1991.

Ellwood, P.M., Jr., Anderson, N.N., Billings, J.E., et al. Health Maintenance Strategy. *Medical Care* 9(3):291-298, 1971.

Enthoven, A. Consumer Choice Health Plan. *New England Journal of Medicine* 298:650-658 and 709-720, 1978.

Enthoven, A. Managed Competition: An Agenda for Action. *Health Affairs* 7(3):25-47, 1988a.

Enthoven, A. *Theory and Practice of Managed Competition in Health Care Finance.* Amsterdam: North Holland, 1988b.

Enthoven, A. Management of Competition in the FEHBP. *Health Affairs* 8(3):33-50, 1989.

Enthoven, A., and Kronick, R. Universal Health Insurance Through Incentives Reform. *Journal of the American Medical Association* 265(19):2532-2536, 1991.

Ermann, D. Hospital Utilization Review: Past Experience, Future Directions. *Journal of Health Policy, Politics and Law* 13(4):683-704, 1988.

Etheredge, L. A Pro-Competitive Regulatory Structure. Unpublished discussion paper for Jackson Hole Conference. Jackson Hole, Wyo., August 1990.

Etheredge, L. System Reform Alternatives: Who Should Purchase and Manage Health Plans? Presentation at Symposium on Extending Coverage to the Uninsured, sponsored by the Institute for Health Policy Solutions, Minneapolis, Minn., August 12, 1992.

Executive Office of the President. *Budget of the United States Government: Fiscal Year 1993.* Washington, D.C.: U.S. Government Printing Office, 1992.

Faulkner, E. *Accident-and-Health Insurance.* New York, N.Y.: McGraw-Hill Book Company, Inc., 1940.

Faulkner, E. *Health Insurance.* New York, N.Y.: McGraw-Hill Book Company, Inc., 1960.

Fein, R. *Medical Care Medical Costs: The Search for a Health Insurance Policy.* Cambridge, Mass.: Harvard University Press, 1986.

Feingold, E. *Medicare: Policy and Politics.* San Francisco, Calif.: Chandler Publishing Company, 1966.

Feldblum, C. Employment Protections. *Milbank Quarterly* 69(Suppl. 1/2):81-110, 1991.

Feldman, R., and Dowd, B. Biased Selection: Fairness and Efficiency in Health Insurance Markets. Paper prepared for Conference on American Health Policy:

Critical Issues for Reform, sponsored by American Enterprise Institute for Public Policy Research, Washington, D.C., October 3-4, 1991.

Fielding, J.F. The Challenges of Work-Place Health Promotion. In: *Health at Work*. S. Weiss, J. Fielding, and A. Baum, eds. Hillsdale, N.J.: Lawrence Erlbaum Associates, Publishers, 1991a, pp. 13-28.

Fielding, J.F. Cost-Benefit and Cost Effectiveness Analysis in Work-Place Health Promotion Programs. In: *Health at Work*. S. Weiss, J. Fielding, and A. Baum, eds. Hillsdale, N.J.: Lawrence Erlbaum Associates, Publishers, 1991b, pp. 170-177.

Firshein, J. Anatomy of a Waiver: Oregon Plan Stumbles. *Medicine and Health Perspectives* 46(3):unnumbered, August 24, 1992a.

Firshein, J. ERISA Sets Roadblock for State Health Reform. *Medicine and Health Perspectives* 46:unnumbered, June 15, 1992b.

Fitzpatrick, T.B. Utilization Review and Control Mechanisms: From the Blue Cross Perspective. *Inquiry* 2(2):16-29, 1965.

Fletcher, M. '24-hour' Cover Explored. *Business Insurance*, May 4, 1992, pp. 2, 49.

Flora, P., and Heidenheimer, A., eds. *The Development of Welfare States in Europe and America*. New Brunswick, N.J.: Transaction Books, 1981.

Fox, D.M., and Leichter, H.M. Rationing Care in Oregon: The New Accountability. *Health Affairs* 10(2):7-27, 1991.

Frank, R., and McGuire, T. Mandating Employer Coverage of Mental Health Care. *Health Affairs* 9(1):31-42, 1990.

Frank, R., Goldman, H., and McGuire, T. A Model Mental Health Benefit in Private Health Insurance. *Health Affairs* 11(3):98-117, 1992.

Freudenheim, M. Business and Health: Single Coverage for On Job and Off. *New York Times*, March 3, 1992a, p. D2.

Freudenheim, M. Rochester Serves as Model in Controlling Health Cost. *New York Times*, August 25, 1992b, pp. 1, D5.

Freudenheim, M. The Unquiet Future of Commercial Health Insurance. *New York Times*, July 12, 1992c, p. F11.

Frieden, J. Hershey's Newest Nonfat Product: Wellness. *Business and Health* 9(12):56-60, 1991.

Fuchs, V.R. The Basic Forces Influencing Costs of Medical Care. In: U.S. Department of Health, Education and Welfare, *Report of the National Conference on Medical Costs*, June 27-28, 1967. Washington, D.C.: U.S. Government Printing Office, 1968, pp. 16-31.

Fuchs, V.R. The Competition Revolution in Health Care. *Health Affairs* 7(3):5-24, 1988.

Fuchs, V.R. The Health Sector's Share of the Gross National Product. *Science* 247:534-538, 1990.

Fuchs, V.R. National Health Insurance Revisted. *Health Affairs* 10(4):7-17, 1991.

Fuchs, V.R. The Best Health Care System in the World? *Journal of the American Medical Association* 268(7):916-917, 1992.

GAO (General Accounting Office). *Employee Benefits: Extent of Companies' Retiree Health Coverage*. GAO/HRD-90-92. Washington, D.C., 1990a.

GAO. *Health Insurance: Cost Increases Lead to Coverage Limitations and Cost Shifting.* GAO/HRD-90-68. Washington, D.C., 1990b.

GAO. *Canadian Health Insurance: Lessons for the United States.* GAO/HRD-91-90. Washington, D.C., 1991a.

GAO. *Defense Health Care: Champus Mental Health Benefits Greater Than Those Under Other Health Plans.* GAO/HRD-91-20. Washington, D.C., 1991b.

GAO. *Medicaid Expansions: Coverage Improves but State Fiscal Problems Jeopardize Continued Progress.* GAO/HRD-91-78. Washington, D.C., 1991c.

GAO. *Medicare: Further Changes Needed to Reduce Program and Beneficiary Costs.* GAO/HRD-91-67. Washington, D.C., 1991d.

GAO. *Private Health Insurance: Problems Caused by a Segmented Market.* GAO/HRD-91-114. Washington, D.C., 1991e.

GAO. *Access to Health Care: States Respond to Growing Crisis.* GAO/HRD-92-70. Washington, D.C., 1992a.

GAO. *Employee Benefits. States Need Labor's Help Regulating Multiple Employer Welfare Arrangements.* GAO/HRD-92-40. Washington, D.C., 1992b.

GAO. *Federal Health Benefits Program: Stronger Controls Needed to Reduce Administrative Costs.* GAO/T-GGD-92-20. Washington, D.C., 1992c.

Garamendi, J. *California Health Care in the 21st Century: A Vision for Reform.* Sacramento, Calif.: Office of the Insurance Commissioner, February 1992.

Garrison, L.P., Jr. Assessment of the Effectiveness of Supply-Side Cost-Containment Measures. *Health Care Financing Review* 1991 Annual Supplement:13-20, 1991.

Geigel, R., and Jones, S. Outcomes Measurement: A Report from the Front. *Inquiry* 27(1):7-13, 1990.

Geisel, J. Some Relief on Health Costs. *Business Insurance*, January 27, 1992, pp. 1, 78.

Gertman, P.M., and Lowenstein, S. A Research Paradigm for Severity of Illness: Issues for the Diagnosis-Related Group System. *Health Care Financing Review* 1984 Annual Supplement:79-90, 1984.

GHAA (Group Health Association of America, Inc.). *HMO Industry Profile.* Washington, D.C., 1991.

Ginsburg, P. Impact of the Economic Stabilization Program on Hospitals. In: *Hospital Cost Containment—Selected Notes for Future Policy.* M. Zubkoff, I.E. Raskin, and R.S. Hanft, eds. New York, N.Y.: PRODIST for the Milbank Memorial Fund, 1978, pp. 293-323.

Glaser, W. *Health Insurance in Practice: International Variations in Financing, Benefits, and Problems.* San Francisco, Calif.: Jossey-Bass Publishers, 1991.

Gold, M. DataWatch: HMOs and Managed Care. *Health Affairs* 10(4):189-206, 1991.

Gorham, W. Medical Care Price Trends. In: U.S. Department of Health, Education and Welfare, *Report of the National Conference on Medical Costs*, June 27-28, 1967. Washington, D.C.: U.S. Government Printing Office, 1968, pp. 3-16.

Gosfield, A. *PSROs: The Law and the Health Consumer.* Cambridge, Mass.: Ballinger Publishing Co., 1975.

Gosfield, A. PROs: A Case Study in Utilization Management and Quality Assurance. In: *1989 Health Law Handbook*. New York, N.Y.: Clark Boardman Co., Ltd., 1989.

Gosfield, A. Value Purchasing and Effectiveness: Legal Implications. In: *1991 Health Law Handbook*. New York, N.Y.: Clark Boardman Co., Ltd., 1991.

Gostin, L., and Roper, W. UpDate: The Americans with Disabilities Act. *Health Affairs* 11(3):248-258, 1992.

Grazier, K., Richardson, W., Martin, D., et al. Factors Affecting Choice of Health Care Plans. *HSR: Health Services Research* 20(6):659-682, 1986.

Greenfield, S. Flaws in Mortality Data: The Hazards of Ignoring Comorbid Disease. *Journal of the American Medical Association* 260:2253-2255, 1988.

Hadley, J. *More Medical Care, Better Health?* Washington, D.C.: The Urban Institute Press, 1982.

Hadley, J., and Swartz, K. The Impact on Hospital Costs Between 1980 and 1984 of Hospital Rate Regulation, Competition, and Changes in Health Insurance Coverage. *Inquiry* 26(1):35-47, 1989.

Hadley, J., Steinberg, E., and Feder, J. Comparison of Uninsured and Privately Insured Hospital Patients: Condition on Admission, Resource Use and Outcome. *Journal of the American Medical Association* 265(3):374-379, 1991.

Hall, M.A. Sounding Board. Reforming the Health Insurance Market for Small Businesses. *New England Journal of Medicine* 326(8):566-570, 1992.

Harris, R. *A Sacred Trust*. Baltimore, Md.: Penguin Books, Inc., 1969. (Reprint: Originally published by The New American Library, Inc., New York, N.Y., 1966.)

Havighurst, C. Practice Guidelines as Legal Standards Governing Physician Practice. *Law and Contemporary Problems* 54:87-117, Spring 1991.

Hay/Huggins Company, Inc. *Psychiatric Benefits in Employer-Provided Healthcare Plans*. Report prepared for the National Association of Private Psychiatric Hospitals. Washington, D.C., 1992.

*Health Benefits Letter*. New Study Shows 992 Mandated Benefits in the States. *Health Benefits Letter* 1(15):1-4, August 29, 1991.

Hellinger, F. An Empirical Analysis of Several Prospective Reimbursement Systems. In: *Hospital Cost Containment—Selected Notes for Future Policy*. M. Zubkoff, I.E. Raskin, and R.S. Hanft, eds. New York, N.Y.: PRODIST for the Milbank Memorial Fund, 1978, pp. 370-400.

Hellinger, F. Selection Bias in Health Maintenance Organizations: Analysis of Recent Evidence. *Health Care Financing Review* 9(2):55-63, 1987.

Helms, W.D. Linking Public and Private Efforts: Initiatives at the State and Local Level. Presented at Symposium on American Employers and Health Care: Roles, Responsibilities, and Risk, sponsored by the Academy Industry Program of the National Research Council and the Institute of Medicine's Committee on Employer-Based Health Benefits, Washington, D.C., May 19-20, 1992.

Helms, W.D., Gauthier, A., and Campion, D. Mending the Flaws in the Small-Group Market. *Health Affairs* 11(2):7-28, 1992.

HIAA (Health Insurance Association of America). *Providing Employee Health Benefits: How Firms Differ*. Washington, D.C., 1990.

HIAA. *Critical Distinctions: How Firms That Offer Health Benefits Differ from Those That Do Not*. C. Lippert and E. Wicks, eds. Washington, D.C., 1991a.

HIAA. *Health Care Financing for All Americans: Private Market Reform and Public Responsibility.* Washington, D.C., 1991b.

HIAA. *Source Book of Health Insurance Data.* Washington, D.C., 1991c.

HIAA. *Group Life and Health Insurance.* Parts A, B, and C. Washington, D.C., 1992.

Hill, R.B.; and Anderson, R.E. The Autopsy Crisis Reexamined: The Case for a National Autopsy Policy. *Milbank Quarterly* 69(1):51-78, 1991.

Holoweiko, M. Health Care Blunders: Is Your Company Liable? *Business and Health* 10(1):26-31, 1992.

Hornbrook, M., ed. *Advances in Health Economics and Health Services Research,* Vol. 12. Greenwich, Conn.: Jai Press, Inc., 1991.

Howland, J., Stokes, J., III, Crane, S.C., et al. Adjusting Capitations Using Chronic Disease Risk Factors: A Preliminary Study. *Health Care Financing Review* 9(2):15-24, 1987.

Hoy, E., Curtis, R., and Rice, T. Change and Growth in Managed Care. *Health Affairs* 10(4):18-36, 1991.

Iezzoni, L.I. Measuring the Severity of Illness and Case Mix. In: *Providing Quality Care: The Challenge to Clinicians.* N. Goldfield and D.B. Nash, eds. Philadelphia, Pa.: American College of Physicians, 1989, pp. 70-105.

Iezzoni, L.I., Schwartz, M., and Restuccia, J. The Role of Severity Information in Health Policy Debates: A Survey of State and Regional Concerns. *Inquiry* 28(2)117-128, 1991.

Immerwahr, J. *Faulty Diagnosis: Public Misconceptions About Health Care Reform.* New York, N.Y.: The Public Agenda Foundation, 1992.

Independence Blue Cross and Pennsylvania Blue Shield. *Independence and Leadership in Health Care: Community Health Care Report, 1988.* Philadelphia, Pa., 1988.

Intindola, B. Attack on Classifying Risks Endangers Industry. *National Underwriter,* June 10, 1991, p. S23.

IOM (Institute of Medicine). *Controls on Health Care.* Papers of the Conference on Regulation in the Health Industry, January 7-9, 1974. Washington, D.C.: National Academy of Sciences, 1975.

IOM. *Assessing Quality in Health Care.* Washington, D.C.: National Academy of Sciences, 1976.

IOM. *Health Planning in the United States: Selected Policy Issues* (2 volumes). Washington, D.C.: National Academy Press, 1981.

IOM. *Assessing Medical Technologies.* Council on Health Care Technology. Washington, D.C.: National Academy Press, 1985.

IOM. *Controlling Costs and Changing Patient Care? The Role of Utilization Management.* B. Gray and M. Field, eds. Washington, D.C.: National Academy Press, 1989.

IOM. *Effectiveness and Outcomes in Health Care.* Washington, D.C.: National Academy Press, 1990a.

IOM. *Medicare: A Strategy for Quality Assurance.* K. Lohr, ed. Washington, D.C.: National Academy Press, 1990b.

IOM. *Kidney Failure and the Federal Government.* R. Rettig and N. Levinsky, eds. Washington, D.C.: National Academy Press, 1991.

IOM. *Guidelines for Clinical Practice: From Development to Use.* M. Field and K. Lohr, eds. Washington, D.C.: National Academy Press, 1992a.

IOM. *Medical Innovation at the Crossroads.* Vol. 3, *Technology and Health Care in an Era of Limits.* A. Gelijns, ed. Washington, D.C.: National Academy Press, 1992b.

IOM. *Access to Health Care in America.* M. Millman, ed. Washington, D.C.: National Academy Press, 1993.

IOM. *Assessing Health Care Reform.* Washington, D.C.: National Academy Press, forthcoming.

Jackson-Beeck, M., and Kleinman, J.H. Evidence for Self-selection Among Health Maintenance Organization Enrollees. *Journal of the American Medical Association* 250(20):2826-2829, 1983.

Jencks, S., and Schieber, G. Containing U.S. Health Care Costs: What Bullet to Bite? *Health Care Financing Review* 1991 Annual Supplement:1-12, 1991.

Jones, N. Essential Requirements of the Act: A Short History and Overview. *Milbank Quarterly* 69(Suppl. 1/2):25-54, 1991.

Jones, S. Perspective: Can Multiple Choice Be Managed? *Health Affairs* 8(3):51-59, 1989.

Jose, W.S., II. An Idea Whose Time Has Come. *Health Action Managers.* February 25, 1991, pp. 1, 6.

*Journal of Health Politics, Policy and Law.* 16(4), 1991.

Juengst, E. Priorities in Professional Ethics and Social Policy for Human Genetics. *Journal of the American Medical Association* 266:1835-1836, 1991.

Kane, N.M., and Manoukian, P.D. The Effect of the Medicare Prospective Payment System on the Adoption of New Technology: The Case of Cochlear Implants. *New England Journal of Medicine* 321(20):1378-1383, 1989.

Kaplan, R.M., Anderson, J.P., Wu, A.W., et al. The Quality of Well-Being Scale: Applications in AIDS, Cystic Fibrosis, and Arthritis. *Medical Care* 27(3, Suppl.):S27-S43, 1989.

Kempe, A., Wise, P.H., Barkan, S.E., et al. Clinical Determinants of the Racial Disparity in Very Low Birth Weight. *New England Journal of Medicine* 327:969-973, 1992.

Kent, C. Easing the Way Toward Managed Care: Point of Service. *Medicine and Health Perspectives*, July 27, 1992a, np.

Kent, C. Hawaii: Universal Care in Hawaii. *Medicine and Health Perspectives*, May 25, 1992b, np.

Kent, C. Liability Lawsuits: Casting a Wider Net. *Medicine and Health Perspectives*, May 4, 1992c, np.

Kerr, P. Vast Amount of Fraud Discovered in Workers' Compensation System. *New York Times*, December 29, 1991, pp. 1, 14.

Kirkman-Liff, B.L. Health Insurance Values and Implementation in the Netherlands and the Federal Republic of Germany: An Alternative Path to Universal Coverage. *Journal of the American Medical Association* 265(19):2496-2506, 1991.

Knowles, J. The Hospital. In: *Life and Death and Medicine.* San Francisco, Calif.: W.H. Freeman and Company, 1973, pp. 91-100.

Kramon, G. New Incentives to Take Care. *New York Times*, March 21, 1989, p. D2.

Kronick, R. Health Insurance, 1979-1989: The Frayed Connection Between Employment and Insurance. *Inquiry* 28(4):318-332, 1991a.

Kronick, R. Managed Competition: Why We Don't Have It and How We Can Get It. Paper prepared for Conference on American Health Policy: Critical Issues for Reform, sponsored by American Enterprise Institute for Public Policy Research, Washington, D.C., October 3-4, 1991b.

Kronick, R. Empowering the Demand Side: From Regulation to Purchasing. *Inquiry* 29(2):213-230, 1992.

Law, S. *Blue Cross: What Went Wrong?* New Haven, Conn.: Yale University Press, 1974.

Levit, K., and Cowan, C. Business, Households, and Governments: Health Care Costs, 1990. *Health Care Financing Review* 13(2):83-93, 1991.

Levit, K., Lazenby, H., Cowan, C., et al. National Health Expenditures, 1990. *Health Care Financing Review* 13(1):29-54, 1991.

Lewin/ICF. *The Health Care Financing System and the Uninsured.* Prepared for U.S. Department of Health and Human Services. Washington, D.C.: 1990.

Lewin/ICF and Alpha Center. *Evaluation of the Ohio Certificate of Need Program.* Report prepared for the Certificate of Need Study Committee and Ohio Department of Health, June 28, 1991.

Lichtenstein, R., Thomas, W., Adams-Watson, J., et al. Selection Bias in TEFRA At-Risk HMOs. *Medical Care* 29(4):318-331, 1991.

Light, D.W. The Practice and Ethics of Risk-Rated Health Insurance. *Journal of the American Medical Association* 267(18):2503-2508, 1992.

Liu, K., Moon, M., Sulvetta, M., and Chawla, J. International Infant Mortality Rankings: A Look Behind the Numbers. *Health Care Financing Review* 13(4):105-118, 1992.

Lohr, K.N., ed. Advances in Health Status Assessment: Conference Proceedings. *Medical Care* 27(3, Suppl.):S1-S294, 1989.

Lohr, K.N., ed. Advances in Health Status Assessment: Proceedings of a Conference. *Medical Care* 30(5, Suppl.):S1-S293, 1992.

Lohr, K.N., Brook, R.H., Kamberg, C.J., et al., *Use of Medical Care in the Rand Health Insurance Experiment: Diagnosis- and Service-Specific Analyses in a Randomized Controlled Trial.* Santa Monica, Calif.: Rand Corporation, 1986.

London, M. Medical Staff Utilization Committees. *Inquiry* 2(2):77-95, 1965.

Long, S.H., and Marquis, M.S. Gaps in Employment-Based Health Insurance: Lack of Supply or Lack of Demand? In: U.S. Department of Labor, *Health Benefits and the Workforce.* Washington, D.C.: U.S. Government Printing Office, 1992, pp. 37-42.

Long, S.H., and Settle, R.F. Medicare and the Disadvantaged Elderly: Objectives and Outcomes. *Milbank Memorial Fund Quarterly/Health and Society* 624(4):609-656, 1984.

Lubitz, J., Beebe, J., and Riley, G. Improving the Medicare HMO Payment Formula to Deal with Biased Selection. In: *Advances in Health Economics and Health Services Research*, Vol. 6, *Biased Selection in Health Care Markets.* R.M. Scheffler and L.F. Rossiter, eds. Greenwich, Conn.: Jai Press, Inc., 1985, pp. 101-122.

Luft, H. *Health Maintenance Organizations: Dimensions of Performance.* New

Brunswick, N.J.: Transaction Books, 1987. (Originally published: New York: Wiley, 1981.)

Luft, H. Problems and Prospects in Multiple Option Health Plan Settings. Paper prepared for Conference on American Health Policy: Critical Issues for Reform, sponsored by American Enterprise Institute for Public Policy Research, Washington, D.C., October 3-4, 1991.

Luft, H., and Miller, R. Patient Selection in a Competitive Health System. *Health Affairs* 7(3):97-119, 1988.

Luft, H., Trauner, J., and Maerki, S. Adverse Selection in a Large, Multiple-Option Health Benefits Program: A Case Study of the California Public Employees' Retirement System. In: *Advances in Health Economics and Health Services Research* Vol. 6, *Biased Selection in Health Care Markets.* R.M. Scheffler and L.F. Rossiter, eds. Greenwich, Conn.: Jai Press, Inc, 1985, pp. 197-229.

Luft, H., Robinson, J., Gardner, L., et al. *A Method for Risk-Adjusting Employer Contributions to Competing Health Insurance Plans Using Variables in Personnel Files.* Final Report for Research Project Predicting Medical Care Use and Expenditures with Variables in Administrative Files. San Francisco, Calif.: Institute for Health Policy Studies, University of California at San Francisco, 1989.

Lurie, M., Ward, N.B., Shapiro, M.F., et al. Termination from Medi-Cal: Does It Affect Health? *New England Journal of Medicine* 311(7):480-484, 1984.

MacIntyre, D. *Voluntary Health Insurance and Rate Making.* Ithaca, N.Y.: Cornell University Press, 1962.

Madlin, N. Coalitions Strive for Quality. *Business and Health* 9(10):22-31, 1991a.

Madlin, N. Wellness Incentives: How Well Do They Work? *Business and Health* 9(4):70-74, 1991b.

Marion Merrell Dow, Inc. *Marion Merrell Dow Managed Care Digest.* HMO Edition 1992. Kansas City, Mo.: 1992.

Marmor, T. *The Politics of Medicare.* Chicago, Ill.: Aldine Publishing Company, 1973. (Reprint: originally published by Routledge & Kegan Paul, Ltd., 1970.)

McCarthy, E.G., and Widmer, G.W. Effects of Screening by Consultants on Recommended Elective Surgical Procedures. *New England Journal of Medicine* 291(25):1331-1335, 1974.

McDowell, I., and Newell, C. *Measuring Health. A Guide to Rating Scales and Questionnaires.* New York, N.Y.: Oxford University Press, 1987.

McEvilla, J. The Patient, Prescription Practices, and Pharmacy Services. In: U.S. Department of Health, Education and Welfare, *Report of the National Conference on Medical Costs*, June 27-28, 1967. Washington, D.C.: U.S. Government Printing Office, 1968, pp. 249-258.

McGuire, T. An Evaluation of Diagnosis-Related Group Severity and Complexity Refinement. *Health Care Financing Review* 12(4):49-60, 1991.

McIlrath, S. Panel Wants Most Paper Claims to Go the Way of the Dinosaur. *American Medical News*, August 10, 1992, pp. 1, 39.

McLaughlin, C., and Zellers, W. Shortcomings of Voluntarism in the Small-Group Market. *Health Affairs* 11(2):28-40, 1992.

McLeod, D., and Geisel, J. Congress Seeks to Curb MEWA Abuse. *Business Insurance*, March 16, 1992, pp. 1, 30.

Mechanic, D., Ettel, T., and Davis, D.  Choosing Among Health Insurance Options: A Study of New Employees.  *Inquiry* 27(1):14-23, 1990.

Mehr, R.  *Fundamentals of Insurance.*  Homewood, Ill.:  Richard D. Irwin, Inc., 1983.

Mercer-Meidinger-Hansen.  *Retiree Health Benefits: Plan Designs for a Changing World.*  Louisville, Ky.: William M. Mercer-Meidinger-Hansen, Incorporated, 1989.

Merlis, M.  Controlling Health Care Costs.  In:  *A Call for Action. Supplement to the Final Report of the Pepper Commission.*  U.S. Bipartisan Commission on Comprehensive Health Care.  Washington, D.C.:  U.S. Government Printing Office, September 1990, pp. 27-42.

Merrill, J., and McLaughlin, C.  Competition vs. Regulation: Some Empirical Evidence.  *Journal of Health Politics, Policy and Law* 10:613-623, 1986.

Miller, A., and Bradburn, E.  Shape Up—Or Else.  *Newsweek*, July 1, 1991, pp. 42-43.

Miller, F.  Practice Guidelines and Medical Malpractice Liability.  Paper commissioned for the Institute of Medicine Study of Clinical Practice Guidelines.  April 1991.

Miller, R., and Luft, H.  Diversity and Transition in Health Insurance Plans.  *Health Affairs* 10(4):37-47, 1991.

Mills, W.  Rising Health Costs: A View from Congress.  In:  U.S. Department of Health, Education and Welfare, *Report of the National Conference on Medical Costs*, June 27-28, 1967.  Washington, D.C.:  U.S. Government Printing Office, 1968, pp. 50-55.

Moffit, R.E.  *Consumer Choice and Health: Learning from the Federal Employees Health Benefits Program.*  Washington, D.C.:  Heritage Foundation, February 6, 1992.

Moses, R.  Evaluating and Avoid the Pitfalls of Managed Health Care Benefits.  Paper prepared for the 1992 Managed Health Care Congress.  Washington, D.C., Michales and Wishner, P.C., August 1992.

Moskowitz, D.B.  High Courts Tackle Case of Corporate Health Benefit Cuts.  *Washington Post*, June 1, 1992, Business Section, p. 11.

Muchnick-Baku, S., and McNcil, C.  *Healthy People 2000 at Work: Strategies for Employers.*  Washington, D.C.:  The National Resource Center on Worksite Health Promotion, Washington Business Group on Health, 1991.

Muchnick-Baku, S., and Orrick, S.  *Working for Good Health: Health Promotion and Small Business.*  Washington, D.C.:  The National Resource Center on Worksite Health Promotion, Washington Business Group on Health, 1991.

Mullan, F.  *Plagues and Politics.*  New York, N.Y.:  Basic Books, Inc., 1989.

Mulley, A.  The Question of Value: A Clinician Researcher's Perspective.  Presented at Symposium on American Employers and Health Care: Roles, Responsibilities, and Risk, sponsored by the Academy Industry Program of the National Research Council and the Institute of Medicine's Committee on Employer-Based Health Benefits, Washington, D.C., May 19-20, 1992.

Munts, R.  *Bargaining for Health: Labor Unions, Health Insurance and Medical Care.*  Madison, Wisc.:  University of Wisconsin Press, 1967.

National Association of Insurance Commissioners. *Report of the Health Care Insurance Access Working Group.* Washington, D.C.: 1991.

National Association of Manufacturers. *Employer Cost-Shifting Expenditures.* Prepared by Lewin/ICF. Washington, D.C.: 1991.

National Health Policy Forum. *Regulating Health Insurance in the Small-Group Market: Proposals to Increase Availability and Affordability.* Issue Brief No. 581. Washington, D.C., 1991.

National Health Policy Forum. *Multiple Employer Purchasing Groups: The Challenge of Meshing ERISA Standards with Health Insurance Reform.* Issue Brief No. 604. Washington, D.C., 1992.

Neipp, J., and Zeckhauser, R. Persistence in the Choice of Health Plans. In: *Advances in Health Economics and Health Services Research,* Vol. 6, *Biased Selection in Health Care Markets.* R.M. Scheffler and L.E. Rossiter, eds. Greenwich, Conn.: Jai Press, Inc., 1985, pp. 47-72.

Nelson, A.R. Lessons from the Past. *The Internist* 25(1):7-8, January 1984.

Newhouse, J.P. Medical Care Costs: How Much Welfare Loss? *Journal of Economic Perspectives* 6(3):2-21, 1992.

Newhouse, J.P., Manning, W.G., Morris, C.N., et al. Some Interim Results from a Controlled Trial of Cost Sharing in Health Insurance. *New England Journal of Medicine* 305(25):1501-1507, 1981.

Newhouse, J.P., Manning, W.G., Keeler, E.B., et al. Adjusting Capitation Rates Using Objective Health Measures and Prior Utilization. *Health Care Financing Review* 10(3):41-54, 1989.

Northwestern National Life Insurance Company. Employers Plan to Restrict Dependent Health Care Coverages. *Medical Benefits* 6(14):10, 1989.

NYBGH (New York Business Group on Health). Risk-Rated Health Insurance: Incentives for Healthy Lifestyles. May 1990, pp. 1-9.

OTA (Office of Technology Assessment). *The Hemodialysis Equipment and Disposables Industry.* Washington, D.C.: U.S. Government Printing Office, 1984.

OTA. *Genetic Monitoring and Screening in the Workplace.* Washington, D.C.: U.S. Government Printing Office, 1990.

Park, R.E., Brook, R.H., and Kosecoff, J. Explaining Variation in Hospital Death Rates. *Journal of the American Medical Association* 264:484-490, 1990.

Pauly, M.V. Overinsurance and Public Provision of Insurance: The Roles of Moral Hazard and Adverse Selection. *Quarterly Journal of Economics* 88(1):44-62, 1974.

Pauly, M.V. Effectiveness Research and the Impact of Financial Incentives on Outcomes. In: *Improving Health Policy and Management: Nine Critical Research Issues for the 1990s.* S.M. Shortell and U.E. Reinhardt, eds. Ann Arbor, Mich.: Health Administration Press, 1992, pp. 151-194.

Pauly, M.V., Danzon, P., Feldstein, P., et al. A Plan for "Responsible National Health Insurance." *Health Affairs* 10(1):5-25, 1991.

Payne, S. Identifying and Managing Inappropriate Hospital Utilization: A Policy Synthesis. *HSR: Health Services Research* 22(5):709-769, 1987.

Pierce County Medical. *A Brief History of the Nation's First Successful Prepaid Health Plan.* Takoma, Wa.: May, 1992.

Polk, J. Presentation at National Health Policy Forum on Multiple Employer Purchasing Groups: The Challenge of Meshing ERISA Standards with Health Insurance Reform. Washington, D.C., September 24, 1992.

Poullier, J. Health Data File: Overview and Methodology. *Health Care Financing Review* 1989 Annual Supplement:111-118, 1989.

Poullier, J. Administrative Costs in Selected Industrialized Countries. *Health Care Financing Review* 13(4):167-172, 1992.

Poynter, N. *Medicine and Man.* Middlesex, England: Pelican Books, 1971.

PPRC (Physician Payment Review Commission). *Annual Report to Congress.* Washington, D.C.: 1988, 1989, 1990, 1992a.

PPRC. *Monitoring Access of Medicare Beneficiaries.* Report to Congress. Washington, D.C.: 1992b.

Pressman, J., and Wildavsky, A. *Implementation: How Great Expectations in Washington Are Dashed in Oakland.* Berkeley, Calif.: University of California Press, 1973.

Price, J.R., and Mays, J. Selection and the Competitive Standing of Health Plans in a Mutiple-Choice, Mutiple-Insurer Market. In: *Advances in Health Economics and Health Services Research,* Vol. 6, *Biased Selection in Health Care Markets.* R.M. Scheffler and L.F. Rossiter, eds. Greenwich, Conn.: Jai Press, Inc., 1985, pp. 127-147.

Priest, D. How Hawaii Stands Above Health-Care Fray. *Washington Post,* October 18, 1992, pp. A4-A5.

ProPAC (Prospective Payment Assessment Commission). *Report and Recommendations to the Secretary,* U.S. Department of Health and Human Services, April 1, 1986, Washington, D.C.

ProPAC. *Medicare and the American Health Care System.* Report to the Congress, June 1992, Washington, D.C.

Reinhardt, U.E. West Germany's Health Care and Health-Insurance System: Combining Universal Access with Cost Control. In: *A Call for Action. Supplement to the Final Report of the Pepper Commission.* U.S. Bipartisan Commission on Comprehensive Health Care. Washington, D.C.: U.S. Government Printing Office, September 1990, pp. 3-17.

Resnick, R. Health Reform Plans Adapted from Jackson Hole Vie for Support. *Business and Health* 10(11):41-44, 1992.

Rettig, R.A. Technology Assessment—An Update. *Investigative Radiology* 26:165-173, 1991.

Rich, S. Health Care Coverage Gaps Widespread. *Washington Post,* June 25, 1992, p. A30.

Robinson, J.C., Luft, H.S., Gardner, L.B., et al. A Method for Risk-Adjusting Employer Contributions to Competing Health Insurance Plans. *Inquiry* 28(2):107-116, 1991.

Roemer, M., and Shain, M. *Hospital Utilization under Insurance.* American Hospital Association Monograph Series No. 6, Chicago, Ill.: American Hospital Association, 1959.

Roper, W., Winkenwerder, W., Hackbarth, G., and Krakauer, H. Effectiveness in Health Care: An Initiative to Evaluate and Improve Medical Practice. *New England Journal of Medicine* 319:1197-1202, 1988.

Rorem, C.R.  Sickness Insurance in the United States. *Bulletin of the American Hospital Association*, June 1932 (reprinted in Rorem, 1982).

Rorem, C.R.  *A Quest for Certainty: Essays on Health Care Economics, 1930-1970.* Ann Arbor, Mich.: Health Administration Press, 1982.

Rosenbloom, D., and Gertman, P.M.  An Intervention Strategy for Controlling Costly Care. *Business and Health* 1(8):17-21, 1984.

Rosko, M.  A Comparison of Hospital Performance Under the Partial-Payer Medicare PPS and State All-Payer Rate-Setting Systems. *Inquiry* 26(1):48-61, 1989.

Rothstein, M.A.  Genetic Discrimination in Employment and the Americans with Disabilities Act. *Houston Law Review* 29:23-84, 1992.

Rowland, M.  Matching Life Styles to Benefits. *New York Times*, March 1, 1992, p. 14.

Russell, L.  *Is Prevention Better Than Cure?* Washington, D.C.: The Brookings Institution, 1986.

Russell, L.  *Medicare's New Hospital Payment System: Is It Working?* Washington, D.C.: The Brookings Institution, 1989.

Russell, L.  Are Worksite Health Promotion Programs a Good Investment? In: *The Economy of New Jersey: Health Care Issues,* Vol. III. J.R. Chelius, ed. Trenton, N.J.: New Jersey Business and Industry Association, 1990.

Rutgow, I., and Sieverts, S. Surgical Second Opinion Programs. In: *Socioeconomics of Surgery.* I. Rutgow, ed. St. Louis, Mo.: C.V. Mosby Co., 1989.

Sailors, R.  Linking Public and Private Efforts: The Florida Experience. Presentation at Symposium on American Employers and Health Care, Institute of Medicine and Academy Industry Program of the National Research Council, Washington, D.C., May 20, 1992.

Salkever, D.S., and Bice, T.W.  Certificate-of-Need Legislation and Hospital Costs. In: *Hospital Costs Containment—Selected Notes for Future Policy.* M. Zubkoff, I.E. Raskin, and R.S. Hanft, eds. New York, N.Y.: PRODIST for the Milbank Memorial Fund, 1978, pp. 429-460.

Saltman, R.  Single-Source Financing Systems: A Solution for the United States? *Journal of the American Medical Association* 268:774-779, 1992.

Schachner, M.  MCA Extends Benefits to Same-Sex Partners. *Business Insurance*, May 25, 1992, p. 6.

Scheffler, R.M., Gibbs, J.O., and Gurnick, D.A.  *The Impact of Medicare's Prospective Payment System and Private Sector Initiatives: Blue Cross Experience, 1980-1986.* Final report on HCFA Grant No. 15-C-98757/5. Berkeley, Calif.: University of California, Berkeley, 1988.

Scheffler, R.M., Sullivan, S.D., and Ko, T.H.  The Impact of Blue Cross and Blue Shield Plan Utilization Management Programs, 1980-1988. *Inquiry* 28(3):263-275, 1991.

Schieber, G.J., and Poullier, J.P.  Overview of International Comparisons of Health Care Expenditures. *Health Care Financing Review* 1989 Annual Supplement:1-7, 1989.

Schieber, G.J., and Poullier, J.P.  International Health Spending: Issues and Trends. *Health Affairs* 10(1):106-116, 1991.

Schieber, G.J., Poullier, J.P., and Greenwald, L.M.  Health Care Systems in Twenty-Four Countries. *Health Affairs* 10(3):22-38, 1991.

Schiller, Z., Kondrad, W., and Anderson, S. If You Light up on Sunday, Don't Come in on Monday. *Business Week,* August 26, 1991, pp. 68-72.

Schneider, M., Sommer, J., and Keceki, A. *Gesundheitssyteme im Internationalen Vergleich.* Augsberg, West Germany: BASYS GmbH, 1987.

Schoendorf, K.C., Hogue, C.J.R., Kleinman, J.C., et al. Mortality Among Infants of Blacks as Compared with White College-Educated Parents. *New England Journal of Medicine* 326(23):1522-1527, 1992.

Schur, C., and Taylor, A. Health Insurance and the Two-Worker Household. *Health Affairs* 10(1):155-163, 1991.

Schwartz, R.M., Michelman, T., Pezzullo, J., et al. Explaining Resource Consumption Among Non-Normal Neonates. *Health Care Financing Review* 13(2):19-28, 1991.

Schwartz, W. The Inevitable Failure of Cost Containment Strategies: Why They Can Provide Only Temporary Relief. *Journal of the American Medical Association* 257:220-224, 1987.

Seeman, R.F. An Employer's Experiences. Presented at Symposium on American Employers and Health Care: Roles, Responsibilities, and Risk, sponsored by the Academy Industry Program of the National Research Council and the Institute of Medicine's Committee on Employer-Based Health Benefits, Washington, D.C., May 19-20, 1992.

Segal Company. *Survey of State Employee Health Benefit Plans 1991: Summary of Findings.* Prepared by C. Yaggy. New York, N.Y.: Segal Company, 1991.

Shannon, B. The Brain Gets Sick, Too—The Case for Equal Insurance Coverage for Serious Mental Illness. Draft paper, 1992.

Showstack, J.A., Blumberg, B.D., Schwartz, J., et al. Fee-for-Service Physician Payment: Analysis of Current Methods and Their Development. *Inquiry* 16(3):230-246, Fall 1979.

Sipress, A. Cigarettes, Other Habits, Can Cost Someone a Job. *Washington Post,* April 30, 1991, Health Section, p. 7.

Snook, T. NAIC Small Group Health Model Law. Milliman and Robertson Research Report, April 1991 (no city).

Somers, A.R. *Hospital Regulation: The Dilemma of Public Policy.* Princeton, N.J.: Industrial Relations Section, Princeton University, 1969.

Somers, A.R., and Somers, H.M. National Health Insurance: Story with a Past, Present, and Future. In: *Health and Health Care: Policies in Perspective.* A.R. Somers and H.M. Somers, eds. Germantown, Md.: Aspen Systems Corporation, 1977a, pp. 179-192.

Somers, A.R., and Somers, H.M. National Health Insurance: Criteria for an Effective Program and a Proposal. Excerpt from H.M. Somers and A.R. Somers, Major Issues in National Health Insurance, presented to Sun Valley Health Forum, 1971; published in *Milbank Memorial Fund Quarterly* April 1972: Part 1, pp. 177-210 and in *Health and Health Care: Policies in Perspective.* A.R. Somers and H.M. Somers, eds. Germantown, Md.: Aspen Systems Corporation, 1977b, pp. 192-203.

Somers, H.M., and Somers, A.R. *Doctors, Patients, and Health Insurance.* Washington, D.C.: The Brookings Institution, 1961.

Somers, H.M., and Somers, A.R. *Medicare and the Hospitals: Issues and Prospects.* Washington, D.C.: The Brookings Institution, 1967.

Sorensen, A., Saward, E., and Wersinger, R. The Demise of an Individual Practice Association: A Case Study of Health Watch. *Inquiry* 17(3):244, 1980.

Span, P. Smokers' New Hazard: No Work. Health Costs Behind Job Bias Issue. *Washington Post,* November 12, 1991, pp. A1, A14.

Spilker, B., ed. *Quality of Life Assessments in Clinical Trials.* New York, N.Y.: Raven Press, 1990.

Starfield, B. Primary Care and Health: A Cross-National Comparison. *Journal of the American Medical Association* 266:2268-2271, 1991.

Starr, P. *The Social Transformation of American Medicine.* New York, N.Y.: Basic Books, Inc., 1982.

Steinwachs, D.M. Redesign of Delivery Systems to Enhance Productivity. In: *Improving Health Policy and Management: Nine Critical Research Issues for the 1990s.* S.M. Shortell and U.E. Reinhardt, eds. Ann Arbor, Mich.: Health Administration Press, 1992, pp. 275-310.

Steinwald, B., and Sloan, F.A. Regulatory Approaches to Hospital Cost Containment: A Synthesis of the Empirical Evidence. In: *A New Approach to the Economics of Health Care.* M. Olson, ed. Washington, D.C.: American Enterprise Institute for Public Policy Research, 1981.

Stern, L. Coalitions: The Convergence Continues. *Business and Health* 9(10):9-16, 1991.

Stern, R.S., Weissman, J.S., and Epstein, A.M. The Emergency Department as a Pathway to Admission for Poor and High-Cost Patients. *Journal of the American Medical Association* 266(16):2238-2243, 1991.

Stevens, R. *In Sickness and in Wealth: American Hospitals in the Twentieth Century.* New York, N.Y.: Basic Books, 1989.

Stewart, A.L., and Ware, J.E., Jr., eds. *Measuring Functioning and Well-Being: The Medical Outcomes Study Approach.* Durham, N.C.: Duke University Press, 1992.

Sullivan, C., and Rice, T. The Health Insurance Picture in 1990. *Health Affairs* 10(2):104-115, 1991.

Sullivan, J.F. Judge Voids Health Subsidy Covering New Jersey's Poor. *New York Times,* May 28, 1992, pp. A1, B7.

Swartz, K. A Research Note on the Characteristics of Workers Without Employer-Group Health Insurance Based on the March 1988 Current Population Survey. In: U.S. Department of Labor, *Health Benefits and the Workforce.* Washington, D.C.: U.S. Government Printing Office, 1992, pp. 13-20.

Taylor, H., Leitman, R., and Kramer, E. Rochester Health Care Experiences. Study conducted for Blue Cross Blue Shield of the Rochester Area by Louis Harris and Associates, Inc., New York, April 1992.

Taylor, P. *The Health Care System of Rochester, New York: Its History and Achievements.* Rochester, N.Y.: Finger Lakes Health Systems Agency, 1987.

Temkin, N.R., Dikmen, S., Machamer, J., et al. General Versus Disease-Specific Measures: Further Work on the Sickness Impact Profile for Head Injury. *Medical Care* 27(3, Suppl.):S44-S53, 1989.

1

Thorpe, K. Health Care Cost Containment: Results and Lessons from the Past 20 Years. In: *Improving Health Policy and Management: Nine Critical Research Issues for the 1990s.* S.M. Shortell and U.E. Reinhardt, eds. Ann Arbor, Mich.: Health Administration Press, 1992a, pp. 227-274.

Thorpe, K. Inside the Black Box of Administrative Costs. *Health Affairs* 11(2):41-55, 1992b.

Todd, J.S., Seekins, S.V., Krichbaum, J.S., and Harvey, L.K. Health Access America—Strengthening the U.S. Health Care System. *Journal of the American Medical Association* 265(19):2503-2506, 1991.

Towers, Perrin, Forster & Crosby, Inc. Study of the Federal Employees Health Benefits Program. Prepared for the U.S. Office of Personnel Management, Washington, D.C., April 1988.

Traska, M.R. Workers' Comp Costs Front and Center. *Medical Utilization Review* 20(10):5-6, 1992.

Trauner, J. From Benevolence to Negotiation: Prepaid Health Care in San Francisco, 1850-1950. Doctoral Dissertation, University of California, San Francisco, 1977.

U.S. Chamber of Commerce Research Center. *Employee Benefits: Survey Data from Benefit Year 1990.* Washington, D.C.: 1991.

U.S. Department of Health and Human Services. *Health United States, 1990.* Washington, D.C.: U.S. Government Printing Office, 1991.

U.S. Department of Health, Education and Welfare. *Report of the National Conference on Medical Costs,* June 27-28, 1967. Washington, D.C.: U.S. Government Printing Office, 1968.

U.S. Department of Health, Education and Welfare. *Trends Affecting U.S. Health Care System.* Prepared by the Cambridge Research Institute. DHEW Pub. No. HRA 76-14503. Washington, D.C.: U.S. Government Printing Office, January 1976.

U.S. House of Representatives, Committee on Post Office and Civil Service. *The Federal Employees Health Benefits Program.* Washington, D.C.: U.S. Government Printing Office, 1989.

U.S. Public Health Service. *Healthy People 2000: National Health Promotion and Disease Prevention Objectives.* Washington, D.C.: U.S. Government Printing Office, 1990.

U.S. Senate. Medicare and Medicaid: Problems, Issues and Alternatives, Report of the Staff to the Committee on Finance, U.S. Senate, Washington, D.C., February 9, 1970.

U.S. Senate, Committee on Governmental Affairs, Permanent Subcommittee on Investigations. *U.S. Government Efforts to Combat Fraud and Abuse in the Insurance Industry.* Interim report on combatting fraud and abuse in employer sponsored health benefit plans. Washington, D.C.: U.S. Government Printing Office, 1992a.

U.S. Senate, Special Committee on Aging. *Developments in Aging: 1991.* Vol. 1. Washington, D.C.: U.S. Government Printing Office, 1992b.

Ware, J.E., Jr., and Sherbourne, C.D. The MOS 36-Item Short-Form Health Survey (SF-36). I. Conceptual Framework and Item Selection. *Medical Care* 30:473-483, 1992.

Warner, K. Wellness at the Worksite. *Health Affairs* 9(2):63-79, 1990.

Warner, K., Wickizer, T., Wolfe, R., et al. Economic Implications of Workplace Health Promotion Programs: Review of the Literature. *Journal of Occupational Medicine* 30:106-112, 1988.

Warren, S., and Gerst, S. Workers' Compensation and Managed Care. *AAPPO Journal*, pp. 11-17, Feb./March 1992.

*Washington Post.* OMB to Review Standards of Health Covering 6 Million. March 26, 1992, p. A19.

Weeks, L.E., and Berman, H.J. *Shapers of American Health Care Policy: An Oral History.* Ann Arbor, Mich.: Health Administration Press, 1985.

Weir, M., Orloff, A., and Skocpol, T., eds. *The Politics of Social Policy in the United States.* Princeton, N.J.: Princeton University Press, 1988.

Weisbrod, B. The Health Care Quadrilemma: An Essay on Technological Change, Insurance, Quality of Care, and Cost Containment. *Journal of Economic Literature* 24:523-552, 1991.

Weiss, S., Fielding, J., and Baum, A., eds. *Health at Work.* Hillsdale, N.J.: Lawrence Erlbaum Associates, Publishers, 1991.

Welch, W.P. Medicare Capitation Payments to HMOs in Light of Regression Towards the Mean in Health Care Costs. In: *Advances in Health Economics and Health Services Research*, Vol. 6., *Biased Selection in Health Care Markets.* R.M. Scheffler and L.F. Rossiter, eds. Greenwich, Conn.: Jai Press, Inc., 1985, pp. 75-96.

Welch, W.P. Restructuring the Federal Employees Health Benefits Program: The Private Sector Option. *Inquiry* 26(3):321-334, 1989.

Welch, W.P. Defining Geographic Areas to Adjust Payments to Physicians, Hospitals, and HMOs. *Inquiry* 28(2):151-160, 1991.

Wennberg, J.E. Dealing with Medical Practice Variations: A Proposal for Action. *Health Affairs* 3(2):6-32, 1984.

Wennberg, J.E. What is Outcomes Research? In: Institute of Medicine, *Medical Innovations at the Crossroads*, Vol. 1, *Modern Methods of Clinical Investigation.* A. Gelijns, ed. Washington, D.C.: National Academy Press, 1990, pp. 33-46.

Wennberg, J.E. Unwanted Variations in the Rules of Practice. *Journal of the American Medical Association* 265:1306, 1991.

Werlin, S. Cost Control Methods in Health Care Delivery. In: *PSRO: Organization for Regional Peer Review.* B. Decker and P. Paul, eds. Cambridge, Mass.: Ballinger Publishing Co., 1973, pp. 132-173.

Wickizer, T. The Effect of Utilization Review on Hospital Use and Expenditures: A Review of the Literature and an Update on Recent Findings. *Medical Care Review* 47(3):327-363, 1990.

Wiener, J.M. Federal Benefits Revisions: Reform or Cost Control? *Medicine and Health Perspectives*, no page numbers, April 16, 1990.

Wiener, J.M. Oregon's Plan for Health Care Rationing. *The Brookings Review*, pp. 26-31, Winter 1992.

Wilensky, G., and Rossiter, L. Patient Self-Selection in HMOs. *Health Affairs* 5(4):66-80, 1986.

Wilensky, G., and Rossiter, L. Coordinated Care and Public Programs. *Health Affairs* 10(4):62-77, 1991.

Wilson, F., and Neuhauser, D. *Health Services in the United States.* Cambridge, Mass.: Ballinger Publishing Company, 1974.

Woolhandler, S., and Himmelstein, D.U. The Deteriorating Administrative Efficiency of the U.S. Health Care System. *New England Journal of Medicine* 324(18):1253-1258, 1991.

Woolsey, C. Benefit Self-Funding Gaining New Converts. *Business Insurance,* January 27, 1992a, pp. 3, 10.

Woolsey, C. Employers Alter Retiree Benefits in Light of FAS 106. *Business Insurance,* May 4, 1992b, pp. 1, 33.

Woolsey, C. Employers Monitor Lifestyles. *Business Insurance,* February 17, 1992c, pp. 3-6.

Woolsey, C. Linking Wellness to Health Care Costs. *Business Insurance,* February 17, 1992d, p. 12.

Woolsey, C. Off-Duty Conduct: None of Employer's Business. *Business Insurance,* February 17, 1992e, pp. 10-11.

Woolsey, C. UNISYS to Drop Retiree Health Care. *Business Insurance,* November 9, 1992f, p. 2.

Woolsey, C. Varied Paths Lead to Common Goal of Wellness. *Business Insurance,* February 17, 1992g, p. 16.

Wysong, J., and Abel, T. Universal Health Insurance and High-Risk Groups in West Germany: Implications for U.S. Health Policy. *Milbank Quarterly* 68(4):527-560, 1990.

Yordy, K.D. National Planning for Health: An Emerging Reality. *Bulletin of the New York Academy of Medicine* 48(1):32-38, January 1972.

Young, L. Utilization Review and Control Mechanisms: From the Blue Shield Perspective. *Inquiry* 2(2):5-15, 1965.

Zellers, W., McLaughlin, C., and Frick, K. Small-Business Health Insurance: Only Healthy Need Apply. *Health Affairs* 11(1):174-180, 1992.

# APPENDIXES

# A

# Opinion Surveys on Employment-Based Health Benefits and Related Issues

The following questions were part of surveys conducted by the Gallup Organization for the Employee Benefit Research Institute (EBRI). Unless otherwise indicated, responses to questions represent combined results for November and December 1991 surveys. For these surveys, IOM staff worked with Dallas Salisbury, William Custer, and Laura Bos of EBRI to develop the questions. For some questions, certain response categories have been omitted in this summary. As a result, and also because of rounding errors, the totals below may not add up to 100.

**Do you currently have health care coverage through either a health insurance plan, a health maintenance organization, or a government program?**

Yes                                                                85%

Of "Yes" respondents, source of coverage (could list more than one):
Employer (own/family member) program      63
Government program                        18
Purchased on own                          13
Other answer                              11

**Have you or a family member ever passed up a job opportunity or stayed in a job you would have preferred to have left solely because of health benefits?** (November 1991 survey)

Yes                                                                11%

Aged 18–34                                17
Aged 35–54                                10
Aged 55 and over                           4

**Which of the following best describes the reason you or your family member chose not to change jobs?** (November 1991 survey)

Prospective employer did not offer health benefits    26%
You or someone in your family had a medical condition
    the prospective employer's health plan did not cover    9
Health benefits provided less coverage than you or a
    family member had previously    24
The prospective employer's health plan cost too much    19
None of these    20

**For your own health care and that of your family, which of the following is your biggest concern?** (December 1991 survey)

Cost    49%
Quality    36
Access and availability    12
Everything/all    1

**For society as a whole, what do you think the biggest problem in health care is?** (December 1991 survey)

Cost    79%
Access and availability    13
Quality    6

**In the last few years, has your health insurance coverage?** (November 1991 survey)

Gotten better overall    16%
Gotten worse overall    24

**Which best describes your satisfaction with your health benefits?** (November 1991 survey)

Satisfied    64%
Would rather have additional health benefits and less salary    20
Would rather have additional salary and fewer health benefits    7

**How much more money would you or your family member's employer have to give you each year to make you willing to give up your current employer-provided health benefits?** (September 1991 EBRI/Gallup survey)

0–$1,000    11%
$1,001–$3,000    19

| | |
|---|---|
| $3,001–$5,000 | 15 |
| $5,001 or more | 22 |
| Don't know | 29 |

**How would you characterize your health plan?** (November 1991 survey)

| | | |
|---|---|---|
| Most of it is too hard to understand | | 10% |
| <12 grade education | 15 | |
| Some college | 12 | |
| College graduate | 5 | |
| Some of it is hard to understand | | 36 |
| It is easy to understand | | 52 |

**Does your employer offer you a choice of two or more health insurance plans or is only one plan available to you?** (November 1991 survey)

| | |
|---|---|
| Offers choice | 36% |
| Only one plan available | 36 |
| Not applicable/no employer | 26 |

**How do you rate your current health insurance benefits?**

| | |
|---|---|
| Excellent | 27% |
| Good | 46 |
| Fair | 20 |
| Poor | 6 |
| Don't know | 3 |

**You are confident that your employer (your spouse's employer) contracts with the best available health insurance plan(s) for its employees.** (November 1991 survey)

| | |
|---|---|
| Agree | 71% |
| Disagree | 24 |
| Don't know | 5 |

**Many companies, insurers, and government programs have adopted measures to eliminate unnecessary expenditures on health care and to save costs by promoting cost-effective care. Have these cost management measures resulted in any of the following?** *("Yes" respondents)* (November 1991 survey)

| | |
|---|---|
| Your being denied health care services you think you needed? | 9% |
| Your experiencing unreasonable hassle or delays in obtaining health care services? | 17 |
| Your being required to receive health care services from a physician you would not have otherwise chosen? | 16 |

**If your doctor recommends that you have a diagnostic test or treatment that is not covered by your health insurance, would you:** (November 1991 survey)

| | |
|---|---|
| Follow his or her advice and pay for it yourself | 34% |
| Attempt to weigh the benefits of the recommendation against the cost before making a decision | 20 |
| Approach your employer or insurance company to see if an exception could be made | 38 |

**Does your household maintain a relationship with a physician who could be called your personal or family doctor?**

| | |
|---|---|
| Yes | 76% |
| Male | 72 |
| Female | 80 |
| Aged 18–34 | 69 |
| Aged 35–54 | 78 |
| Aged 55 and over | 84 |
| Income under $20,000 | 70 |
| Income $20,000 to <$75,000 | 79 |
| Income $75,000 and > | 83 |
| White | 78 |
| Minority | 69 |

**In the last five years, has your household had to involuntarily change your personal or family physician?**

| | |
|---|---|
| Yes | 18% |

**If yes to [above question], which of the following statements best describes the reason for that change?** (December 1991 survey)

| | |
|---|---|
| Doctor moved/closed practice/retired | 26% |
| Respondent moved | 15 |
| Respondent changed jobs | 15 |
| Health plan required change/employer changed plan | 17 |
| Selected another health plan from employer | 4 |
| Other | 24 |

**Which of the following groups is in the best position to make decisions about the quality of health care provided by a hospital or physician?** (December 1991 survey)

| | |
|---|---|
| Employer | 10% |
| Individual | 55 |
| Government | 32 |
| All the same | 1 |

**Which of the following groups do you think is in the best position to influence the cost of health care?** (December 1991 survey)

| | |
|---|---|
| Employer | 11% |
| Individual | 14 |
| Government | 28 |
| Doctor | 23 |
| Insurers | 20 |
| All the same | 2 |

**Who do you think should be most responsible for providing health benefits for full-time employees and their dependents in the U.S.?** (December 1991 survey)

| | |
|---|---|
| Employers | 48% |
| Federal government | 31 |
| Individual | 14 |
| All the same | 3 |

**If you had the choice, which of the following organizations would you prefer to purchase your health benefits through?** (November 1991 survey)

| | |
|---|---|
| An employer | 39% |
| A trade association, union or professional group | 8 |
| State government | 5 |
| Federal government | 16 |
| On your own | 25 |

**Do you think employers should be required to provide health insurance if the employees pay a portion of the costs?** (July 1991 survey)

| | |
|---|---|
| Yes | 83% |
| No | 16 |

In general, do you strongly favor, favor, oppose or strongly oppose the implementation by the U.S. government of some type of national health insurance system? (January 1992 survey)

| | |
|---|---|
| Strongly favor | 25% |
| Favor | 54 |
| Oppose | 14 |
| Strongly oppose | 4 |

Which of the following do you think is the better way to deal with our nation's health care problems? (Gallup poll for CNN and USA Today, January 28, 1992)

| | |
|---|---|
| Reform of our current private health care system | 64% |
| Government-sponsored national health insurance | 30 |

# B

# Regulation of Employment-Based Health Benefits: The Intersection of State and Federal Law

*Edward F. Shay**

The regulation of employment-based health benefits by state governments and the federal government intersect and diverge in complex ways. This paper surveys some, but not all, aspects of each regulatory arena and their interrelations.

States regulate health and other insurers. State regulation varies widely in both scope and intensity but may cover insurer formation, taxation and operation, insurance contracts and rates, unfair insurance practices, and other types of insuring organizations such as health maintenance organizations (HMOs), preferred provider organizations (PPOs), and related managed care organizations (MCOs).

Federal laws, on the other hand, regulate employee health benefits. Most significant is the Employee Retirement Income Security Act of 1974 (ERISA). It is primarily concerned with reporting, disclosure, and fiduciary duties related to the establishment and administration of employee health benefit plans. The most noteworthy aspect of current federal law, in particular, ERISA, may be the federal preemption of most state regulatory power relating to employee benefits. Federal tax policies, antidiscrimination laws, coordination with Medicare, and concurrent federal regulation of some HMOs also affect employee health benefits.

State regulation of health benefits arises from the historic role of the states as regulators of insurance. Federal regulation of health benefits arises from the federal role in taxation and in regulating the relationships between

---

*Paper prepared by Edward F. Shay, partner at Saul, Ewing, Remick & Saul in Philadelphia, Pennsylvania. Some editing of the paper, which initially covered a broader range of legal issues, was undertaken by IOM committee members and staff.

employers and employees. Compared to current federal regulation of health benefits, state insurance regulation tends to be more extensive and explicit.

To some extent, state regulation of health insurance and federal regulation of health benefits overlap and at times conflict. ERISA's preemption provisions, which are discussed below, coordinate the relationship between these concurrent systems for regulating health benefits. The nature of that coordination has important practical consequences for those being regulated.

## LEGAL FOUNDATIONS OF STATE INSURANCE REGULATION

The role of the states as regulators of insurance evolved from the nineteenth-century view expressed by the Supreme Court of the United States in *Paul v. Virginia[1]* that "commerce" under the Commerce Clause of the U.S. Constitution did not include making an insurance contract. Because an insurance contract was not interstate commerce, the Supreme Court upheld state regulation of insurance within state borders. With the blessing of the Supreme Court, the states for the next 75 years incorporated domestic insurance companies of every type, regulated and taxed foreign insurance companies within state borders, licensed their products, and regulated the relationship between the insurer and the insured. During this same period, the federal government did not regulate insurance companies.

In 1944 the Supreme Court decided *United States v. South-Eastern Underwriters Association[2]* and redefined dramatically the federal state balance in the regulation of insurance. In *United States v. South-Eastern Underwriters Association*, the Supreme Court reviewed a direct appeal from a federal district court that had dismissed an indictment against 200 insurance companies for fixing prices in interstate commerce in violation of the Sherman Anti-Trust Act. In order to maintain the paradigm of insurance regulation established by *Paul v. Virginia* and its sequelae, the *South-Eastern Underwriters* case would have required the Supreme Court to limit an act of Congress rather than regulatory efforts by a state. The Supreme Court reviewed 75 years of decisional law that held that insurance contracts were "local" commerce and not "commerce" under the Commerce Clause. Then the Court reviewed the size, complexity, and volume of insurance transactions and observed that only a "technical legal conception" rather than a "practical one, drawn from the course of business" could continue to sustain the doctrine of *Paul v. Virginia.[3]* The Court concluded that modern insurance transactions were "commerce" subject to the Sherman Act and the Commerce Clause.

The states and the insurance industry were stunned by the "precedent-shattering decision in the *South-Eastern Underwriter* case." Together, they gave their "overwhelming endorsement" to remedial legislation intended to restore by statute what the Supreme Court no longer conferred by constitutional right.[4] On March 9, 1945, Congress restored to the states their primary role as the regulators of insurance by enacting the McCarran-Ferguson Act.[5] Under the McCarran-Ferguson Act, the states could regulate and tax insurance companies without the limitations posed by the Commerce Clause.[6] However, the McCarran-Ferguson Act reserved a federal regulatory role "to the extent that such business is not regulated by state law."[7]

Rather than encourage federal regulation in the absence of adequate state regulation, the state insurance commissioners formed the National Association of Insurance Commissioners (NAIC) shortly after the passage of the McCarran-Ferguson Act. The NAIC prepared model acts for adoption by the states to preclude a federal regulatory role.[8] The NAIC continues today as a resource to which both regulators and the regulated may look for information on regulation of insurance and for model regulations and guidelines.

## EARLY REGULATION OF HEALTH INSURANCE

Regulation of group health insurance began at the state level for other reasons of historical and legal importance. Initially, group health insurance was a tentative experiment at the local level. In the 1930s, hospitals and medical societies began one of the earliest forms of group health benefits, which evolved over two decades into Blue Cross and Blue Shield plans.[9] By 1945, Blue Cross and Blue Shield covered 19 million subscribers through 80 plans nationwide.[10]

Initially, Blue Cross and Blue Shield plans were organized as nonprofit service plans. As service plans, the Blue Cross and Blue Shield plans applied rudimentary, but community-based, rates and relied on direct contracts with hospitals and physicians to provide for their insureds a service benefit (e.g., hospital room and board) rather than a cash (indemnity) payment. Many Blue Cross and Blue Shield plans were initially exempted from taxation by early enabling legislation that also conferred upon state insurance commissioners considerable regulatory authority to review and approve premiums and provider and subscriber agreements.[11]

Prior to 1950, commercial insurers generally did not offer group health policies, relying instead on individual accident and health policies offered in conjunction with disability coverage for lost income.[12] Commercial insurers did not contract with hospitals and physicians and paid instead a fixed cash indemnity to their insureds, which varied with the nature of the loss involved. State regulation of commercial insurers often involved less burdensome "file and use" rate setting, which allowed commercial insurers to use a filed rate unless it was specifically disapproved by state insurance regulators.[13]

## OVERVIEW OF CURRENT STATE REGULATION
## OF HEALTH INSURANCE

As envisioned by the drafters of the McCarran-Ferguson Act, the states have played the dominant role in regulating the health insurance products and their vendors that may be chosen by employers to provide insurance-funded health benefits. Logically, regulation by 50 states permits considerable variation in the scope and intensity of regulation. This overview summarizes state regulation of insurance company formation and financial matters; insurance contracts and rates; unfair insurance practices; health insurer coverage and mandates; managed care; and so-called anti-managed-care laws.

### Formation and Financial Matters

Through laws on incorporation and laws on the licensing of insurance companies, states regulate the organizational structure and financial affairs of insurance companies. Most states permit insurance companies to organize under general corporate statutes and to comply with industry-specific requirements by obtaining a license, sometimes called a certificate of authority.

The purpose of licensing is to protect the public against ineptly managed or financially unsound insurance companies. Prospectively, regulators may condition initial licensure on compliance with requirements for minimum capital and surplus, security deposits with the state, and participation in a state guaranty association that allows a state to assess companies to make up some or all of the losses of a failed insurer. Once a company is licensed, state regulators use periodic reporting and audits to assess the current financial condition of a company. This monitoring focuses on loss and claim reserves, unearned premium reserves, and other financial indicators.

State regulation of health insurers also includes taxation on insurance companies and on the premiums paid by purchasers of health and accident insurance.[14] Some Blue Cross and Blue Shield plans are exempt from taxation. However, in most states, Blue Cross and Blue Shield pay taxes or some equivalent to taxes.

### Insurance Contract and Rate Regulation

States regulate health insurance contracts and seek to balance the interests of consumers in obtaining fair and reasonable coverage against the interests of insurers in avoiding unreasonable or undisclosed risks. However, the intensity with which state regulators pursue this objective may vary greatly from state to state. A representative approach to contract regulation could involve statutes or regulations that by their terms fix the definitions of important terms in health insurance contracts, require a grace period prior to cancellation for nonpayment of premiums, and require written disclosure of any coverage limitations or exclusions for preexisting conditions.[15]

Juxtaposed to contract regulation that protects insureds is regulation enabling insurers to fully and fairly assess the risks that they underwrite. For example, regulators may permit or require a contract provision that allows an insurer to examine the person of an insured for whom a claim is made,[16] a contractual right that permits an insurer to enforce an exclusion for preexisting conditions and facilitates the investigation of questionable claims.

Rate regulation seeks to ensure that the price of insurance is not excessive, inadequate, or unfairly discriminatory. This standard for rate setting was first propounded in 1946 by the NAIC in model legislation drafted after enactment of the McCarran-Ferguson Act.[17] In reviewing rates, state regulators follow one of two basic procedures. Under the "file and use" approach, companies are deemed approved to use their rates if they receive no pertinent communication from state regulators after a prescribed period, perhaps 60 days after filing. Under a "review and approval" process, companies (especially Blue Cross and Blue Shield plans) may use rates only following approval.

## Unfair Insurance Practices

Insurance regulators rely upon unfair insurance practice laws in many states to regulate discriminatory or deceptive behavior by insurers. Although plainly intended to protect consumers, these laws have been widely interpreted by the courts to prohibit injured consumers from suing deceptive insurers.[18] Instead, insurance regulators must initiate a lawsuit on behalf of the government. Typically, unfair insurance practice laws are generic and regulate broadly all types of insurance companies and their dealings. They prohibit specific unfair practices in considerable detail. Typical unfair practices include misrepresenting benefits, making false or misleading statements, engaging in false advertising, or engaging in unfair discrimination. Unfair discrimination includes making unfair or unreasonable distinctions between individuals of the same class and essentially the same level of risk.[19]

With mixed results, regulators have applied unfair insurance practice laws to accident and health insurance to expand or maintain the availability of insurance for classes of persons to whom insurance is not readily available. One court has held it unfairly discriminatory for insurers to apply individual medical underwriting to small groups while not applying the practice to large groups.[20] Another court has found no unfair discrimination where insurers used HIV testing results to deny coverage because HIV-positive individuals were held not to be in the "same class" as persons who did not test positive for HIV.[21]

## Coverage and Mandates

States seek also to regulate the type of health insurance coverage that is available to their residents. Many require health insurers to offer specified benefits or to make payments to particular types of practitioners. One recent survey of these laws reports that 992 requirements in various states are applicable to some or all types of health insurance.[22] Known as "mandates," these laws typically follow two approaches. The first involves mandated coverage for specific conditions such as premature birth or substance abuse and dependency. The second type of mandate specifies those practitioners such as nurse midwives or optometrists who may receive payment under group health insurance policies.

In some states where concern for the availability of insurance for small employers and for uninsured individuals has commanded legislative attention, states have abandoned their emphasis on mandates in favor of so-called "bare bones" policies.[23] These policies offer a limited array of basic benefits and are intended to provide an affordable alternative to group health policies whose cost has been increased by mandated benefits.

## Managed Care

States also regulate insurancelike, or risk-assuming, entities in what has come to be called managed care. In a broad sense, managed care involves organized systems of cost containment achieved through management of consumer and provider patterns of consumption of health care services. HMOs and PPOs are the most widely regulated types of managed care organizations. Cost containment methods in managed care vary widely, and state regulatory activities are equally varied in scope and intensity. For example, some states do not regulate PPOs that do not assume risk.

To protect the public against insolvency, undertreatment, and poor quality care, state regulators rely upon initial licensing and ongoing supervision that address these concerns. Typically, state laws prohibit any person from offering or establishing an HMO or risk-assuming PPO without obtaining a license.[24] Some regulation of HMOs and PPOs has, historically, been intended to protect conventional health care providers and discourage prepaid group practices and network health plans. (See Chapter 2 of this report.)

Both HMOs and PPOs in many states are also subject to some degree of ongoing supervision, although the degree varies from state to state. This supervision may involve periodic reporting of financial information and utilization experience. In the case of HMOs, subsequent setting of premiums is subject to ongoing review and approval, as are the rates paid to providers.

Beyond HMOs and PPOs, managed care has spawned an array of other entities that have become involved in managing the cost of health benefits and health care services. State regulation of utilization review organizations, third-party administrators, and related vendors of information systems is increasing. Many of these entities are vendors who market their services specifically to the health benefit plans of large employers. Again, some state regulation has been hostile to these organizations and activities.

In response to the growth and diversification of managed care, state legislators have increased their oversight through legislation. Industry sources report that legislatures considered 306 bills in 1991 that dealt with managed care. Seventy bills aimed to regulate such utilization review activities, which are now regulated in 24 states.[25] Again, the extent of this regulatory trend varies greatly from state to state.

Many managed care laws attempt to balance enrollee choice and access against certain cost containment strategies. They may regulate provider selection and participation in PPO networks or the selection of reviewers and hours of operation of utilization review organizations.[26]

The proliferation of state managed care laws has faced opposition. Especially when employment-based health benefits are involved, such laws have been challenged on the grounds that state regulators are encroaching upon the activities that under federal law must be left to federal regulation.[27]

### Practical Consequences of Opting for a Fully Insured Health Benefits Plan

When an employer provides a fully insured employee benefit plan (i.e., transfers risk to a commercial insurer or Blue Cross and Blue Shield plan), the insured benefits are regulated by the applicable state insurance laws. Thus, they are subject to state benefit mandates, state premium taxes, and state managed care and utilization review laws, as well as laws intended to protect consumers. The number of applicable state laws may be multiplied by the number of states in which the employer does business or its employees reside. The practical consequences of opting for self-insured employee health benefits are discussed in the next section of this paper.

## FEDERAL REGULATION OF HEALTH BENEFITS

Federal law affects private employment-based health benefits in ways that are fundamentally different from those arising from state regulation. Federal law addresses the contractual aspects of health benefits provided as part of a benefits package in the context of a private employer-employee relationship; state health benefits regulation focuses on benefits in the context of an insurance arrangement.

For example, the provision of health benefits in the employer-employee context is affected by the Labor Management Relations Act of 1947 (LMRA).[28] LMRA bans broadly most payments by employers to labor organizations, but it permits labor and management to establish jointly administered health and welfare trusts, sometimes called Taft-Hartley trusts.[29] Foreshadowing ERISA, LMRA has never included any substantive requirement on the amount of health benefits to be provided.

In addition to LMRA, several other federal laws regulate health benefits. These laws, which are briefly discussed at the end of this paper, include the following:

• Federal tax law, which generally makes the economic value of conferring health benefits a largely nontaxable event and provides separate rules for certain specific types of plans, including medical spending accounts and voluntary employee benefit associations (VEBAs).

• Antidiscrimination laws, which broadly prohibit discrimination based on race, gender, age, and disability in employee benefit plans.

• Federal regulation of HMOs, which includes rules applicable to employers and requires employers to offer health benefits through federally qualified HMOs.

• Medicare's secondary payer rules, which define when an employer's health benefit plan must pay before Medicare will pay for an otherwise eligible Medicare beneficiary covered by employment-based health benefits.

ERISA, however, is the centerpiece of federal regulation of health benefit plans. It defines many specific federal roles as well as how the federal and state regulatory systems relate to each other. In general, regulation of employee health benefits under ERISA focuses on process: how employers disclose and report information about their health benefit plans; how employers and others must behave as fiduciaries of these health benefit plans; how special rules on continuation of health benefits must be applied; and how the federal regulatory effort relates to state regulation. Although the statute and associated regulations are quite detailed in many respects, ERISA does not explicitly regulate the substantive content of employee health plans nor require that such a plan be offered.

## Health Benefit Plans Under ERISA

Without understating the importance of other federal regulation of health benefits, ERISA[30] defines the federal role in regulation of private employment-based health benefit plans. It was enacted in 1974 as an attempt at omnibus regulation of pension and welfare benefits and an effort to prevent recurrence of past abuses. The original legislation and its later amendments[31] present a uniform and fairly cohesive federal policy.

ERISA has its roots in the common law of trusts. Its provisions governing the establishment of trusts and the requirements for fiduciaries have been derived from trust law. This body of law has also influenced the manner in which ERISA is enforced. Consequently, courts approach violations of ERISA from the perspective of trust law, not from the perspective of tort law.

ERISA is made up of four titles, of which Title I covers reporting, disclosure, and fiduciary conduct in the provision of health and other employee benefits.[32] Tax aspects of pensions,[33] obtaining IRS determinations,[34] and termination of defined benefit pension plans[35] are dealt with elsewhere in ERISA. Title I of ERISA demarcates the boundary between federal and state regulation of employee health benefits through ERISA's much litigated preemption provision.

For present purposes, Title I can be subdivided into several topics for discussion. Title I begins with legislative findings and purposes.[36] It then sets forth controlling definitions,[37] reporting and disclosure requirements,[38] requirements for fiduciaries and fiduciary responsibilities,[39] provisions on administration and enforcement,[40] and, finally, requirements dealing with continuation coverage under the Consolidated Omnibus Budget Reconciliation Act of 1985 (COBRA).[41] ERISA's important preemption provisions, which govern the relationship between federal and state regulation of employee benefit plans, are a part of Title I's section on administration and enforcement.

### Legislative Focus and Definitions

The legislative history of ERISA emphasizes private pension plan reform. When considering ERISA, Congress expressed concern about whether pension contributions by working Americans would be available to sustain the workers in their retirement.[42] Motivating this concern was discernible growth in the private pension system and a sense that regulation had not kept pace with the system's changes.[43] To improve pension plan regulation, Congress set out to regulate vesting, assure adequate funding, and establish minimum standards for disclosure and fiduciary responsibility.[44]

Although mentioned in the House and Senate reports on the legislative history of ERISA,[45] welfare plans—of which health benefit plans are a subset—received far less congressional attention in the legislative process. There was concern, however, about multiple and conflicting state regulation of these plans.

Under ERISA, "employee welfare benefit plans" include

> Any plan, fund, or program which was heretofore or is hereafter established or maintained by an employer or by an employee organization, or both, to the extent that such plan, fund or program was established or is maintained for purposes of providing for its participants or their beneficiaries, through the purchase of insurance or otherwise, (A) medical, surgical or hospital care or benefits. . . .[46]

Except for government plans, church plans, certain educational organization plans, and excess benefit plans, all employee welfare benefit plans (including health benefit plans) are covered by ERISA.[47,48] Other terms in ERISA's definitional provision include "employer," "employee," "participant," "beneficiary," "employee organization," and "multiple employer welfare arrangement" (MEWA).[49]

Nothing in the statutory definition of what is a "welfare plan" or in the required contents of a summary plan description dictates that even a barebones level of benefits must be provided under the health benefit plan. The Supreme Court's seminal statement on an employer's duty to provide health benefits, or to provide a particular mix of benefits, is direct and clear. The Court has simply stated that "ERISA does not mandate any particular benefits, and does not itself proscribe discrimination in the provision of employee benefits."[50] In effect, the Supreme Court looks upon an employer's offer to provide health benefits to employees as a private contract. ERISA does not require such a contract, nor does ERISA regulate the offer, acceptance, and adequacy of consideration of the private contract between employer and employee.

ERISA also does not require that health benefits vest, or become nonforfeitable by a plan participant. The basic line of reasoning followed by most courts on the question of vesting of health benefits begins with ERISA's definitional section. Under ERISA, "nonforfeitable" is defined "with respect to a *pension* benefit or right" (emphasis added) and excludes by omission any reference to welfare plan benefits such as health benefits.[51] Other provisions of ERISA state that "vesting" does not apply to "an employee welfare benefit plan."[52]

Reasoning that Congress would not inadvertently omit employee health benefits (i.e., welfare plans) from the vesting provisions of the statute, the courts have repeatedly ruled that a plan participant acquires no vested or future expectation of a fixed level of health benefits unless the plan specifically provides for it. For example, a federal court has held that nonunion retirees of a large industrial manufacturer could not rely on ERISA for substantive protection of the health and other welfare benefits that the company terminated in bankruptcy.[53] Likewise, the parents of a hospitalized child could not acquire a vested expectation to full payment for the hospital admission if health plan trustees properly reduced coverage and payment levels during the course of the admission.[54] In sum, the federal courts look at the private contract between employer and employee to provide health benefits and conclude that nothing in ERISA regulates the terms of that contract with respect to its modification or termination.

### Reporting and Disclosure Requirements

ERISA articulates detailed reporting and disclosure requirements for employee benefits. These requirements apply unevenly to welfare plans and pension plans because the latter are required to furnish to the Secretary of Labor considerable additional information.[55] With respect to welfare plans, three basic requirements sum up ERISA's disclosure and reporting provisions, although the details may be quite complex and vary for different kinds of plans.

First, welfare plans must periodically furnish to participants and beneficiaries a summary plan description.[56] The Secretary of Labor has added by regulation a requirement that the description explain what medical benefits are covered by the plan.[57] Second, the administrator of a welfare plan must file with the Secretary of Labor the summary plan description and must also file material modifications to the plan.[58] Third, plan participants must be furnished with a summary annual report.[59] In addition, plans with more than 100 participants, and certain others, must file an annual return (form 5500), which may include detailed financial information, with the Internal Revenue Service.

The summary plan description is the primary disclosure document about the plan that is made available to participants and their beneficiaries. Reflecting congressional concern, ERISA states that the summary plan description "shall be written in a manner calculated to be understood by the average plan participant, and shall be sufficiently accurate and comprehensive to reasonably apprise such participants of their rights and obligations under the plan."[60] Plans that are fully insured and have fewer than 100 participants are exempt by regulation from the annual reporting requirements. Depending on their financing arrangements, other plans face reporting requirements of varying complexity. The procedural character of the reporting and disclosure requirements in ERISA is apparent from the text of the statute and implementing regulations.

ERISA requires that the following information be included in the summary plan description:

- the plan name;
- the type of administration;
- the name and address of the agent designated for service of process;
- the name and address of the administrator;
- applicable collective bargaining terms;
- ineligibility requirements;
- grounds for disqualification, ineligibility, or loss of benefits;
- source of funding;
- identity of organization providing benefits;
- year-end date of plan;
- fiscal or recordkeeping year of plan;
- claims-making procedures; and
- remedies for denial of benefits.[61]

### Fiduciaries

ERISA does impose standards upon welfare plan fiduciaries. ERISA defines who is a fiduciary, sets forth duties and standards of conduct for fiduciaries, prohibits fiduciaries from engaging in certain transactions, and creates liability for fiduciaries. ERISA's rather detailed approach to these questions reflects directly Congress's well-documented concern in the legislative history of ERISA with the lack of adequate fiduciary standards.[62]

ERISA requires that each plan must provide for one or more "named fiduciaries."[63] Named fiduciaries have ultimate responsibility for the plan and provide visible and accountable management for the plan. Beyond "named fiduciaries," ERISA includes other individuals whose duties bring them within the definition of "fiduciary." The touchstone of the definition of "fiduciary" is discretion and the exercise of discretion in plan management, plan administration, and investment of plan assets.[64] ERISA's definition of who is a fiduciary turns primarily upon an analysis of the tasks performed by persons involved in plan administration, asset management, and distribution of benefits. Within the context of health benefit plans, sorting out the fiduciary status of trustees, insurers, third-party administrators, case managers, consultants, and others has been left to the courts. Looking to ERISA's definition of a "fiduciary," the courts have emphasized that a fiduciary must enjoy the ability to make discretionary decisions.[65] For example, those who process claims as the agents of other decisionmakers lack discretion and hence are not fiduciaries. Some fiduciary activities have been recognized by regulation, and others vary by circumstance. Insurers that pay or deny claims have been seen to be fiduciaries.[66] Third-party administrators may or may not be fiduciaries, depending upon their behavior.[67]

Fiduciaries must comply with ERISA's stringent fiduciary standards of conduct. A fiduciary must discharge his or her duties "solely in the interests of participants and beneficiaries."[68] Moreover, a fiduciary must act "for the exclusive purpose" of providing benefits to participants and beneficiaries and defraying the reasonable expenses of the plan.[69] In the discharge of his or her duties, the ERISA fiduciary must use the care, skill and prudence of a "prudent man" in a "like capacity."[70] Furthermore, a fiduciary must not only observe the standards of conduct set forth by ERISA but must also enforce those standards on other plan fiduciaries or face personal liability for a breach of fiduciary standards by cofiduciaries.[71]

ERISA creates personal liability for a breach of any obligation or duty imposed on a fiduciary under Title I of ERISA.[72] Such a fiduciary must restore any illicit profits generated by the fiduciary and make up any resulting plan losses. Courts may impose equitable or remedial relief, including removal of a fiduciary.[73] The Supreme Court has limited recovery of losses arising from a violation of a fiduciary duty to the plan entity and denied recovery (beyond receipt of the benefits themselves) to beneficiaries and participants seeking individual relief for improper denial of claim benefits.[74] In general, fiduciaries of a welfare plan may not be held liable for extra-contractual compensatory damages or punitive damages to a participant or beneficiary.

ERISA, itself, does not set forth the standard or level of scrutiny that a federal court must apply when a court reviews the decision of a fiduciary. However, because ERISA embodied many of the principles of the law of trusts, federal courts traditionally have approached the review of fiduciary functions under ERISA in the same manner in which they have traditionally approached the review of actions taken by a trustee. Generally speaking, when a fiduciary has exercised his or her discretion in granting or denying benefits reasonably, a reviewing court will overturn or disturb the decision only if the decision is considered to be an abuse of discretion or arbitrary and capricious.

Recently, the traditional judicial view of how to review fiduciary decisions under ERISA has been reexamined. In *Firestone Tire & Rubber Company v. Bruch ("Firestone")*,[75] the Supreme Court concluded that the reflexive judicial application of the arbitrary and capricious standard of review was no longer appropriate. In *Firestone*, individual claimants for funds under a severance benefit plan were denied severance benefits when parent company Firestone Tire & Rubber sold a subsidiary to another company. Because the claimants were immediately rehired, Firestone determined that there was no "reduction in work force," the qualifying event under the plan. Applying the arbitrary and capricious test, the federal district court upheld Firestone's reading of its severance plan.

In its decision, the Supreme Court held that the written terms of the plan must confer explicit discretion on a fiduciary before the courts can defer to the fiduciary's discretion. Absent written, plan-conferred discretion, the Supreme Court stated that a different standard of review would be used (the de novo standard), under which the Court would consider competing interpretations of a plan and decide which interpretation the Court deemed most reasonable.

The *Firestone* decision has changed how ERISA fiduciaries administer health benefit plans to some extent. To minimize judicial scrutiny, some plans have been amended to clearly confer on fiduciaries the discretion to grant or deny certain health benefits. Plan-conferred discretion is a particularly important factor in granting or denying benefits for experimental treatment or extracontractual benefits under a plan. However, in dealing with benefits that are clearly conferred under the plan and expected by a participant, the role of discretion is limited and the role of the courts on review of denials has been clearly enlarged.

## Administration, Enforcement, and Preemption

Part 5 of Title I of ERISA addresses administration and enforcement. This part establishes criminal and civil remedies,[76] requires every employee benefit plan to establish a claims procedure,[77] and confers rule-making authority on the Secretary of Labor.[78] Consistent with the rest of Title I, the thrust of Title I's provisions on administration and enforcement is largely procedural. The Department of Labor has an active ERISA enforcement program.

One important provision in this part of Title 1 relates to federal preemption of state laws. Federal preemption derives from the supremacy clause of the U.S. Constitution, which provides that federal law will supersede conflicting state law. When federal law preempts state law, the federal law negates enforcement of the state law with respect to those matters on which Congress has made federal law supreme.

Section 514 of ERISA provides for federal preemption of state laws that relate to employee health benefit plans.[79] Preemption under ERISA is important because it defines the spheres of federal jurisdiction to regulate health benefits plans and state jurisdiction to regulate health insurance. State and federal jurisdictions coexist because of how Congress both defined and limited preemption under ERISA.

Congress deliberately defined the scope of ERISA preemption broadly, rejecting a narrower proposal. Although the legislative history is silent in this respect, congressional staff members who worked on ERISA have stated that the preemption provision was a direct reaction to the actions of states, such as Missouri,* which attempted to subject employers' employee health

---

*The Missouri State Superintendent of Insurance attempted to prohibit the Monsanto Company's self-insured health plan from paying benefits because such payments would constitute

plans to state insurance laws. Consistent with this historical perspective, Senator Harrison Williams stated at the time that

> [i]t should be stressed that with the narrow exceptions specified in the bill, the substantive and enforcement provisions of [the bill] . . . are intended to preempt the field for Federal regulations, thus eliminating the threat of conflicting or inconsistent State and local regulation of employee benefit plans.

In 1983, a limited exception to ERISA preemption was crafted for the Hawaii Prepaid Health Care Act, a law that predates ERISA. This exception was strictly limited to the provisions of the Hawaii Prepaid Health Care Act that were in existence on September 2, 1974, the date of ERISA's enactment. The amendment explicitly stated that preemption continued with respect to any Hawaiian tax law relating to employee benefit plans. The legislative history with regard to this limited exemption indicates Congress's desire to broadly preempt state laws related to health and welfare benefit plans. Both state and federal courts have given full credit to the breadth of ERISA's preemption provision.

Section 514 contains three interrelated concepts, which are referred to as (1) the "preemption" clause, (2) the "insurance savings" clause, and (3) the "deemer" clause. Taken together, these three clauses delineate those activities that through preemption require uniform federal treatment under ERISA or that remain within the regulatory purview of the states.

The breadth of preemption, and the scope of federal jurisdiction, is driven by the preemption clause of Section 514, which requires federal primacy over any state law that relates to any health benefit plan. Limiting the preemption clause is a savings clause, which restores to the states their traditional role in the regulation of insurance, banking, and securities. However, the deemer clause states that no employee benefit plan shall be deemed to be an insurance company or to be engaged in the business of insurance for the purpose of any state law purporting to regulate insurance companies.

The threshold question in any analysis of ERISA preemption begins with an inquiry into whether the challenged state law "relates to" any employee benefit plan.[80] The Supreme Court has given the phrase "relates to" an "expansive sweep"[81] to apply to state laws that relate to employee benefit plans "in the usual sense of the phrase, if it has a connection with or reference to such a plan."[82] The Supreme Court has explained that a challenged state law has a "connection with" a benefit plan if it makes an impact upon it and a "reference to" a benefit plan if it "makes mention of" a plan. Preempted state laws include not only state statutes and regulations but also lawsuits based upon state common law.

---

the transaction of "insurance business," in violation of Missouri law. *State v. Monsanto Company*, 517 S.W. 2d 129 (Mo. 1984).

The potential reach of ERISA's preemption clause is best explained by illustration. The federal courts have found that the following types of state laws "related to" employee benefit plans:

• a state law seeking to integrate workers' compensation benefits with employer-sponsored pension benefits.[83]
• a state law requiring employers to pay sick leave to employees unable to work owing to pregnancy.[84]
• common law tort and breach of contract for failure to pay benefits under an insurance policy.[85]
• a state antisubrogation statute forbidding employer health plans from seeking contributions from automobile carriers for claims for injuries.[86]
• a state wrongful discharge suit motivated by an employer's desire to avoid pension contributions.[87]
• a wrongful death action in which termination of benefits was alleged to cause heart attack.[88]
• a state statute of general applicability directing that all bonds, bills, notes, and contracts for the payment of money shall be assignable.[89]

In contrast, the following state laws have been held too remote, peripheral, or tenuously related to employee benefit plans to fall to preemption under ERISA:

• a patient's medical malpractice action against a health maintenance organization.[90]
• a state garnishment statute.[91]
• a state escheat law.[92]
• a common law suit for wrongful termination that did not involve the employer's avoiding paying benefits.[93]

Despite the breadth of preemption of state law under ERISA, and with it federal jurisdiction over health benefit plans, Congress has carved out an exception that preserves state regulation of insurance, and with it an indirect state role in the regulation of health benefits funded by insurance. Practically speaking, judicial interpretation of the insurance savings clause defines the jurisdictional limits within which states may regulate health insurance used to fund health benefit plans.

Whether a challenged state regulatory policy must be "saved" from preemption by ERISA depends upon analysis and application of the savings clause (Subsection 514(b)(2)(A)). The savings clause generally restores to the states their regulatory role by declining to extend ERISA's preemption "to exempt or relieve any person from any law of any state which regulates insurance, banking or securities."[94]

In *Metropolitan Life Insurance Company v. Massachusetts*,[95] the Supreme Court construed the savings clause of ERISA and gave it a "common sense" reading. Thus interpreted, the savings clause applies to laws that comport with a state's traditional role regulating insurance. The Supreme Court has also stated that the savings clause protects state laws that fall within the ambit of the McCarran-Ferguson Act as the "business of insurance."[96] In *Metropolitan Life Insurance Company v. Massachusetts*, the Supreme Court upheld a Massachusetts-mandated mental health benefit requirement insofar as it applied to insurers selling insurance contracts to employee health benefit plans. Thus, ERISA's savings clause can save from federal preemption certain state laws that indirectly regulate employee benefit plans.

Beyond the "common sense" test, the Supreme Court also applies the McCarran-Ferguson Act concepts of what constitutes the business of insurance to ascertain if a challenged state law addresses an activity that is considered the "business of insurance." Whether an activity is the "business of insurance" depends upon

• whether the practice has the effect of transferring or spreading a policyholder's risk,
• whether the practice is an integral part of a policy relationship between an insurer and the insured, and
• whether the practice is limited to entities within the insurance industry.[97]

In a steady stream of cases, the federal courts have labored to apply the Supreme Court's guidance on the savings clause and to sort out where federal jurisdiction over employee benefit plans ends and state regulation over insurance begins. Three examples illustrate circumstances in which the savings clause has excepted a state law from preemption:

• a premium tax on stop-loss insurance was not preempted even where calculated with reference to amount of uninsured benefits paid.[98]
• a state statute requiring employers and insurers to notify employees of their right to individual coverage upon conversion from group coverage regulates insurance and cannot be preempted.[99]
• a state statute that required an insurer to issue an individual conversion policy to a member of a group after the insurer terminated group coverage was not preempted.[100]

In contrast, in other cases, courts have limited the savings clause and applied preemption as follows:

• a state statute authorizing the insured to sue the insurer for wrongful cancellation does not spread risk and will not escape preemption.[101]
• a state law regulating prepaid dental plans will be preempted because prepaid service plans are not regulated as business of insurance.[102]

• the judicial rule of construing the terms of an insurance contract against the insurer does not regulate the insurance industry and will be preempted.[103]

As these examples illustrate, the federal courts have not applied the savings clause in a manner that would expand the sway of state jurisdiction over the broader context of employer-sponsored health benefits.

ERISA's deemer clause further refines the jurisdictional balance between federal and state regulation of health benefits. The deemer clause is an exception to the exception created by the savings clause. In essence, the deemer clause provides that in the guise of regulating insurance companies and insurance contracts, states may not regulate employee benefit plans by deeming them to be engaged in the business of insurance.[104]

The import of the deemer clause rests upon how the Supreme Court explained it and applied it in *Metropolitan Life Insurance Company v. Massachusetts*.[105] The Supreme Court explained that permissible regulation under the savings clause was restricted to insurance companies and insurance contracts. To give meaning to the deemer clause, the Supreme Court observed that uninsured or self funded employee benefit plans could not be regulated by the states.

Consistent with the decision in *Metropolitan Life Insurance Company v. Massachusetts*, federal courts have preempted state laws that individuals have attempted to apply to self-funded health benefit plans. The following examples illustrate how the deemer clause makes preemption particularly applicable to self-funded employee benefit plans:

• a state unfair trade practices act that imposed duties on insurers could not be deemed applicable to a self-funded disability plan.[106]
• a state antisubrogation law barring a self-funded plan from seeking a contribution for claims from an automobile carrier was an insurance regulation but was preempted when it was deemed applicable to a self-funded plan.[107]
• a state law prohibiting coverage exclusion for injuries resulting from motor vehicle accidents was preempted when it was deemed applicable to exclusions in a self-funded plan.[108]
• state laws imposing terms in a contract between third-party administrators and self-funded plans and requiring the administrator to carry a fidelity bond were not regulation of insurance and were preempted by ERISA.[109]

With respect to self-funded plans, the federal courts have carried forward in these and other cases the process begun by the Supreme Court's discussion of the deemer clause in *Metropolitan Life Insurance Company v. Massachusetts*. Repeatedly, the federal courts have stated that especially when employers self-fund their benefit plans, those plans fall almost exclusively under the jurisdictional umbrella of ERISA to the exclusion of state regulation.

Preemption under ERISA also extends to common law state causes of action as they "relate to" a health benefit plan. In *Pilot Life Insurance Company v. Dedeaux*,[110] the Supreme Court rejected the argument that the tort of bad faith denial of benefits regulated insurance. Thus, while the tort of bad faith denial of insurance claims clearly related to a health benefit plan, the savings clause of ERISA did not bar its preemption. The significance of *Pilot Life* is about damages. Those claimants who must proceed under ERISA rather than state law can obtain no more than the amount of the benefits wrongfully denied them. In short, *Pilot Life* appears to have removed the threat of exemplary damages from processing ERISA claims, although the U.S. Solicitor General has taken the position that Section 502(a)(3) authorizes the award of monetary damages for foreseeable losses directly resulting from breach of plan terms or substantive provisions of ERISA (personal communication to Marilyn Field from Gerald Lindrew, Department of Labor, November 23, 1992).

## Practical Consequences of Opting for a Self-Insured Health Plan

By choosing to self-fund an employee health benefits plan, an employer remains subject to federal regulation but is no longer subject indirectly to state insurance regulation. Partly for this reason, self-funded health benefits have become a widespread funding method in employment-based health benefits.[111] The practical consequences of an employer's choice of funding method are instructive from even the briefest point-by-point comparison of state insurance regulation versus regulation under ERISA. Consider the following comparisons:

• states license insurers and require managers experienced in risk assessment and asset management; ERISA has virtually no similar substantive qualifications for fiduciaries.

• states require insurers to maintain minimum capitalization, which promotes solvency; ERISA has no minimum capital requirements for health benefit plans and does not address solvency.

• states require insurers to maintain reserves and to invest them conservatively; ERISA has no similar requirement for health benefit plans, although plan fiduciaries are subject to certain statutorily specified fiduciary obligations.

• states require health insurance policies to meet minimum requirements on coverage; ERISA requires disclosure of benefits in summary plan descriptions, but there are, in general, no minimums.

• states mandate some benefits that protect against catastrophic losses (e.g., coverage of premature newborns); ERISA has no benefit mandates for health benefit plans.

• states prohibit unfair underwriting practices such as permanent exclusion of preexisting conditions; ERISA has no such restrictions.

• states prohibit unilateral reduction or termination of benefits by a carrier during the effective period of a policy; apart from coverage required under 1985 amendments to ERISA (for which the enrollee must pay), ERISA permits unilateral reduction or termination of benefits during the plan year unless the terms of the plan itself or some contractual arrangement provides otherwise.

• states can review premium rates and reject them if they are inadequate; ERISA requires no review of the adequacy of an employer's funding commitment to pay for benefits.

ERISA's burden of regulation on a self-funded health benefit plan appears to be much lighter in terms of organization, substance, and administration than the burden of state regulation on insurance companies. Some observers may see ERISA's lack of substantive regulatory safeguards for beneficiaries of health benefit plans as troublesome. However, as the following comparisons show, de facto deregulation of employee health benefit plans under ERISA yields many advantages for employers. For example,

• ERISA limits beneficiary claims to the value of lost benefits; state judicial proceedings routinely target insurers as deep-pocket defendants who must pay punitive damages for bad faith denial of claims.

• ERISA permits cost containment incentives in terms of precertification and copayments; states frequently prohibit such practices with anti-managed-care laws.

• ERISA permits rapid design of innovative health plans such as employer-sponsored point-of-service HMOs; states have been less flexible in allowing state-regulated HMOs to diversify into similar lines of business.

• ERISA allows employers to determine the subrogation and coordination of benefit priorities for their health benefit plans; states frequently favor other types of accident and health insurance through antisubrogation laws.

• ERISA does not tax the employer's contribution to a self-funded health benefit plan; states tax health insurance premiums.

For many of the foregoing reasons, ERISA offers apparent incentives to large employers to self-fund their health benefit plans. Self-funded plans are not subject to state mandates,[112] and ERISA requires no minimum benefits.[113] Plan managers are free to design cost containment features such as copayments[114] and to reduce payments to providers who frustrate cost containment techniques.[115] In the case of legal disputes, ERISA makes the award of lawyer's fees discretionary, which is advantageous to plan sponsors. As explained above, under recent Supreme Court decisions, plan sponsors can also avoid the ruinous costs of exemplary damages in litigation about denied claims for benefits.

From 1985 to the present, the courts have hammered out the foregoing legal environment under ERISA for self-funded health benefit plans. During this same period, premiums for conventional health insurance have escalated. Many employers have opted out of insured funding of health benefits and state regulation of insurers and into self-funding and the system of federal regulation of health benefits described above.

## COBRA Continuation Coverage

In 1985, Congress amended ERISA and the Internal Revenue Code to allow qualified health plan participants and beneficiaries who would otherwise lose their benefits due to certain defined events to elect continued coverage.[116] These provisions are widely referred to as COBRA continuation coverage, or simply COBRA coverage, an abbreviation of the Consolidated Omnibus Reconciliation Act of 1985. The coverage continuation requirements apply to employers with 20 or more employees.[117]

COBRA requires that the continuation coverage must be "identical"[118] to what is provided to similarly situated plan participants. Modifications of the plan must also be uniform and identical as to active employees and persons covered by COBRA.[119] COBRA coverage also prohibits eligibility based upon evidence of insurability.[120] COBRA caps the premium that can be charged for continuation coverage at 102 percent of the applicable premium under the plan.[121]

Eligibility under COBRA's continuation coverage provisions arises when certain qualifying events take place that would otherwise result in a loss of coverage for a qualified beneficiary or participant. Qualifying events include:[122]

• Death of a covered employee.
• A termination or reduction in hours for a covered employee.
• A divorce or separation of a covered employee from his or her spouse.
• A dependent child ceasing to be dependent under the terms of the plan.
• A reorganization and bankruptcy by the employer of a retired employee.

To inform eligible participants and beneficiaries of their options, COBRA relies upon detailed notice and election requirements. To begin, COBRA requires that a general notice of COBRA continuation coverage must be provided when benefit coverage first begins.[123] Typically, a summary plan description includes a recitation of COBRA coverage qualifying events, employer obligations, and employee obligations.

Notice of a qualifying event must be provided to the plan administrator by an employer when a qualifying event involves an employee's death, termination or reduction in hours, or entitlement to Medicare or the employer's bankruptcy.[124] A covered employee must notify the plan administrator in the event of a divorce, legal separation, or the end of a child's dependency status.[125] Once a plan administrator has been notified of a qualifying event, the plan administrator must give notice to any qualified beneficiary affected by the qualifying event.[126] Upon receipt of notice, COBRA requires that a qualified beneficiary be given at least a 60-day period to elect coverage. If coverage is elected, COBRA then prohibits the plan from requiring payment of any premium for another 45 days.[127]

Properly elected coverage must extend from the date of the qualifying event until the end of the prescribed period, which generally ranges from 18 to 36 months. In the case of a termination or reduction in hours, the required period is 18 months. COBRA requires a maximum of 36 months of dependent coverage for the death of a covered employee, a divorce or legal separation, entitlement to Medicare by the covered employee, and loss of dependent child status.[128]

COBRA coverage is not unconditional, and it may be lost by the occurrence of a so-called terminating event. Terminating events include failure by the qualifying beneficiary to pay premiums, commencement of actual coverage under another plan, and entitlement to Medicare.[129] Continuation coverage also ends if the employer terminates the health benefit plan.

Since its enactment in 1986, COBRA coverage has undergone minor amendments. Essentially, these amendments have attempted to clarify objectives that have been part of the statutory scheme since 1986. Some amendments have been added to broaden and add qualifying events under which continuation coverage will apply.[130]

## THE MEWA PROBLEM

One current jurisdictional problem in the regulation of health benefits that perplexes regulators involves multiple employer welfare arrangements (MEWAs).[131] As defined in ERISA, a MEWA is an employee welfare benefit plan or other arrangement that is established to offer benefits to the employees of two or more employers. Conversely, a MEWA cannot be established pursuant to one or more collective bargaining agreements, a characteristic that usually distinguishes MEWAs from Taft-Hartley trusts. Also, a MEWA cannot be an aggregation of a group of trades or businesses under common control.[132] In practice, these rules have generally made MEWAs a health benefit vehicle for small employers.

For those entities that are MEWAs, ERISA's preemption provisions do not prescribe preemption of state laws as ERISA does for other employee welfare benefit plans. Specifically, the preemption provisions applicable to MEWAs declare that fully insured MEWAs must comply with state insurance laws that set standards for reserves. Self-funded MEWAs must also comply with state insurance laws to the extent not inconsistent with Title I—unless exempted by the Secretary of Labor in accordance with regulations.[133] To date, the Secretary of Labor has not promulgated regulation to exempt self-funded MEWAs from state law.

MEWAs have presented at least two problems for regulators that have prompted considerable attention from both state and federal regulators. First, fraudulent MEWAs have tried to avoid regulation by manipulating their circumstances to escape classification as a MEWA or by erroneously arguing that they are not subject to state regulation because of ERISA. Second, because MEWAs tend to serve pools of small employers, their sponsors frequently lack the time or sophistication to investigate the solvency of the MEWA. To redress the shortcomings of current regulation, some propose that MEWAs be subject entirely to federal jurisdiction and be required to obtain federal certification, but other proposals are also pending.

## FEDERAL LAWS SUPPLEMENTING ERISA

This discussion emphasizes ERISA and the nexus between federal and state regulation of health benefits. The scope of federal regulation also includes other important laws that affect employment-based health benefits but do not profoundly limit state regulation of health insurance.

Much simplified, these laws can be summarized as follows:

### Taxation

Topic:    Taxation on the value of employee health benefits.
Source:    Internal Revenue Code, Sec. 162, 106, and 105.
Features:  Sec. 162 allows an employer to deduct the cost of health benefits; Sec. 106 excludes employer contributions to a plan from an employee's income; Sec. 105 excludes payments from a plan from a employee's income.
Effect:    Encourages higher contributions for health benefits and insulates employees from the cost of health coverage.
Comment: Policy concerns focus on the growth of tax expenditures and on equity on health benefits.[134]

## Medicare Secondary Payor

Topic:     Coordination of large employer health benefits with Medicare.
Source:    Sec. 1862, Social Security Act; 42 U.S.C.A. 1395y.
Features:  Requires employers with 20 or more employees to provide
           primary coverage for certain otherwise eligible Medicare
           beneficiaries (e.g., workers aged 65 to 69 and those with end-
           stage renal disease). Individuals and government may enforce
           this by lawsuit and obtain double damages.
Effect:    Subordinates Medicare payment to employers' plans and
           reduces outlays by Medicare.
Comment: Subject of current nationwide recoupment effort; topic of past
           investigations.[135]

## The Civil Rights Act

Topic:     Discrimination in employment practices.
Source:    Civil Rights Act of 1964, Title VII; 42 U.S.C.A. 2000e-2.
Features:  Employment practices include health benefits. Protected
           classes for race, color, sex, religion, and national origin.
Effect:    Bans discrimination in health benefits based on a suspect
           classification.
Comment: Few cases have been reported based on race discrimination;
           more cases arise under the Pregnancy Discrimination Act of
           1978, an amendment.[136]

## The Age Discrimination in Employment Act

Topic:     Discrimination in employment practices.
Source:    29 U.S.C.A. 621 et seq.
Features:  Employment practices include health benefits. Protects work-
           ers who are at least 40 years of age. Age-based distinctions are
           allowed pursuant to a "bona fide" benefits plan, provided that
           the distinctions are not a "subterfuge."
Effect:    Provides equal access to health benefits for older workers.
Comment: Older Workers Benefit Protection Act[137] codified the "equal
           benefits/equal cost" rule from EEOC regulations,[138] which
           allows employers to either provide the same amount of benefits
           or to spend an equal amount to provide reduced coverage to
           older workers.

## The Americans with Disabilities Act

Topic:     Discrimination in employment practices.
Source:    42 U.S.C.A. 12101.

Features: Employment practices include health benefits. Protects physically or mentally impaired persons working for employers with 25 or more employees after July 26, 1992.

Effect: Protects general access to health benefits in the employment of impaired individuals. Does not affect most insurance underwriting practices.

Comment: Sec. 501(c) of ADA was not intended to change underwriting practices as permitted by state insurance regulation or the regulatory structure of self-insured plans.[139] Plans must base distinctions on "sound actuarial principles" and plan provisions cannot be used as "subterfuges" for prohibited discrimination.[140]

As the courts begin to interpret this last piece of legislation, which became effective in 1992, their judgments about which health plan practices constitute sound distinctions and which constitute subterfuges for discrimination may limit plan discretion in ways that ERISA does not. For example, although federal courts held, in *McGann v. H&H Music*,[141] that ERISA did not preclude an employer from reducing coverage for AIDS-related medical expenses after an employee had begun to submit claims, the result might have been different if the disability act had been in effect when the case first arose.

## CONCLUSION

Under current state regulation of health insurance and federal regulation of health benefits, the states continue to exercise regulatory control over those core activities that are recognized as the business of insurance. Through ERISA and other federal laws, the federal government retains jurisdiction over employee health benefit plans. The intersection of these competing regulatory schemes is defined by the ERISA preemption clause, a circumstance that, in the eyes of some, leaves important aspects of employee health benefits insufficiently defined in law.

## NOTES

1. *Paul v. Virginia*, 75 U.S. 168 (1868). In this case, the Supreme Court upheld the conviction and $50 fine of Samuel Paul for writing a contract of fire insurance for a New York insurance company that was not licensed as a foreign insurance company under an 1866 Virginia statute. Paul challenged his conviction and the statute by arguing that the Commerce Clause of the U.S. Constitution reserved exclusively to Congress the regulation of commerce among the states. The Supreme Court acknowledged that the Commerce Clause regulated interstate commerce but held that an insurance contract was not an "article of commerce in any proper meaning of the word."

2. 322 U.S. 533, 64 S.Ct. 1162, 88 L.Ed. 1440 (1944).

3. 322 U.S. 533, 547.

4. 1945 *U.S. Code, Cong. and Admin. News*, pp. 670-673.

5. 59 Stat. 33 (1945). In the McCarran-Ferguson Act, Congress declared that "the regulation and taxation by the several States of the business of insurance is in the public interest, and that silence on the part of the Congress shall not be construed to impose any barrier to the regulation or taxation of such business by the several States." 59 Stat. 33 (1945), 15 U.S.C. §1011.

6. *Prudential Insurance Company v. Benjamin*, 328 U.S. 408 (1946). The state of South Carolina was not constrained by the Commerce Clause from taxing foreign insurers. Prudential, incorporated in New Jersey, was taxed 3 percent of premiums, a rate higher than domestic carriers.

7. 59 Stat. 33 (1945).

8. Keeton, R.E., and Widiss, A.I. Insurance Law, *A Guide to Fundamental Principles, Legal Doctrines and Commercial Practices*, West Pub. Co. (1988), p. 932.

9. Anderson, O.W. *Blue Cross Since 1929: Accountability as the Public Trust*, Ballinger (1975), pp. 29-44.

10. *Id.*, pp. 45-52.

11. Rorem, C.R. "Enabling Legislation for Nonprofit Hospital Services Plans," 6 *Law and Contemp. Problems*, 528 (1939).

12. Somers, H.M., and Somers, A.R. "Private Health Insurance," 46 *Calif. Law Rev.*, 508, pp. 510-511 (1958).

13. Congressional Research Service, *Health Insurance and the Uninsured: Background Data and Analysis* (June 9, 1988), p. 119.

14. Commerce Clearing House, *State Tax Guide*, para. 88-000.

15. National Association of Insurance Commissioners (NAIC), *Model Insurance Laws, Regulations and Guidelines* (1989), pp. 100-1.

16. NAIC, *Model Insurance Laws, Regulations and Guidelines* (1989), pp. 100-8 [Sec. 5(M)].

17. Dirlam, J.B., and Stelzer, I.M. "The Insurance Industry," 107 *U. Pa. L. Rev.* 199 (1958).

18. NAIC, *Model Insurance Laws, Regulations and Guidelines* (1989), pp. 880-15 to 19. The NAIC lists cases from several jurisdictions in which courts have declined to infer a private right of action in state unfair insurance practices acts.

19. NAIC, *Model Insurance Laws, Regulations and Guidelines* (1989), p. 880-2.

20. *Insurance Federation of Pennsylvania v. Foster* 587 A.2d 865 (1991).

21. *Health Insurance Association of America v. Corchoran*, 531 N.Y.Supp.2d 456 (Sup., 1988).

22. *Health Benefits Letter*, No. 15, p. 1 (1991).

23. *Health Benefits Letter*, No. 8, p. 1 (1991).

24. The NAIC Model HMO Act, section 3 states that "no person shall establish or operate a health maintenance organization in this state, without obtaining a certificate of authority under the Act."

25. Health Insurance Association of America, *State Legislation and Litigation Report 1991*, Washington, D.C. (1992), p. 3.

26. Helvestine, W.A., "Legal Implications of Utilization Review," *Controlling Costs and Changing Patient Care*, Institute of Medicine (1989), p. 186.

27. See, for example, *Self-Insurance Institute of America v. Gallagher*, 11 E.B.C.-2162 (N.D. Fla., 1989) involving preemption of state regulation of TPAs.

28. The Labor Management Relations Act (LMRA) was enacted on June 23, 1947, 61 Stat.

157. The act is frequently referred to as the Taft-Hartley Act, a reference to the sponsors of the legislation. LMRA has been amended several times since its passage.
    29.  29 U.S.C.A. §186(c)(5).
    30.  29 U.S.C.A. §1001 *et seq.*, P.L. 93-406, 88 Stat. 829.
    31.  ERISA has been amended on a piecemeal basis on several occasions, as follows: P.L. 96-364, Sept. 26, 1980; P.L. 97-473, Jan. 14, 1983; P.L. 99-272, Apr. 7, 1986; P.L. 99-509, Oct. 21, 1986; P.L. 101-239, Dec. 19, 1989; P.L. 101-508, Nov. 5, 1990. The amendments have generally had more impact on the regulation of pensions than on welfare plans.
    32.  29 U.S.C.A. §1001-1168.
    33.  26 U.S.C.A. Chap. 1, Internal Revenue Code of 1986, §401-425.
    34.  29 U.S.C.A. §1201-1242.
    35.  29 U.S.C.A. §1301-1461.
    36.  29 U.S.C.A. §1001(a), (b), and (c).
    37.  29 U.S.C.A. §1002.
    38.  29 U.S.C.A. §1021-1028.
    39.  29 U.S.C.A. §1101-1113.
    40.  29 U.S.C.A. §1131-1134.
    41.  29 U.S.C.A. §1161-1168.
    42.  In reporting S.4, the Senate Committee on Labor and Public Welfare reported: "The provisions of S.4 are addressed to the issue of whether American working men and women shall receive private pension plan benefits which they have been led to believe would be theirs upon retirement from working lives." Sen. Rpt. No. 93-127, 1974 *U.S. Code, Cong. and Admin. News*, p. 4838, 93rd Cong., 2nd Sess.
    43.  The House Committee on Education and Labor states that the Welfare and Pension Plans Disclosure Act was "weak in its limited disclosure requirements and wholly lacking in substantive fiduciary standards." House Rpt. No. 93-533, 1974 *U.S. Code, Cong. and Admin. News*, p. 4642, 93rd Cong., 2nd Sess.
    44.  *Id.*, pp. 4643-4645.
    45.  House Rpt. No. 93-1280 states that the proposed reporting and disclosure requirements would apply to "all pension and welfare plans established or maintained by an employer or employee organization. . . ." 1974 *U.S. Code, Cong. and Admin. News*, p. 5039, 93rd Cong. 2nd Sess.
    46.  29 U.S.C.A. §1002(1).
    47.  29 U.S.C.A. §1002(3).
    48.  29 U.S.C.A. §1003(a).
    49.  29 U.S.C.A. §1002(5), (6), (7), and (8).
    50.  *Shaw v. Delta Air Lines, Inc.*, 463 U.S. 91 (1982).
    51.  29 U.S.C.A. §1002(19).
    52.  29 U.S.C.A. §1051(1).
    53.  In *White Farm Equipment Company*, 788 Fed.2d 1186 (6th Cir., 1986).
    54.  *Coonce v. Aetna Life Insurance Company*, 777 F.Supp. 759 (W.D.Mo., 1991).
    55.  For example, in annual reports, only pension plans must file a statement of assets and liabilities and an actuarial statement. 29 U.S.C.A. §1023(c)(2) and (d).
    56.  29 U.S.C.A. §1021(a).
    57.  29 C.F.R. 2520.102-1.
    58.  29 U.S.C.A. §1021(b).
    59.  29 U.S.C.A. §51023(a).
    60.  29 U.S.C.A. §1022(a)(11).
    61.  29 U.S.C.A. §1022(b).
    62.  The legislative history of ERISA shows that Congress believed that existing standards

of conduct were inadequate, and legislation was needed to make clear who are fiduciaries and what would be their standards of accountability. House Rpt. No. 93-533, 1974 *U.S. Code, Cong. and Admin. News*, p. 4643, 93rd Cong., 2nd Sess.

63. 29 U.S.C.A. §1102(c).

64. 29 U.S.C.A. §1002(21)(A).

65. *Pappas v. Buck Consultants, Inc.*, 923 F.2d 531 (7th Cir., 1991), where the court distinguishes between nonfiduciary lawyers, accountants, and actuaries who advise trustees of a plan and the trustee fiduciaries who exercise discretion to take advice and act on it.

66. See *Eaton v. D'Amato*, 581 F.Supp. 743 (D.D.C. 1980).

67. See *Eaton v. D'Amato*, 581 F.Supp. 743 (D.D.C. 1980); and *Baxter v. C.A. Muer Corporation*, 941 F.2d 451 (6th Cir., 1991).

68. 29 U.S.C.A. §1104.

69. *Id.*

70. *Id.*

71. 29 U.S.C.A. §1105.

72. 29 U.S.C.A. §1109.

73. *Id.*

74. *Massachusetts Mutual Life Insurance Company v. Russell*, 473 U.S. 134, 105 S.Ct. 3085 (1985).

75. 109 S.Ct. 948 (1989).

76. 29 U.S.C.A. §1132.

77. 29 U.S.C.A. §1133.

78. 29 U.S.C.A. §1135.

79. 29 U.S.C.A. §1114.

80. 29 U.S.C.A. §1114(a).

81. *Pilot Life Insurance Company v. Dedeaux*, 481 U.S. 41, 107 S.Ct. 1549 (1987).

82. *Shaw v. Delta Airlines, Inc.*, 463 U.S. 85, 103 S.Ct. 2890 (1983).

83. *Alessi v. Raybestos-Manhattan, Inc.*, 451 U.S. 504, 101 S.Ct. 1895 (1981).

84. *Shaw v. Delta Airlines, Inc.*, 463 U.S. 85, 103 S.Ct. 2890 (1983).

85. *Pilot Life Insurance Company v. Dedeaux*, 481 U.S. 41, 107 S.Ct. 1549 (1987).

86. *FMC Corp. v. Holliday*, 112, S.Ct. 403 (1990).

87. *Ingersoll Rand Co. v. McClendon*, 111, S.Ct. 478 (1990).

88. *Settles v. Golden Rule Insurance Co.*, 927 F. 2d 505 (10th Cir., 1991).

89. *Arkansas Blue Cross and Blue Shield v. St. Mary's Hospital*, 947 F.2d 1341 (8th Cir., 1991).

90. *Independence HMO v. Smith*, 733 F.Supp. 983 (E.D. Pa., 1990).

91. *American Telephone and Telegraph v. Mercy*, 592 F.2d 118 (3rd Cir., 1979).

92. *Aetna Life Insurance Company v. Borqes*, 869 F.2d 142 (2nd Cir., 1989).

93. 29 U.S.C.A. §1144(b)(2)(A).

94. 29 U.S.C.A. §1144(b)(2)(A).

95. 471 U.S. 724, 105 S.Ct. 2380 (1985).

96. 471 U.S. at 743.

97. 471 U.S. at 743.

98. *General Motors v. California Board of Equalization*, 815 F.2d 1305 (9th Cir., 1987).

99. *Hall v. Pennwalt Group Comprehensive Medical Expense Benefits Plan*, 46 F.Supp. (E.D. Pa., 1988).

100. *International Resources, Inc. v. New York Life Insurance Company*, 950 F.2d 294 (6th Cir., 1991).

101. *Anschultz v. Connecticut General Life Insurance Company*, 850 F.2d 1467 (11th Cir., 1988).

102. *Oracare DPO v. Mermin*, 1991 Lexis 8732 (D.C. N.J., 1991).
103. *Brewer v. Lincoln National Life Insurance Company*, 921 F.2d 150 (8th Cir., 1990).
104. 29 U.S.C.A. §1144(b)(2)(B).
105. 471 U.S. 724, 105 S.Ct. 2380 (1985).
106. *Powell v. Chesapeake and Potomac Telephone*, 780 F.2d 419 (4th Cir., 1985).
107. *United Food and Commercial Workers v. Pacyga*, 801 F.2d 1157 (9th Cir., 1986).
108. *Thompson v. Talguin Building Products Company*, 928 F.2d 649 (4th Cir., 1991)
109. *SIAA v. Gallagher*, 11 E.B.C. 2162 (N.D. Fla., 1989).
110. 418 U.S. 41, 107 S.Ct. 1549 (1987).
111. Eighty-five percent of large employers self-fund their health benefits. *Health Care Financing Review*, Sp. 1989, pp. 84-85. Recent news reports of contemporary surveys of employers state that self-insured health benefits are being used by 41 percent of employers with 500 employees or fewer. *Business Insurance*, January 27, 1992, p. 3.
112. *Metropolitan Life Insurance Company v. Massachusetts*, 471 U.S. 724, 105 S.Ct. 2380 (1985).
113. *Shaw v. Delta Airlines, Inc.*, 463 U.S. 85, 103 S.Ct. 2890 (1983).
114. *Nazay v. Miller*, 14 E.B.C. 1953 (3rd Cir., 1991).
115. *Kennedy v. Connecticut General Life Insurance Company*, 924 F.2d 698 (7th Cir., 1991).
116. P.L. 99-272, 100 Stat. 82 (1986).
117. Internal Revenue Code of 1986, §498OB(d); *Kidder v. H. and B. Marine, Inc.*, 925 F.2d 857 (5th Cir., 1991).
118. Internal Revenue Code of 1986, §498OB(f)(2)(A).
119. *Id.*
120. Internal Revenue Code of 1986, §498OB(f)(2)(C).
121. Internal Revenue Code of 1986, §498OB(f)(2)(C)(i).
122. Internal Revenue Code of 1986, §498OB(f)(3).
123. Internal Revenue Code of 1986, §498OB(f)(6)(A).
124. Internal Revenue Code of 1986, §498OB(f)(6)(B).
125. Internal Revenue Code of 1986, §498OB(f)(6)(C).
126. Internal Revenue Code of 1986, §498OB(f)(6)(D).
127. 29 U.S.C.A. §602(c)(3).
128. Internal Revenue Code of 1986, §498OB(f)(2)(B)(i)).
129. Internal Revenue Code of 1986, §498OB(f)(2)(B)(ii-v).
130. For example, the Tax Reform Act of 1986, P.L. 99-514, extended maximum coverage from 18 to 36 months for persons who experience a second qualifying event. OBRA 1989, P.L. 101-239, extended coverage from 18 to 29 months for disabled persons who are entitled to Social Security.
131. *The Wall Street Journal* has editorialized that MEWA fraud goes unchecked because in the early 1980s Congress gave the states jurisdiction over MEWAs but MEWAs continue to argue that they are subject to federal jurisdiction only. *The Wall Street Journal*, p. B2, May 15, 1990.
132. 29 U.S.C.A. §1002(40).
133. 29 U.S.C.A. §114(b)(6).
134. Steuerle, C.E. "Finance-Based Reform: The Search for Adaptable Health Policy," unpublished paper presented at American Health Policy: Critical Issues for Reform, an American Enterprise Institute conference, October 3, 1991, Washington, D.C.
135. General Accounting Office, *More Hospital Cost Should Be Paid by Other Insurers* (HRD-87-43), January 1987; and General Accounting Office, *Incentives Needed to Assure Private Insurers Pay Before Medicare* (HRD-89-19), November 1988.

136. P.L. 95-555, 92 Stat. 2076.

137. *Id.*, 109 S.Ct. at 2866.

138. 29 C.F.R. §1625.10.

139. House Rpt. No. 101-485(II), 1990 *U.S. Code, Cong. and Admin. News*, p. 419.

140. *Id.*, 420. The language of the legislative history is borrowed verbatim from the NAIC's Model Regulation on Unfair Discrimination in Life and Health Insurance on the Basis of Physical or Mental Impairment, §3.

141. *McGann v. H&H Music Co.*, 946 F.2d 401 (5th Cir. 1991).

# C

# Participants in Meetings Held in Conjunction with Project

*Committee Members and Staff Present*

Harold T. Shapiro, Ph.D.
Princeton University, *Chair*

David Edwards
Eastman Kodak Company

Allen Feezor
North Carolina Department of
    Insurance

Marilyn J. Field, Ph.D.
Study Director

Jo Harris-Wehling
Staff Officer

George F. Sheldon, M.D.
University of North Carolina

K. Peter Schmidt, J.D.
Arnold and Porter

Donna D. Thompson
Senior Project Assistant

Joan B. Trauner, Ph.D.
Coopers & Lybrand

*Oral Testimony*

Roger Bulger, M.D.
Association of Academic Health
Centers

Paul P. Cooper III, C.L.U.
Business Roundtable

Mary Jane England, M.D.
Washington Business Group on
Health

Daniel H. Johnson, Jr., M.D.
American Medical Association

Richard M. Niemiec
Blue Cross and Blue Shield
Association

Charles M. O'Brien, Jr.
American Hospital Association

John Ott, M.D.
Group Health Association of
America

Michael O. Roush
National Federation of Independent
Business

Elliot K. Wicks, Ph.D.
Health Insurance Association of
America

Joy Johnson Wilson
National Conference of State
Legislatures

*Written Testimony*

American Federation of Labor and
Congress of Industrial
Organizations (AFL-CIO)

American Federation of State,
County and Municipal
Employees (AFSCME)

Association of Private Pension and
Welfare Plans

Children's Defense Fund

Consumers Union

## WORKSHOP ON BIASED RISK SELECTION

**February 20, 1992**
**Washington, D.C.**

PARTICIPANTS LIST

*Invited Panel*

Gerard Anderson, Ph.D.
Director, Johns Hopkins Center
for Hospital Finance and
Management

George Berry, F.S.A.
Milliman & Robertson, Inc.

John M. Bertko, F.S.A.
Principal, Coopers & Lybrand

Bruce D. Bowen, Ph.D.
Director, Medical Economics and
Statistics
Kaiser Family Health Plan

James Charling, F.S.A.
Second Vice President
Principal Financial Group

Alice Rosenblatt, F.S.A.
Senior Vice President and Chief
Actuary
Blue Cross/Blue Shield of
Massachusetts

Gordon R. Trapnell, F.S.A.
President, Actuarial Research
Corporation

*IOM Committee and Staff*

David Edwards
Director of Corporate Employee
Benefits
Eastman Kodak

Allen Feezor
Chief Deputy Commissioner of
  Insurance
North Carolina Department of
  Insurance

Marilyn J. Field, Ph.D.
Study Director, Institute of
  Medicine

Jo Harris-Wehling
Staff Officer, Institute of Medicine

Stanley Jones
Independent Consultant

K. Peter Schmidt, J.D.
Partner, Arnold and Porter

Harold T. Shapiro, Ph.D.
President, Princeton University

George F. Sheldon, M.D.
Chair, Department of Surgery
University of North Carolina

Donna D. Thompson
Senior Project Assistant
Institute of Medicine

Joan B. Trauner, Ph.D.
Principal, Coopers and Lybrand

Karl D. Yordy
Director, Division of Health Care
  Services
Institute of Medicine

*Observers*

David A. Bryant
Assistant Director of Government
  Information
American Academy of Actuaries

Michael M. Hagan
Economist
Agency for Health Care Policy and
  Research

Gary D. Hendricks
Director of Government
  Information
American Academy of Actuaries

## SYMPOSIUM PROGRAM

Academy Industry Program of the National Research Council and
Committee on Employment-Based Health Benefits
of the Institute of Medicine

American Employers and Health Care:
Roles, Responsibilities, and Risks

May 19-20, 1992
Washington, D.C.

Tuesday, May 19, 1992 ─────────────────────────────────────────

1:00 p.m.  **Welcome & Introductions**
Frank Press, President, National Academy of Sciences
Karl Yordy, Director, Division of Health Care Services,
Institute of Medicine
Dallas L. Salisbury, President, Employee Benefit Research
Institute, *Symposium Chair*

1:15  **KEYNOTE ADDRESS: AMERICAN EMPLOYERS
AND HEALTH CARE**
Dallas L. Salisbury, Employee Benefit Research Institute

1:45  **THE QUESTION OF VALUE AND EMPLOYMENT-
BASED HEALTH BENEFITS**
Moderator: Alan R. Nelson, M.D., American Society of
Internal Medicine

**A Clinician-Researcher's Perspective**
Albert G. Mulley, Jr., M.D., Massachusetts General Hospital

**An Employer's Perspective**
Charles R. Buck, Jr., Sc.D., General Electric Company

3:30  **RISKY BUSINESS: SHARING AND SHUNNING THE
BURDEN OF COSTLY ILLNESS**
Moderator: Stanley B. Jones, Independent Consultant

**A Consulting Actuary's Overview**
George Berry, F.S.A., Milliman and Robertson

**An Employer's Experience**
Robert F. Seeman, American Airlines

5:20  **HEALTH CARE COSTS AND BUSINESS
COMPETITIVENESS**
Moderator: W.H. Krome George (retired), Aluminum
Company of America

**Evidence and Its Limits**
David J. Brailer, M.D., The Wharton School

**Controversy and Context**
Howard Rosen, Competitive Policy Council

9:00 a.m.  **BEYOND THE BENEFITS PACKAGE:  BUILDING A HEALTHY WORKFORCE**
Moderator:  Marilyn J. Field, Ph.D., Institute of Medicine

**Implementing and Evaluating a Worksite Strategy**
Barbara L. Decker, Southern California Edison Company

**Legal and Ethical Cautions**
Mark A. Rothstein, Health, Law and Policy Institute, University of Houston

10:30  **LINKING EFFORTS OF PUBLIC AND PRIVATE SECTORS**
Moderator:  Harry P. Cain II, Ph.D., Blue Cross and Blue Shield Association

**Initiatives at the State and Community Levels**
W. David Helms, Ph.D., The Alpha Center

**Lessons and Observations from One State**
Ree Sailors, Florida Health Access

1:30 p.m.  **HEALTH CARE REFORM AND THE ROLE OF THE EMPLOYER**
Moderator:  Judith Feder, Ph.D., Center for Health Policy Studies, Georgetown University

**Focusing on the Individual and Market Forces**
Robert E. Moffit, Ph.D., Heritage Foundation

**Building on the Employment-based System**
Walter B. Maher, Chrysler Corporation

**Moving to National Health Insurance**
Theodore R. Marmor, Ph.D., Yale University

**Confronting the Perception Gaps**
John Immerwahr, Ph.D., The Public Agenda Foundation

3:30  **PATIENTS, PHYSICIANS, AND EMPLOYERS: CHANGE AND CHALLENGE**
Jerome H. Grossman, M.D., New England Medical Center

# D

# Biographies of Committee Members

**HAROLD T. SHAPIRO, Ph.D.,** is Princeton University's 18th president. Dr. Shapiro, who received his Ph.D. in economics from Princeton in 1964, holds a faculty appointment as a professor of economics and public affairs. He came to Princeton from the University of Michigan where he served on the faculty for twenty-four years as professor of economics and public policy and as president from 1980 to 1988. He is a member of President Bush's Council of Advisors on Science and Technology. He also serves on the boards of Alfred P. Sloan Foundation, the Universities Research Association, the Consortium on Financing Higher Education, Interlochen Center for the Arts, the Dow Chemical Company, and the National Bureau of Economic Research. He has been elected a member of the Institute of Medicine of the National Academy of Sciences and the American Philosophical Society and is a Fellow of the American Academy of Arts and Sciences. He is a native of Montreal with dual American and Canadian citizenship and received his bachelor's degree from McGill University.

**HARRY P. CAIN, II, Ph.D.,** is Senior Vice President, Federal Programs, Blue Cross and Blue Shield Association. He is responsible for the contracts with the federal government, primarily those related to the Federal Employees Health Benefits Program and to the administration of the Medicare program. From 1978 to 1982, he was Executive Director of the American Health Planning Association and before that held several health-related positions in the Department of Health, Education and Welfare, including: Director, Office of Policy Development and Planning, Office of Assistant Secretary for Health; and Assistant Director, National Institute of Mental Health. His undergraduate degree is from Stanford University and his Ph.D. from Brandeis University.

*328*

**DAVID E. EDWARDS** is the Director, Benefits, of Eastman Kodak Company. Mr. Edwards was formerly manager of Employee Benefits for Eastman Chemicals Division. A native of the State of Washington, Mr. Edwards graduated from East Tennessee State University where he earned a bachelor's degree in business administration. Mr. Edwards serves on the Board of Directors of the ERISA Industry Committee, the Hospital Reimbursement Task Force and the Health Committee of New York State Business Council, the Industrial Management Council Health Care Vision Strategy Committee, and the Technical Advisory Committee of the State of New York Insurance Department.

**ALLEN FEEZOR** has served as Chief Deputy Commissioner of the North Carolina Department of Insurance since 1985. From 1985 to 1987 he also served as executive administrator for the Teachers' and State Employees' Comprehensive Major Medical Plan, a 430,000 member health benefit plan. Mr. Feezor's health care benefits background includes positions with Blue Cross and Blue Shield including the position of senior Washington representative with the Blue Cross and Blue Shield Association. He is a faculty member of the National Academy for State Health Policy; president and board member of the Utilization Review Accreditation Commission; chairman of the National Association of Insurance Commissioners Small Group Market Reform Task Force; and co-founder, past president, and board member of the Washington Area State Relations Group. Mr. Feezor lectures on politics and health policy at Duke University, University of North Carolina School of Public Health, and the Medical College of Virginia. He has testified before congressional panels, numerous national groups and in many state capitols on a variety of health payment issues. He received his bachelor's and master's degrees from Duke University.

**W.H. KROME GEORGE** was the Chairman of the Executive Committee of Aluminum Company of America (ALCOA) from 1977 to 1986. He had held various positions with ALCOA beginning in 1942, including chairman of the board and chief executive officer from 1975 to 1983, vice-president for finance from 1965 to 1967, and vice-president for economic analysis and planning from 1964 to 1965. Mr. George holds directorships with the International Primary Aluminum Institute of Norfolk Southern Corporation, with TRW, Inc., and with Todd Shipyards Corporation. He was formerly Metro Chair of the National Alliance of Businessmen and is a member of the World Affairs Council of Pittsburgh, a member of the Council on Foreign Relations, a member of the Management Executive Society, and a member of the Allegheny Health Education and Research Corporation. Mr. George was educated at the Massachusetts Institute of Technology.

**WILLIAM S. HOFFMAN,** Ph.D., is Director of the International Union, United Automobile, Aerospace and Agricultural Implement Workers of America (UAW) Social Security Department. He is responsible for health care, retirement, disability and layoff income protection issues, both in the public policy and collective bargaining arenas. He serves on the Council on Graduate Medical Education of the U.S. Department of Health and Human Services and the Prospective Payment Assessment Commission of the U.S. Office of Technology Assessment. He recently completed three-year terms with the ERISA Advisory Council of the U.S. Department of Labor and the Certificate-of-Need Commission for the State of Michigan. He served on the Institute of Medicine Committee to Design a Strategy for Quality Review and Assurance in Medicare. He has over seventeen years of negotiating and program administration experience within the automobile, aerospace, and agricultural implement industries and with numerous other companies across the United States and in Canada. He is presently principal investigator of a longitudinal study into the effects of General Motors plant closings on workers and their families. He is a director of two social research foundations, is an Adjunct Professor of Sociology at Wayne State University and represents the UAW on several private and governmental boards and committees.

**STANLEY B. JONES,** is a consultant to private foundations on competitive private health insurance markets and the roles of public policy in improving these markets. He was a founding partner of the Washington consulting firm, Health Policy Alternatives, Inc., and has served as Vice President for Washington Representation of the Blue Cross and Blue Shield Association, and staff director of the Senate Health Subcommittee. He is a member of the Institute of Medicine and author of many articles and papers on private health insurance, structural reform of the health system, and health care competition. He is currently serving as chairman, Advisory Committee to the Robert Wood Johnson Foundation State Initiatives in Health Care Financing Reform Program; member, Kaiser Family Foundation National Health Care Expenditure Limit Study; member, U.S. Comptroller General's Health Advisory Committee; and member, U.S. Office of Technology Assessment Advisory Panel on "International Differences in Health Technology, Services, and Economics." He did undergraduate work at Dartmouth College and graduate work at Yale in philosophy and religion.

**NICOLE LURIE,** M.D., M.S.P.H., is an Associate Professor of Medicine and Public Health at Hennepin County Medical Center and the University of Minnesota. Following her residency training in internal medicine at UCLA, she became a Robert Wood Johnson Clinical Scholar. Following her move to Minnesota she was awarded a Henry J. Kaiser Family Foundation Faculty Scholar Award, which supported her work on physician prescribing and pharmaceutical industry advertising. She is currently the Director of the Program in Clinical Epidemiology, Effectiveness and Policy at Hennepin County Medical Center. Her research interests are in access to care, quality of care, and health care cost containment.

**ALAN R. NELSON,** M.D., became the American Society of Internal Medicine's (ASIM) chief executive officer in March 1992. Prior to assuming this full-time staff position of the 26,000-member organization, he was in the private practice of internal medicine and endocrinology in Salt Lake City for 27 years. From November 1991–1992, Dr. Nelson also served as president of the World Medical Association and he is a past president of the American Medical Association and the Utah Medical Association. In 1989 Dr. Nelson was named "Distinguished Internist of the Year" by ASIM. He is a graduate of Northwestern University School of Medicine, a fellow of the American College of Physicians, and a member of the Endocrine Society and the American Association of Clinical Endocrinologists. Also in 1990, he was appointed by U.S. Department of Health and Human Services Secretary Louis Sullivan to the advisory committee to the Food and Drug Administration. Throughout much of his career he has been involved in peer review and quality assurance and served four years as a commissioner of the Joint Commission on Accreditation of Healthcare Organizations. He is also a member of the board of Intermountain Health Care Inc., and chairman of its professional standards committee.

**JOHN K. ROBERTS, JR.,** F.S.A., is President and Chief Executive Officer, Pan-American Life Insurance Company, New Orleans, Louisiana. His life insurance industry activities include: Vice Chairman, Board of Directors, Life Office Management (LOMA), 1988; Chairman of LOMA Board, 1989; Board of Directors, Health Insurance Association of America, 1990; Board of Directors, American Council of Life Insurance, 1992. He serves on the Board of Directors of the Whitney National Bank of New Orleans and Whitney Holding Corporation. He was also President of the Southeastern Actuaries Club. His community involvement includes: past Chairman, Board of Trustees 1988, United Way of Greater New Orleans Area; General Campaign Chairman 1983, United Way Campaign of Greater New Orleans Area; Board of Trustees, YMCA; Board of Trustees, Children's Hospital of New Orleans; past Chairman, Tulane University Parents' Council; former member, Board of Directors, Children's Bureau of New Orleans; Board of Directors, Metropolitan Area Committee; Campaign Chairman Corporate, 1990; Campaign Chairman for Major Gifts, 1991, New Orleans Symphony.

**DALLAS L. SALISBURY** is President of the Employee Benefit Research Institute, a Washington-based nonprofit, nonpartisan, public policy institution. Before that he served as Assistant Executive Director of the Pension Benefit Guaranty Corporation, and as Executive Assistant to the Administrator of Pension and Welfare Benefit Programs, at the U.S. Department of Labor and as Acting Assistant Administrator for Policy, Planning, and Research. In the latter position he played a major role in implementation of the Employee Retirement Income Security Act of 1974 (ERISA). He also served as a consultant to the Speaker of the House, Washington State House of Representatives. He received a Master's Degree in Public Administration from the Maxwell Graduate School of Citizenship and Public Affairs School at Syracuse University in 1973, and an undergraduate degree in finance from the University of Washington in 1970.

**K. PETER SCHMIDT** is a partner in the Washington, D.C. law firm of Arnold & Porter, serving as the head of its Benefits and Employment Law Group. He joined Arnold & Porter after his graduation, *magna cum laude*, from the University of Wisconsin Law School. He has written and spoken extensively on employee benefits including papers and seminars for, among others, American Law Institute; American Bar Association; Practicing Law Institute; New York University Institute of Labor; New York Law Journal; Warrent, Gorham & Lamont; and the Employee Benefit Research Institute.

**GEORGE F. SHELDON,** M.D., is Professor and Chairman of the Department of Surgery at the University of North Carolina at Chapel Hill. He formerly was Professor of Surgery and Chief of the Trauma Service at the University of California, San Francisco, at San Francisco General Hospital. He served as a charter member of the Council on Graduate Medical Education in 1986. He was Chairman of the American Board of Surgery (1989–1990) and has served on the Surgery Test Committee of the National Board of Medical Examiners. He has also served on the Accreditation Council on Graduate Medical Education's Residency Review Committee and remains on the Standing Panel for Accreditation Appeals. Dr. Sheldon is currently a regent of the American College of Surgeons and Secretary of the American Surgical Association. He previously was President of the American Association for the Surgery of Trauma. He served as a member of the Association of American Medical Colleges (AAMC) Graduate and Professional Education of the Physician Committee 1983–1984. He also served on the AAMC Committee on Teaching in the Ambulatory Setting and served as Chairman of the Veterans Administration Merit Review Board for Surgery. He has served on the National Institutes of Health Working Groups, was Vice-Chairman of the Conjoint Council on Surgical Research and currently is on the American Institute of Biological Sciences Study Section. He serves on 10 editorial boards and also serves on the Board of Directors of the Hill-Physick-Keith House of the Historical Trust in Philadelphia, Pennsylvania.

**KENNETH E. THORPE,** Ph.D., is Associate Professor in the Department of Health Policy and Administration, University of North Carolina (UNC) at

Chapel Hill. Prior to moving to UNC, Dr. Thorpe was Director of the Program on Health Care Financing and Insurance at the Harvard University School of Public Health. Thorpe received his Ph.D. in policy analysis at the Rand Graduate School. During the past five years, Dr. Thorpe has served as an adviser to the Pepper Commission, the Advisory Council on Social Security, the National Leadership Coalition for Health Care Reform, and the New York State Department of Health and was a gubernatorial appointee to Massachusetts' Universal Health Care Commission. He has written dozens of articles on health care financing issues and is co-author of *Competition and Compassion, Conflicting Roles for Public Hospitals*. Dr. Thorpe is currently completing work on examining the medical malpractice system and is engaged in ongoing efforts with state and national groups in developing national health policy proposals and legislation.

**JOAN B. TRAUNER,** Ph.D., is an Executive Consultant at Coopers & Lybrand in Actuarial, Benefits and Compensation Consulting Group in San Francisco. Prior to this position, she was a Principal in the San Francisco office, with national responsibility for Governmental Programs and Managed Care. She is also an Assistant Adjunct Professor of Health Policy at the Institute for Health Policy Studies, University of California San Francisco, where she served previously as a full-time health services researcher from 1979–1986. Dr. Trauner currently serves on the Health Benefits Advisory Committee to the California Public Employees' Retirement System and has recently completed services on the Health Insurance Reform Taskforce within the California Department of Insurance. She is also a technical advisor to the state of Hawaii, having been responsible for the design of Hawaii's State Health Insurance Program for the uninsured. Dr. Trauner regularly advises large payers, including HMOs, insurers, and state governments about the design and operations of managed care programs. She is the author of a paper on utilization management that appeared in the 1989 publication by the IOM Committee on Utilization Management by Third Parties.

**GAIL L. WARDEN** is president and chief executive officer of Henry Ford Health System in Detroit, a vertically integrated regional health care system. The system includes a tertiary care hospital, two community hospitals, 35 ambulatory care centers in four Michigan counties, a 900-member physician medical group, a 410,000-member health maintenance organization, and other programs and services. Before joining Henry Ford Health System, Warden was president and chief executive officer of Group Health Cooperative of Puget Sound in Seattle, executive vice president of the American Hospital Association, and executive vice president and chief operations officer of Rush-Presbyterian-St. Luke's Medical Center.

# Glossary and Acronyms

**access**  The timely use of personal health services to achieve the best possible health outcomes.

**acute care**  Services within a hospital setting intended to maintain patients for medical and surgical episodic care over a relatively short period of time.

**administrative expenses**  For health insurance, expenses incurred in one or more of the following general categories: claims administration; general administration; interest credit; risk and profit charge; commissions; and premium taxes.

**administrative services only (ASO) agreement**  A contract for the provision of certain services to a group employer or similar entity by an insurer or its subsidiary. Such services often include actuarial services, benefit plan design, claim processing, data collection and analysis, employee benefit communications, financial advice, and stop-loss coverage.

**admission review**  Assessment of the appropriateness of urgent or emergency admissions that must occur within a limited period (e.g., 24 to 48 hours) after hospitalization.

**adverse selection**  The disproportionate enrollment of individuals with poorer-than-average health expectations in certain health plans (see biased risk selection).

**ambulatory care**  Medical services provided on an outpatient (nonhospitalized) basis. Services may include diagnosis, treatment, surgery, and rehabilitation.

**appropriate care**  Care that is clinically justified; sometimes used interchangeably with necessary care and sometimes used only to refer to whether the use of a particular site of care (for example, hospital) is justified.

**benefit** Conventionally defined as the amount payable for a loss under a specific insurance coverage (indemnity benefits) or as the guarantee that certain services will be paid for (service benefits).

**biased risk selection** Exists (1) when the individuals or groups that purchase insurance differ in their risk of incurring health care expenses from those who do not or (2) when those who enroll in competing health plans differ in the level of risk they present to different plans.

**cafeteria plan** A flexible benefit plan that allows employees to choose benefits from a number of different options, such as group health insurance and dependent care assistance.

**capitation** A fixed rate of payment, usually provided on a per member per month basis, to cover a defined set of health services for members of a health plan.

**carrier** An entity providing insurance or administering a medical expense protection plan; under Medicare, the private organization administering claims and certain other tasks for Part B.

**case management** A planned approach to organizing medical and other services for an individual with a serious medical problem. When applied to members of a health benefit plan, exceptions to coverage limits or exclusions may be used to permit the most cost-effective mix of services.

**catastrophic expense protection (or out-of-pocket limit)** A health plan benefit that limits the amount the enrollee must pay out-of-pocket for coinsurance or other required cost sharing for covered services. Once the limit is reached, plans generally pay for any additional covered expenses in full.

**Civilian Health and Medical Program of the Uniformed Services (CHAMPUS)** A government health plan for dependents of active and retired members of the uniformed services (e.g., Army, Navy).

**claim** An itemized statement of services provided to a specific patient by a health care provider. It is submitted to a health plan for payment.

**coalitions** Regionally based groups of employers and/or providers, insurers, and labor representatives who may disseminate information on health care issues, collect and analyze data, and provide other services for members.

**coinsurance** The percentage of a covered medical expense that a health plan or a beneficiary must pay (after the deductible is met).

**collective bargaining** A negotiation between organized labor and employer(s) on matters such as wages, hours, working conditions, and health and welfare programs.

**community rating** Setting health insurance premiums at the same level for all individuals or groups in a defined community. Modified community rating may set different rates for certain major subgroups (e.g., individuals or small businesses).

**contract** A binding agreement between two or more parties to perform or not perform certain actions. A contract of insurance is embodied in a written document usually termed a policy.

**contribution** That share of an insurance premium paid by a covered individual or by an employer (or government) (see premium).

**controllable risks** Risks associated with choices and behaviors that individuals are thought to be able to control to some degree (e.g., smoking and skydiving).

**conventional health plan** Plan that offers health benefits with few if any restrictions on the participant's choice of practitioners and providers and that pays for medical care largely or entirely on a fee-for-service basis.

**coordination of benefits** A method of integrating benefits payable under more than one health plan so that the insured's benefits from all sources do not exceed 100 percent of allowable medical expenses.

**copayment** A fixed payment per service (e.g., $5 per office visit) paid by a health plan member.

**cost sharing** The portion of health care expenses that a health plan member must pay, including deductibles, copayments, and coinsurance.

**cost shifting** Transfer of health care provider costs that are not reimbursed by one payer to other payers through higher charges for services.

**covered charges** Charges for medical care or supplies that, if incurred by a health plan member, create a liability for the health plan.

**covered services** Services eligible for payment by a health plan.

**deductible** The amount of medical expense that must be incurred and paid by an individual (generally during a calendar year) before a third party will assume any liability for payment of benefits. Health plans may have separate deductibles for some services.

**demographics** Statistical descriptions of populations' characteristics, such as age, income, marital status, and employment.

**dependent** An insured's spouse (not legally separated from the insured) and unmarried child(ren) who meet certain eligibility requirements and who are not otherwise insured under the same group policy. The precise definition of a dependent varies by insurer or employer.

**diagnosis-related groups (DRGs)** A system used by Medicare and some other payers to determine hospital reimbursement on the basis of the medical condition of a patient and certain other factors (e.g., patient age and significant complications).

**direct employer coverage** Individual receives benefits through his or her own current or former employer or union.

**effectiveness** Probability of benefit to patients from a specific medical service under average conditions of use.

**efficacy** Probability of benefit to patients from a specific medical service under ideal conditions of use.

**efficiency** Level of benefit from a fixed level of input *or* amount of input cost to achieve a defined level of benefit.

**eligible employee** An employee who has met the requirements (e.g., hours of employment) for coverage set forth by the employer (in accord with any applicable statutes).

**employee assistance programs (EAPs)** Health-related counseling or referral programs provided by employers that typically emphasize reduction of stress, chemical dependency, and similar problems.

**employer coverage** Benefits an individual has as an employee (direct) or as a dependent of an employee (indirect).

**enrollee** Individual covered by a health benefit plan.

**exclusions** Health care and related services (e.g., cosmetic surgery and long-term care) explicitly not covered by a health plan.

**experience rating** Setting health insurance premiums based in whole or part on past claims history of a particular group or its anticipated future claims.

**family head** The family member with the highest reported personal earnings. In families of nonworkers, the family head is the family member with the highest reported income from any source.

**fee-for-service** Payment for health care on a service-by-service basis (e.g., office visit or lab test) rather than a salaried or capitated basis; this is the method used by conventional health plans and sometimes by network health plans.

**fiduciary** According to ERISA, person charged with the legal responsibility for the operation and administration of an employee benefit plan.

**501(c)(9) trust** This trust takes its name from the section of the Internal Revenue Code that permits more favorable tax treatment to qualifying trusts.

**flexible benefits** A benefit program that allows employees to select the type and amount of benefits from a set of options defined by the employer (see cafeteria plan).

**full-year, full-time worker** Individual who worked at least 35 weeks during the year, 35 or more hours in a typical week, and spent no time looking for work during the year.

**full-year, part-time worker** Individual who worked at least 35 weeks during the year, fewer than 35 hours in a typical week, and spent no time looking for work during the year.

**gatekeeper** A designated health care practitioner who provides primary care services and coordinates specialist and other care for health plan members, who face extra costs for care that is not so provided or coordinated.

**gross domestic product (GDP)** The value of all goods and services produced in a country.

**gross national product (GNP)** The value of all goods and services produced in a country plus income earned in foreign countries less payments to foreign sources.

**group model HMO** A health maintenance organization that contracts with one or more group medical practices for delivery of health services.

**guaranteed issue** Insurance coverage that does not require the insured to provide evidence of insurability.

**health maintenance organization (HMO)** An entity that accepts responsibility and financial risk for providing specified health care services to a defined population during a defined period of time at a fixed price; enrollees generally have no coverage for nonemergency care provided outside the HMO panel of practitioners and providers (see also group model HMO and individual practice association).

**health plan** An organization or arrangement that provides defined medical expense protection (and sometimes medical services) to enrolled members (see also conventional health plan and network health plan).

**indemnity** An amount payable under an insurance policy for an insured loss.

**indirect employer coverage** Individual is provided benefits through another individual, usually a family member, who has direct employer coverage.

**individual practice association (IPA)** A health maintenance organization that contracts with private physicians who serve HMO enrollees in their offices, often on a discounted fee-for-service basis.

**insurable event** An event that is (1) individually unpredictable and unwanted, (2) relatively uncommon and significant, (3) precisely definable and measurable, (4) predictable for large groups, and (5) unlikely to occur to a large portion of insured individuals simultaneously.

**insurance** Conventionally, the protection against significant, unpredictable financial loss from defined adverse events that is provided under written contract in return for payments (premiums) made in advance.

**insurer** Organization that bears the financial risk for the cost of defined categories of services for a defined group of enrollees.

**loading factor** The amount added to the net premium rate determined for a group insurance plan to cover the possibility that losses will be greater than statistically expected because of hazardous industry, large percentage of unskilled employees, or other factors.

**managed care** A term used (1) broadly to describe health care plans that add utilization management features to indemnity-style coverage or (2) more narrowly to identify group or network-based health plans that have explicit criteria for selecting providers and financial incentives for members to use network providers, who generally must cooperate with some form of utilization management.

**manual rate** The premium rate developed for a group from an insurer's standard rate tables, usually contained in its rate or underwriting manual.

**maximum benefit** The highest amount any one individual may receive under an insurance contract.

**Medicaid** A state and federally financed program administered by states that covers certain categories of low-income individuals for health care services as required or permitted under the Social Security Act.

**medical necessity** The need for a specific medical service based on clinical expectations that the health benefits will outweigh the health risks; sometimes used interchangeably with appropriateness.

**medical underwriting** See underwriting.

**Medicare** The federal health care financing program for aged and disabled people who are covered under the Social Security Act. The program has two distinct parts: Part A, Hospital Insurance, and Part B, Supplementary Medical Insurance.

**minimum premium plan** A health plan that an employer self-funds at a fixed percent (e.g., 90 percent) of the estimated monthly claims, with the insurance company insuring claims in excess of that amount.

**moral hazard** A value-laden term—not used in this report—to describe the tendency of insured individuals to behave differently from uninsured individuals (in particular, to use or be provided with more appropriate or inappropriate health care services), sometimes used interchangeably with adverse risk selection.

**multiemployer plan** A plan established or maintained pursuant to a collective bargaining agreement and including more than one employer.

**multiple employer trust (MET)** A legal trust established by a plan sponsor that brings together a number of small, unrelated employers for the purpose of providing group medical care coverage on an insured or a self-funded basis.

**multiple employer welfare association (MEWA)** A benefit plan to which more than one employer contributes but which is not collectively bargained.

**network health plan**  A health plan that restricts coverage in whole or part to services provided by a specified network or group of physicians, hospitals, and other health care providers; see also health maintenance organization, independent practice association, open-ended HMO, preferred provider organization, and point-of-service plan.

**nonelderly population**  Individuals under age 65. (As used in reporting data from the Employee Benefit Research Institute's analysis of the Current Population Survey, the term excludes institutionalized individuals and those in the armed forces and members of their families.)

**nonworker**  Persons aged 18 and over who neither worked nor looked for work during the year.

**open-ended HMO**  A health plan option offered by a health maintenance organization (HMO) that in contrast to typical HMO coverage provides some benefits for nonemergency care provided by non-HMO providers; see also point-of-service plan.

**open enrollment**  Period during which a health plan accepts new enrollees without requiring evidence of insurability; some Blue Cross and Blue Shield plans offer continuous open enrollment; in an employer health plan, new employees and certain others can typically join at other times.

**open season**  See open enrollment.

**other private coverage**  Individual or group insurance not offered through an individual's (or family member's) current or former employer or union. This category consists primarily of individually purchased private insurance.

**other worker**  Individual aged 18 or over who worked or looked for work during the year but who was not a full-year, full-time worker. Unless otherwise indicated, the worker may have been unemployed during the year.

**outcome**  The result of a medical intervention.

**out-of-pocket expenses**  Payments made by a plan enrollee for medical services that are not reimbursed by the health plan. Out-of-pocket expenses can include payments for deductibles, coinsurance, services not covered by the plan, provider charges in excess of the plan's limits, and enrollee premium payments.

**panel**  A defined set of health care practitioners or providers that serve a network health plan, usually on a contractual basis.

**participating practitioner or provider**  One who has an agreement to serve members of a health plan under defined conditions.

**part-year worker**  Individual aged 18 or over who worked or looked for work fewer than 35 weeks during the year.

**point-of-service (POS) plan** A health plan, often based on an existing health maintenance organization (HMO), that offers enrollees some coverage for out-of-network care but provides more extensive coverage for in-network care coordinated by a designated primary care physician; enrollees can make the choice of network or nonnetwork care at the time they need service (see also open-ended HMO).

**pooling** The combining of expenses for certain groups (usually small), types of coverage (e.g., all mental health business), or other classes (e.g., classes in group health insurance that have claims in excess of normal limits) in order to spread risk.

**portability** Feature of an insurance policy that allows an insured to accumulate and transfer insurance benefits from one employer to another, or among employed, self-employed, or nonemployed statuses.

**practice patterns** Aggregate characteristics of a practitioner's use of medical resources over time.

**practitioner** A physician or medical care professional.

**preadmission review** Assessment of the clinical justification for a proposed hospital admission.

**preexisting condition** A physical or mental condition that exists prior to the effective date of coverage.

**preferred provider organization (PPO)** A health plan that offers enrollees greater coverage for services provided by a practitioner or institution that has, in most cases, agreed to price discounts and that may have agreed to abide by various kinds of utilization management requirements.

**prefunding** Method of funding the cost of retirement coverage during an employee's active working years.

**premium** An amount paid periodically to purchase health benefits; for self-insured groups that do not purchase insurance, the term may refer to the per employee or per family cost of health benefits and may be used for planning and analysis purposes even when no contribution to coverage is collected from the employee.

**premium tax** An assessment levied by a federal or state government, usually on the net premium income collected in a particular jurisdiction by an insurer.

**prepaid group practice** A term used before the term health maintenance organization was coined to refer to multispecialty physician groups paid on a salaried or capitated basis.

**primary care physician** A physician who provides basic first-line medical care, such as a family practitioner, general pediatrician, obstetrician/ gynecologist, and general internist.

**primary payer** Payer obligated to pay for covered care before the liability of any other payer applies.

**profile analysis** Use of aggregate statistical data on an institution or practitioner to compare practice and use patterns, identify inappropriate practices, or assess other characteristics of practice.

**prospective payment system** A payment system under which health care providers are paid a predetermined, fixed amount for patient care. Although prospective payment rates may be related to the costs providers incur in providing services, the amount a provider is paid for a service is unrelated to the provider's actual cost of providing that specific service to a given individual. Medicare and CHAMPUS use prospective payment systems to pay for inpatient hospital services (see DRGs).

**provider** An organization or individual that gives medical services (see also practitioner).

**purchasing cooperative** A term broadly used in discussions of health care reform to describe an entity that would buy health coverage on behalf of some group (e.g., small employers or all residents of a geographic area) and that would generally operate to pool risk, reduce marketing and other administrative costs, provide coverage that was portable from one job to another, and otherwise attempt to overcome problems that particularly affect individual or small-group purchasers of insurance.

**quality assessment** Evaluation of the technical and interpersonal aspects of medical care.

**quality assurance** An organized program to protect or improve quality of care by evaluating medical care, correcting problems, and monitoring corrective actions.

**quality of care** The degree to which health services for individuals and populations increase the likelihood of desired health outcomes and are consistent with current professional knowledge.

**referral** An arrangement for a patient to be evaluated and treated by another provider.

**reinsurance** Acceptance by one insurer (the reinsurer) of all or part of the risk of loss underwritten by another insurer (the ceding insurer).

**reserve** Premium amounts set aside by insurers to pay for current and future claims liabilities.

**retention** Administrative expense charged by an insurer and/or employee organization. These expenses may include claims payment (administration) expenses, state premium taxes, and risk charges.

**retrospective payment** A payment method for health care services in which hospitals (or other providers) are paid for services rendered after the service has taken place.

**retrospective utilization review** Assessment of the appropriateness of medical services on a case-by-case or aggregate basis after the services have been provided.

**risk** The chance of loss. In health insurance, risks relate to the chance of health care expenses arising from illness or injury.

**risk-adjusted payment** Employer or government share of a health plan premium adjusted for the age, health status, past claims experience, or other characteristics of the health plan's enrollees.

**risk charge** That portion of a group insurer's retention intended to be used (1) to spread the cost of catastrophic or epidemic losses over all groups, (2) to pay certain claims that may be pooled and not charged against the experience of a particular group, (3) to cover the deficits arising on the poorer risks in a given class, or (4) to contribute to the insurer's general surplus as protection against major losses affecting its entire group business.

**risk factors** Characteristics of individuals (e.g., age, gender, health status, and life-style) correlated with higher probability of health care expenses.

**risk pool** The population of individuals (or groups) across which costs for insured expenses are spread through premiums or other mechanisms.

**risk rating** Term broadly used to describe the linking of an individual's health behavior or risk of medical expenses to a financial penalty or reward borne by the individual, such as a higher or lower premium or a rebate for low users of care.

**risk segmentation** The clustering of higher- and lower-risk individuals in different health plans or the exclusion of higher-risk individuals from coverage altogether.

**risk selection** See biased risk selection.

**risk sharing/pooling/spreading** The degree to which individuals collectively bear the cost of protecting against loss (e.g., medical care expenses) rather than individually bear the cost based on their past or expected future expenses.

**second opinion** An opinion about the appropriateness of a proposed treatment provided by a practitioner other than the one making the original recommendation; some health benefit plans require such opinions for selected services.

**selective contracting** Negotiation by third-party payers of a limited number of contracts with health care professionals and facilities in a given service area. Preferential reimbursement practices and/or benefits are then offered to patients seeking care from these providers.

**self-funding** See self-insurance.

**self-insurance** Funding of medical care expenses in whole or part through internal resources rather than through transfer of risk to an insurer.

**self-paying patients** Health care users not covered by health insurance or public assistance who assume personal responsibility for paying their hospital and medical bills.

**service benefits**   Coverage for defined types of medical care rather than cash (indemnity) benefits.

**site of service**   Location where care is provided, for example, an inpatient facility or home.

**social insurance**   Old age, disability, health, or other insurance that is mandated by statute for defined categories of individuals or the entire population, usually financed by payroll and other taxes.

**staff model HMO**   A health maintenance organization that pays providers through salaried arrangements.

**statutory health insurance**   Health insurance required or provided automatically by law.

**stop-loss insurance**   Coverage by an insurer for expenses above a predetermined amount.   Specific stop loss defines the expense threshold on an individual basis; aggregate stop loss defines the expense threshold for an entire group.

**third-party administrator (TPA)**   Organization that processes health plan claims without bearing any insurance risk.

**third-party payer**   An organization other than the patient (first party) or health care provider (second party) involved in the financing of personal health services.

**triple-option plan**   An experience-rated program for an employer group in which a single insurance carrier, Blue Cross and Blue Shield plan, or health maintenance organization provides indemnity or service benefits in conjunction with various managed care or HMO plans.

**trust**   An arrangement for the care and management of property or funds by a person or third party for the benefit of another.

**uncompensated care**   Health care rendered to persons unable to pay and not covered by private or governmental health insurance plans; includes both unbilled charity care and bad debts (services billed but not paid).

**uncontrollable risks**   Risks associated with events not thought to be under an individual's control.

**underwriting**   Determining whether to accept or refuse individuals or groups for insurance coverage (or to adjust coverage or premiums) on the basis of an assessment of the risk they pose and other criteria (e.g., insurer's business objectives).

**utilization management**   A set of techniques used on behalf of a purchaser of health benefits to manage costs through case-by-case assessments of the clinical justification for proposed medical services (e.g., hospitalization and specific types of surgery).

**wage and salary workers** All workers aged 18 to 64 who are not self-employed.

**waiting period** The time a person must wait from the date of entry into a health plan or application for coverage to the date that coverage is effective.

**workers** Individuals aged 18 to 64 who worked or looked for work during the year. Unless otherwise indicated, the worker may have been unemployed during the year.

**workers compensation law** A statute imposing liability on employers to pay benefits and furnish care to employees injured and to pay benefits to dependents of employees killed in the course of and because of their employment.

## ACRONYMS

ADA       Americans with Disabilities Act of 1990
AHCPR     Agency for Health Care Policy and Research

CBO       Congressional Budget Office
COBRA     Consolidated Omnibus Budget Reconciliation Act of 1985
CRS       Congressional Research Service

DHHS      (U.S.) Department of Health and Human Services
DOL       (U.S.) Department of Labor
DRG       Diagnosis-related group

EAPs      Employee assistance programs
EBRI      Employee Benefit Research Institute
ERISA     Employee Retirement Income Security Act of 1974

FEHBP     Federal Employees Health Benefits Program
FFS       Fee-for-service (plan)

GAO       General Accounting Office

HCFA      Health Care Financing Administration
HMO       Health maintenance organization

IBNR      Incurred but not reported (claims)
IOM       Institute of Medicine
IPA       Independent practice association

NAIC    National Association of Insurance Commissioners

POS     Point-of-service (plan)
PPO     Preferred provider organization
PPS     Prospective payment system
PRO     Peer review organization
PSRO    Professional standards review organization

TPA     Third-party administrator

# Index

## A

Access, 7, 334
  public subsidies to improve, 18–19
  risk selection affecting, 182–183
  vs. coverage, 7, 234
Accountability, 237
Actuarial techniques
  early development of, 56
  fairness issues in, 179–182
Administration of health benefit plans
  administrative services only
    agreements, 113, 334
  in Canadian system, 110
  case studies in, 128–145
  complexity of, in U.S., 11–12, 149–
    152, 232, 240–241
  cooperatives for, 127
  cost of, 108–110, 151–152, 206, 240
  early cost containment strategies,
    73–77
  employer functions in, 5–6, 11, 121–
    127, 149–152, 232–233
  ERISA on, 303–304
  legal issues in, 152–153

  risk selection through practices in,
    174–175
  size of employer and, 121–122, 124–
    126
  state regulation of, 296, 298–299
  third-parties for, 113, 126, 152–153,
    344
Admission review, 334
Adverse selection, 46, 169, 334, *see
  also* Risk selection
Age
  coverage for elderly, 77, 90
  discrimination, protection against,
    316
  of health plan, related to enrollment
    age, 178
  of individual, vs. group, enrollees,
    168 n.1
  premiums related to, 173
  of uninsured workers, 93
Agency for Health Care Policy and
  Research, 226
Ambulatory care, definition of, 334
American Association for Labor
  Legislation, 58–59

*347*

American College of Surgeons, 63
American Medical Association
  opposition to group health plans by,
    70
  opposition to social insurance
    proposals by, 59–60, 63, 65
American Risk and Insurance
  Association, 41 n.6
Americans with Disabilities Act of
  1990, 117–118, 148, 316–317
  application to risk selection, 185–
    187
  confidentiality provisions of, 246
  legal uncertainties in, 186
  medical records management in, 17
  medical underwriting in, 182

**B**

Benefit, definition of, 43, 335
Benefit design, 114–115
  basic benefits, 19–20, 193, 249, 258
  cost management in, 74–75
  cost sharing in, 74, 103–106
  diversity in, 10, 122–126, 237–238,
    242
  employee assistance programs in,
    118–119
  employee concerns about, 136–137,
    145–149
  ERISA on, 84, 302
  evolution of, 101–102
  flexible, 119, 218, 337
  in health maintenance organizations,
    102
  health promotion programs in, 116–
    119
  influence on risk selection of, 171–
    172, 173–174
  innovation in, 10, 71–72, 238–239,
    242
  insurable events in, 44–45, 338
  Medicare, 78–79
  mental health care in, 104–106
  planning, in case study, 130–133,
    137–139
  regulating, 19–20, 193–194, 249, 258

risk selection affecting, 184–185
  in sample request for proposal, 156–
    158, 162–165
  in social insurance, 41–42, 56–57
  state-mandated, 101, 249, 298
  in workers' compensation programs,
    115–116
Biased risk selection, see Risk
  selection
Blue Cross plans
  costs of, 219
  HMO sponsorship by, 126
  origins of, 66–69, 71–72, 295
Blue Shield plans
  HMO sponsorship by, 126
  in Medicare program, 78–79
  origins of, 54 n.3, 68–69, 295
Bureau of the Census, Current
  Population Survey, 88, 93, 96

**C**

Cafeteria plan, 335
California, 37, 108, 250
Canada, 22, 32, 33, 110, 151, 252
Capital expenditures, regulation of,
  208–209
Capitation, 335
Carve-outs, for retirees, 94–95 n.6
Case management, 335
Case study
  contrasting cases, 142–145
  employee advisory group in, 135–
    137
  evaluating benefit plans in, 131–
    133
  evaluating proposals in, 137–140
  financial management in, 133
  goal setting in, 130
  implementing new benefit plan in,
    140–142
  legal issues in, 134
  request for proposals in, 137, 155–
    166
  small business concerns in, 143
Catastrophic expense protection, 335
Certificates of need, 209

Civilian Health and Medical Program of the Uniformed Services (CHAMPUS), 335
Claims management
definition of "claim," 335
in ERISA, 83
in sample request for proposal, 160–161
COBRA, see Consolidated Omnibus Budget Reconciliation Act of 1985
Coinsurance, 104, 335
Commercial insurence, 55–56, 71–72
Committee on the Costs of Medical Care (1927), 60–64, 66–67
Community rating, 257
definition of, 336
in early insurance plans, 67
experience rating vs., 47
in social insurance, 42
theoretical basis of, 181
Competition
ability of, to regulate health care, 207, 220–223, 240
among purchasing cooperatives, 18
effect of risk selection on, 169
managed, 37, 38, 81, 190–194
risk selection as basis for, 183
Complexity of U.S. health care system, 11–12, 149–152, 240–241
Compulsory coverage in social insurance, 41–42, 56–57
recommendations, 251–254
Confidentiality
in Americans with Disabilities Act, 185–186, 246
recommendations for, 16–17, 246
worker concerns about, 148
Consolidated Omnibus Budget Reconciliation Act of 1985, 85, 313–314
Consultants, in planning health benefits, 124–126
Continuity of care
problems with, 10–11, 146, 239
research on, 259
Continuity of coverage, 10–11, 239, 259

under COBRA, 85, 313–314
termination benefits, ERISA on, 84
Cooperatives
health-plan purchasing, 18, 127, 214–215, 247–248, 342
regulating competition through, 191–192
Coordination of benefits, 94–95 n.6, 336
Copayment, 336
Cost management
benefit designs for, 74–75
cost sharing strategies in, 217
early efforts in, 73–77
early federal initiatives, 82
flexible benefits and, 218
growth of government role in, 207–211
health planning in, 75–76, 208–209
health promotion programs in, 218
issues in, 202–204
market-based strategies for, 220–223, 240
in Medicare program, 208–209
in network plans, 217–218
obstacles to, 11, 239–240
private sector strategies for, 212–220
prospective payment system for, 211
rate-setting programs for, 208–210
risk pool management for, 74
role of, in health care reform, 20, 250–251
self-insurance and, 218
see also Costs of health care; Utilization management
Cost sharing, 74, 103–106
definition of, 336
effect on cost of care, 217
income-adjusted, 181 n.7
Cost shifting
definition of, 336
employer concerns about, 232
government role in, 211–212
recommendations for controlling, 248
uncompensated care and, 21, 184, 252

Costs of health care
 administrative expenses in, 108–110,
  151, 206, 240
 caps on enrollee spending, 104
 concept of value in, 203–204, 223–
  227
 consumer concerns about, 202
 consumer spending on, 4, 204
 distribution of spending on, 3, 4, 5,
  27–28, 167
 in early insurance plans, 67–68
 economic effects of, 202–203
 employer spending on, 4, 27–28, 71
  n.17, 207
 factors in rise of, 4, 7, 202–204, 221
 growth of, 4, 28–29, 61, 78, 108,
  204–207
 individual's health status affecting,
  178–179
 inflation as factor in, 204
 inpatient vs. outpatient services in, 204
 international comparisons of, 4–5,
  29–30
 market forces in, 220–223
 medical care component of, 204–205
 medical technology in, 203, 204–
  206, 224
 as obstacle to small group benefit
  plans, 94
 population growth as factor in, 204
 premium costs in, 106–108
 public program spending on, 5, 207,
  274
 public subsidy of, 18–19, 248
 reform and, 20, 248, 250–251
 risk selection and, 183–184
 size of group and, 183
 tax expenditures in, 110
 trends in, 204–206
 uncompensated care in, 184, 252
 in workers' compensation programs,
  115
 *see also* Cost management
Council of Smaller Enterprises, 127
Coverage
 continuity of, 10–11, 85, 239, 259,
  313–314

direct employer, 90, 337
indirect employer, 90, 338
issues in legislative reform, 256
mandated continuity of, 313–314
state-mandated, 298
state regulation of, 296–297, 298
vs. access, 7, 234
*see also* Benefit design

## D

Deductibles, 103–104, 336
Demographic risk adjustment, 196–197
Dental benefits, 102
Department of Health and Human
 Services, 88, 89
Department of Labor, Bureau of Labor
 Statistics, 88–89
Diagnosis-related groups, 197, 211, 336
Disability insurance, 43 n.8
 in origins of medical insurance, 51–
  54
Discrimination
 age, protection against, 316
 health related, 117–118, 148, 185–
  187, 236–237
 in workplace health promotion
  programs, 118–119

## E

Economic Stabilization Program, 208
Elderly
 employment-based insurance for, 90
 private insurance for, 77
Eligibility
 defining family members for, 89–90
  n.5
 state-mandated, 101
 workplace rules, 93–94
Employee advisory groups, in case
 study, 135–137
Employee assistance programs, 24,
 118–119, 258–259, 337
Employee Benefit Research Institute,
 31, 88
 survey, 148–149, 287–292

Employee Retirement Income Security
    Act of 1974 (ERISA), 82–85,
    231–232, 293, 300–313
  deemer clause of, 310
  definitions in, 302, 304
  employer liability for managed care
    and, 152–153
  federal legal supplements to, 315–
    317
  fiduciary standards in, 304–306
  government regulation before, 82
  multiple employer welfare
    arrangements and, 315
  preemption of state law by, 306–
    311
  recommendations for amending, 16,
    19, 249–250
  regulation of self-funded plans
    under, 310–313
  reporting requirements of, 303–304
  savings clause of, 307–310
  underwriting in, 182
  vesting in, 302–303
Employment-based health coverage
  case study of, 128–145
  costs of, 106–111
  defining, 40–41, 44
  development of, 3, 27, 49–56, 65–
    71, 67–71
  employee responsibilities in, 145–
    149
  in health care reform, 23–24, 26–27,
    36, 207, 230–231, 242–243, 260–
    261
  management activities in, 5–6, 121–
    127, 149–152, 232
  mandated, 21–23, 251–254
  participation in, 5–6, 8–9, 26, 27–
    28, 89–98, 232–233
  private initiatives to control costs in,
    212–220
  types of, 98–106, 114–119
Employment practices
  discontinuity in benefit coverage,
    10–11, 239
  effect of Americans with Disabilities
    Act on, 185–187

  encouraging enrollment in spouse's
    benefit plan, 92
  hiring of smokers, 117–118 n.16,
    186
  medical screening in hiring, 9, 117–
    118
ERISA. *See* Employee Retirement
    Income Security Act of 1974
European experience, *see* International
    comparisons
Experience rating, 47, 112–113, 133,
    197, 337

**F**

Families
  deductibles in coverage for, 103
  of insured workers, benefits for, 89–
    92
  of uninsured workers, 92–94
Federal Employees Health Benefits
    Program
  features of, 170, 175
  origins of, 73
  risk selection in, 175–177
Federal regulation
  in development of employment-
    based health plans, 70–71
  early social insurance proposals, 60–
    65
  encouraging HMOs, 210
  before ERISA, 82, 300
  of mental health benefits, 106 n.11
  need for, 19, 245–246, 248–250,
    251–254
  of pre-employment medical
    screening, 9
  *see also* Employee Retirement
    Income Security Act of 1974
    (ERISA); State regulation
Fee-for-service plans
  definition of, 337
  modified, in network plans, 100
Fiduciary
  definition of, 337
  standards in ERISA, 304–306

Financial Accounting Standards Board,
95
Financial management
ERISA requirements, 84
evaluating benefit options, in case
study, 133
retiree benefits as corporate
liabilities, 95, 113–114
tax expenditures in health benefits,
110–111
Flexible benefits, 119, 218, 337
Foundations for medical care, 76
France, health care spending in, 30, 32
Fraud, 116

**G**

Gatekeeper physician, 100, 338
Gender, premiums related to, 173
Geographic variations in coverage, 98,
101
Germany, 36–37 n.3
development of medical insurance
in, 53
health care spending in, 30, 32t
premium costs in, 106
risk segmentation in, 46 n.9, 168 n.2
role of employers in, 217 n.5
sickness funds of, 46 n.9, 56, 57
social insurance in, 41 n.6, 42, 57
Group Health Association, 69
Group practice
origins of, 66, 69
prepaid, 341

**H**

Hawaii, 37, 83, 108, 219, 307
Health Care Financing Administration,
88, 89
Health Insurance Association of
America, 88, 89, 188 n.13
Health Maintenance Organization Act
of 1973, 82
Health maintenance organizations
benefit coverage in, 102
definition of, 338

evaluating, in case study, 130, 132–
135
evidence of cost savings in, 218
government encouragement of, 210
group model, 338
growth of, 100
Medicare-contracted, 197
numbers of, 126
open-ended, 340
relative restrictiveness of, 98
risk selection in, 174, 177–178, 179
staff model, 344
state regulation of, 298–299
Health planning, 75–76, 208–209
Health Planning and Resources
Development Act of 1974, 209
*Healthy People 2000*, 116
Heritage Foundation, 37
High-risk individuals, 117–118, 171–
172, 199–200
Historical developments, 3, 27
Blue Cross plan, 66–69
in cost management, 73–77
early social insurance proposals, 57–
65
government efforts to control health
care costs, 207–212
growth of cost of care, 78
key dates of, 52
origins of employment-based health
plans, 69, 70–72
origins of medical insurance, 51–56
private insurance initiatives, 65–71
in regulation of insurance, 293–295
in social insurance, 56–57
in utilization review, 76–77
Hospice care, 102
Hospitals
administrative expenses in, 110
cost of uncompensated care in, 184,
252
cost shifting in, 211–212
development of, 53
government cost control programs
in, 208–210
prospective payment system in, 211
resource management of, 75–76

**I**

Indemnity insurance, 98–99, 338
  evaluating, in case study, 132–133
Independent practice associations, 126,
    338
  employee concerns about, in case
    study, 135–136
  evaluating, in case study, 130, 132
  evidence of cost savings in, 218
  origins of, 75
  relative restrictiveness of, 98
  risk selection in, 174
Information management
  under Americans with Disabilities
    Act, 185–186
  analyzing health care data, 88
  in establishing health status
    measures, 198–199, 225
  evaluating benefit plans, case study
    of, 131–133
  in risk-adjustment methodologies,
    18, 197–198
  *see also* Confidentiality
Innovation
  in benefit plan design, 10, 24, 238–
    239
  by commercial insurers, 71–72
  in health research, 238
  in medical technology, 10, 31, 50
  in state regulatory efforts, 249–250
Insurable event, 44–45, 338
Insurance
  actuarial fairness in, 180
  administrative costs of, 109–110
  administrative practices, regulation
    of, 296
  basis for state regulation of, 293–
    295
  definition of, 43, 338
  disability, defining, 43 n.8
  ERISA preemption and state
    regulation of, 308–310
  growth of, 71–72
  indemnity, 98–99
  insurable event in, 44–45, 338
  language of, 40–47

  moral hazard in, 45–47
  origins of, 51–56
  prepayment, definition of, 44
  private, enrollment in, 90
  rate regulation of, 296–297
  social, 41–42, 56–57, 58–60, 60–65,
    181, 344
  unfair practices in, 297–298
Insured workers, 89–92
  concerns of, in benefit plan, 145–
    149
  employee advisory group, in case
    study, 135–137
  full-year, full-time, 92–93, 337
  full-year, part-time, 337–338
  health care spending by, 106
International comparisons
  defining employment-based systems
    in, 36
  early medical insurance in, 51–56
  in health care reform, 36–37
  in health care spending, 4–5, 29–34,
    239–240
  universal coverage, 56–57, 236
  *see also specific country*

**J**

Japan, health care spending in, 30, 33
Job "lock," 32, 239

**K**

Kaiser plan
  origins of, 69
  underwriting in, 127 n.2, 219

**L**

Labor Management Relations Act of
    1947, 300
Legal issues
  in authority of ERISA, 301
  employer liability for managed care,
    152–153
  federal preemption of state laws by
    ERISA, 306–311

fiduciary standards in ERISA, 304–
306
foundations of state insurance
regulation, 294–295
in multiple employer welfare
arrangements, 314–315
in review of benefit plan options, in
case study, 134
unfair insurance practices, state
regulation of, 297–298
Lifestyle factors, 180, 186–187
Loading factor, 339
Louisiana, 108
Low-wage workers
extent of coverage for, 92–93
subsidizied coverage, 248, 251
tax deductions for health care for,
111

**M**

Managed care, 100, 339
Managed competition, 190–194
Managed coverage, *see* Compulsory
coverage in social insurance
Marketing practices, risk selection
through, 175
Maryland, 209
Massachusetts, 108
McCarran-Ferguson Act, 82, 295,
309
Medicaid, 2, 42, 79–80, 339
administrative expenses, 108, 110
cost shifting and, 212
Oregon plan for restructuring, 193
Medical organizations
early opposition to health plans by,
69–70
*see also* American Medical
Association
Medical records, *see* Information
management
Medical services
in cost of care, 204–206, 223–226
regulation of, 75–77, 208–211
Medical technology
assessing value of, 225–226

cost of care and, 203, 205–206, 218,
224
development of, 51–53
innovation in benefit design and, 10,
31, 50
Medicare prospective payments and,
211
risk assessment methodologies and,
195–196
role in cost of health care, 205–206
Medicare, 2, 12, 78–79, 208–209, 339
administrative expenses, 108, 110
enrollment history, 79
HMOs in, 20
integrating retiree employment-
related coverage with, 94–95 n.6
pharmacy benefits in, 102
prospective payment system in, 211,
212
risk assessment in, 195–196
secondary payors in, 316
use of utilization measures in, 197
Mental health care
cost of, as percentage of health
expenditures, 104–106
coverage limits on, 104–106
employee assistance programs for,
118–119
Mississippi, 108
Moral hazard, 45–47, 339
Multiemployer plans, 85, 339
Multiple employer welfare associations,
84, 314–315, 339

**N**

National Association of Insurance
Commissioners, 82, 188 n.13, 295
National Conference on Medical Costs,
212
National Labor Relations Board, 70–71
National Medical (Care) Expenditures
Survey, 92
Netherlands, 106, 145–146
Network health plans
coinsurance in, 103–104
definition of, 340

effect on cost of care by, 217–218
risk selection in, 174
state regulation of, 298–299
types of, 100–101
Norway, health care spending in, 30

## O

Oregon, 19, 193 n.15

## P

Part-time workers, 90, 337–338
Peer review, 76
Peer review organizations, 210–211
Pepper Commission, 37
Pharmacy benefits, 102, 147 n.4
Physician(s)
  early opposition to health insurance, 55
  as gatekeepers, 100
  impact of employment-based benefits on, 149–152
  importance of, in consumer choice, 170
  in Medicare program, 78–79
  payment, 211
  primary care, 341
  risk selection in restricted network of, 174
  role of, 53
  types of, in state-mandated benefits, 101
Point-of-service plans
  definition of, 341
  features of, 191
  growth of, 100
  relative restrictiveness of, 98
Preadmission review, 341
Preferred provider organizations, 218, 341
  coinsurance in, 104
  relative restrictiveness of, 98
  risk selection in, 174
  state regulation of, 298–299
Premiums
  age related to, 173

considerations in regulating, 255
cost of, 106–108
definition of, 341
effect of risk selection on, 175–176
evaluating benefit plan options, in case study, 133
gender related to, 173
risk rating of individuals and cost of, 117
for self-insured groups, 112, 113
workers' compensation, 115
Private insurance, enrollment in, 90
Professional standards review organizations, 210
Prospective Payment Assessment Commission, 212
Prospective payment system
  cost shifting and, 211–212
  definition of, 342
  effect of, 211
  origins of, 211
Public opinion
  on administration of health care system, 232
  compulsory employment-related coverage in, 31
  cost concerns in, 202
  delivery of health care in, 1–2, 22–23, 31
  Employee Benefit Research Institute survey on, 148–149, 287–292
  of health benefits system, 12–13
Public spending
  early social insurance proposals, 57–65, 60–65
  financing through reform, 20, 248
  international comparisons, 4–5, 32–33, 56–57
  for Medicaid, 80
  need for, 18–19, 248
  public understanding of, 202
  in risk-adjusted payment plans, 17–18
  statistics, 4, 27
Purchasing cooperatives, *see* Cooperatives

## Q

Quality assurance, 342
Quality of care, 342
  definition of, 184
  effect of risk selection on, 184–185
  health care spending and, 33 n.2
  for the uninsured, 21, 252

## R

Redlining, 97–98
Reform of health care system
  administrative issues in, 151–152
  alternatives proposed for, 37–38
  amending ERISA in, 16, 19, 248–
    250
  American Medical Association
    stance on, 59 n.8
  basic benefit design in, 19–20, 193,
    249, 258
  confidentiality issues in, 16–17
  continuity of care in, 259
  cooperatives in, 18, 247–248
  cost of, 250–251
  employee assistance programs in,
    258–259
  employer size and, 219–220
  high risk individuals in, 199–200
  impact of private cost control
    strategies, 216–220
  issues in, 1–3, 35–40, 48, 50, 254–
    256
  managing competition in, 190–194
  mandated universal coverage in, 21–
    23, 251–254
  market-oriented approaches to, 7,
    22, 207, 220–223, 240
  mental health care in, 106 n.11
  need for, 1, 14, 17, 47–48, 260
  pace of, 227–228
  proposals in other countries, 36–37
  public subsidy of, 18–19, 248
  to reduce risk selection, 14–17, 175–
    176, 187, 242
  research needs for, 256–259

risk-adjusted payments in, 17–18,
    194–196, 247, 257
  risk sharing and, 261
  role of employer in, 14, 22, 23–24,
    31, 36, 216–220, 230–231, 242–
    243, 260–261
  role of private sector in, 227–228,
    229–230, 260–261
  state experimentation in, 249–250
  underwriting practices in, 16, 47,
    187–190, 245–246, 257
  within voluntary system, 243
  workers' compensation system in,
    115–116
Reimbursement systems
  cost shifting and, 211–212
  development of, 75
  evaluation of, in case study, 133
  in Medicare program, 79
  in network plans, 100
  physician, 211
  prospective payment, 211
  resource-based relative value scale,
    211
Reinsurance, 199–200, 342
Request for proposals, in case study,
    137–139, 155–166
Research needs
  basic benefit design, 19–20, 258
  on continuity of care, 259
  employee assistance programs,
    effects of, 258–259
  for health care reform, 23, 256–259
  methodologies for risk adjusting, 18,
    257
  technology assessment, 226–227
  underwriting reforms, consequences
    of, 257
Resource-based relative value scale, 68,
    211
Responsible National Health Insurance
    plan, 37
Retirees, 94–95
  benefits for, as corporate liability,
    95, 113–114
Retrospective payment, 342
Risk, definition of, 43, 343

Risk-adjusted payments, 17–18, 194–
    196, 247, 343
  demographic approach to, 196–197
  health status measures in, 198–199
  methodologies for, 196–199, 257
  prior use data for, 197–198
Risk pools, see Risk sharing
Risk rating, 47, 117, 343
Risk segmentation
  arguments for, 13, 242
  causes of, 47, 168
  definition of, 46–47, 343
  strategies for reducing, 187, 245–
    246
Risk selection, 167–169, 200–201
  benefit design affecting, 171–174
  biased, 46, 167, 335
  causes of, 170–175, 178–179
  definition of, 46, 168
  discrimination and, 9, 236–237
  in early insurance plans, 67, 69
  effect of Americans with Disabilities
    Act, 185–187
  effect on access, 182–183
  effect on costs of care, 183–184
  effect on premiums, 175–176
  effect on quality of care, 184–185
  employer factors contributing to,
    170–172
  equity issues in, 179–182
  evidence of, 177–179
  in Federal Employees Health
    Benefits Program, 175–177
  high risk individuals and, 199–200
  moral hazard and, 46
  in network plans, 174
  regulating competition to discourage,
    190–194
  risk-adjusted payments to reduce,
    17–18, 194–196
  size of group and, 168
  strategies for reducing, 14–16, 187,
    245
  through administrative practices,
    174–175
  through individual medical records,
    16–17

through marketing practices, 175
  underwriting practices and, 173,
    187–190, 245–246
  universal coverage and, 22, 252
Risk sharing
  definition of, 343
  importance of, 26
  risk pools for, 43, 74–76, 199–200,
    343
Rochester, New York, 113, 127, 181
    n.8, 218–219

## S

Second opinion, 76, 343
Self-insured groups, 343
  advantages of, 111–112
  in case study, 133
  cost savings by, 218
  ERISA regulation of, 83–85, 310–
    313
  funding mechanisms for, 111
  liability for managed care in, 153
  medical underwriting within, 16
  premiums for, 112, 113
  related to employer size, 111
  risk segmentation and, 47, 168
  risk-sharing arrangements for, 112–
    113
  state regulation of, 101, 250, 310–
    313
  stop-loss insurance for, 113
  taxing of, 248
  trends in, 189
  types of, 44
Size of employer
  administration of health plan and,
    110, 121–122, 124–126
  benefit design and, 5–6, 9–10, 99
  cost containment strategies related
    to, 214
  costs of health care and, 106, 183,
    237
  coverage availability related to, 5,
    96–97, 232–233
  employee assistance programs,
    118

employer-financed coverage for
    retirees and, 95
evaluating benefit plans and, in case
    studies, 142–145
flexible benefit plans and, 119
health care reform and, 16, 219–220
health promotion programs and, 5–6,
    117
risk selection and, 16, 168
self-insurance practices and, 16, 111
underwriting and, 16, 245–246
Small businesses
cooperative efforts by, 18, 127, 214–
    215, 247–248
definition of, 5, 42–43
HMO offerings by, 99, 214
limiting underwriting practices in,
    187–190
reasons for not offering health
    benefits in, 94
see also Size of employer
Smokers, hiring of, 117–118 n.16, 186
Social insurance
definition of, 41–42, 344
development of, 56–57
early proposals for, 58–65
in Germany, 41 n.6, 42, 59
theoretical basis of, 181
Social Security Act, 64, 78, 80
Amendments of 1972, 208–209
Société Française de Bienfaisance
    Mutuelle, 53
State regulation
benefits mandated by, 19–20, 101,
    249, 298
ERISA and, 82–85, 249–250, 306–
    313
experimentation in, 249–250
extent of, 293
of insurance company management,
    296
of insurance rates, 296–297
limiting risk selection through, 181–
    182
of managed care organizations, 298–
    299
of Medicare, 79–80

of multiple employer welfare
    arrangements, 315
origins of, in health care, 293–295
of self-insured groups, 310–313
social insurance initiatives, 58–60
of unfair insurance practices, 297–
    298
Statistics
administrative expenses, 108–110
benefit design, 102
coinsurance arrangements, 104
in Committee on the Costs of Health
    Care report (1928–1932), 60–61
consumer concerns about cost of
    care, 202
cost of mental health care, 104–106
coverage related to size of company,
    96, 99
data sources for, 88–89
deductibles, 103
employment-based plans, enrollment
    in, 1, 27, 71, 236
flexible benefit plans, 119
health care in Rochester, New York,
    219
health care spending, 3, 4, 27–28,
    78, 204–206, 207
HMO enrollment, 210
industry type as variable in coverage
    availability, 97
insured populations, 3, 26, 27, 28,
    236
insured workers, 89–92
Medicaid, 80
Medicare, 79, 236
network plan enrollments, 100
premium costs, 106–108
publicly funded health coverage, 4,
    27
regional variation in coverage
    availability, 98, 99
retirees, 94–95
self-insured groups, 111
taxation of health benefit
    expenditures, 110–111
types of plans offered, 99
uninsured populations, 1, 4, 27, 236

uninsured workers, 92–94
worker attitudes toward benefit
    plans, 148–149, 287–292
workers' compensation benefits, 115
Steelman Commission, 37
Stop-loss coverage
    definition of, 113, 344
    extent of, in self-insured groups, 111
    for self-insured groups, 113
    types of, 113
Switzerland, 42

**T**

Taft-Hartley Act of 1947, 70
Tax Equity and Fiscal Responsibility
    Act of 1982, 85
Taxes, 110–111
    deductibility of contributions to
        health plans, 71, 110–111
    flexible benefit packages and, 119
    legal supplements to ERISA, 315
    in market-based reforms, 222
    retiree health benefits as corporate
        liabilities, 95, 113–114
    for self-insured groups, 248
Technology. *See* Medical technology
Terminating benefits, ERISA provisions
    on, 84
Third-party administrators, 113, 126,
    152–153, 344
Traveler's Insurance Company, 55 n.4
Triple-option plan, 344
Trusts, for self-insurers, 113, 344

**U**

U.S. Chamber of Commerce, 37
U.S. Public Health Service, origins of,
    57
Uncompensated care, 21, 184, 252, 344
Underwriting
    in Americans with Disabilities Act,
        185, 186
    in cooperative plans, 127 n.2
    by Council of Smaller Enterprises,
        127

definition of, 344
    risk selection and, 173, 182, 187–
        190, 245–246
    role of, 47
    in small-group market, 16
    strategies for limiting, 16, 181–182,
        187–190, 245–246, 251–252, 255,
        257
Uninsured populations
    age of, 93
    health care for, 21, 234, 252
    health of, 183
    statistics, 1, 4, 27, 236
    workers as, 8–9, 87, 92–94
    working, vs. nonworking, in
        generating uncompensated care,
        184 n.9
Unions
    in development of employment-
        based health plans, 70–71
    in development of medical
        insurance, 54, 55, 76
United Kingdom
    health care spending in, 30, 33
    origins of medical insurance in, 51,
        55–56
Universal coverage, 236
    employment-based, 21–23, 251–254
    lack of, 22–23, 254
    need for, 21, 251–252
Utilization management
    definition of, 344
    effect of, on cost of care, 217
    employer liability for managed care
        and, 152–153
    extent of, in employer benefit plans,
        213–214
    as measure in risk-adjusting, 197–
        198
    in Medicare, 208
    origins of, 76–77
    retrospective, 342

**V**

Voluntary employee beneficiary
    association, 113

Voluntary system of coverage, 1, 8, 26,
    235, 237
  early history, 51–56
  improving, 243–251
  limitations of, 21, 251–252
  marketplace effects of, 9–10
  replacing, 251–254

## W

Welfare capitalism, 54
Well baby care, 102
Wellness programs, 116–119, 218
Workers' compensation, 114, 115–116,
    345